DEATH TO THE FRENCH

AN ALMANAC OF BRITISH VICTORIES OVER THE FRENCH

1106-1942

PHILIP H. WHITE

To Helen and Garde,
With my
warm regards.
Philip H. White,

TRAFFORD

The cover is a representation of the Sketch "The British Lion and the French Peacock" by Philippe de Loutherbourg, c.1797, by kind permission of the Trustees of the British Museum

Note for Librarians: A cataloguing record for this book is available from Library and Archives Canada at www.collectionscanada.ca/amicus/index-e.html

ISBN 1-4251-0368-5

Printed in Victoria, BC, Canada. Printed on paper with minimum 30% recycled fibre. Trafford's print shop runs on "green energy" from solar, wind and other environmentally-friendly power sources.

Offices in Canada, USA, Ireland and UK

Book sales for North America and international:
Trafford Publishing, 6E–2333 Government St.,
Victoria, BC V8T 4P4 CANADA
phone 250 383 6864 (toll-free 1 888 232 4444)
fax 250 383 6804; email to orders@trafford.com
Book sales in Europe:
Trafford Publishing (UK) Limited, 9 Park End Street, 2nd Floor
Oxford, UK OX1 1HH UNITED KINGDOM
phone +44 (0)1865 722 113 (local rate 0845 230 9601)
facsimile +44 (0)1865 722 868; info.uk@trafford.com
Order online at:
trafford.com/06-2125

10 9 8 7 6 5 4

To Poossie Nancy

CONTENTS

ACKNOWLEDGEMENTS

I have worked on this book intermittently for a long time, and I am greatly indebted to my wife and family who have not only patiently waited its completion but continued to believe that it would be. Other friends who have encouraged me to continue and have supplied me with material germane to the subject are: Professor Martin Hattersley, and Mr. Wallace J. Mackay, and there are a number of others who have strongly encouraged me to carry on.

The librarians at the Universities of British Columbia and of Victoria, and the public library of Greater Victoria have always been painstakingly helpful and a credit to their profession.

The efficiency of the staff of the British Museum in supplying me with the electronic image of the Sketch from which the cover has been produced is particularly noteworthy.

I am also indebted to Roy Diment of Vivência Resources Group for creating the cover and to the staff at Trafford Publishing for their patience and help in the final stages of publication.

Cari Taylor provided expert assistance in adapting my text to the arcane formatting procedures of the computer; and my wife, Nancy, and our daughter, Angela Monahan, did sterling work in proof reading and in editing the text.

My best thanks to all of these people and with sincerest apologies to any I have inadvertently omitted.

Any errors, and other shortcomings are entirely my own.

INTRODUCTION

Schopenhauer observed that: "Every nation ridicules other nations, and all are right", and this expresses tolerably well the spirit in which this book has been written. In England, the celebration of military and naval victories is a very old tradition – Shakespeare's Henry V referring to those who would fight with him at Agincourt and live to tell the tale forecasts that they "will yearly on the vigil feast [their] neighbours", and at least as far back as the Napoleonic War, in the public schools, masters were encouraging the boys to celebrate military and naval victories. This tradition prompted the idea to compile a comprehensive list of anniversaries of military and naval victories over the perennial enemy, the French, in order to provide a reason for a party; '385 dates to celebrate', and the title is one of the oldest toasts in the language. As the work progressed, it was suggested that it would be an improvement if there were also a narrative account of the wars during which the battles took place, and in response, synopses of the seventeen wars between the twelfth and twentieth centuries in which victories were achieved are provided in Part One. Part Two is an annotated almanac of the anniversaries arranged by month, day, and year, but in Part One the battles are listed in strict time sequence by year, month, and day, and are cross-referenced to the description in Part Two. Although the total number of victories is greater than days in the year, they are not evenly spaced, on some days there have been more than one and none on others, so that if a celebration is desired on a blank day, the obvious solution is to adopt one of multiple entries; after all, the Queen finds it convenient to celebrate an official birthday on a day different from her birth date.

From time to time, I have been asked why French victories were not to be included. The short answer is that defeats are not usually something to celebrate, but there is a better explanation. After Napoleon's second abdication, such a volume of apologia was produced that it has become known as the Napoleonic Legend, and part of it, in 28 volumes, is "*Victoires et Conquêtes des Français*", to which those wishing such information are respectfully referred.

The general dislike of the British for the French, and vice versa, is well-known, and the history of hostilities over more than nine hundred years goes a long way to explain how it has evolved and continued. The attitude does not rest on stereotypes; historians have analyzed this element in the British character. Dr. A.L. Rowse citing some of the work of Professor Sir Lewis Namier goes on to say that: "... in a nation collectivity adds up to something more than the sum of the individuals. One may love France and appreciate the French, but the French collectivity is selfish, self-interested, and short sighted (witness 1940), egotistic and rhetorical (witness Louis XIV, Napoleon, de Gaulle)". Professor Colley has written a book, "Britons: Forging the Nation 1707 – 1837", in persuasive explanation of her thesis that the sense of British identity was forged through the prolonged conflict with France during the eighteenth century and the early years of the following one: "... men and women came to define themselves as Britons – in addition to many other ways – because circumstances impressed them with the belief that they were different from those beyond their shores, and in particular from their prime enemy, the French." The fact that the perceived differences with French characteristics and manners might be based on quite erroneous notions of what those characteristics and manners were did not affect the outcome, Britons were not "superstitious (read Roman Catholic), militarist, decadent, and unfree" [words in parentheses added], but the French were. If 'English' is substituted for 'Briton' the effect on the national character of frequent wars with France can be traced back to at least the fourteenth century, since when it has always been easy "to fire their blood (of the people) and draw forth their subsidies by promising an expedition for the conquest of France". These feelings were common in all levels of society and have carried forward into the present. The mass of citizens are usually more unabashedly chauvinistic, sometimes expressing it in surprising ways. Professor Sir John Plumb has recorded that in the eighteenth century "the general consumption of roast beef, beer, and white bread was regarded as one of the foundations of an Englishman's superiority over the French". Some substance to this curious claim is given by the Cambridge History of World Food where it is reported that contractors found that an Englishman could commonly do the work of two and a half Frenchmen, but when the latter were given as ample a ration of meat as the former, the difference was insignificant.

The cover of this book is an illustration of how British-French relations were seen at the end of the eighteenth century. The original Sketch is by Philippe de Loutherbourg, a French artist who, like Voltaire and other Philosophes, was an Anglophile. Loutherbourg had achieved recognition for his work in France by election to the Academy at an age below that required by the law of that institution. A few years later he settled in London and quickly established himself in a number of genres including the painting of naval victories over the French. The Sketch –'The British Lion and the French Peacock' – is an expression of the popular view of British naval superiority over the French.

The Laudable Association of Anti-Gallicans was the first of many patriotic societies formed from the mid-eighteenth century onwards. The founders were tradesmen, and it was aimed principally against French imports but reached out further; for example, by commissioning four times a year a sermon on the need for greater civic exertion against the iniquities of France; these sermons were then published at the Association's expense. These societies had such an appeal that they were even founded in the colony of Massachusetts.

One of Nelson's biographers has described his mother, the wife of an Anglican parson, as being of strong character, devout, patriotic, and one who hated the French as almost personal enemies.

Looking for examples in this vein, one is spoiled for choice, but here are three that are less well known. William Hazlitt displayed some of the ambivalence noted by Dr. Rowse. He was an ardent supporter of the French revolution and Napoleon whose biography in four volumes he regarded as his major work. Nevertheless ,only a few years after Waterloo he wrote that: "The French have to me a character of littleness (sic) in all about them; but they have produced three great men that belong to every country, Molière, Rabelais, and Montaigne." Bertrand Russell, brought up by his grandmother, the widow of the first Earl Russell, a Liberal prime minister, wrote: "When I was young, France was still regarded as the traditional enemy of England, and I gathered as unquestionable truth that one Englishman could defeat three Frenchmen." Maynard Keynes while at Eton witnessed the funeral procession of Queen Victoria and wrote to his parents that he was "… most pleased with the small band of picked Germans" and the only blot "was the French mission, they chatted and strolled along as if they were smoking cigarettes on their native boulevards". Robert Skidelsky, Keynes' biographer, states that with these pro-German, anti-French emotions Keynes saw out the Victorian era and has speculated if these opinions were due to his early conditioning. Keynes' parents (his father was a professor at Cambridge) "… were not unusual, either, in holding the French in fairly low esteem".

Professor Colley quotes Margaret Thatcher's father, the Methodist grocer of Grantham, as describing the French nation as "corrupt from top to bottom", and she, too, speculates on how much of his vilification of France he might have passed on to his daughter. Be that as it may, in present times, Britain and France find themselves often in opposition in a new but bloodless arena – the European Union. The real issues are that Britain presses a liberalising market-driven agenda whereas the French prefer a 'social Europe', that is, some form of a European welfare state; for the French, the common agricultural policy is a foundation stone of the EU, but for the British it is a protectionist monstrosity and a serious obstacle to expanding free trade globally; France would like Europe to form a political block capable of confronting the United States, an idea totally unacceptable to Britain. And in all of these and other differences, a constant and acute irritation for France is the the way the English language has become universal, and the language of choice within the EU; this could be seen as the crowning British victory.

It is common knowledge that the promotion of an external threat is an effective way of diverting attention from domestic problems, and the British government of the day was always alert to the advantage of encouraging anti-French sentiment. Allegedly, in 1754, a mob of artisans went through the streets of Bristol shouting: 'No French … No lowering the wages of labouring men to fourpence a day and garlic.' (note the similarity to current complaints in all manner of richer countries against immigrant labour). A contemporary example of the foreign threat is a coarse assertion by an aide of Mrs. Thatcher that the cry "Bugger France! Bugger Europe!" always pays off, particularly in an election.

In reverse, the French authorities were at least as adept at playing a similar card; thus Napoleon addressing his troops immediately before the Battle of Ulm (against the Austrians):"Soldiers, but for the army now in front of you, *we should this day have been in London; we should have avenged six centuries of insults, and restored the freedom of the seas."*

Taking a wider view, criticisms and dislike of the French are not a British peculiarity.In 2005, Olivier Clodong, a professor of social and political communication at the École Supérieure de Paris and José-Manuel Lamarque reported on their investigation of what other Europeans thought about the French, and the picture is not a flattering one.The Germans view the French as pretentious, off-hand, and frivolous; to the Dutch, they are agitated, talkative, and shallow; in Spanish eyes, cold, distant, vain, and impolite; the Portuguese opinion is conceited; the Italian response, snobs, arrogant, flesh-loving, righteous, and self-obsessed; the Swedes find them disobedient, immoral, disorganized, neo-colonialist, and dirty; and the Greeks see them as stupid, egocentric bon vivants. By comparison, the British opinion is not extreme – chauvinists, stubborn, nannied, and humourless; in turn the French describe the British in almost the same words except for adding insular and hate the French. Since the invasion of Iraq, Francophobia in the United States has reached the vitriolic level and fuels a popular e-mail correspondence in terms that surpass the best efforts of those patriotic societies of colonial Massachusetts.

The subject matter of this book has required two unavoidable approximations, and both arise from the long period of time, nine centuries, over which it extends. The first relates to nomenclature - who were the antagonists? The second is the date on which they fought.

Nation is very difficult to define, it is a chameleonic word the colour of which is in the eye of the beholder, and nation-state is a comparatively recent concept. At the Conquest, England, Wales, Scotland, and Ireland were separate entities with approximately the present boundaries but inhabited by different races. The Normans were in a minority in England, and Anglo-Saxons outnumbered them. When the Normans were not at war in France, they tried to extend their dominion into Wales, Scotland, and Ireland. After two or three hundred years, they had conquered most of Wales, made some inroads in Scotland and Ireland, and with the passage of time had assimilated with the Anglo-Saxons in England. Wherever they succeeded, feudal tenure was imposed leading to contingents from these territories appearing in their mainly English armies. Shakespeare is not, to say the least, an infallible historical source, but in his dramatized representation of the battle of Agincourt his four officers in Henry V's army are an English, Welsh, Irish, and Scottish captain respectively. After Edward I's conquest in 1294, most of Wales was annexed to the English crown and has been subsumed under the word English. Scotland is a different case. Often invaded but never conquered by the English, from the end of the thirteenth century until the middle of the sixteenth it was periodically allied with France against England in what is known as the Auld Alliance; then, after one hundred and four years of a joint monarchy, it was united with England by an Act of Union in 1707. Ireland is a different case again. English conquest was more successful than in Scotland but not as complete as in Wales. Irish nationalists usually sought – and often received – active help from France against England, but the king of England ruled distinctly as king of Ireland until an Act of Union in 1801. However, until at least the middle of the eighteenth century, Scots and Irish hostile to England were organized respectively into regiments in the French army. In another sphere, during the larger part of the seventeenth and eighteenth centuries, when the opportunity arose, the American colonists fought the French as subjects of the English king. The pragmatic solution to the problem of identity is to label as English (with a trivial exception) the victors in battles won before the Scottish Act of Union and as British after that time. The French are those fighting for the king of France, or on rare occasions as allies of that monarch.

In a book of anniversaries dates are obviously important, but during the period covered the calendar system was changed, and to complicate the effect the changes were not made universally. The old system, established by Julius Cæsar, was based on slightly inaccurate calculations and became increasingly out of kilter. Once it had been finally accepted that disputing the accuracy of the Julian calendar did not constitute heresy, Pope Gregory XIII by papal bull in 1582 established a more accurate calendar and corrected the errors in the previous one. Unfortunately, many of the Protestant countries flatly refused to accept any rulings from Rome, and so there were now two calendar systems in Europe. Britain adopted the Gregorian calendar in September 1752 by a statute decreeing that eleven days in September 1752 were eliminated, and the immediate effect was rioting in which the cry of the mobs was "Give us back our eleven days"; this was quite properly ignored. As a result, a date in a month old style is relatively speaking not the equivalent of the same date new style. A notable example is the date of the battle of the Boyne, it was fought in 1690 on 1 July old style, but the anniversary is always celebrated by the Orange Order and its supporters on 12 July new style. Concurrently, it was also decreed that the year would begin on January 1 and not March 25. In this book, dates are those in the source from which they have been taken, and no attempt at absolute uniformity has been made.

The titles of commanders have led to another approximation. Wellington, for example, began life as the Honourable Arthur Wellesley and progressed through knighthood and the several levels of the peerage to a dukedom; Nelson's only rank, as a younger son of a parson, was a naval one until he was knighted and rose to be a viscount and a Sicilian duke. Without tracking these changes in title, these two are always referred to as Wellington or Nelson, and similarly with the French commanders.

Footnotes are thought to be unnecessary in a book of this kind, but the principal sources are listed in the References, and sincere apologies are offered for any omissions.

For those who are not persuaded that the Schopenhauer aphorism at the beginning truly expresses the spirit of the book, here is another Schopenhauer maxim to provide a Hegelian anti-thesis: "Every miserable fool who has nothing at all of which he can be proud, adopts as a last resource pride in the nation to which he belongs; he is ready and happy to defend all its faults and follies tooth and nail, thus reimbursing himself for his own inferiority."

Finally, with great pleasure, I acknowledge that the subject is politically incorrect, and enjoyment of this knowledge has sustained me through the inevitable periods of ennui.

Philip H. White
Victoria,
British Columbia.
Canada

1

SYNOPSES OF THE WARS

GENERAL

This part of the book briefly describes the wars in which were fought the battles recounted individually in Part Two; and here the battles of those wars are listed by year in calendar order so that they can be followed in chronological order.

Although Anglo-French conflicts have occurred in every century for the last nine, and in that time there have been many changes in the methods of warfare, and in the places in which battles have been fought, there is a general point to be made about the relative resources of the antagonists that will provide a better perspective.

The resources in question are population, particularly the proportion available for military service, the economy, the efficiency of government in mobilizing the resources including taxable capacity, and diplomatic skills in forming alliances against the enemy. Sometimes the difference between particular items is more apparent than real, for example, on the battle-field it may make little difference whether some of the opposing troops are there as allies with a subsidy from the principal, or stand as mercenaries paid directly by the principal.

In the earlier part of the period especially, the data are very approximate, but in comparing estimates of population from different sources the differences are much smaller when the comparison is made by reference to the ratio of the respective populations. From 1200 to1707, the French population was generally between three to three and a half times as large as the English one, and when, after the Act of Union, Scots are added to the English number the ratio is not substantially reduced. The ratio of the respective armed forces is about the same; at its maximum the army of Louis XIV was about 250,000 compared with 75,000 English supplemented by mercenaries, and this disparity existed at sea where Louis XIV's navy was larger than the combined fleets of England and Holland.

Until the end of the Napoleonic war, mercenaries were employed by all combatants, but here too, on balance, the French probably increased their numerical advantage, and the quality of such forces was not necessarily inferior, for example, the Swiss regiments in the French Revolutionary Wars were among the élite. However, one aspect of military policy added to the French advantage in numbers. In France with its absolute monarchy, there was no hindrance or objection to the creation of a standing army, and it had its beginning in the fifteenth century culminating in the introduction of the *levée en masse* by the Committee of Public Safety in 1793. Experience in Britain was quite different, royal ambitions to create a standing army were strongly resisted by Parliament, although Cromwell's New Model Army made itself an exception, and the issue was finally settled by the Bill of Rights in 1689 which declared it to be illegal to raise or keep a standing army within the kingdom in time of peace without the consent of Parliament. The result was that at the height of the Napoleonic War the French had an army of 1,500,000 reinforced by armies of various allies whereas the British army was only 220,000.

The imbalance in population and its concomitants was offset by Britain's superior performance in industrial output (it was the country in which the industrial revolution first occurred), foreign trade, and taxable capacity. It has been estimated that between 1688 and 1815 Britain's gross national product increased three times but tax receipts went up fifteen times and the government was able to spend twice the French proportion of national income; its capacity to raise revenue was unequalled.

Until the nineteenth century, France was the European super power. Germany comprised dozens of small duchies, electorates and principalities in which Prussia and Bavaria were the only exceptions; Italy was also fragmented; from the seventeenth century the power of Spain deteriorated steadily; and the heterogeneous Austro-Hungarian Empire was not able to match the centralized French resources. To redress the imbalance, England, and later Britain, had to proceed in alliance with other countries, and naturally the French sought to counter these efforts so that diplomacy was usually an important strategic element in the wars.

It would require a much larger book than this one to attempt to isolate the part played in any given battle by the English or British on the one hand, and the French on the other, from the contribution of respective allies and mercenaries – Wellington's heterogeneous army at Waterloo is a notable example – and the approximations, sometimes heroic, are admitted.

Popular discussion crudely subsumes these considerations into simple equations, such as Winston Churchill's assertion in 1940 that one Pole is equal to three Frenchmen, countered by Field Marshal Gort and Air Chief Marshal Dowding who thought the ratio was nearer to ten. In a similar vein is Nelson's dictum that "one Englishman is equal to three Frenchmen", but here Nelson is repeating what Shakespeare had already put in the mouth of Henry V at Agincourt and in so doing was probably only repeating an opinion already in common usage. In spite of going to sea at the age of 12, Nelson seems to have been well-versed in Shakespeare's 'Henry V' because Nelson's renowned reference to his 'band of brothers' is taken verbatim from the same passage in the play.

Finally, all attempts to quantify the balance of resources, irrespective of the base, must have regard to the intangibles. Said Napoleon, whose opinion in such matters commands respect: "Morale makes up three quarters of the game, the relative balance of manpower accounts for only the remaining quarter."

ANGLO-FRENCH WARS 1066 - 1337

The explanation of the causes of any war is complex, but in this instance it is particularly the case. The period runs from the Norman Conquest to the outbreak of the Hundred Years' War, and for roughly the first half of that time English political and military history is not much more than an adjunct of the activities of the territorial magnates of northern France, and in particular of the Dukes of Normandy who were often kings of England as well.

Originally, the Normans were Vikings from Scandinavia, they had begun to settle in northern France late in the ninth century and their regular raiding and pillaging took them to the walls of Paris on several occasions. They so intimidated the indigenous population that in 911 the king, Charles the Simple, created their leader, Rollo, Duke of Normandy (the word is derived from *Normanni* or Northmann) and granted him lands in the lower Seine valley and around what is now Rouen. Displaying characteristic valour, ferocity, craftiness, and cunning extending to downright treachery when the ends called for it, the Normans embarked on campaigns of expansion. First, they pushed westwards into Lower Normandy, and then farther afield into southern Italy and Sicily where their audacity and martial skills gave them victory over enemies that were far more numerous.

The Italian conquests were already approaching completion when William, Duke of Normandy and a descendant of Rollo, decided to put a slender claim to the throne of England to trial by force of arms. He took his army across the Channel and at Hastings was able to defeat the Anglo-Saxon army wearied by a rapid forced march from Stamford Bridge, near York, where it had just defeated an invading Norwegian army. Ever since this victory, William has been styled 'the Conqueror'.

William quickly demonstrated superior administrative skills. The feudal system of France with Norman improvements was imposed, the famous Domesday record was made, and extensive land grants were made to his principal supporters. The language of the court and the new aristocracy was the French of northern France as were the customs and religion, all of which had been grafted onto Scandinavian roots. The key to consolidation of the Norman conquest was that the Duchy of Normandy and the kingdom of England should be in the same hand because under the feudal system all land was deemed to be held from the ruler to whom the feudal tenants, from the highest to the lowest, were obliged to swear fealty; many Norman nobles now had large estates in the Duchy and in the kingdom, and it was essential that they should not have divided loyalties. This vital condition did not survive the Conqueror's death, and the Anglo-French Wars became inevitable, but even before he died, William was intermittently at war with the French king, Philip I. In 1087, he had burned Mantes, about 25 miles west of Paris, and while riding through the burning town his horse stumbled. William sustained injuries when he fell from his horse that proved fatal, and he was buried at Caen in the abbey which he had founded. Like his immediate successors, William had been an infrequent visitor to England after the rebellions following Hastings had been put down.

William had three sons; in order of seniority, Robert, William, and Henry. Under the feudal law of succession, the eldest son succeeded to his father's patrimony that is the property his father had inherited, and for Robert this was the Duchy. On his death bed at Rouen, William bequeathed England to William, and Henry was given a substantial sum of money with which to buy estates in Normandy. Not for the first time and certainly not the last, the eldest son had many disagreements with his father, the king, and finally with the support of Philip I of France he revolted unsuccessfully and was allowed to go into exile in France. The stage was now set for the commencement of the wars in earnest.

Soon after he had succeeded to the throne, many of the Norman nobles in England revolted against William, known as Rufus, in favour of his brother, Robert, the new Duke of Normandy. The rebellion was suppressed in England, but hostilities continued in Normandy until 1091, when a truce was made. A temporary unification of Normandy and England then occurred in an unusual way. Duke Robert was so exhilarated and enthused by the preaching of Pope Urban II that nothing could restrain him from joining the First Crusade against the Turks in order to liberate Jerusalem. Robert had not been a capable ruler in Normandy, and in order to equip himself and his army for the long journey from Normandy, he mortgaged the Duchy to his brother, William Rufus, for 10,000 marks.

Rufus was anything but a passive lender content with the revenues of the Duchy, instead with energy and military skill he set about restoring the boundaries of Normandy to those at the time of his father's death. Maine and the Vexin, the lands between Rouen and Paris, which had been lost by Robert, were recovered. On the other side of the Channel, he took better control of the Scottish frontier and suppressed rebellions of those nobles who thought their lot would be improved with Robert as the single ruler of Normandy and England. Not lacking the support of the laity, William also managed to advance the interests of the monarchy against the church. All things considered, William was proving to be a capable ruler when he died in the New Forest in a hunting accident, although there is a view that he was assassinated, perhaps on the orders of his younger brother Henry.

The evidence of an assassination is only circumstantial, but the facts are that William died without heirs and that only three days after his death, in a model *coup d'état,* Henry was crowned as Henry I at Westminster having thoughtfully seized the royal treasure along the way. Immediately, a coronation proclamation was made renouncing alleged abuses of William II, (showing the way to many a democratically-elected politician later), and he made efforts to ingratiate himself with the church. Then, mindful that the Anglo-Saxons had been defeated only 34 years before, he married Matilda of the old Anglo-Saxon royal line and the daughter of the king of Scotland; this was in face of the general Norman opinion that the Anglo-Saxons were decidedly inferior, and they mocked Henry for his marriage.

Meanwhile, Robert, who might be thought to have had a better claim to the English throne in right of the eldest son, was on his way back from the Crusade trailing clouds of glory honestly earned (he had fought in the streets of Jerusalem itself when it was taken), and with a rich wife. Within a year of Henry's coronation, Robert was ready to contest it and he invaded England. As at Rufus' accession, some of the nobility rebelled in favour of Robert, but with the support of most of the Anglo-Saxons and the church, the insurgents were beaten. Henry had not been strong enough to inflict a decisive defeat, and so he bought Robert's acquiescence to his succession in consideration for an annuity of 3,000 marks. As an aside, assuming market prices in both transactions, Rufus' mortgage loan of 10,000 marks for the revenues of the Duchy of Normandy compared with the annuity paid from the English revenues suggests that the latter were decidedly more substantial. Given what happened only five years later, such a comparison might require different assumptions because Henry, responding to considerable dissatisfaction with Robert's self-indulgent and vacillating rule in the Duchy, first bribed important Norman barons, made alliances with neighbouring princes, and then invaded Normandy.

The battle of Tinchebrai, south-west of Falaise, settled the issue between Robert and Henry once and for all; fighting as the king of England Henry routed Robert's army, took Robert prisoner and kept him captive successively in the castles of Wareham, Devizes, Bristol and Cardiff for the rest of his life. Unquestionably, the most able of the Conqueror's sons, Henry proceeded aggressively to enforce his rule in northern France against William Clito, Robert's only legitimate son, who was supported by Louis VI of France, and disgruntled Norman barons who had backed the wrong man. By 1120, Henry had triumphed, the barons had sworn fealty to him, and Louis VI had been defeated. At this point, circumstances beyond his control caused Henry's plans for his succession to unravel. Although Henry is said to have acknowledged more than twenty illegitimate children (not remarkable by regal standards - Augustus II of Poland and Saxony is reputed to have sired 354), but Henry had only one legitimate son, William the Atheling, who at the age of 17 was drowned when the *White Ship* in which he was travelling to England struck a rock on leaving Barfleur and sank. According to William of Malmesbury, William's death was a dynastic tragedy because as the son of a Norman father and an Anglo-Saxon mother he represented a real hope for the reconciliation of the two peoples; this now had to wait for about two hundred years.

Henry's queen, Matilda, had died two years previously and less than three months after the *White Ship* went down, Henry had married again to Adela of Louvain. Ensuring an incontrovertible succession was now Henry's paramount concern, but although the new queen was only about twenty years old and Henry fifty-two, there was no heir (for the record it seems the failure lay with Henry since on her re-marriage after his death, Adela bore the Earl of Arundel a son).When Henry finally accepted this disappointment to be immutable, he recalled from Germany his widowed daughter, Matilda, Dowager Roman Empress, compelled the barons to swear to accept her as his heir, and married her to Geoffrey Plantagenet, Count of Anjou and Maine, territories immediately south of Normandy. In furtherance of his policy of alliances by means of diplomatic marriages, no fewer than eight of his illegitimate daughters were married to neighbouring princes, from Alexander of Scotland in the north to the count of Perche in the south; a policy that prompted William of Malmesbury to assert that for Henry sex was not a matter of pleasure but of policy; in today's jargon, however, it might be described as a 'win-win strategy'.

After five years of anything but wedded bliss, Matilda gave birth to a son, the future Henry II, and an orderly succession seemed secure, but when Henry I died at Lyons-la-Forêt, near Rouen, his favourite nephew, Stephen of Blois, following his uncle's example, executed a lightning *coup d'état.* Within a week or two of Henry's death and unscrupulously disregarding his oath to accept Matilda's succession, Stephen seized the throne and was subsequently accepted as Duke of Normandy. The pope obligingly confirmed these dishonourable actions, and Stephen appeared to have met the basic requirement of ruling in England and in Normandy, but it was all too good to last. With support from her husband who had succeeded his father as Count of Anjou and from her half-brother Richard, Earl of Gloucester, an illegitimate son of Henry I, Matilda invaded England, and a civil war broke out that continued for fourteen years. Mistakes were made on both sides, but Stephen was always in decline; Count Geoffrey conquered Normandy in 1144 and became duke; the pope withdrew his support and refused to accept Stephen's son, Eustace, as his heir, and instead recognized Matilda's son as Stephen's successor. Stronger support for son Henry came from the barons in Normandy where he had become duke when his father abdicated in his favour in 1150. To general relief, the English civil war finally came to an end in 1153; by the treaty of Winchester, Stephen acknowledged Henry as his heir, and he came to the throne a year later on Stephen's death.

At the age of 21, Henry was now King of England, Duke of Normandy, Count of Greater Anjou, and in addition by his marriage to Eleanor, the heiress to the vast duchy of Aquitaine, his empire was extended from the Scottish border to the Pyrenees. This was a larger and richer territory than that of the king of France, and in it England was only a province. It has been estimated that during his reign Henry was twice absent from England for more than four years at a time and that he was in France for 21 years out of a total of 35. Apart from the huge task of governing such a geographical spread when travel was so difficult, living in France in this period was attractive. The concept of chivalry as a code of behaviour expected of a knight demanding personal honour, loyalty, generosity and courage was developing in northern France, and if practice always fell short of the ideal, it did create a social bond between monarch, nobility and gentry. Chivalry also inspired poetry, art, architecture, and music, and notions of courtly love provided an elegant compensation for the dissatisfactions of dynastic marriages. Louis VII of France summed it up in a few words, observing that Henry enjoyed "… all in abundant plenty. We in France have only bread, wine and gaiety."

Henry possessed extraordinary energy, organising abilities, and qualities of leadership; he was constantly on the move to the extent that Louis VII was said to be convinced that he could fly. In England, in the aftermath of the near-anarchy of Stephen's reign, he was able to continue the work of Henry I and extend the power of the monarchy by a series of administrative and judicial reforms that centralised government and created an efficient management system that functioned effectively during the king's absences. In the familiar struggles between king and church, Henry is notorious for his part in the assassination of Thomas Becket in Canterbury cathedral, but in time he was able to overcome the effect that this had on his contemporaries. In short, he can be regarded as one of the most able monarchs of England, but, again like Henry I, Henry's shortcoming was failure to establish an orderly succession.

After twenty years on the throne, Henry had decided how the Angevin empire was to be divided between his sons. Eight children had been born – five sons and three daughters, but one son, William, had died aged three. The surviving sons in order of seniority were: Henry; Richard; Geoffrey; and John, and in the first plan no territory was to be bequeathed to John. Henry was to have his father's patrimony, namely, Anjou, Normandy, and England; Richard's share was his mother's inheritance, Aquitaine; and Brittany, conquered by Henry, was to go to Geoffrey. Later, after Henry had completed a partial conquest, Ireland was to be John's portion. Expectations were raised but were not met because Henry kept control. Soon, with the support of Eleanor, John and Richard, joined later by Geoffrey, rebelled and were supported by the kings of Scotland and France. The rebels were no match for Henry, and in a few months he had re-established his authority throughout his empire, but the succession plans continued to fall apart. Son Henry died during a second, lesser rebellion in 1183 and two years later Geoffrey, Duke of Brittany, was trampled to death at a tournament in Paris where he was plotting with the king of France. A contemporary opinion of Geoffrey offers a persuasive view of the poisonous relationships in the royal family: "overflowing with words, smooth as oil, a hypocrite in everything, capable by his syrupy eloquence of corrupting two kingdoms with his tongue." The Oscar-winning film 'The Lion in Winter' is a dramatized version of these family feuds, but it does seem a pity that the pageantry of Henry's vivid reign did not inspire Shakespeare to add it to his historical plays. In 1189, at the end of his life, Henry II was defeated by Richard and Philip II in alliance who chased him from Le Mans to Saumur, and he died at Chinon, his favourite castle. Henry and Eleanor are buried in the abbey church of Fontevrault.

Richard, invariably described as 'the Lionheart' or *Coeur de Lion,* has always been a popular and heroic figure in English history, and the striking equestrian statue in Old Palace Yard, Westminster is a tribute to his outstanding military ability not only as a commander in the field but also in planning campaigns – the organization of the Crusade invasion fleet to sail from northern waters to Palestine is a mediæval masterpiece. His brilliant performance in the Third Crusade, notably a defeat of Saladin, the capture of Acre, and the treaty of Jaffa, are commemorated in a Memorial Chapel in All Hallows by the Tower in which there is also the crusading altar originally in Richard's castle at Athlit in Israel. The fact that Richard was decidedly French - by birth, in character and upbringing - has not dimmed his popular image in England.

He returned from the Crusade to find that in his absence King Philip II had been able to seize a large part of Normandy, thanks in no small part to the treacherous behaviour of brother John. Richard set about making good these losses and had largely succeeded when he died from a wound suffered at the siege of Chalus-Chabrol. As he lay dying, he ordered that he should be buried at Fontevrault with his father but that his heart should be interred at Rouen, the capital of Normandy.

Henry II and Richard are both recognized as excellent English monarchs, but regrettably John, who succeeded Richard, was one of the worst. On his accession in 1199, there was an immediate fissure in the Angevin empire; the barons in Normandy opted for John; those in Brittany for John's nephew, Arthur, (the son of Geoffrey); while Aquitaine continued to be held by Queen Eleanor on John's behalf. Starting in the manner in which he continued, John's first essay into foreign policy had a decidedly Pyrrhic flavour, he made a 2 years' truce with Philip II in consideration for which he handed over parts of Normandy that were part of the original grant to Rollo, recognized Philip as the overlord of all the English possessions in France and paid Philip a large sum of money into the bargain. The only thing that might be said in John's defence is that he had no intention of honouring the terms he had agreed. Two years later, John was fighting Philip who had recognized Arthur, the son of John's brother Geoffrey, as the rightful ruler of Normandy and of Anjou. Arthur was besieging Mirebeau in Aquitaine where John's mother, Eleanor the Dowager Queen, was holding out in the castle, when he was taken prisoner by the English relieving force. He was taken to Falaise and then to Rouen, where it is generally accepted he was murdered either personally by his uncle, John, or on his orders. Arthur was never seen alive again although his body was eventually recovered from the Seine. John proved incapable of organizing an effective military defensive campaign and by the end of

1203 he had been obliged to withdraw to England. Philip II overran all of the English territories in France with exception of Gascony, and John, nick-named 'Lackland' by his father, now became scornfully known to his English subjects as 'Softsword'.

John had no choice but to spend virtually all the remaining years of his reign in England, and this did nothing to improve his reputation. Overall, his aim was to recover the lost territories in France, and to this end he was forced to increase royal revenues by taxation and from any other sources that could be found. A bout of inflation reduced fiscal capacity and provoked oppressive measures by the king which from time to time descended into tyranny. Confirming the unfavourable impressions created by Arthur's murder were the death by deliberate starvation of the wife and son of a rebel baron, William de Boase, in a dungeon in Windsor Castle, and the hanging of 28 hostages, sons of rebel Welsh chieftains. Imprudently, John added the pope to his powerful opponents, and by 1212 Philip II was preparing to invade England. John reacted to this threat by ingeniously making his peace with the pope and even securing his support. He was able to send a fleet across the Channel and to destroy the French fleet at Damme. Emboldened by this success, John took an army to Poitou and reinforced the army of the German Emperor, Otto IV, but Philip II took his revenge for Damme at Bouvines in 1214 and added to John's miserable military record.

The preferred method of dealing with an unpopular ruler in this period was to promote the cause of a rival with some claim to right of succession, but Arthur's involuntary demise had ruled this out. The method chosen to constrain the activities of this secretive, suspicious, jealous, and capricious monarch was the unusual one of reform. The dissatisfied barons marched on London, captured it, and forced John to sign Magna Carta in a meadow at Runnymede in June 1215. This document and the reissues of 1216, 1217, and 1225 have had a far greater long term effect than the immediate one. John never intended to observe the limitations it imposed on royal rights, and three months later civil war began in earnest. John made a bad start, he lost part of his baggage train while crossing the Wash, and shortly afterwards he died at Newark. The barons in rebellion had invited the son of Philip II to replace John as king, and he came to England to lead the rebels. At first, Louis was successful, but after John's death the rebellion lost impetus and defeats followed. Louis had some compensation at the Treaty of Kingston in the form of a secret payment of 10,000 marks, and he went on to have a brief reign in France during which he took the English province of Poitou. In seventeen years, John had lost the Angevin empire on the continent except for Gascony and the Channel Islands.

Academic research frequently takes the form of seeking to disprove current doctrine, and in the natural sciences controlled experiments make proof easier to establish than in the social sciences in which opinion is often as far as enquiry can lead. Nineteenth century historians treated John very roughly, but modern historians have disputed their more extreme opinions, nevertheless, we might reasonably take the balance of opinion to be that "[John] had the mental abilities of a great king but the inclinations of a petty tyrant".

It should not be thought that the events in this period were played by an all-male cast. Several women took an active part. Matilda, the Conqueror's consort, in addition to succeeding in the primary task of ensuring succession by bearing nine children, proved to be a very able deputy, often acting as regent during William's absences from Normandy. Unusually, her marriage seems to have been exceptionally successful, and Matilda was able to ameliorate the always-strained relationship between William and Robert, their eldest son. Like her husband, she founded an abbey at Caen in which she was buried.

Matilda's daughter-in-law, the first wife of Henry I was also named Matilda and she, too, proved to be a competent deputy for her husband, frequently acting as regent of England during Henry's absence in France.

A minor complexity in this fragment of the history is that the next character is also named Matilda, she is the daughter of Henry I and his wife Matilda. Her opportunity to show her mettle came when her only legitimate brother was drowned in a ship-wreck. Matilda had been sent to Germany when only 8 years old in order to marry the Holy Roman Emperor, Henry V, the ceremony took place four years later but when Henry died in 1125 the child bride had not borne any children. Her father recalled her to England where he forced his barons to accept her as his heir to the English throne and to the duchy of Normandy, and in the following year he arranged her marriage to Geoffrey, the heir of the Count of Anjou. This time Matilda's situation was reversed – she was 26 but the groom was only 14 – and it was not a happy marriage, nevertheless after five years the future Henry II was born and as his father had become the Count of Anjou the foundation of the Angevin empire was laid. A major hitch occurred when Henry I died; instead of Matilda's succession, her cousin, Stephen executed a *coup* by which he became king of England and Duke of Normandy. Matilda, showing plenty of fighting spirit, organised an army and in alliance with her illegitimate half-brother Robert, Earl of Gloucester, invaded England in 1139. Civil war now began and Matlida's early successes were crowned when Stephen was captured at the battle of Lincoln, but Matilda failed to exploit this advantage due in no small measure to the efforts of Stephen's queen, another formidable woman. In turn, Robert was taken prisoner at the battle of Winchester and subsequently had to be exchanged for Stephen; after Robert's death Matilda withdrew to Normandy but continued to maintain her position in England on behalf of her son Henry. The anarchy that her efforts ensured came to an end when Henry succeeded Stephen. Matilda is known as an impetuous, haughty but indomitable woman to whom Henry was greatly indebted for her determination to maintain his right to succession.

Yet another Matilda deserves mention; this one is Matilda of Boulogne, the queen of Stephen. She was the heiress to the lands of the counts of Boulogne in France and in England which provided her husband with substantial resources and a power base for the *coup* that put him on the throne. After he had been captured she not only organized resistance to Matilda but brought an army to Winchester where the Earl of Gloucester was defeated and taken prisoner; this was the means of securing Stephen's release. A strategic triumph was the arrangement of the marriage of her son, Eustace, to a daughter of Louis VI of France, although this plan failed when Eustace died before his father.

The career of Eleanor of Aquitaine is the outstanding example that gender did not bar an active participation and leadership in these times; in the development of her spectacular career, she had the advantage of longevity, she lived for 82 years compared with the average of 51 years for the four Matildas described above. She was the heiress of the Duke of Aquitaine and Count of Poitiers whose territories were greater than those of the king of France, and at fifteen she brought this glittering dowry with her on her marriage to Louis VII. Beautiful and capricious, Louis adored her, and, not always beneficially, she had considerable influence over him. When he went on the Second Crusade, Eleanor joined him leading her own troops and dressed as an Amazonian warrior. By the time they returned, the relationship had soured, and after fifteen years, Louis divorced Eleanor nominally because of consanguinity but more probably because Eleanor had borne only two daughters. Whatever the reason, this divorce has been described as one of the greatest political blunders in the history of mediæval France, because two months later Eleanor married Henry, Count of Anjou, and two years after that Eleanor, now 32 years old, had become queen of England, duchess of Normandy and much else besides. Although eleven years older than Henry, Eleanor had five sons and three daughters, and during her child-bearing years she participated actively in the administration of the realm and even more actively in the management of her own domains where she maintained a court at Poitiers that became a centre of poetry and a model of courtly life and manners. These activities came to an end in 1173 when Eleanor took the side of her sons' revolt against their father and gave them considerable military support. The revolt failed and Eleanor was taken prisoner while seeking refuge in France; until Henry's death sixteen years later, Eleanor was kept in close confinement in England from which she emerged to play a greater political role than ever before. Immediately, she made preparations for Richard's coronation, and while he was away crusading, Eleanor managed the realm during which time she was active in thwarting the intrigues of the treacherous John with Philip II of France. On his way back from the Crusade, Richard was seized and held for ransom by the Duke of Austria; Eleanor led the efforts to raise the ransom money and then went in person to escort him home. Richard's death without an heir stirred Eleanor into further action. Across the Pyrenees she went in order to bring her granddaughter, Blanche, from the court of Castile to marry her to the son of the French king, a marriage intended to ensure peace between Angevin and the French monarchy-a courageous but futile attempt. Then, nearly 80 years old we find Eleanor in the thick of the defence of Anjou and Aquitaine against the attack of her grandson, Arthur. After the relief of Mirebeau, Eleanor finally retired to the monastery at Fontevrault where she is buried. In addition to taking an active part in current affairs, Eleanor showed an understanding of strategy in arranging the marriages of her daughters – Matilda to the duke of Saxony and Bavaria; Eleanor to the king of Castile; Joan to the king of Sicily, and then to the count of Toulouse. It has been suggested that she might well be called "the grandmother of Europe", but much later Queen Victoria had a better claim to the title. After her death, the nuns of Fontevrault wrote of her that she "surpassed almost all the queens of the world".

A minor change in fashion marked by John's death in 1216 is in historical nomenclature. Henry II, Richard I, and John are normally described as the Angevin kings, but their successors up to Richard II (1399) are known as Plantagenets. The name Plantagenet is derived from *Planta genesta,* the botanical name of broom, traditionally the emblem of the counts of Anjou, and it came into common usage after Richard III called himself by it.

A change of much larger significance in relations between England and France occurred in the early years of the reign of Henry III, John's son, who was only nine when he came to the throne. Unsuccessful in his attempt to take the English crown, Louis VIII, as he became in France, captured Poitou so that the only part of France left in English hands was Gascony in the south west corner. The territorial balance of the twelfth century was now entirely reversed. Under the Angevins, England was a province in a continental empire, and its kings were frequently abroad for long periods, but under the Plantagenets it was an independent kingdom that occupied most of the monarch's attention and his presence.

During Henry's minority, the country was governed by a council of barons, and the civil war in which the rebels sought to put the French dauphin on the throne in place of John ended with a victory over the rebels. Henry declared himself to be of age in 1227 and began a reign generally marked by failure at home and abroad. Civil war broke out in 1264 and the king was defeated by Simon de Montfort at Lewes and taken prisoner, but a year later the result was reversed at Evesham by Henry's son, Edward, and de Montfort was killed and dismembered on the field; this gruesome end had an unwelcome result in the rapid emergence of a cult that defied efforts to suppress it. The remains had been interred at Evesham Abbey which became the centre of a pilgrimage, and within thirteen years of Simon's slaughter over 200 miracles had reputedly occurred. In the few years remaining to Henry he was obliged to accept some limitations to the absolute authority of the crown in which his belief and practice were at the root of his failures. Henry had a genuine admiration of the arts and spent lavishly on a wide range of objects with which to embellish royal palaces, and his enduring legacy was the rebuilding of Westminster Abbey in which he is buried near to his idol, Edward the Confessor.

Henry's son, Edward, succeeded as Edward I. He was in Sicily returning from the Eighth Crusade when he heard of his father's death and made a leisurely return home for his coronation. A man of imposing height, skilled in warfare and in government, his reign is best remembered for great improvements in administrative efficiency and for legal reforms; he was able to mobilize resources of men, money and supplies to unprecedented levels and this capacity gave England a valuable advantage in future wars against the French. Edward's own military campaigns were aimed at securing and enlarging the frontiers of England. He proceeded first against the Welsh and substantially succeeded in making Wales a part of England, but although he pressed hard, he was not as successful against the Scots. The 'Auld Alliance', the series of treaties for mutual defence between Scotland and France against the English, dates from 1295 and was a factor in Anglo-French conflicts until the sixteenth century. Queen Eleanor died seventeen years before Edward (perhaps after bearing fourteen children it is not surprising), and two years later Robert Burnell, Edward's lifelong friend and chancellor, also died. After the death of these two sound advisers, Edward's performance deteriorated; he became embroiled in an inconclusive war against the French over Gascony from which he extricated himself by marrying Marguerite, the French king's sister, but his love for Eleanor is demonstrated by his memorial to her memory. He ordered a cross to be erected at every place the funeral cortege stayed overnight on its way back to Westminster. There were twelve in all and Charing Cross is the best known, although the cross now standing there is not original but a fanciful reproduction; three originals still stand at Waltham Cross, Geddington, and Hardingstone.

The period of the Anglo-French Wars ends with the reign of Edward II, son of Edward I, which was even worse than that of Henry III; and in comparison to these two, the reign of Edward I is like a slice of prime roast beef between two slices of mouldy bread. Tall and good looking, Edward II looked like a king, but he lacked any of the other attributes. He showed a strong predilection for favourites that might have been based on homosexual attraction, and these men were given leading roles in government. The leading barons strongly objected, and five years after his coronation Edward was forced to accept the beheading of his prime favourite, Piers Gaveston, by the Earl of Warwick and a group of nobles; the site of the execution, Blacklow Hill near Warwick, is still marked by a monument. However, the violent nobles were no better at government than those chosen by the king, the Scots won a famous victory at Bannockburn, and a civil war broke out. Rather surprisingly, the royalist faction quickly routed their opponents, and there followed what has been described as:"one of the most unpleasant and ultimately ineffectual regimes ever to rule England". The Scottish war went badly for the English as did a conflict with France over Gascony. Queen Isabella, the daughter of Philip IV of France, had become estranged from Edward and had found refuge at the French court with her brother, Charles IV; it was there she became the lover of Roger Mortimer, Earl of March. Mortimer had been one of the rebel barons defeated by Edward, and after a dramatic escape from the Tower of London, he got away to France. In 1327, Isabella and Roger had been able to assemble a sufficient force with which to invade England where they met only feeble opposition and found popular support. Edward was deposed by Parliament and incarcerated in Berkeley Castle where he was soon murdered. For three years Isabella and Roger ruled on behalf of Edward's heir then only fifteen years old, but the regime was corrupt and incompetent, and there were few regrets when the young Edward III plotted a *coup* and took Mortimer prisoner. After a trial in Parliament, Mortimer was executed; Isabella was more fortunate, she was sent into a comfortable retirement, and in her declining years, perhaps in contrition, she joined the Order of the Poor Clares.

Christopher Marlowe wrote a fine historical tragedy in blank verse, 'Edward II', which is thought to have had an important influence on Shakespeare; and out on the lunatic fringe, those who believe that Marlowe was the real author of Shakespeare's plays would say this helps to prove our point.

The few English victotries in the Anglo-French Wars were:

1106	Sep.28	Tinchebrai	1213	May.30	Damme
1119	Aug.20	Brenneville	1217	May.20	Lincoln
1194	Jul.3	Fréteval	1217	Aug.24	Sandwich
1202	Aug.1	Mirebeau-en-Poitou			

HUNDRED YEARS' WAR 1337 – 1457

In the reign of the four kings of England immediately preceding Edward III, there had been civil war in three of them, and preoccupation with domestic crises meant there was little inclination to join in foreign campaigning even if the resources for it had not been exhausted at home. Edward III completely changed this state of affairs and launched England on a plan to establish a great continental empire principally on French territory. The effort continued through four reigns not in a continuous war, but in a series of wars that collectively have come to be known as the Hundred Years' War. From an English perspective, there were four phases: I, 1337-1360; II, 1361-1413; III, 1414-1420; IV, 1421-1457.

At the beginning, the considerable advantage of France in numbers and interior lines of communication was offset by English superiority in the quality of troops, notably archers armed and skilful in the use of the formidable longbow, who were directed by superior commanders, and in more efficient government. The English who now confronted the French were markedly different people from those who were ruled by John. The seamless amalgamation of the Anglo-Saxon and Norman races was well on the way to completion, and the population was more than willing to support their king in a war against the French. The immediate causes of the war were: to keep the important trade with Flanders free from French domination; constant French attempts to exercise feudal authority over Gascony, the one remaining English territory in France; and what was seen as French meddling in Scotland. These reasons were comprehensively combined in the claim to the French crown put forward by Edward III after the French king, Charles IV, died in 1328 without heirs. Through his mother, Edward was the nephew of Charles IV, and the other – successful – claimant was Philip VI, Charles' cousin, but Edward did not abandon his claim, and neither did any of his successors until 1802!

Philip became embroiled in a civil war in Flanders on the side of the count who had appealed for his help. England took the other side and hostilities began with the naval battle at Cadsand. They continued with another civil war in Brittany in which Philip VI supported the claims of Charles de Blois (of King Stephen's family) to the Duchy, and Edward those of John de Montfort (whose ancestor had led the barons' revolt against Henry III; thus were the monarchies and nobilities of England and France still writhing together at this period). Final settlement of the Brittany succession was not made until 1365, with the Montforts victorious, but in the meantime the war took on much larger dimensions. Edward III invaded France with the main English army and routed the French at Crécy, but natural causes then reduced the scale of operations on both sides. A devastating plague called the 'Black Death' struck Europe with a death rate not previously experienced, it raged from about 1347 to 1354, and it is estimated that between a third and a half of the population died. The economic and social effects were huge and affected military operations, but in roughly the same proportions. After Crécy, Calais was taken and the English were ascendant for the rest of Phase I culminating in the Black Prince's victory at Poitiers and the capture of the French king, John II, who spent most of his remaining years as a prisoner in England where he died. The Treaty of Brétigny 1360 marks the end of Phase I.

Edward III had proved to be the man for the hour. He took great care in planning his campaigns, was able to inspire his troops, and to choose exceptional commanders; to these talents he added a sure grasp of strategy. Before commencing operations on the continent, Edward had secured his northern frontier by dealing the Scots a heavy defeat at Halidon Hill, and throughout the French campaigns he changed his strategy in the light of experience and opportunities. His domestic policies were pragmatic.He skilfully managed the nobility relying on patronage and a willingness to compromise even if he sometimes refused to honour commitments he had given, and not the least of his achiuevements was to declare English as the official language. Unusually, he had no problems with his immediate family of seven sons and five daughters. He was able to provide the elder sons with adequate estates, and the war provided them with sufficient opportunities for independent action. Edward's stature in Europe was such that he was invited to become the Emperor of Germany, but Parliament forced him to decline the honour.

Phase II of the War represents something of a hiatus in both England and in France. In England there were financial problems arising from the economic decline following the Black Death and the cost of the war in France, and these difficulties enabled the Commons to enlarge its powers at the expense of the king's. In the later years of his life Edward suffered senility, and when his eldest son, the Black Prince, died a year before him leaving a boy as his heir, the stage was set for a re-run of the disastrous succession to Edward I.

Richard II was nine years old at his accession, and at the beginning government was largely in the hands of John of Gaunt, Edward's third son, who had been virtually the regent during his father's dotage. In France, England had been forced on the defensive and was not holding ground, financial difficulties continued and the imposition of a particularly heavy poll tax provoked a serious uprising known as the 'Peasants' Revolt' (if Mrs. Thatcher had studied history instead of chemistry she might not have persisted in her own version of this inefficient and wildly unpopular levy). This uprising came to an end with a dramatic intervention by the fourteen years-old king, but he was not able to build on this success. He developed ideas of royal supremacy which led him directly into conflicts with Parliament led by some of the powerful barons. Richard's supporters were defeated in the field, and Richard survived as king only because the victors could not agree on who should be put in his place. After several years' absence in Spain, where improbably he had been King of Castile, John of Gaunt now returned and steadied his nephew sufficiently to quieten opposition for about eight years. The end of this uneasy peace came because of opposition to Richard's policy of negotiating a peace with France, and to a plan to re-establish English supremacy in Ireland. At one point Richard intimidated Parliament with his archers, exiled John of Gaunt's son, Henry, then confiscated his very rich inheritance, and set off for Ireland with an expedition. A month later, Henry, now Duke of Lancaster, invaded England where he met with little resistance, and when Richard returned from Ireland he got no further than North Wales before he was seized, forced to abdicate, and was deposed by Parliament.

Henry came to the throne as Henry IV and almost immediately was met with a rebellion by some of Richard's courtiers now abruptly cut off from preferment. The main result was that Richard was kept in custody and died mysteriously shortly afterwards, but there is no reliable evidence to support allegations that he was murdered. Shakespeare has left us with a dramatic study of the final years of Richard's reign, including his 'murder', the play is written entirely in blank verse and contains some of Shakespeare's best known speeches such as his panegyric of England: "This royal throne of kings, this sceptred isle... ...", and the scene of Richard's deposition in Parliament is one of the most famous in Shakespeare's works.

A more serious rebellion occurred three years later in which leading magnates who had supported Henry's usurpation, notably the Percys of Northumberland were now against him. Henry, ably assisted by his son, the future Henry V, triumphed at the battle of Shrewsbury, only to find that Wales was well on the way to independence under the leadership of Owain Glyndwr. War with Scotland fomented by the defeated Earl of Northumberland, continuous conflicts with the French on land and sea, and the burden of taxation to meet the concomitant expenses presented Henry with daunting problems that he overcame by energy, perseverance, and decisiveness. The exceptional efforts he made probably weakened his health, and in 1406 he had the first of a series of strokes. To a considerable degree, Henry's rule was sustained by the ability of his sons, Henry, Thomas, John, and Humphrey, and when he died in 1413 he passed on a kingdom that was sufficiently united and peaceful at home, and buttressed by alliances in Germany, Scandinavia, Brittany, and Flanders, for son Henry to contemplate campaigning in France.

Shakespeare wrote two historical plays about Henry IV dealing with the early phase of the power struggle between the York and Lancaster families. Part 1 is set in the rebellion of the Percys and Owen Glyndwr and introduces the extraordinary character Sir John Falstaff. In Part 2 the war against the Welsh insurgents continues; on his death bed Henry IV is reconciled with his eldest son Henry (V) who has been leading an aimless, hedonistic life with Falstaff, and Henry V is seen as a reformed character who renounces Falstaff and his way of life. The play ends with Henry's brother John forecasting war with France.

In France, Phase II of the War began more successfully. In De Guesclin, they found a much more capable leader than his predecessors. He shrewdly avoided pitched battles and proceeded by sieges and guerilla tactics to recover substantial areas of lost territory and, at one point, even an invasion of England was contemplated. De Guesclin died a soldier's death during a siege, and a series of diplomatic failures, as well as the succession of Charles VI at the age of eleven, led to near-anarchy. Two rival nobles, the Duke of Burgundy and the Duke of Orleans, strove to secure power to rule, and their pursuit of self-interst allowed civil disorder to flourish. Bands of brigands, many of whom were former soldiers, roamed through the country living by robbery and intimidation, and efforts to restore order were hampered by the bouts of madness from which Charles VI now suffered.

The English prospects in Phase III of the War were bright. In Henry V, they had a capable, fearless, and authoritarian monarch backed by enthusiastic, popular support, whereas the French king was feeble and the country disunited. Henry was a man to press such an advantage, and barely two years after his coronation he was in France at the head of his army. His strategy was realistic, it was to make an alliance with a powerful French noble, otherwise it would be impossible to sustain the programme of conquest and colonization on which he embarked after his astounding success at Agincourt had revealed the possibilities. Four years after Agincourt, the Duke of Burgundy was murdered by the Orleanists and his heir made an alliance with Henry. This quickly led to the Treaty of Troyes in 1420 (May 21) by which Charles VI agreed to disinherit the Dauphin in favour of the succession of Henry (and his heirs) as king of France, in the meantime Henry was to be the regent of France. Not surprisingly, the Dauphin rejected these terms thereby ensuring that fighting would continue. The better to consolidate the Treaty, Charles' daughter, Catherine, was betrothed to Henry, and they were married shortly afterwards. This proved to be the pinnacle of the English achievement.

Shakespeare's 'Henry V' emphasises his hero's qualities and popularity, and while full of patriotic fervour, the whole is uplifted by some wonderful poetry, and considering that Shakespeare never served in the military, his perception and portrayal of men about to go into battle is noteworthy. This play is the final one in the tetralogy of 'Richard II', 'Henry IV, Parts 1and 2'.

In the final Phase of the War, Henry continued to campaign successfully, but he died in 1422 of disease contracted in the field, leaving a nine months old son, Henry VI of England and Henri II of France. Henry's brother John, Duke of Bedford, took over the military command and was more than competent, but the rising cost of continual warfare was creating problems in England that were no longer dimmed by the charisma of Henry; in France allied support wavered, especially after a resurgence of the Dauphin's forces led by Joan of Arc, and then in 1435 the Burgundians decided to change sides. This marked the end of English efforts to create an empire on the continent. Without some French support the position was untenable, and only the pace of the withdrawal remained to be decided. There were some victories, and Henry VI was crowned king of France in 1431 as Henri II, but the final defeat came at Castillon in 1453 after which only Calais and the Channel Islands remained in English hands.

The English were now free to fight each other, and they proceeded to do so in the War of the Roses that was concluded in 1485 at the Battle of Bosworth during which Richard III was killed and Henry Tudor took the crown as Henry VII.

Shakespeare has another tetralogy of plays in which the Wars of the Roses is the setting– 'Henry VI, Parts 1, 2, and 3' and 'Richard III'.

English Victories in the Hundred Years War were:

1337	Nov.10	Cadsand	1415	Oct.25	Agincourt
1340	Jun.24	Sluys	1415	Sep.22	Harfleur
1342	Sep. 30	Morlaix	1416	Mar.11	Valmont
1345	Aug.26	Bergerac	1416	Aug.15	Seine Mouth
1345	Oct.21	Auberoche	1417	Jul.25	Harfleur
1345	Dec.2	Aiguillon	1417	Sep.20	Caen
1346	Jan.4	La Réole	1418	Jan.2	Falaise
1346	Jun.9	St. Pol	1418	Jul.20	Pont L'Arche
1346	Jul.26	Caen	1419	Jan.20	Rouen
1346	Aug.20	Aiguillon	1419	Jul.2	Pontoise
1346	Aug.24	Blanchetaque	1420	Mar.5	Fresnay
1346	Aug.26	Crécy	*1420*	*May.21*	*Tr.of Troyes*
1346	Sep.21	St.Jean d'Ang.	1420	Jun.13	Sens
1346	Oct.4	Poitiers	1420	Nov.18	Melun
1347	Jun.20	Roche Derrien	1420	Jul.1	Montereau
1347	Aug.4	Calais	1421	Jul.20	Dreux
1349	Dec.31	Calais	1422	May.2	Meaux
1351	Apr.8	Taillebourg	1423	Jul.31	Cravant
1352	Aug.14	Mauron	1424	Aug.17	Verneuil

1355	Oct.5	Major Sweep	1425	Aug.10	Le Mans
1356	Jun. 22	Major Sweep	1426	Mar.6	St. James
1356	Sep.19	Poitiers	1429	Feb.12	Rouvray
1358	Jul.5	Rennes	1436	Jan.15	Ry
1360	May.8	*Tr. of Bretigny*	1437	Feb.16	Pontoise
1364	Sep.30	Auray	1438	Jul.15	Le Crotoy
1367	Apr.3	Nájera	1439	Dec.23	Avranches
1370	Sep.19	Limoges	1440	Oct.2	Harfleur
1387	Mar.24	Margate	1441	Jul.20	Pontoise

THE WAR OF THE HOLY LEAGUE 1511 – 1522

There are two victories that belong to the period between the end of the Hundred Years' War and this one , but neither is part of a War because the triumphs were bloodless. The first began with a foray into France by Edward IV in the later stages of the War of the Roses. Edward was the Yorkist contender for the throne, and his opponent was the enfeebled Henry VI; the latter was deposed after his defeat at the Battle of Towton in 1461, but briefly regained the crown ten years later. Henry and his supporters were defeated first at Barnet and then at Tewkesbury, and Edward wasted no time in ordering the murder of Henry who was his prisoner.

At the beginning of the second instalment of his reign, Edward planned to re-unite his kingdom through war with France. There was popular support for this policy, and Parliament voted liberal increases in taxation to fund the enterprise. Alliances were made with Brittany and Burgundy and a truce negotiated with Scotland. In 1475, Edward landed in France with the largest English army since the days of Edward III, but before the French could be brought to battle, the English allies deserted, and Edward agreed to the generous terms offered by Louis XI. By the Treaty of Picquigny (29 August), the English army withdrew from France in consideration of a substantial payment. Louis' desire to avoid war was due to the threat to the monarchy from several powerful nobles, and to a belief that war was a precarious business that should be made only reluctantly.

Although Edward was a brilliant general who never lost a battle, and he improved administration and the treasury, his besetting sins were lechery and gluttony, and he was incapable of sustained attention to business.

The second victory belongs to Henry VII whose victory over Edward's brother, Richard III, ended the War of the Roses. Henry was an unusual king in that he was not attracted by the prospect of military glory, not even at the expense of the French; he was extremely diligent in his attention to the affairs of state especially government finances; and acted as if his purpose was not to be merely solvent but rather to increase the monetary reserves of the kingdom. Generally, he favoured a good-neighbour policy – an alliance with Spain and peace with Scotland – it being obvious to him that peace was cheap and trade profitable.

These commendable ambitions suffered a set back in 1492 under the threat of a union between the duchy of Brittany and France. Spain, the Roman Empire, and Burgundy were opposed, and Henry felt compelled to join them. He invaded France and laid siege to Boulogne, but the heiress to Brittany married the French king thereby making the campaign pointless, and Henry negotiated the unheroic Treaty of Étaples (3 November). In the Treaty, Henry renounced all claims on French territory except for Calais and in return received a large annuity as an indemnity, but Henry's successors did not regard his renunciation of the French crown to be binding.

When Henry VIII succeeded to the throne at the age of seventeen, he was athletic, musically gifted and determined to promote the style and splendour of the monarchy; in popular opinion, he was the most handsome and accomplished prince of his time. He was also wildly extravagant. Vanity impelled him to seek a greater prominence in European affairs than his resources and ability could properly sustain. At first, he supported his father-in-law, the king of Aragon, in a disastrous campaign against France, but England joined the Holy League – an alliance formed by Pope Julius II against Louis XII of France - comprising Spain, Venice, the Holy Roman Empire, and Switzerland. Henry took a large army to France and enjoyed several small scale victories, including the capture of Tournai; simultaneously, another English army commanded by the Earl of Surrey inflicted a devastating defeat on the Scots at Flodden. Unfortunately, these successes did not amount to much because the Holy League had started to fall apart with each participant making a separate peace with France. England made its own *rapprochement* with France in the Treaty of London 1518, but it did not hold. After fresh overtures from Charles V, now the Holy Roman Emperor, another English army was sent to France but it accomplished nothing of value. The expense of this policy caused Henry to abandon it, and he did so shortly before Charles won a great victory over the French with the result that he had no advantage from it.

In spite of his moderate performance and victories of no particular consequence, Henry remained popular, but modern opinion is that he squandered his many advantages.

English victories in this War were:

1512	Aug.10	Brest	1513	Sep.9	Flodden
1513	Aug.16	Guinegate	1513	Sep.25	Tournai
1513	Aug.23	Thérouanne	1522	Sep.4	Lottinghen

WAR OF THE SPANISH ALLIANCE 1543-1546

In the last years of his life, Henry was profoundly depressed at being cuckolded by his fifth wife, Catherine Howard, and the revenge of her death on the block was not sweet enough to make it palatable. By accident or design, Henry threw himself into diplomacy and war. Following their defeat at Flodden, the Scots were more than usually attracted to the Auld Alliance, and the French faction at court became increasingly powerful. James V married successively Madeleine, the daughter of Francis I, forever Henry's *bête noire,* and on her death, Mary of Guise, but these plans were derailed by the heavy defeat of the Scots at Solway Moss, and James V's death three weeks later leaving a baby girl as his sole heir. Notwithstanding his previous experience of Charles V's unreliabitity as an ally, Henry now agreed to another alliance with Spain against Francis I of France in the form of a joint invasion. There was no coordination, and the English invasion was poorly organized and ill supplied, but this miserable effort was better than Charles' who soon made a unilateral peace with France. Henry's troops were able to capture Boulogne, but the crippling expense of maintaining the occupation forced Henry to negotiate the terms for the eventual evacuation of his prize. The final phase of the war was some naval action on both sides of the Channel in which the English had the last word.

The English victories in this War were:

1544	Sep.14	Boulogne
1545	Jul. 21	Isle of Wight
1545	Sep.2	Le Tréport

NORTH AMERICAN COLONIAL WARS 1613 – 1654

The conflicts in this period were conducted by different agencies of the English government, but all were similar in that they arose from the expansion of English colonization of what are now the United States and Canada. The first phase of colonization by the English, the French, and the Dutch was usually undertaken by private investors organized under a government charter. The charter companies had to organize their own defences which meant that simultaneously they had an offensive capability as well; from which it is a short step to argue in favour of an offensive-defensive, or pre-emptive strike. The early settlers took a realistic view of their situation and were not overly concerned by moral justifications of their policies, thus it was that fighting around the frontiers sometimes occurred even though the respective nations were not in a state of war.

The northern New England colonies in particular were soon in competition with the settlers of New France both in ways of approaching the Divine for favour and support as well as in mundane matters of trade and economic activities. The earliest victory came from Virginia where each settler, women and children included, had been given a military rank with prescribed duties and a rigorous discipline backed by severe penalties for offences. Alarmed by evidence of French settlements in what is now Nova Scotia, the Company of Virginia, acting under the authority of the Great Seal of England, appointed Samuel Argall as Admiral of Virginia with orders to expel the French from all territory claimed by England and provided him with three ships (two of which had been captured from the French) and supplies for the purpose. Argall easily destroyed the offending settlements and returned to Jamestown.

France and England were not at war while Argall's belligerent activities were in course, but the elaborate, diplomatic etiquette demanded a formal enquiry into his campaign after it had been concluded. Unsurprisingly, the verdict was that it was perfectly legal and proper, but his principal ship that had been taken from the French was returned to its owner, a Mme. de Guercheville of the French court, although her claim for damages was denied. On the intervention of the French ambassador, two French Jesuits who had been taken prisoner were allowed to return to France.

The action of the Kirke brothers against the French colony in Quebec was also financed privately by a group of merchants commissioned by Charles I, but this was done while England was engaged in an indecisive war against France to enforce the marriage treaty (read payment of the dowry) made when Charles married the sister of the French king. The Kirke brothers captured Quebec, took the French leader, Champlain, prisoner, and held it for three years, but then found, as later colonists did, that their successes were traded away in the bargaining that took place in treaty negotiations in Europe.

Massachusetts, more precisely the Massachusetts Bay Company, was responsible for another attack on Acadia (Nova Scotia) during the brief period that England was a Protectorate. Cromwell was happy to commission Robert Sedgwick, the major general of Massachusetts, as general of the fleet and commander-in-chief of the entire New England coast authorizing him to make reprisals against French commerce for the attacks of French privateers commissioned by the exiled Stuart princes, Rupert and Charles. Sedgwick never took a conservative view of any authority given to him, and he decided that to seize Acadia for Massachusetts and England was no more than his duty. He sailed from Boston in early July 1654 and less than three months later he was back in Boston attending a public service of thanksgiving for his conquest.

Sedgwick saw his son-in-law appointed military governor of Acadia, and departed for England with the French commander of Acadia as his prisoner. Sedgwick found favour with Cromwell, and just before his death, he was appointed as supreme commander in Jamaica.

The English victories were:

1613	Jul.15	Port Royal
1629	Jul.19	Quebec
1654	Jul.3	Acadia

ANGLO-DUTCH WARS 1665-1667

There were four Anglo-Dutch Wars in the seventeenth and eighteenth centuries, but it was only in the second, 1665-1667, that the French fought, towards the end, with the Dutch. Except for the last one when the Dutch fought in support of the insurgents in the American War of Independence, the Anglo-Dutch Wars were the ultimate extension of commercial rivalry between the antagonists. The English fought the French mainly in the West Indies, and St. Kitts and Fort St. Pierre were naval victories. This inconclusive war was formally concluded by the Treaty of Breda (31 July 1667) in which England recovered Antigua, Montserrat and St. Kitts from the French but had to yield Acadia.

The English victories were:

1667	May. 10	St. Kitts
1667	Jun. 25	Fort St. Pierre

WAR OF THE LEAGUE OF AUGSBURG 1688-1697

This war is also known as War of the Grand Alliance, or the NineYears' War, or in the United States as King William's War; and it was the prologue to the War of the Spanish Succession. The root cause was the rivalry between the French and Austrian monarchies – respectively the Bourbons and Habsburgs. Louis XIV of France nurtured two imperial aspirations – to become the ruler of the huge Spanish empire and to be elected Holy Roman Emperor, and at this date both positions were held by a Habsburg. In Spain, Charles II had by some physiological miracle continued to live albeit with such bouts of imbecility that he became known as Charles the Mad, but now his demise was near. The Holy Roman emperor was an elective office, and the electors were the rulers of various jurisdictions in Germany, but the domination of the Austrian Habsburgs was such that in fact the title had almost become hereditary. Charles II was childless, and it could reasonably be assumed he would remain so, which left the way open for Louis to advance the hereditary claim of his grandson; as for the imperial election, Louis calculated that with his armies to threaten and his money to bribe, he could beat the Habsburgs at the poll. Opposition to these bold plans came from those with much to fear from an enlarged influence and integration of

Catholic countries under Bourbon hegemony – only three years before the war began, Louis had expelled from France tens of thousands of Protestants after decades of persecution – and the prospect of increased competition in colonization was alarming.

Hostilities began when Louis, believing the Austrians were fully occupied in repelling a Turkish invasion of Hungary, invaded the Rhineland Palatinate and proceeded to devastate it. William of Orange, who now ruled England jointly with Mary his wife (and cousin), was prominent in organizing an alliance against France, and at its peak it included the Holy Roman Empire, Holland, Savoy, England, Sweden, Bavaria and Brandenburg. In practice, this dazzling array of powers merely served to illustrate that coalitions are rarely as effective as they promise to be. Much of the European fighting took place in and around the Spanish Netherlands where the French proved that they had the best armies with generals to match, but they did not perform as well at sea or overseas in India and North America. The fact was that France had not been prepared for a world wide war, and when the contest turned into a war of attrition, the allies proved able to stay the course. A feature of the North American engagements was the strong participation of the Indian tribes – on both sides, and the more independent role assumed by the colonists in planning and executing their military activities. There was nothing indecisive in the war at sea. After an early success, the French suffered a series of setbacks culminating in the destruction of the fleet at Barfleur & La Hougue.

At length, the unexpected costs of the war and general weariness led all sides to the table, and the Treaty of Rijswijk brought an end to the war, but it did nothing to resolve the rivalry between the houses of Bourbon and Habsburg, and the English–French conflicts had been revived and were to continue. For the most part, conquered territories were restored, but there were changes. After a century of disengagement England became active in European politics, and it was forced to build up its fleet and develop a naval policy that led on to economic power. On the other hand, France became committed to sacrificing colonial expansion for continental gains, and it had to reckon with a huge increase in its annual deficit and in the national debt. Of particular importance to William and his wife was that in the Treaty Louis formally acknowledged a Protestant king of England, and the right of succession of a Protestant princess (Anne).

As in a number of previous wars between England and France, the rival monarchs were related. Louis XIV was a nephew of a grandmother of William and Mary.

The English victories were:

1689	Aug.1	Londonderry	1692	May.19	Barfleur & La Hougue
1689	Aug.25	Walcourt	1694	Aug.31	Ferryland
1690	May.21	Port Royal	1695	Sep.1	Namur I
1690	Jul.1	Boyne	1696	Aug.15	York Fort
1691	Jul.12	Aughrim			

WAR OF THE SPANISH SUCCESSION 1701-1713

In effect, this War (also known as Queen Anne's War) was a continuation of the War of the League of Augsburg, but it was on a much larger scale. In what might be termed the underpinnings of military success, England entered the war stronger than France in finance, banking, commerce, and in treasury control and management, and shortly before he died at the age of 52, William III was able to use diplomacy to offset further France's superiority in sheer numbers. Another Grand Alliance was formed in which England, the Dutch Republic, and Austria were the core and Hanover, Prussia and other German states, except Bavaria and Cologne, also joined.

Charles II, the last Habsburg monarch of Spain, died in 1700 without issue, and although the event had been anticipated and agreement reached between some of the major European powers on an orderly and peaceful succession, *realpolitik* confounded good intentions. Two attempts were made. By a Treaty of Partition in 1698 it was decided that Spain, the Spanish Netherlands, and the colonies would pass to Joseph Ferdinand, son of the Elector of Bavaria, and a nephew of the King of Spain, who was generally considered to be the most neutral, meaning the least dangerous, to the signatories; Austria and France were to share the other not inconsiderable territories, mainly large parts of Italy and islands in the Mediterranean. The countries making this agreement were England, the Dutch Republic, and France. Within months, and as always treating prince and pauper just the same, smallpox carried off Joseph Ferdinand; all had now to be done again, and time was running short. A second Treaty of Partition was made by which Archduke Charles, a younger son of the Emperor Leopold I of Austria, was to have Spain, the Spanish Netherlands, and the colonies, while France was to have the Spanish territories in Italy. The English and the Dutch were satisfied because the considerable danger to their trade that would have resulted if France acquired the Spanish Netherlands was averted, and Louis XIV was unusually accommodating in agreeing to these generous terms. Unfortunately, the Austrian Emperor adamantly refused to sign, and he was supported by the Spanish nobles who effectively were the government. In the last few weeks of his sad life, Charles II was persuaded, possibly coerced, into signing a will by which he bequeathed to Philip of Anjou, grandson of Louis XIV, the monarchical possessions in their entirety, and if the bequest was not accepted they should pass to Archduke Charles.

It has been said that Leopold's rejection of the terms of the second Partition Treaty "was a blunder only surpassed in the catalogue of costly Austrian follies by the ultimatum to Serbia in July 1914". Relatively speaking, it had a similar result; Europe was plunged into a war that extended into North America. The will meant that if Louis declined to accept the whole of the Spanish empire on behalf of his grandson, then it would revert to the Habsburgs, and this was no choice at all. Within weeks of Charles' death Louis acted so precipitately as to make further negotiation impossible. French troops poured into the Spanish Netherlands and the Dutch barrier towns, and Spain was compelled to transfer to the French the monopoly of the slave trade to the Spanish West Indies. Then, as if to ensure that England would fight against him, in flagrant disregard of his agreement in the Treaty of Rijswijk to recognize William and Mary's succession to the English crown and subsequently that of Anne, Louis declared the son of the deposed James II to be the rightful king of England as James III.

At the beginning, Austria was joined by England and the Dutch Republic or United Provinces, and later Hanover, Prussia, Savoy and Portugal entered the alliance; Bavaria and Cologne stood with France. England and the United Provinces fought under the command of the brilliant John Churchill, Duke of Marlborough, later joined by imperial forces commanded by another outstanding general, Prince Eugene of Savoy, and with the important exception of the victory at Blenheim on the Danube, their campaign was in Flanders and along the lower Rhine.

Marlborough never lost a battle or a siege but his Dutch allies were excessively cautious, and opportunities to bring an earlier end to the war were lost. Another impediment to an earlier peace was a strategic one. The Portuguese alliance was crucial to England because Lisbon provided a naval base essential to sustain fleet operations in the western Mediterranean, and the Portuguese insisted on a campaign in Spain in support of the Austrian claimant to the throne, but early successes in the north east were not maintained and the French gained supremacy.

The war was on a scale not previously experienced, and the financial burden on both sides was serious. In the field, it was largely a stalemate and both sides were ready to negotiate a peace; the more so in the case of the English and the Dutch because in 1711 Archduke Charles, for whose claim to the Spanish throne they had been fighting, succeeded to the Austrian throne on the death of his brother and the prospect of this territory being added to that of Spain was decidedly unattractive. It says something about the disjointed nature of the alliance that instead of one treaty, there was a number between France, Spain and the members of the alliance.

A small but important change that occurred during the war was the Act of Union between England and Scotland so that the 'English' treaty was made in the name of Anne, Queen of Great Britain. The treaties gave territories to Britain that were important to a trading and colonizing power, and the war had given other advantages. During it English sea power had increased whereas the Dutch and French navies had declined, and the Treaty of Utrecht marked the rise of Britain as a colonial power at the expense of France and Spain. The wide expansion of foreign trade and the navy to support and protect it evolved into what has been called a 'maritime-imperial' system based on shipping and trade much more than on extent of territory. Islands, strategically placed not only for naval operations but also for trade, were now a principal objective of Britain at peace settlements. One such example, now often forgotten, was Heligoland in the mouth of the River Elbe, it was a spoil of the Napoleonic War at the expense of Denmark and held until 1890 when it was exchanged with Germany for territories in east Africa.

English victories in the War were:

1702	Jun-15	Kaiserswerth	1705	Jul. 18	Elixhem	1708	Sep. 19	Port Mahon
1702	Sep-25	Venlo	1705	Sep. 6	Leau	1708	Sep. 28	Wyandael
1702	Oct. 2	Stevenswaert	1705	Oct. 9	Barcelona	1708	Dec. 9	Lille
1702	Oct. 6	Ruremonde	1705	Oct.29	Santoliet	1708	Dec. 30	Ghent
1702	Oct. 12	Vigo Bay	1706	May. 23	Ramillies	1708	Dec. 31	Bruges
1702	Oct. 29	Liege & Fort Ch.	1706	May. 25	Louvain	1709	Sep. 3	Tournai
1703	May. 15	Bonn	1706	May. 26	Vilvorde	1709	Sep. 11	Malplaquet
1703	Aug. 26	Huy	1706	May. 28	Brussels	1709	Oct. 20	Mons
1703	Sep. 27	Limbourg	1706	Jun 1	Alcantara	1710	Jun .1	Douai
1704	Jun. 20	Chignecto Bay	1706	Jun 6	Antwerp	1710	Aug. 29	Bethune
1704	Jul. 2	Donauwoerth	1706	Jul. 9	Ostend	1710	Oct. 2	St. Venant
1704	Aug. 13	Blenheim	1706	Aug. 22	Menin	1710	Oct. 13	Port Royal
1704	Aug. 13	Velez Malaga	1706	Sep. 9	Dendermonde	1710	Nov. 8	Aire
1704	Oct. 26	Trier	1706	Oct. 1	Ath	1711	Sep. 13	Bouchain
1704	Dec. 20	Trarbach	1707	Jul. 17	Toulon	1712	Jul. 4	Le Quesnoy
1705	Mar. 10	Marbella	1708	Mar. 21	East Scotland	*1713*	*Apr. 11*	*Treaty of Utrecht*
1705	Jul. 11	Huy	1708	Jul. 11	Oudenarde	1713	Jun. 1	Placentia

WAR OF THE AUSTRIAN SUCCESSION 1740-1748

Macauley, writng about Frederick the Great, described the cause of this war in dramatic terms: “In order that he might rob a neighbour whom he had promised to defend, black men fought on the coast of Coromandel [India], and red men scalped each other by the Great Lakes of North America”, but although this describes the opening of hostilities, there were in fact three wars that are subsumed under this title. The predicament that eventually led to world-wide fighting arose even while the terms for concluding the previous war (of the Spanish Succession) were still being negotiated. Archduke Charles, the Habsburg claimant to the Spanish throne, became the Austrian emperor in 1711 on the death of his elder brother who died leaving daughters to grieve his passing but no sons, and under the ancient Salic Law observed in Austria and other parts of Europe but not, to its great advantage, in England, females were barred from inheriting crowns, consequently Charles succeeded as Charles VI.

Shortly after his accession Charles devised the Pragmatic Sanction in order to ensure that in the event that he had no male heirs, females were entitled to succeed to his undivided territories; in effect this abrogated the Salic Law in the Habsburg dominions. By 1720, Charles accepted that he would not have a son, and he devoted much time and effort in persuading the countries of Europe and Russia formally to recognize the validity of the Pragmatic Sanction, and when he died in 1740 all had done so. Immediately after Charles' death, Frederick, later to be known as the Great, who had only just ascended to the throne of Prussia, invaded the rich Austrian province of Silesia, and Charles Albert of Bavaria pressed a claim to be elected emperor of the Holy Roman Empire. Maria Theresa, who had just succeeded Charles, found herself with a depleted treasury and a weak army. Prussia quickly captured Silesia, and the prospect of easy conquests proved irrestible to other European countries notwithstanding that it meant repudiating their undertakings to accept Maria Theresa's right of succession; in a few words – "what is an obligation to an opportunity?" Although by this time the British king was also the elector of Hanover, and he fought in person at the battle of Dettingen, the principal interest of Britain lay beyond the continent. Three sufficiently distinct smaller wars can be identified.

First, French policy was to weaken the Austrian empire, and so France supported Bavaria, Saxony, and Spain in their claims to various pieces of Austrian territory, and the candidancy of Charles Albert of Bavaria for election as emperor of the Holy Roman Empire. Secondly, there were two invasions of Silesia by Prussia, and in the second the French actively supported Prussia. Thirdly, France, Britain and Spain engaged in colonial wars in which rights to trade were at least as important as territorial possession, and in fact Britain was already at war with Spain (the War of Jenkin's Ear), but there was also the traditional hostility between France and Britain which could be relied on to arouse popular support in England.

The fighting in all areas was hard, and it is estimated that in total 500,000 were killed, but no nation had been able to establish a clear advantage when finally general fatigue, including financial, led all to sign the Treaty of Aix-la-Chapelle. The Treaty promised no permanent solution for any of the issues: neither the colonial and commercial rivalry between Britain and the two Bourbon monarchies; nor the Silesian dispute between Prussia and Austria; nor the struggle for hegemony in Italy. There was, however, something new to be observed, a major European power, Prussia, had emerged and demonstrated formidable capabilities with attributes that were alarmingly different from the general run.

This war witnessed a rare event, namely, a battle in Britain itself. With some help from France, the Stuarts in the person of the Young Pretender, 'Bonnie Prince Charlie', raised a rebel army in the Scottish Highlands that was able to march south as far as Derby until it was forced to retreat to Culloden and crushing defeat. The lack of tangible support during the march south showed that England was Protestant and unwilling to accept a Roman Catholic monarchy – like France's, for example.

The British victories in this war were:

1743	Jun.27	Dettingen	1746	Dec.19	Fort St. David
1745	Jun.16	Louisbourg I	1747	May.3	Cape Finisterre I
1745	Jun.20	Porte-La-Joye	1747	Oct.14	Cape Finisterre II
1746	Mar.25	HMS Sheerness v.Pr.Wales.	1748	Jun.28	CuddaloreI
1746	May.3	Loch nam Uamh	*1748*	*Oct.18*	*Tr.of Aix la Chapelle*

CARNATIC WAR 1746 – 1763

Strictly speaking, there was a series of military conflicts in this part of southern India in the east Ghats and the Coromandel Plain which were sometimes, but not always, part of the War of the Austrian Succession and the Seven Years War. Those who see globalization as corporate expansion into foreign countries might cite the Carnatic war as an early example because it began with competition in its extreme form between the *Compagnie des Indes* of France and the East India Company of England, each of which had been granted certain trading monopolies (a contemporary parallel in Canada was the Hudson's Bay Company and the Company of New France (a.k.a. *La Compagnie des Cents Associés*). Naturally, a French company did not recognize a monopoly granted by a British monarch, or vice versa, and at first each sought to enforce its mandate through agreements with indigenous rulers; this was diplomatic competition in which the French gained some advantage. Rivalry between the respective Indian clients of the Companies led to hostilities in which the Companies provided European military skills as well as personnel, and during the Seven Years' War in Europe, the French and British sent armies and navies to carry on the fighting in India. The French lost their initial advantage due to the performance of three outstanding British commanders in succession, Stringer Lawrence, Robert Clive, and Eyre Coote who showed a particular talent for training and inspiring the Indian troops under their command.

By 1761, the French had nothing left of their Indian empire, but for another forty years by supporting and inciting Indian rulers in the regions important to British trade, they continued to harass the East India Company. A decisive end was made to all such activity in 1799 at Srirangapatam where Tipu Sultan was beaten; commanding a division in this battle was a Colonel Arthur Wellesley who just a few years later in Portugal and then in Spain beat a series of French marshals and finally, now the Duke of Wellington, defeated Napoleon at Waterloo.

British victories in this War were:

1751	Nov.25	Arcot	1752	Sep. 6	Bahur
1751	Dec.3	Arni	1752	Sep.16	Covelong
1751	Dec.15	Conjeveram	1753	Apr. 2	Seriungham
1752	Feb.28	Kaveripak	1753	Jul. 7	Trichinopoly II
1752	May.29	Volconda	1753	Oct. 2	Trichinopoly III
1752	Jun. 13	Trichinopoly	1753	Nov.28	Trichinopoly IV

FRENCH AND INDIAN WARS 1754-56

This war, begun two years before the Seven Years' War formally recognized that Britain and France were again at war, was an inevitable consequence of the inconclusive end to the War of the Austrian Succession, and it then continued as a part of the larger one. The sphere of operations for the French and Indian Wars was North America, and more particularly the St. Lawrence River, the Great Lakes and the upper reaches of the Mississipi and Ohio Rivers. By the middle of the eighteenth century, French and British settlers were in confrontation, and a conference in Paris had failed to resolve the differences. Seriously over-estimating their capacity and resources, the French government ordered the Marquis Duquesne to take possession of the Ohio Valley and remove all Britsh presence from the area; to this end, he erected a number of forts, while Robert Dinwiddie, lieutenant-governor of Virginia was making grants of land in the Ohio Valley in support of the drive for settlement across the Appalachian mountains. Hostilities were inevitable, and the young George Washington began his military career in command of a contingent of the Virginia militia which secured a victory over the French by means of a pre-emptive strike – a tactic that contemporary U.S. Presidents have not hesitated to employ. As in the Carnatic War, in the first two years the French established a slight advantage, but once the Seven Years' War began, the British steadily took control, largely because naval supremacy enabled regular troops to be brought to North America along with supplies of all kinds. In 1758, control of the Ohio Valley was secured with the capture of Fort Duquesne, several other key points including Louisbourg were also taken, and the way had been prepared for the triumph in the following year when Quebec, the strongest French fortress in North America and the lynch pin of its power, was surrendered. The *de facto* British control of North America was established in 1760 with the capture of Montreal and Detroit, and formally recognized in the Treaty of Paris in 1763.

An unlooked for consequence of the complete defeat of the French in North America was that it removed the major external threat to the colonies of New England and contributed significantly to ideas of independence, because the need of the protection afforded by the British armed forces was greatly reduced.

British victories in this war were:

1754	May.27	Youghioghenny	1755	Jun.16	Bay of Fundy Exped.
1755	Jun.10	Newfoundland	1755	Sep.8	Crown Point

SEVEN YEARS' WAR 1756 – 1763

This was the war made inevitable by the disreputable beginning and the inconclusive end of the War of the Austrian Succession. The prelude was a change-over in some traditional alliances.The Hanoverian dynasty in Britain had brought continental territory with it, and the startling performance of Frederick the Great's Prussia in the previous war suggested that Austria was not likely to be able to provide adequate protection for Hanover against Prussian or French aggression; accordingly, early in 1756, Britain entered into an alliance with Prussia. In response, France discarded its customary rivalry with Austria to ally with it, and a little later these two were joined by Russia; the circle round Prussia was closed when Sweden and Saxony chose to participate with them. The whole process has been described as a 'diplomatic revolution'.

Before Austria could launch an offensive to recover the lost province of Silesia, Frederick the Great took the initiative and attacked Saxony followed by an invasion of Bohemia. France, Russia, and Sweden now advanced from different directions and Prussia was forced to fight defensively on several fronts. Aid was solicited from Britain, and a Hanoverian and a Hessian army were deployed in western Germany under the command of the king's son, the Duke of Cumberland. It was defeated and replaced by another force commanded by the Duke of Brunswick. At this point, the British cause was hugely improved by a remarkable leader, William Pitt the Elder who inspired the military and the population as well as commanding the respect of Prussia, and above all he showed an excellent grasp of strategy. With the French too preoccupied in Europe to defend their overseas possessions, he saw the war as an opportunity to secure British colonial hegemony and with it trading supremacy in North America, India, and the West Indies. Military activity on the continent was a means to this end, and as he put it "America has been conquered in Germany". As the various armies marched backwards and forwards across Europe, the Britsh fought the French, and later the Spanish as well, around the world. A great part of the British success is due to Pitt's leadership, and he is one of the great British prime ministers.

For a time the Prussian position deteriorated to a point that reduced Frederick to despair from which he was rescued by the providential death of Tsarina Elizabeth of Russia. Her successor, Peter III, was a great admirer of Frederick, and not only did he promptly make peace and mediate peace with Sweden, but he also supported Prussia with Russian troops. This brought the end of the war in sight. Without the assistance of Russia, Austria lost hope of recovering Silesia, France had no further interest, and Britain wanted only to make certain of the gains made overseas. The Treaty of Paris awarded the fruits of conquest to Britain, and shortly afterwards a separate treaty between Austria and Prussia confirmed that Silesia was now Prussian.

British victories in the War were:

1757	Mar.25	Chandernagore	1759	Sep.10	Pondicherry
1757	Jun. 23	Plassey	1759	Sep.13	Plains of Abraham
1758	Feb.28	HMS Monmouth v Foud.	1759	Oct.21	Cape François
1758	Apr.4	Ile de Rhé	1759	Nov.20	Quiberon Bay
1758	Apr.29	Cuddalore	1760	Jan.22	Wandiwash
1758	Jul.6	Trout Brook	1760	Feb.28	Three Frigates v.
1758	Jul.27	Louisbourg II	1760	Apr.5	Karikal
1758	Aug.3	Negapatam	1760	May.16	Quebec
1758	Aug.27	Fort Frontenac	1760	Jul.8	Restigouche
1758	Nov.24	Fort Duquesne	1760	Jul.31	Warburg
1758	Dec.7	Condore	1760	Aug.25	Fort de Lévis
1758	Dec.9	Rajamundry	1760	Sep.8	Montreal
1758	Dec.29	Gorée Island	1760	Nov.29	Detroit
1759	Feb.17	Madras	1761	Jan.15	Pondicherry
1759	Apr.8	Masulipatam	1761	Apr.5	Gingee Forts
1759	May.1	Guadeloupe	1761	Jun.7	Belle Isle
1759	Jul.25	Fort Niagara	1761	Jul.15	Vellinghausen
1759	Jul.26	Fort Ticonderaga	1761	Aug.13	HMS Bellona v.
1759	Jul.31	Fort St. Frédéric	1762	Feb.12	Martinique
1759	Aug.1	Minden	1762	Jun.24	Wilhelmstahl
1759	Aug.17	Lagos Bay	1762	Sep.18	St. John's
			1763	*Feb.10*	*Treaty of Paris*

AMERICAN WAR OF INDEPENDENCE 1775-1783

This war began as a civil war between Britain and the New England colonies, but as in the case of earlier civil wars in both France and England, these countries took the opportunity to support the insurgents in retaliation for previous events - of which there were many- and to further other policies. France in 1778, Spain in 1779 and The Netherlands in 1780, formally declared war on the side of the colonists but failed to exploit to the full British weakness caused by political rivalries and a government often in disarray which affected military and naval performance. As is often the case, some of the antagonists suffered in unforeseen ways. The costs France incurred in the venture greatly aggravated the parlous public finances in France, and more disastrously the spectacle of the colonists triumphant provided the increasing number of critics of the *ancien regime* with empirical evidence to substantiate their radical ideas. Dangerous sentiments were released that a few years later went totally out of control.

Nine years after the loss of the New England colonies, Britain and France were again at war as principals, and with only a short break it lasted for over twenty years.

There were French troops fighting with Americans, but the Britsh victories were nearly all naval and did not affect the result of the war itself. Their victories were:

1778	.Oct 16	Pondicherry	1781	.Apr 16	Porto Praya Bay
1778	.Dec 29	St. Lucia	1781	.Dec 14	Ushant
1779	.Jul 6	Grenada	1782	.Apr 12	The Saintes
1779	.Oct 9	Savannah	1782	.Apr 19	HMS Foudroyant
1781	.Jan 6	Jersey	1783	.Jun 13	Cuddalore

FRENCH REVOLUTIONARY WARS 1792 – 1802

When the American War of Independence was over and the British had lost an empire, the consensus among the rulers of continental Europe was that Britain was now in irreversible decline from the peak of prestige at the end of the Seven Years' War. The incompetent conduct of the American war and its unpopularity aroused dissatisfaction with corruption in public life and grossly inadequate political representation, but not for the first time in the country's history, a long war with France was enough to promote a sense of national purpose and to reduce discontent to manageable proportions. Unexpected assistance came from the forces released by the industrial revolution now well under way and far in advance of any other country.

The revolution in France that led to major European wars was of the traditional kind and brutally executed. The first phase of egalitarian fervour led to anarchy which gave way to a series of dictatorships enforced by public executions on an unprecedented scale in which the king and queen had starring parts. The dangerously radical ideas that led to the turmoil were seen as a serious threat to the whole political and social order of Europe, and Austria and Prussia were the first to call on all countries to support the French king against the revolutionaries. The French reply was a declaration of war in the expectation that the spirit of the revolution would inspire other oppressed populations to follow their example. A Prussian-Austrian army was defeated, Belgium was occupied, and Holland threatened; at home the security of the Republic was thought to require the execution of Louis XVI and Marie Antoinette, and these events brought into existence the First Coalition against France comprising Prussia, Austria, Spain, the United Provinces, and Britain.

The Coalition was not a success. Prussia and Austria were preoccupied with the second and third partitions of Poland; the Dutch were beaten into submission and converted to the Batavian Republic in concert with the conqueror; Prussia and Spain made separate peace with France; and a year later Spain came back into the war but on the French side. Napoleon had now appeared as commander of the French army in Italy where he decisively defeated the Austrians forcing them to acknowledge the French conquest of the Austrian Netherlands, and to yield Luxembourg and territory in Italy. A British army in Flanders was not able to make an impact, but there were some important naval successes to relieve the failure of the First Coalition.

About two years after the disintegration of the First Coalition, Britain was able to form a second one; the new allies were Austria, Russia, Portugal, and Ottoman Turkey. In the interim, the Royal Navy struck two heavy blows; Jervis' fifteen ships beat tweny-three Spanish at Cape St. Vincent, putting paid to a French-Spanish invasion of Britain, and eighteen months later Nelson crushed the French fleet in Abukir Bay leaving Napoleon and his army stranded in Egypt. The second Coalition was no more effective than the first. Napoleon had made his way back to Europe in time to beat the Austrians at Marengo and force them to make peace. The Russians left the alliance to join with Sweden, Denmark, and Prussia in the League of Armed Neutrality that was aimed at the the British practice of searching neutral convoys; in retaliation the Navy destroyed the Danish fleet at Copenhagen. The Duke of York proved to be no more effective in Flanders than during the First Coalition, the financial burden was painful, and the war had reached a stalemate; both sides were receptive to a cessation of hostilities. The Treaty of Amiens was signed in 1802, but it proved to be little more than an armed truce and in May 1803 Britain declared war again.

British victories in this War were:

1793	Apr.15	Tobago	1797	Feb.25	Fishguard
1793	May.14	St Pierre&Miquelon	1797	Mar.8	HMS San Fiorenzo v.
1793	May.23	Famars	1797	Dec.20	HMS Phoebe v.
1793	Jun.18	HMS Nymphe v.	1798	Feb.3	HMS Speedy v.
1793	Aug.18	Lincelles	1798	Apr 21	HMS Mars v.
1793	Sep.22	Santo Domingo	1798	Jun.29	HMS Jason v.
1793	Oct.20	HMS Crescent v.	1798	Aug.1	Nile
1793	Oct.22	Nieuwpoort	1798	Sep.8	Ballinamuck
1793	Dec.19	Toulon	1798	Oct.12	Att. Invasion of Ireland
1794	Mar.16	Martinique	1798	Oct.13	HMS Melampus v.
1794	Apr.4	St.Lucia	1798	Oct.18	HMS Anson v.
1794	Apr 26	Beaumont	1798	Oct.20	HMS Fisgard v.
1794	May.10	Willems	1799	Feb.28	HMS Sybille v.
1794	May.20	Bastia	1799	Mar.18	HMS Telegraph
1794	May.22	Tournai	1799	May.18	Cape Carmel
1794	May.29	HMS Caryfort v.	1799	Aug.11	Schiermannikoog
1794	May.30	Port au Prince	1799	Sep.19	Bergen-op-Zoom
1794	Jun.1	Ushant	1799	Oct.2	Egmont-op-Zee
1794	Jun.17	HMS Romney	1799	Nov.23	HMS Courier v.

1794	Jul. 3	Guadeloupe	1799	Dec.26	HMS Viper v.
1794	Aug.1	Calvi	1800	Jan.5	HMS Viper v.
1794	Nov.12	Bois le Duc	1800	Feb.5	HMS Fairy v.
1795	Jan.3	HMS Diamond v.	1800	Feb.18	HMS Foudroyant v.
1795	Jan.4	HMS Blanche v.	1800	Feb.21	HMS Phoebe v.
1795	Mar.13	Genoa	1800	Feb.24	HMS Nymphe v.
1795	Mar.13	HMS Lively v.	1800	Mar.21	HMS Peterell v.
1795	Apr.10	HMS Astraea v.	1800	Mar.30	HMS Lion v.
1795	May.17	HMS Thetis v.	1800	May.11	HMS Phoebe v.
1795	Jun.16	Opns. in Atlantic	1800	Jun.10	St. Croix
1795	Jun.23	Ile de Groix	1800	Jun.22	Quimper River
1795	Jun.24	HMS Dido v.	1800	Jul.29	HMS Viper v.
1795	Jul.13	Hyères Bay	1800	Aug.14	HMS Success v.
1796	Mar.17	HMS Diamond v.	1800	Aug.20	HMS Seine v.
1796	Apr.13	HMS Revolutionnaire	1800	Sep.5	Malta
1796	Apr.20	HMS Indefatigable v.	1801	Feb.19	HMS Phoebe v.
1796	Jun.8	HMS Santa Margarita	1801	Mar.8	Abukir
1796	Jun.10	HMS Southampton v.	1801	Mar.13	Mandora
1796	Jun.13	HMS Dryad v.	1801	Mar.21	Alexandria
1796	Dec.3	HMS Lapwing v.	1801	Jul-13	Algeciras Bay
1796	Dec.22	Bantry Bay	1801	Jul-22	HMS Beaulieu v.
1797	Jan.7	HMS Doris v.	1801	Jul-27	HMS Immortalite
1797	Jan.10	HMS Phoebe v.	1801	Aug-17	Marabout
1797	Jan.13	HMS Indefatigable v.	1801	Sep-10	HMS Viper v.

NAPOLEONIC WAR 1803 – 1815

This war began fourteen months after the Treaty of Amiens because Britain and France were equally dilatory in fulfilling the terms of it making it more like an armed truce than a treaty. France continued to push for expansion in southern Europe and to support British enemies in India, in retaliation Britain again declared war in May 1803. This war is really a continuation of the French Revolutionary Wars but on a much larger scale; before it ended Britain had fought the French in four of the five continents (Australia is the exception). The total cost to Britain was £1,650 million of which three-quarters was paid out of taxation including the new income tax levy. The army had been increased more than five times to about 220,00 with an additional 380,000 in the local militia; the expansion of the navy was even greater – from 16,000 men to 140,000, but the French army was nearly seven times the size of Britain's. The French had another advantage; it was on the way to establishing in the short run a more effective government. Napoleon became First Consul for 10 years in 1799, then First Consul for life in 1802, and finally in 1804 was crowned emperor, and each of these promotions was endorsed by a plebiscite which is more than any of the monarchs arraigned against him could say. Napoleon was a man born to command, and the plebiscites notwithstanding, he was a military dictator, but paradoxically his civil reforms have endured while at the end of the war his military performance had brought no tangible gains. After Pitt the Younger died in 1806, the heads of government in Britain were only moderate, but they were fortunate in the performance of the navy and of Wellington and his troops in Spain, and they plodded on doggedly as one coalition after another was blown apart in a series of continental battles when Napoleon was in his prime.

Faced with French superiority on land, Britain could only proceed by forming coalitions, and, where necessary, by using its financial resources to subsidize its partners. Linking to the previous War, the Third Coalition comprised Britain, Russia, and Austria, but it did not last long, overwhelming French victories over the Austrians at Ulm and Austerlitz forced them to accept the harsh terms of the Treaty of Pressburg including the end of the Holy Roman Empire. Nelson's brilliant victory at Trafalgar and a string of other naval successes had no effect on confrontations far from the sea.

Within months the Fourth Coalition of Britain, Prussia, Russia,and Sweden came into existence, and it, too, can only be desribed as ephemeral. In the last few months of 1806, at Jena, Auerstadt, and Lübeck, the Prussian army was virtually annihilated, and Napoleon, sitting in Berlin, issued his Berlin Decree inaugurating what is known as the Continental System. In the main, this regulation provided that ships entering French controlled ports after calling at British ports were liable to seizure, and the purpose was to prohibit the trade of continental countries with Britain, thus crippling the British economy. The effect was two-edged in that the trade of continental countries was also impaired, and when Britain promptly adopted a similar policy, the effects were felt in France as well. Unexpectedly, Britain was able to develop its colonial trade to the extent that it more than compensated for the losses due to the Continental System, but France's inferiority at sea meant there were no analogous compensations, and the Continental System was a failure.

More immediately, it was Russia's turn next, and it had to be brought within the Continental System. At Friedland, convenient to Prussia, Napoleon and his marshals gained an overwhelming victory which led Czar Alexander I to negotiate a truce in the following week, and shortly after that the Treaty of Tilsit was signed. Russia joined the Continental System and agreed to force Denmark, Sweden, Portugal and Austria to make war on British commerce. These provisions were intended to coerce Britain to seek peace, but the answer was unexpected – George Canning, the young foreign secretary and brilliant disciple of Pitt, seized the Danish fleet, and for the time being Britain carried on the war alone.

The Fifth Coalition was formed two years after Tilsit between Britain and Austria which had recovered sufficiently from its defeats to thirst for revenge and retribution for its losses. It did not last any longer than the predecessors. The Austrian army met the French at Wagram and were beaten by a smaller but better commanded force; shortly afterwards Napoleon sat in Vienna again, and this time his spoils included an unusual one, namely, a dynastic marriage to the daughter of the Austrian emperor. The union required that Napoleon had first to divorce Josphine who was childless; this was not a problem and with a benignity that was not always displayed, Napoleon allowed Josphine to continue to use the title of empress.

Napoleon was now at the peak of his power. Like the last Bourbon king, he had married a Habsburg, and in addition to the extensive French Empire, he controlled the Swiss Federation; the Confederation of the Rhine; the Duchy of Warsaw; the Kingdom of Italy; and Holland had been annexed and his brother Louis deposed. Allied territories included the Kingdom of Spain (his brother, Joseph, was king);the Kingdom of Westphalia (his brother, Jerome, was king); the Kingdom of Naples (his brother-in-law, Murat was king); the Principality of Lucca and Piombino (ruled by another brother-in-law); and Prussia and Austria were obliged to be allies, too. More succinctly and graphically, a man could now walk from Genoa to the Baltic on French soil.

Napoleon's Spanish policy turned out to be a major strategic error that resulted in the Peninsular War, and an opportunity for Britain to mount a land campaign based on its strengths, but a much larger mistake was the French invasion of Russia in 1812. This was caused by Russia renouncing the Continental System and opening up large markets for British trade in the Baltic and in northern Europe. To enforce his will, Napoleon marched with 442,000 men but was not able to manage a decisive victory. Moscow was burning by the time he reached it, and he tarried there for five weeks waiting for a Russian surrender that never came. The Russian winter would not wait, and now Napoleon was forced to pay a staggering price for his tactical errors and the strategic one of believing he could conquer Russia in just one campaign. The retreat from Moscow along the invasion route already stripped of forage and supplies, and in bitterly cold weather in which temperatures fell to -32 degrees C. led to starvation, sickness, privations of every description, and Cossack attacks on stragglers and forage parties. Barely 20,000 of the *Grande Armée* survived, and grievous though the loss of men was, from a military point of view the loss of horses was at least as bad because they were more difficult to replace.

The enormity of the failure of the Russian campaign, and important victories in the Peninsular War so heartened the continental countries that it was relatively easy to form the Sixth Coalition. It comprised the ever-present Britain; Russia; Prussia; Austria; Sweden; a number of German states; and Portugal. Napoleon tried frenetically to re-build his army for the purpose of controlling Germany, and at first he was successful in defeating the Russians and Prussians, but lack of cavalry (all those dead horses in Russia) prevented any pursuit of the enemy as they withdrew. A few months later, the combined coalition force confronted the French at Leipzig to which they had retreated after failing to take Berlin, and fresh, more experienced and better equipped troops in greater numbers carried the day. Bavaria and Saxony changed sides, leaving Napoleon to look to the defence of France that now faced invasion. Fighting with his customary skill against superior numbers, Napoleon won a number of battles east of Paris in 1814 but finally was beaten by the Prussians and the Austrians, and the allies marched into Paris. Napoleon's marshals compelled him to abdicate, and the Treaty of Paris confirmed Napoleon's new title, Emperor of Elba, but a few months later he was back in France, and raising an army.

In response to Napoleon's most unwelcome return, the Seventh Coalition was formed by Britain; Russia; Prussia; Austria; Sweden; a number of German states; and The Netherlands. Napoleon's plan was a conquest on the road which the allied armies intended to use to join together, and Brussels and The Netherlands were the first objective. Moving with a speed that surprised his opponents, Napoleon partially succeeded in driving a wedge between the Prussian army and an army comprising various contingents of different nationalities commanded by the Duke of Wellington, and he advanced on Brussels. The final battle of the war was fought about ten miles from Brussels at Waterloo; Wellington won, and Napoleon was sent to write his memoirs as a prisoner on St. Helena, a remote island in the South Atlantic.

At the end of his reign, Napoleon lost all of his conquered territories and in addition those obtained by the early conquests of the revolutionary period; the result was that the area of France was smaller than when the revolution began.

As a postscript, in the light of the formation of the European Union, it is interesting to note that Napoleon envisaged a commonwealth of Europe under French hegemony, while Pitt, the British prime minister and chief architect of three coalitions, wanted a federal system for the maintenance of European peace.

British victories in this war were:

1803	Jun. 21	St. Lucia	1810	Jul.25	Amanthea
1803	Jul.1	Tobago	1810	Dec.3	Ile de France
1803	Sep.4	Aligarh	1811	Mar.13	HMS Amphion v.
1803	Sep.11	Delhi	1811	May.23	HMS Amazon v.
1805	Jul.22	Cape Finisterre III	1811	Aug.9	Batavia
1805	Oct.21	Trafalgar	1811	Aug.24	Cornelis
1805	Nov.4	Ferrol	1811	Sep.10	Samarang
1806	Jan.8	Blueberg	1812	May.19	HMS Northumberland v.

1806	Feb.6	San Domingo	1812	Aug.31	HMS Bacchante v.
1806	Mar.4	HMS Diadem v.	1812	Sep.18	HMS Bacchante v.
1806	Mar.13	HMS London v.	1813	Jul.3	HMS Milford v.
1806	Jul.4	Maida	1813	Aug.2	HMS Bacchante v.
1808	Nov.10	HMS Amethyst v.	*1814*	*May.30*	*Treaty of Paris*
1809	Feb.24	Martinique	*1815*	*Jun.9*	*Congress of Vienna*
1809	Apr.6	HMS Amethyst v.	1815	Jun.16	Quatre Bras
1809	Apr.11	The Basque Roads	1815	Jun.18	Waterloo
1809	Jul.13	Senegal	*1815*	*Nov.20*	*Treaty of Paris*
1810	Jul.8	Bourbon			

PENINSULAR WAR 1808 – 1814

The Peninsula War is a subset of the Napoleonic War in which all of the fighting took place in the Iberian peninsular except in the final phase when the French had been forced to retreat into south-west France. The basic cause was Napoleon's intention to complete his Continental System by closing the Spanish and Portuguese ports to Britsh trade, and when Portugal was slow to obey his order to do so and to declare war on Britain, a French army marched into Portugal through northern Spain. The conquest was quick, and the French arrived in Lisbon as the royal family was leaving in a British squadron for the colony of Brazil. Napoleon now claimed all of Portugal as well as some provinces in northern Spain. The first reaction of the Spanish king, Charles IV, was to follow the Portuguese royals to South America, but he was thwarted by a *coup* organized in support of his son, Ferdinand, and Charles was forced to abdicate in favour of Ferdinand. With characteristic speed, Napoleon dispatched an army to Madrid under the command of Murat, and enticed Charles and Ferdinand to Bayonne ostensibly for conferences but really to receive their orders. The *coup* was reversed, Ferdinand was obliged to abdicate in favour of his father, and Charles had to abdicate in favour of Joseph Bonaparte, Napoleon's elder brother. To complete this game of regal musical chairs, Joseph had to abdicate the throne of Naples in favour of Murat, Napoleon's brother-in-law, who had declined the kingdom of Portugal. Before all of these changes had been completed, revolution broke out in Madrid and with it a state of war.

The Spanish uprising presented the British with an opportunity to use its small army in a theatre of war in which it could easily be supplied through a major port, and where it had the support and co-operation of the population; Lisbon was also of great value to the Mediterranean fleet. That the opportunity was exploited to the full was due to the employment of a junior commander of genius, Sir Arthur Wellesley later to advance through the ranks of the peerage to become the Duke of Wellington.

The beginning was anything but propitious. Sir Arthur landed with a small army in Portugal in 1808 in which he was only third in command. He won a convincing victory in spite of the pursuit being forbidden by his superiors, and the French requested terms. The Convention of Cintra that settled these terms was thought to be so favourable to the French that it provoked such a public protest that Wellesley and his two superior officers were arraigned before a military tribunal. They were acquitted of any dereliction, and Wellesley was sent back to Portugal in command. While this imbroglio was in course, the Emperor himself had taken an army into Spain to restore Joseph to his new throne, and to give any revolutionaries who stood in his way 'a whiff of grape-shot'. Sir John Moore, in command of the British army in Portugal that was greatly out-numbered by the French, marched out as winter approached to attack Napoleon's line of communication. He was obliged to retreat through the mountains in bitter weather and did so in such a masterly way that his troops were evacuated by sea at Corunna, although Moore was killed in the fighting.

The Emperor returned to France in order to prepare to thrash the Austrians at Wagram, he never returned to Spain, and various marshals were left in command. Wellington's strategy was to secure a base in Portugal that would ensure that if the worst came to the worst the British army could be evacuated; to train the Portuguese army into an effective force; and to assist the Spanish by attacking the French. The ultimate goal was to drive the French out of the Iberian peninsular altogether. The famous Lines of Torres Vedras were constructed in 1809 about 40 miles north of Lisbon and consisted of three lines of interconnected forts and gun emplacements stretching 30 miles from the River Tagus to the sea. They were carefully planned to take advantage of the mountains and other natural features and are regarded as a masterpiece of military engineering. The following year they proved to be impregnable when the French advanced on Lisbon, and their starving army was forced to withdraw.

After the French victory at Wagram, there were seasoned veterans available for service in Spain, and the army strength was increased to 130,000. Although the programme of training the Portuguese army had been a great success, these troops and the British contingent were never close to the numbers of the enemy. Wellington husbanded his resources carefully, preferring to make strategic withdrawals rather than to risk a devastating defeat, as he put it when confronting Marshal Massena from the Lines "…this is the last army England has, we must take care of it". The Spanish were ineffective in the field but supreme in guerrilla warfare and continually harassed the French throughout Spain as Wellington moved carefully onto the offensive. By 1811, with 300,000 French now in Spain, Wellington had cleared Portugal, and his eyes were on the Pyrenees. As the war continued in Spain, a broader French aim gave Wellington an advantage. Napoleon's realization the he would have to attack Russia in order to maintain his Continental System caused him to withdraw tens of thousands of troops and to limit supplies. In July 1812, only one day before the first engagement of the *Grande Armée* in the Russian campaign, Wellington won a brilliant victory at Salamanca after which the French were on the defensive, and the march to the Pyrenees began. By October 1813, Wellington and his army had fought their way into France; they kept moving forward and when news of Napoleon's surrender reached Wellington, he had just beaten Marshal Soult at Toulouse. The Peninsular War was over.

The Peninsular War made an important contribution to Naploleon's defeat. It was a serious drain on the French in men, *matériel,* and money to the extent that Napoleon took to referring to it as the 'Spanish ulcer'; it was also a demonstration that French armies were not invincible even in superior numbers. Wellington's tactics were better, he constantly used the 'reverse slope defence', the concealment of infantry in line along a reverse slope, from which to fire volleys at the critical moment at infantry advancing in column, and in the Peninsular this established the superiority of the line over the column as an infantry formation. The lesson was lost on Napoleon because at Waterloo the French still advanced in column and Wellington had his infantry in line behind the ridge on which he had chosen to make his stand. This time it could not be argued that the line was superior only because the French lacked sufficient artillery and cavalry.

Once the Peninsular War began, the Spanish royals were kept in France and in their absence a central Junta or Council was established first in Seville, and then as the French advance continued it moved to Cadiz. While in Cadiz, the Cortes met and drafted a constitution, a process that created two rival parties, the *Liberales* and the *Serviles*; it is from the former word that that the political term 'liberal' has passed into general use and paradoxically from what was then the most reactionary country in Europe.

British victories in the War were:

1808	Aug. 15	Obidas	1812	Jul. 22	Salamanca
1808	Aug. 17	Rolica	1812	Jul. 23	Garcia Hernandez
1808	Aug. 21	Vimeiro	1812	Aug. 3	Santander
1808	Dec. 21	Sahagon	1812	Aug. 13	Bilbao
1808	Dec.29	Benavente	1812	Oct. 30	Puente Larga
1809	Jan.16	Corunna	1812	Nov.10	Alba de Tormes
1809	May.12	Oporto	1813	Feb.20	Bejar
1809	Jul.28	Talavera de la Reina	1813	Apr.13	Castalla
1810	Sep.27	Busaco	1813	May.31	Esla
1810	Nov.14	Lines of Torres Vedras	1813	Jun.2	Morales
1811	Mar.5	Barossa	1813	Jun.7	Fort Balaguer
1811	Mar.13	Condeixa	1813	Jun.18	Osama
1811	Mar.14	Casal Nova	1813	Jun.18	San Millan de la Cogolla
1811	Mar.15	Foz do Arouce	1813	Jun.21	Vitoria
1811	Apr.3	Sabugal	1813	Jun.26	Tolosa
1811	May.5	Fuentes de Onero	1813	Jul.28	Sorauren
1811	May.16	Albuhera	1813	Aug.13	Sumbilla
1811	Oct.28	Arroyo dos Melinos	1813	Aug.2	Ivantelly
1812	Jan.7	Tarifa	1813	Aug.31	Vera

1812	Jan.19	Ciudad Rodrigo	1813	Sep.8	San Sebastian
1812	Apr.7	Badajoz	1813	Oct.7	Bidassoa
1812	Apr.11	Villagarcia	1813	Oct.31	Pamplona
1812	May.19	Almarez	1813	Nov.10	Nivelle
1812	Jun.22	Lequeitio	1813	Dec.10	Nive
1812	Jun.27	Salamanca Forts	1813	Dec.13	St. Pierre
1812	Jul.6	Castro Urdiales	1814	Feb.27	Orthez
			1814	Apr.10	Toulouse

WORLD WAR II 1939 – 1945

The British and French started off as allies against Germany when the latter invaded Poland in September 1939, but between April and June, 1940, the Germans swept through Denmark, Norway, the Netherlands, Belgium, Luxembourg and France, and the French signed an armistice with Germany in June 1940. Most of the British army (and about half as many French) were successfully evacuated through Dunkirk leaving their equipment behind, and inspired by the leadership of Winston Churchill the British and Commonwealth countries continued the war against Germany – now joined by Italy - on their own. Germany invaded Russia in 1941, an act that greatly relieved pressure elsewhere, and in December 1941 the Japanese attacked the U.S.A. at Pearl Harbour. Two days later Germany and Italy declared war on the United States.

Following the Franco-German armistice, the Germans took control of northern and western France, leaving the French government to rule in the rest of the country with the capital in Vichy. A few thousand French under the leadership of Charles de Gaulle, a general and a cabinet minister who had opposed the surrender, declared their refusal to recognize the armistice and to fight on; this group adopted the name of Free French as opposed to Vichy French. It was this split in the body politic of France that led to the Anglo-French conflicts that are barely noticeable in the wholesale conflagration of this epic war. The immediate and very serious concern of the British in the summer of 1940 was the future of the French fleet. If the Germans were to seize it, they would have the means to attempt the invasion of Britain, without it they had little chance of transporting an invading army across the

Channel because their own navy was not large enough. The French navy took its orders from the Vichy government (officially the French State) and not from de Gaulle with the result that a large part of it was sunk at its North African base. Whether or not this was a strategic error of the British will forever remain a matter of opinion, but it certainly added to the friction in Anglo-French relations.

The second cause of disagreement was the conduct of the French colonies. At first, the chances of Britain defeating the Germans and Italians seemed very small, and most of the colonies recognized the Vichy government. This government collaborated with the Germans in various ways until 1942 when for practical purposes it ceased to have any authority following the German occupation of the remainder of the country. For strategic reasons, the British conquered the French mandated territory of Syria and Lebanon in 1941 and the colony of Madagascar in 1942. Relations with de Gaulle were rarely congenial, and one reason was his suspicion that Britain wanted to reduce the size of the French colonial empire. As Winston Churchill put it: "Each of us has his cross to bear, and mine is the Cross of Lorraine (the emblem of the Free French)".

British victories in this war were:

1940	Jul.3	Mers-el-Kebir
1941	Jun.21	Syria
1942	Nov.5	Madagascar

2

THE DATES OF THE VICTORIES

JANUARY

2 FALAISE 1418, FRANCE (HUNDRED YEARS'WAR)

Commanders: Henry V v. ?

The capture of Caen (see 20 September) had given Henry's Normandy campaign a solid start, and he now wanted to secure the whole of Lower Normandy. By the conventions of the period, the active campaigning season was over until the warmer weather, but Henry, like his great-grandfather, Edward III, was not prepared to let this convention get in his way. His immediate objective was the strongly fortified town and castle of Falaise, the birth place of William the Conqueror. Several lesser towns – Bayeux, Tilly, Villers Bocage, and Argentan - were taken before the attackers set up camp outside Falaise, and in addition to these military precautions, Henry gave an indication of his diplomatic-strategic skills in concluding a truce with the rulers of the contiguous territories of Brittany, Anjou, and Maine. Given the strength of the fortifications and mindful of the necessity of keeping his casualties to a minimum, Henry decided that a blockade and bombardment were to be preferred to assault by storm; and with an eye to reducing loss from disease and the rigours of winter in the open, he ordered huts to be built for his troops. Bombardment was provided by the siege train which included a huge cannon of twenty inches calibre, three balls of which are still displayed in the castle. The attack lasted a month by which time there was a breach in the walls forty yards wide, and the town surrendered followed by the castle a month later.

In spite of the season, the campaign continued. To the west, the Duke of Gloucester took St. Lo, Carenton, Valognes, St. Sauveur le Vicomte, and Cherbourg. In the centre, the Earl of Huntingdon accounted for Coutanes and Avranche, while in the south the Earl of Warwick conquered the formidable castle of Domfront. On now to Rouen (see 20 January and 20 July, Pont de L'Arche).

Note deserves to be taken of a more violent and hotly contested action that took place at Falaise in August 1944 when the Canadians, Poles, British and Americans succeeded in capturing tens of thousands of German troops in the Falaise pocket.

3 H.M.S.DIAMOND (38 GUNS) V. CATON AND OTHERS 1795, FRANCE (FRENCH REVOLUTIONARY WARS)

Commanders: Captain Sir Sidney Smith v. ?

In a daring and unusual enterprise even by the standards of the Royal Navy, Smith rounded Cape Ushant on the north west tip of France and disguised his frigate as French. The next morning he followed a French ship of the line, *Caton*, past the rocks and shoals off Point St. Mathew and into the entrance of the Road of Brest. At sunset, the strong ebb tide setting westerly obliged *Caton* to anchor and Smith did the same astern of her. When the tide changed, Smith weighed anchor and by the light of the moon took his ship into the Road between a French frigate, another vessel and Toulinquet Rocks. Unfortunately for the drama of the story, there were no warships in the Road, and Smith headed *Diamond* for the open sea. His course took him close to *Caton*, and this caused a French corvette to raise the alarm. With considerable presence of mind, Smith spoke to the captain of *Caton* in French and persuaded him that *Diamond* was part of the French Norway Squadron, this was sufficient for the French to call off the pursuit. The originality of this foray was characteristic of Smith (see 18 May, Cape Carmel and 19 December, Toulon).

Author's Note: I can testify that to take a sailing ship into the Road of Brest would have required outstanding skill as well as courage. In the weeks immediately following the D-Day invasion in 1944, the German Army remained in possession of Brittany and the Cherbourg Peninsula, and a naval operation against Brest was ordered that would certainly have met with Sir Sidney Smith's approval. Operating from Falmouth and Plymouth and refuelling en route from a lighter in the Channel, the

64th. M.T.B Flotilla (Senior Officer Lt.Cdr. David Wilkie D.S.C.,R. N.R) in which I was serving as a navigating officer, made two attempts to force passage at night through the Road and into Brest harbour. On each occasion, the star shells, searchlights and other pyrotechnics were such that any effort to go through the 14 miles of the Road would have served only as a naval version of the Charge of the Light Brigade.

4 LA RÉOLE 1346, FRANCE (HUNDRED YEARS' WAR)

Commanders: Earl of Derby v. Agout des Baux.

The siege of La Réole was undertaken to secure Bordeaux against an attack through the valley of the Garonne (see 2 December, Aiguillon). The town and castle enjoyed a strong, natural defensive position that had been enhanced by thick fortifications, and any siege was likely to be a long one. Derby ordered catapaults to be constructed as well as two tall, mobile towers that were to provide archers with a platform from which they could clear the defenders off the walls. The town was soon forced into surrender, but the defenders withdrew into the castle and continued their resistance. Finally, the garrison asked for terms and were permitted to leave with only their arms and horses; they left with just six horses and, as they were leaving, they were reduced to bartering with the English for fresh and better-fed ones. The price is said to have been high. Derby now directed his troops to advance in two columns – one up the valley of the Lot and the other up the valley of the Garonne – and a series of towns were taken up to the boundary with Quercy.

4 H.M.S. BLANCHE (32 GUNS) V. PIQUE (32 GUNS) 1795, WEST INDIES (FRENCH REVOLUTIONARY WARS)

Commanders: Captain Robert Faulkner v. ?

Fought off Guadeloupe, this was a spirited, night action lasting from midnight until 5.00 a.m. when *Pique* surrendered. Faulkner was killed in action and was succeeded in command by Lieutenant Watkins who, with Lieutenant Milne, was promoted to commander in recognition of his part in the success. Two years later, *Blanche* achieved less salutary notice when the crew mutinied against the appointment of Henry Hotham, a captain notorious for the harshness of his discipline. The mutiny was quelled by Horatio Nelson solely by the force of his redoubtable character.

Naval hostilities in the French Revolutionary Wars were not limited to those between the combatants. In 1793, the French fleet at Brest mutinied, and four years later *Blanche's* uprising was small beer compared with major fleet mutinies at Spithead (Portsmouth), the Nore (Chatham), and Yarmouth. All of these mutinies arose from the terrible conditions and hardships of life on board, and they were suppressed with varying degrees of severity. Reforms were promised, and some were made, then, the respective navies were able to resume fighting each other.

5 H.M.S. VIPER (12 GUNS) V. FERRET (14 GUNS) 1800, FRANCE (FRENCH REVOLUTIONARY WARS)

Commanders: Lieut. J.Pengelly v. ?

This fight was one of many in the long history of Anglo–French sea warfare in which one of the antagonists was a privateer. A privateer is not a pirate, but a privately owned vessel armed and operating in time of war against the trade of an enemy under the authority of a letter of marque. Privateers were mostly active in coastal waters against merchant shipping, and in the wars of the eighteenth century the French privateers performed better than their navy. In Britain, unless invasion was threatened, attacks on trade generally excited more public concern and comment than naval battles at a distance. Smaller ships were suitable for keeping privateers in check, and *Viper*, a cutter, was one of them. After a long and bitter fight in which Pengelly and one of his crew were wounded, *Ferret* ('a Tag') surrendered and was taken into Plymouth as a prize. Just ten days before, Pengelly had captured another privateer (see 26 December), and in February he was promoted to commander with command of a troopship.

6 JERSEY 1781. CHANNEL ISLANDS (AMERICAN WAR OF INDEPENDENCE)

Commanders: Major Francis Pierson v. Baron de Rullecourt

Jersey had formally elected to be English and not French (Norman) in 1204, but being so close to France, it was subject to frequent raids and invasions whenever Britain and France were at war. The Battle of Jersey was the last of them. De Rullecourt, something of a ruffian, led a force under the pilotage of a Jersey criminal, but two of the ships struck rocks and sank with loss of life and all of the artillery. Undeterred, the invaders pressed on and landed unopposed. They captured the Governor and forced him to surrender, but the local militia and the regular troops refused to acknowledge the Governor's order to surrender. These units advanced into the market place of the capital, St. Helier, where they confronted the French. After less than thirty minutes of vigorous fighting during which de Rullancourt was mortally wounded, the French surrendered; Pierson had been killed in the early part of the fight and is buried in St. Helier's parish church.

The battle has been commemorated in various ways. There is a magnificent monument to the memory of Major Pierson in Royal Square (formerly the market place) erected by the States of the island; on the 200th Anniversary special £1 coins – one silver and one gold – were struck; and there is a splendid painting of the death of Pierson by the American artist John Copley that hangs in the Tate. In the centre of the portrait is a black soldier, wearing a sergeant's insignia, firing a musket, he is Pompey, the servant of Pierson. He seems to be in the uniform of the militia, but during this war there was a Royal Ethiopa Regiment fighting on the British side and 'Liberty for Slaves' was embroidered on the uniform. It is not known if Pompey was a member of this regiment.

It is usually claimed in Jersey that this battle was the last fought on British soil, but this is not the case (see 25 February, Fishguard), and some might even suggest that Ballinamuck (see 8 September) ought to be counted.

7 H.M.S. DORIS (36 GUNS), UNICORN (32 GUNS), & DRUID (36 GUNS) V. VILLE DE L'ORIENT (40 GUNS), 1797, CHANNEL (FRENCH REVOLUTIONARY WARS)

Commanders: Captain Hon. C. Jones, Captain Sir Thomas Williams & Captain E.Codrington v. ?

A French attempt to invade Ireland in support of the rebels had met heavy gales almost from the time the ships sailed from France. Part of the invasion fleet was scattered, and no troops were landed. *Ville de l'Orient*, carrying 400 hussars, was intercepted by the three British frigates and taken as a prize (see also 13 January H.M.S. Indefatigable et al.). Sir Thomas William's naval service was meritorious (see 8 June H.M.S. Santa Margarita et al.), but Codrington out-shone him. Service early in his career under Howe (see 1 June Ushant) and with Jervis and Nelson led him to command *H.M.S. Orion* at Trafalgar (see 21 October), and at the end of the war with France he was a Knight of the Bath and a rear admiral. Finally, he commanded a combined British, French and Russian fleet against the Turks at Navarino, 1827, – the last major battle to be fought under sail.

7 TARIFA 1812, ANDALUSIA ,SPAIN (PENINSULA WAR)

Commanders: Lt. Col John Skerret & Capt. Genl. Francisco Copons v. Marshal Claude Victor.
Forces: British 1,750, Spanish 1,650 v. French 10,000.

The town had been besieged by the French since December 20 1811, and at first they breached the defences, but subsequent attacks were repulsed and lack of food and other supplies compelled retreat. By January 7 the siege was over, and although French casualties barely exceeded 500, their prestige was badly damaged, and the battalions were so exhausted that they were incapable of further operations.

8 BLUEBERG 1806, SOUTH AFRICA (NAPOLEONIC WAR)

Commanders: Lt. General Sir David Baird v. General Jans Willems Janssens
Forces: British 6,600 v. Dutch & French 5,000.

The British landed at Saldanha Bay from ships commanded by Sir Home Popham and were attacked by the Dutch and French who had marched out from Cape Town. The result was a decisive victory for the British with the loss of only 15 killed.

The French were in Cape Town because in 1806 Napoleon had made his brother, Louis Napoleon, King of the Netherlands, and the Dutch resumed their previous alliance with France. Although the numbers engaged were small, this battle was of considerable importance in that it led to Cape Town becoming a colony of Britain, and a very important port en route to India before the construction of the Suez Canal. The territory was ceded to Britain at the Congress of Vienna 1815 (see 9 June). Janssens met the British again five years later and was thoroughly beaten (see 9 August, Batavia).

10 H.M.S. PHOEBE (36 GUNS) V. ATALANTE (16 GUNS) 1797, IRELAND (FRENCH REVOLUTIONARY WARS)

Commanders: Captain R. Barlow v. Lieut. Dordeli.

This encounter took place about 60 miles south east of Cape Clear in the form of a long chase lasting 8 hours at the end of which *Atalante's* crew of 112 were taken prisoner. A bonus with the prize was that she was coppered. Sheathing ships below the waterline with thin copper sheets fastened with copper bolts as a protection against the teredo worm had only recently come imto service, and additons to the fleet so treated were welcome. Incidentally, this practice is the origin of the phrase 'copper-bottomed'.

Captain Barlow in *Phoebe* exemplifies the contribution of the British frigates, their commanders and crews in the long wars against the French (see 19 February, 21 February, 11 May, and 20 December).

13 H.M.S. INDEFATIGABLE (44 GUNS) & H.M.S. AMAZON (36 GUNS) V. DROITS DE L'HOMME (74 GUNS) 1797, FRANCE (FRENCH REVOLUTIONARY WARS)

Commanders: Captain Sir Edward Pellew & Captain R.C. Reynolds v. Commodore J-R Lacrosse.

This action was fought throughout the night in a heavy gale off Cape Ushant after a long chase from Bantry Bay, where the French had intended to invade Ireland in support of the rebellion (see 7 January, H.M.S. Doris et al.). *Droits de L'Homme* (Rights of Man) had three times the fire power of *Indefatigable*, and including the soldiers on board, five times the manpower. Nevertheless, with 100 killed and 150 wounded, she was driven onto the rocks in Audierne Bay where all of the remaining complement of 1,300, save for 200, were drowned trying to swim ashore. *Amazon* also went aground, and her crew were taken prisoner.

The daring and determination of Pellew in this action were greatly admired, and it was probably the most famous of his victories (see April 20); there is a fine painting of it in the U.S. Naval Academy Museum.

15 (EST.) RY 1436, FRANCE (HUNDRED YEARS' WAR)

Commanders: Sir John Talbot v. La Hire & Poton de Xantrailles
Forces: English 400; French 1,000.

A few months previously, the English committed a serious diplomatic error that ensured their eventual defeat in the Hundred Years' War. Strategically, England required a French ally, and for some years this was the Duke of Burgundy. The enemy was the Dauphin, son of Charles VI, who had been disinherited by his father and replaced by Henry V through the Treaty of Troyes (see 21 May). The Duke sought to bring about an end to the war in a tri-partite negotiation, but the English withdrew, and the Duke entered into an alliance with the Dauphin who now claimed the throne as Charles VII. Talbot emerged as the principal English commander, and he led with an exhilarating verve and dash that was apt to become stupidly reckless at crucial moments. Ry was one of his better performances. The French had advanced up to the gates of Rouen and had hoped the inhabitants of this important town would rise up and let them in. This did not happen, and they withdrew to Ry about ten miles away to wait for reinforcements. Observing the withdrawal, Talbot aroused about 400 stalwarts, and they swept out of Rouen in pursuit. They surprised the French outposts and galloped through their reinforcements into the town. There, Talbot collected his men together, and they were mounted before an alarm could be given. The English were in the streets while the French were still getting out of their billets, and in pandemonium and panic, the French fled, La Hire was wounded, a number of nobles were captured, and all of the baggage was taken. Although on a small scale, the style of this victory did much to restore the military prestige of the English. Talbot now had the bit between his teeth, and it was on to Pontoise (see 16 February).

15 PONDICHERRY 1761, INDIA (SEVEN YEARS' WAR)

Commanders: Col. Eyre Coote & Cdre. C. Steevens v. Comte Thomas-Arthur Lally de Tollendal.
Forces: British about 8,000 including 5,000 Indian troops & naval support; French 11,000 including 9,000 Indian troops.

This was a siege by the British which began on December 10, 1760. The British squadron in support had remained on station long after the date for the annual withdrawal to Bombay for the monsoon season (the opposing French squadron never appeared in 1760). A storm on 1 January wrecked five ships, but gunnery support continued, and on January 15 the French garrison surrendered. Shortly after this battle, the remaining French fortresses in India were taken, effectively ending their jurisdiction in India, and nearly two hundred years of British sovereignty was about to begin. Although the numbers engaged were small, as in the case of Blueberg (see January 8), the outcome was of the greatest importance in the development of the British Empire.

The French commander was the son of an Irish Jacobite loyalist. He served in the Irish Brigade of the French army, the famous 'Wild Geese', and fought at Culloden in the Stuart cause. Seemingly lacking proverbial Irish charm and blarney, in India his lack of tact alienated the Indian princes allied to the French, and this defeat and a previous one at Wandiwash (see 22 January), led to his recall to France where he was indicted for treason. After a long imprisonment, Lally de Tollendal was beheaded publicly in the Place de la Grève. Such a reaction to defeat was not a peculiarly French practice; in 1757 the British admiral, John Byng, was executed on his own quarter deck by a firing squad of Royal Marines for failing to hold Minorca against the French (see 25 March, HMS Sheerness; 19 September, Port Mahon; & 17 August, Lagos Bay). Coote was thirty-four years of age, and he proceeded to establish an excellent military reputation culminating in the appointment of c-in-c India.

At first, Coote declared he had captured Pondicherry for the Crown, but when Governor Pigot of the East India Compnay told him that if that was the case, then the Crown must meet the costs, Coote changed his mind. Coote met a curious end. He was returning to Madras by sea when the ship in which he was travelling was chased by a French warship, this resulted in sea sickness that led to a fever from which the unfortunate Coote died.

16 CORUNNA 1809, SPAIN (PENINSULA WAR)

Commanders: Lt. Gen. Sir John Moore v. Marshal Nicolas-Jean de Dieu Soult, Duke of Dalmatia.
Forces: British 14,000; French 20,000

This battle is a nineteenth century harbinger of Dunkirk. The British had been conducting a long and difficult retreat from Spain with the intention of embarking at Corunna. However, the troops arrived before the transports and were obliged to fight the pursuing French with their backs to the sea. The French were held off, and the embarcation was successfully carried out. British casualties were 800, including Sir John Moore, and the French 2,000. On the face of it, this was a French victory, although it is not so regarded by the British who had not only evacuated the army successfully but had also prevented the conquest of Portugal and southern Spain. While it is not to be compared in its stirring qualities with Shakespeare's representation of Henry V at Harfleur and Agincourt (see 22 September & 25 October), Moore, too, has a poetic eulogy in 'The Burial of Sir John Moore at Corunna' by the Irish poet, Charles Wolfe:

"Not a drum was heard, not a funeral note,
As his corse to the ramparts we hurried
We buried him darkly at dead of night,
The sods with our bayonets turning.
We carved not a line, and we raised not a stone
But we left him alone with his glory."

Marshal Soult made good the lack of a headstone by erecting a monument to Sir John on the ramparts of Corunna with an inscription: "Hic Cecidet Iohannes Moore dux exercitus Britannici, in pugna Ianuarii XVI, 1809, Contra gallos a duce Dalmatiae doctos." ["John Moore general of the British army was killed here January 16, 1809, in battle against the French dedicated by the Duke of Dalmatia"]. There is another monument to Sir John in St. Paul's cathedral. Moore was also admired by Napoleon, not free with accolades, who commented: "His talents and firmness alone saved the British army [in Spain] from destruction; he was a brave soldier, an excellent officer, and a man of talent".

19 CIUDAD RODRIGO 1812 SPAIN, (PENINSULA WAR)
Commanders: Wellington v. Gen. Barrié
Forces: British 20,000; French 2,000

This border fortress covered the northern gateway from Portugal to Spain and was important to the future operations of both sides. Wellington put it under siege, and four days after it began, a major redoubt was captured in a slashing night attack; the bombardment began a few days later. Two breaches were opened in the walls, and the assault was carried out by the 3rd. Regiment (later, The Buffs) and the Light Division, but the two commanders, Maj.Genl. Robert Craufurd and Maj. Genl. Henry Mackinnon were both killed. Craufurd's death seriously weakened Wellington's command structure because Craufurd had already shown exceptional military capacities, not only in the field but also in administration and in the training of the troops under his command. Possibly Craufurd's most notable achievement was leading a forced march to Talavera (see 28 July) in which 43 miles were covered in twenty-six hours, a feat on a par with two of Marlborough's best efforts (see 11 July Oudenarde and 13 September Bouchain). Following the custom of the time, Ciudad Rodrigo was sacked after its capture. British casualities were 1,100; French: 600 killed and 1,300 prisoners.

On the first anniversary of the capture of Ciudad Rodrigo, a great ball was held there with 65 sitting down to dinner, and 200 guests arriving for the dancing. Wellington, now Marquess of Wellington and, courtesy of the Spanish Cortes, Duke of Ciudad Rodrigo, rode 17 miles from his H.Q. to be present – and after taking part in the dance, he rode back in the moonlight. Among the many toasts drunk that evening was "Death to all Frenchmen" in the tradition noted in the Introduction.

20 ROUEN 1419, FRANCE (HUNDRED YEARS' WAR)
Commanders: Henry V v. Guy de Bouteille & Alain Blanchard.

This siege was the culmination of Henry's conquest of Normandy that began at Harfleur (see September 22). The victory at Agincourt (see 25 October) had given Henry and his army a formidable reputation throughout Europe, but at Rouen, one of the major cities in France, the English had too few troops for the usual "breach and storm" tactic and had to resort to a blockade in the course of which Henry showed the ruthless side of his nature. In preparation for the siege, the non-combatants had been expelled from the city, but the English, following the example of the French at Chateau Gaillard 150 years before, refused to let them through the siege lines and 12,000 suffered terrible hardships in the winter weather. However, Henry did allow his soldiers to give some of their own rations to these unfortunates, and at Christmas he distributed a free meal.

After Agincourt, the French had greatly strengthened the fortifications and reinforced the garrison making Rouen the most formidable, fortified city the English had yet encountered. The preparations for the siege were extensive and sometimes extraordinary. In order that the Seine could be blocked downstream, it was decided to bring up the fleet from Harfleur, but in order to do so the town of Caudebec had first to be taken – the Earl of Warwick did so. The ships sailed up the river until it became too shallow, whereupon some of the ships were beached and hauled, with sails set, by the sailors for three miles across land and re-launched to drive the French vessels into the city. Three great chains were then stretched across the river. Upstream, three miles from the city, a large wooden bridge was built to provide quick and easy communication between the north and south wings of the army, and finally a strongly fortified outpost situated on a hill was subdued. The tedium of waiting for hunger to have its effect was relieved by the arrival of a cargo of wine and beer, with 2,500 mugs, the gift of the citizens of London (perhaps the forerunner of Red Cross Parcels). The needs of the besieged were more basic, and they were able to get an appeal for help through to the Duke of Burgundy, then the effective ruler of France because of the insanity of Charles VI. The Duke's reply was to take the Oriflamme (see 25 October Agincourt) from the abbey-church at Saint-Denis and march with it to Pontoise where he went to ground; as at Agincourt, the Oriflamme again proved to be ineffective. The action at Rouen took the form of periodic French sorties that were all beaten back until the city finally surrendered. Always devout, Henry's first act on entering the city was to go to the cathedral and give thanks for all of his blessings.

Such was the effect of the fall of Rouen that the other places in Upper Normandy still in French hands capitulated with indecent haste, usually before being commanded to do so. Before the end of February 1419, Lillebourne, Vernon, Mantes, Dieppe, Gournay, Eu, and Honfleur had thrown in the towel. With a few exceptions, all Normandy had now been conquered, and Henry's supremacy was spelled out the following year in the terms of the Treaty of Troyes (see 21 May). Flushed with success on this scale, Henry gave orders for new coinage to be struck at Caen bearing the inscription " Henricus, Rex Francie" and it was only Henry's early death that made it premature.

22 WANDIWASH I 1760, INDIA (SEVEN YEARS' WAR)

Commanders: Colonel Eyre Coote v. Comte Thomas-Arthur Lally de Tollendal

Forces: British 1,980, 3,350 Indian troops & 16 guns; French 2,250, 4,300 Indian troops & 30 guns.

The French were besieging the fort at Wandiwash when they were engaged by the British relieving force. Action began with an attack on the British position by 3,000 Indian cavalry; close-range gunfire caused the attackers to withdraw with heavy losses, and they took no further part. After a day of fierce fighting, including a bayonet charge by French infantry, the French collapsed and left the field, their losses were 200 men, 160 prisoners and 24 guns; British losses were 63 killed. Among the French prisoners was the Marquis Charles-Joseph Patissier de Bussy-Castelnau, Lally's best general, who had previously been very successful in manipulating the government of Hyderabad in the French interest. All was to no avail because this battle marked the beginning of the end of French dominion in India; Coote proceeded with the subjugation of the central Carnatic blocking the road to Pondicherry where about one year later he delivered the *coup de grâce* (see January 15).

FEBRUARY

3 H.M.S. SPEEDY (14 GUNS) V. PAPILLON (14 GUNS) 1798, SPAIN (FRENCH REVOLUTIONARY WARS)

Commanders: Captain H. Downman v. ?

Fought about six miles west of Vigo, both ships were brigs, although *Papillon* was larger. *Speedy* engaged the enemy for about two-and-a half hours before the French broke off and sailed away. Downman gave chase and continued to fire until light winds separated the ships, but *Papillon* was able to fire at a Spanish brig that *Speedy* had taken as a prize on the previous day and to seize it. The twelve British crew manning the prize battened down twent-six Spaniards and made their escape in a small boat before the French came on board. The wind blew again the next day enabling *Speedy* to continue the chase all through the day and to make an unsuccessful attempt to board *Papillon*. Heavily damaged, *Papillon* was still able to sail away, but as consolation, the Spanish prize was re-taken and ten Frenchmen were found on board together with the Spaniards. Returning to Lisbon for repairs, Downman was gratified to find that the British factory in Oporto had decided to present him with a piece of plate worth £50 for his efforts in protecting their trade.

5 H.M.S FAIRY (16 GUNS) & H.M.S. HARPY (18 GUNS) V. LA PALLAS (42GUNS) 1800, FRANCE (FRENCH REVOLUTIONARY WARS)

Commanders: Captain J.S. Horton & Captain H. Bazely v. Captain J.Epron.

Although fought off Les Sept Isles, the beginning was in St. Aubin's Bay, Jersey where Captain Horton was dining with Captain d'Auvergne, Prince of Bouillon, when they saw a British ship being chased into the Bay by a much larger French one. Horton immediately volunteered to chase the French ship and sailed early the next morning with *Harpy* in company. Contact was made when *Pallas* was sighted sailing westwards and brought to action within pistol shot range. After nearly two hours of heavy fighting, a British frigate and two sloops came up and *Pallas* was forced to strike her colours to *Harpy; Pallas* was a new frigate carrying 350 men and victualled for 5 months.

After repairs, *Pallas* was commissioned into the Royal Navy as *La Pique* (not to be confused with the French ship of that name – see 4 January). The first casualty in *La Pique* was one George, or John, Barnett who in September, 1800, was hanged from the yard arm for mutiny. Barnett had been one of the crew of *Danae,* the frigate that joined the action against *Pallas*, and a few weeks afterwards, mutineers took charge of *Danae* and sailed her to France. The captain and loyal members of the crew were released, and the mutineers took service with the French. In June, *H.M.S. Indefatigable* took a French privateer bound for Brazil out of Bordeaux with a crew of 200; the prisoners were sent to Plymouth for imprisonment, and as they were being marched away, Barnett, one of the leaders of the mutiny, was spotted by the former first lieutenant of *Danae* and brought to trial. Convicted and sentenced to death, after spending some time in prayer, he was run up to the fore-yard arm where the body was left hanging for about an hour. Barnett was from Jersey and spoke fluent French so that his identity might not have come to light but for the chance encounter. Several other *Danae* mutineers were amongst captured French crews, and another was arrested in Wapping masquerading as an American. Tried and hanged from a yard arm, before his death he said that the mutiny had been organised and led by an Irish priest named Ignatius Finney.

6 SAN DOMINGO 1806, WEST INDIES (NAPOLEONIC WAR)

Commanders: Vice Adml. Sir John Duckworth v. Rear Adml. Corentin de Leissègues

Forces: British squadron of 7 ships of the line; French squadron of 5 ships of the line, 2 frigates and a corvette.

After the crushing defeat of the French navy at Trafalgar (see 21 October), Napoleon at first decided to use his remaining ships as powerful raiding squadrons, and de Leissègues had been sent with troops and supplies for the West Indies' colonies with orders to carry out raids afterwards. These plans came to nothing once Duckworth caught up with the French squadron off Cape Nisao. A vigorous action ensued in which three French ships of the line were captured, and the two others, including the flag ship, were driven ashore; the three smaller ships escaped. Tremendous seas were running, and it was not until the afternoon of the following day that the prisoners could be removed and the ships burned. Relatively little damage was done to the British ships, but among the casualties was the Admiral's cook, which brings to mind the story of a Scottish laird. On being told that several of his neighbour's servants, including the cook, had been drowned in the loch the previous afternoon, his first remark was "Good God! What in the world did they do for dinner?"

An incident after the battle illustrates an aspect of the conduct of hostilities in this period. In his public letter, Sir John Duckworth condemned the conduct of the French Captain Henry for running his ship ashore after he had already surrendered (thus robbing the victors of prize money!). Captain Henry and his officers denied they had surrendered maintaining that although the ensign had been shot away, the pendant was always flying, and Duckworth withdrew the charges. The following year Duckworth accomplished a rare feat – he forced the Straight of the Dardanelles, something his successors were not able to do in 1915. As an indication of what life in the Navy could be like in wartime, Duckworth had calculated three years prior to this action that he had been at sea for 10 years and had not seen his daughter for 6 years.

10 TREATY (A.K.A. PEACE) OF PARIS 1763, FRANCE (SEVEN YEARS' WAR).

This was the treaty that concluded the Seven Years' War, the principal parties were France and England, but Spain was also a signatory, and Portugal acceded to its terms. A singularity is that in the Protocol George III of Great Britain is also listed as King of France (thereby asserting the ancient claim) as is Louis XV. The effect of the treaty was to establish Britain's supremacy as a colonial power at the expense of France and Spain, and although its importance was not fully appreciated at the time, a contemporary opinion in Britain was that "it was the most honourable peace this nation ever saw". A clergyman was so exhilarated, he gave his sermon in celebration of the Treaty the title of "The Triumph of the Israelites over the Moabites, or Protestants over Papist." In summary: Britain took from France the entire province of Canada; all of Louisiana east of the Mississipi river; Cape Breton; all the islands in the St. Lawrence River; Tobago; Dominica; St. Vincent and the Grenadines in the West Indies; Senegal; and Minorca. Dunkirk, a hotbed of privateering, had to be de-militarised. In India, France was forced to acknowledge the supremacy of the East India Company, dismantle its fortifications in Bengal, and recognize the British-supported rulers in the Carnatic and Deccan. France was permitted to retain the islands of St. Pierre and Miquelon off Newfoundland; Guadaloupe, Martinique, Marie Galante, Desirade and St. Lucia in the West Indies; Gorée on the African coast; and Belle-Ile-en-Mer, Brittany. As ever, there were those in Britain who were not satisfied; in particular, it was felt that the islands of the West Indies with their valuable sugar trade would have been a better bargain than Canada with its fur trade.

12 ROUVRAY (A.K.A. THE HERRINGS) 1429, FRANCE (HUNDRED YEARS' WAR)

Commanders: Sir John Fastolfe v. Bastard of Orleans.

Sir John was in command of a supply train taking salt fish to the English army covering Orleans (Lent was about to begin), and he was able to repel a French attack inflicting heavy losses and wounding 'The Bastard'. An important reason for the defeat was the impulsive charge of a Scottish contingent in the French army in defiance of orders, this attack suffered such casualties that a rout ensued. The Scottish commander, Sir John Stewart, Constable of the Scots in France, was taken prisoner - again (see July 31, Cravant). At this juncture, French morale was at its nadir, but all this was about to change dramatically as Joan of Arc took her place on centre stage.

Sir John Fastolfe is not the model for Shakespeare's Falstaff - a character in the plays 'Henry IV' and 'Henry V' at the time of the Hundred Years' War. Sir John was a career soldier who fought well at Agincourt (see 25 October) and Verneuil (see 17 August), where he, personally, took Marshall Fayette of France prisoner.; the fortune he made in France was greatly enhanced by Fayette's ransom. Created a knight of the the Garter in 1426, he was acquitted of charges of cowardice in the defeat at Patay, 1429, but his reputation continued to suffer, and Shakespeare makes use of it in his play Henry VI, Part 1, Act IV, Scene 1. When he retired to England he built a castle at Caister; and he appears in the Paston Letters in an unattractive light.

12 MARTINIQUE 1762, WEST INDIES (SEVEN YEARS' WAR)

Commanders: Rear-Admiral Lord George Rodney v. ?

An attempt had been made three years previously to take this island, but the force sent to do so was inadequate, and Guadeloupe was conquered instead (see 1 May). Circumstances were now more propitious, Canada had been taken, and plenty of Major-General Monckton's troops were available for a new effort. The island was conquered after little resistance – Rodney said "We are highly obliged to the inhabitants for their pusillanimous defence.", but another favourable factor was the knowledge of the prosperity of the planters in Guadeloupe that had followed their surrender to the British. After this battle, all the other French colonies in the Lesser Antilles capitulated. A relief force of seven ships of the line arrived from Brest one day too late, and in no condition to undertake offensive operations. In one sense, however, these successes were a labour in vain because at the Treaty of Paris 1763 (see 10 February), Martinique and Guadeloupe were returned to the French.

16 (EST.) PONTOISE 1437, FRANCE (HUNDRED YEARS' WAR)
Commanders: Sir John Talbot v. L'Isle Adam

Flushed with his success at Ry (see 15 January), Talbot, defying the convention that fighting had to be suspended during the winter months because of the weather, decided to attack Pontoise. With only 400 men he left Rouen in bitter winter weather and made a forced march to his objective. The surprise was complete, and it enabled Talbot to send a small party across the frozen river Oise dressed as peasants carrying baskets for the market. This bold imposture deserved to succeed, and it did. As soon as the English had entered the town, they shouted loudly "The town is ours! St. George! Talbot!", and this was the signal for the assault party to climb the scaling ladders, enter the town and straight away open the gates for the rest of their comrades. L'Isle Adam and the garrison scrambled out of Pontoise as best they could, leaving behind all their belongings and stores (a rich looting opportunity). The town was strongly fortified, and its fall opened the way to Paris. In spite of the small number of troops, Talbot marched on the city, and when they arrived they crossed the moat on the ice but were unable to find a way of scaling the walls and were obliged to withdraw. This victory and others in Normandy boosted English morale at a time when they had no allies in France. Somewhat ironically Talbot and L'Isle Adam, as leader of the Burgundians, had fought side by side at the siege of St. Denys two years previously.

On the death of the Duke of Bedford two years earlier, Talbot had become in practice, if not in name, the English commander in France and so continued until his death, fighting side-by-side with his son, at the battle of Castillion in 1453 (in his play 'Henry VI, Part 1' Shakespeare, with a poetical disregard for historical fact, has a dramatic scene in which Talbot tries, unsuccessfully, to persuade his son to escape the approaching disaster). Talbot's ardour and performance on the battlefield were such as to establish a moral ascendancy over the French to whom he was known as the 'English Achilles', and although they were said to regard him "with terror and dismay", nevertheless, they erected a monument to him at Castillion (analogous to Sir John Moore's monument at Corunna – see 16 January). In Patay, the site of another French victory, there is still a road named rue Talbot, and he became the subject of contemporary French poems. While he could still reasonably claim to be King of France, Henry VI made Talbot Marshal of France, and later the first Earl of Shrewsbury. Originally, Talbot's body was buried at Falaise (a most suitable place for a mighty man of valour – see 2 January), but the head was taken separately to England; subsequently the body was taken to England and interred with the head. This rather bizarre procedure was concluded in 1860 when the remains were exhumed, and it was established beyond peradventure of doubt that Talbot had been killed by a blow to the head from a battle axe. At the last report, he was still buried, with all of the pieces in the same place, in the parish church of Whitchurch, Shropshire.

17 MADRAS 1759, INDIA (CARNATIC WARS)

Commanders: Colonel Stringer Lawrence v. Comte Thomas-Arthur Lally de Tollendal
Forces: Britsh 1,750 + 2,200 Indian troops, French 2,300 + 5,000 Indian troops.

Recently appointed to supreme command in southern India, Tollendal determined to force the British out of Madras and the Coromandel coast. French troops were recalled from the Deccan, and the march on Madras began, but it did not go well. The siege started early in January, and a month later it had had little effect, but the British had been able to reinforce the garrison at Chingleput in the French rear. Aware of the danger, Tollendal detached a substantial force to attack Chingleput, but it was beaten back with heavy losses, and while he was considering the deterioration in his position, Admiral Sir George Pocock brought his squadron into the roads. The ships were enough to tip the balance, and on 17 February the French were in full retreat to Arcot leaving behind 52 guns and all their stores and ammunition. This defeat was the beginning of the end of French jurisdiction in India (see 22 January, Wandiwash and 15 January, Pondicherry).

18 H.M.S.FOUDROYANT (80 GUNS) & OTHERS V. LE GÉNÉREUX (74 GUNS) & OTHERS 1800, MEDITERRANEAN (FRENCH REVOLUTIONARY WARS)

Commanders: Rear Adml. Horatio Nelson v. Rear Adml. Jean Baptiste Pérrée.

Le Généreux was one of only two ships of the line to have escaped from the total disaster at the battle of the Nile (see 1 August), and now it was escorting several smaller ships with nearly 4,000 troops and supplies for the relief of Malta, then under blockade and siege. As an introduction to the main event, the first to be attacked was a French frigate, *La Ville de Marseilles*, which surrendered after only a few shots had been fired and proved to be a most welcome prize being loaded with salt meat, brandy, wine, and other useful but less delectable stores in the eyes of sailors obliged to spend long periods at sea. *Le Généreux* did not resist very long – a few broadsides were exchanged, and she struck her colours, perhaps because the Rear Admiral, hit in the left eye by a musket ball and with his right thigh shattered by a cannon ball, was dying from his wounds. Nelson's flag captain, Sir Edward Berry, brought the admiral's sword to Nelson, but Berry enjoyed a triumph of his own. Immediately following the Nile, Nelson had sent him to Lord St. Vincent, the c-in-c, with his official dispatch, and the ship in which he was travelling was attacked and captured by *Le Généreux*. Berry was severely wounded in the fighting and imprisoned at Corfu, but now he had played a major role in seizing his captor.

Pérrée was a serious loss to the French navy. Three years younger than Nelson, his career was already distinguished by successes in the Atlantic and against British possessions along the west coast of Africa. In general, Napoleon had a poor opinion of French naval officers, Pérrée was an exception to whom Napoleon had given the nickname 'the Intrepid Pérrée', and presented him with a sword of honour. He had been given the important, personal service of taking to Toulon the art treasures that Napoleon had plundered in Italy – and which were not to be returned to their rightful owners (see 30 May Treaty of Paris).

19 H.M.S. PHOEBE (36 GUNS) V. AFRICAINE (44 GUNS) 1801, STRAIT OF GIBRALTAR (FRENCH REVOLUTIONARY WARS)

Commanders: Captain R. Barlow v. Captain Majendie.

Africaine was sighted about six miles from Gibraltar sailing eastwards, and *Phoebe* chased her for about two and a half hours. Closing to within pistol-shot, after two hours of steady bombardment, the British frigate reduced *Africaine* to a wreck, the guns dismounted, and the decks strewn with dead and wounded. *Africaine* had sailed from Rochefort six days earlier carrying 400 troops, including a general and other senior officers, as well as a ship's company of 315, apparently bound for Egypt where the French army had been marooned after the battle of the Nile (see 1 August) . The carnage was increased because the French soldiers insisted, as a point of honour, on remaining on the upper deck during the fighting, although they served no useful purpose there. French casualties were at least 200 killed and 143 wounded; British casualties were very light. *Africaine* was repaired and taken into service in the Royal Navy with the same name; those members of *Phoebe's* crew who lived so long received Navy medals in 1849.

Captain Barlow in *Phoebe* exemplifies the contribution of the British frigates, their commanders and crews in the long wars against the French (see 10 January, 21 February, 11 May, and 20 December).

20 BEJAR 1813, SPAIN (PENINSULA WAR)

Commanders: Lt. General Viscount Rowland Hill v, General Maximilien Foy.

This is a small engagement. The French made a surprise attack on the town which the British had chosen for their winter quarters, but the British were on the alert and the French were obliged to beat a hasty retreat. Although this action did not provide Hill with an opportunity to show his considerable military skills, he did so on a number of other occasions in the Peninsular War and commanded the 2nd Corps at Waterloo (see 19 May, Almaraz; 28 October, Arroyo dos Molinos; 30 October, Puente Larga; 13 December, St. Pierre).

21 H.M.S. PHOEBE (36 GUNS) V. BELLEGARDE (14 GUNS) 1800, EASTERN ATLANTIC (FRENCH REVOLUTIONARY WARS)

Commanders: Captain R. Barlow v. ?

This was a small action, and so routine that it might almost be classed as a training exercise. The frigate came up with the French privateer out of St. Malo, home port for many privateers, and promptly took her into custody. *Bellegarde* had been at sea for 16 days and had taken two merchant ships, one of which was recovered.

For other examples of the contribution of British frigates, their commanders and crews in the long wars against the French, see 10 January, 19 February, 11 May, and 20 December.

24 H.M.S. NYMPHE (36 GUNS) WITH H.M.S. AMETHYST (36 GUNS) V. MODESTE 1800, FRANCE (FRENCH REVOLUTIONARY WARS)

Commanders: Captain P. Frazer v. ?

Modeste, a French East Indiaman, had sailed from Ile de France (Mauritius) nine weeks previously carrying a valuable cargo of cotton, coffee, tea, sugar, and indigo, and when in sight of home, to the great anguish and frustration of the officers and crew, she was seized by *Nymphe* and *Amethyst* and escorted to Plymouth to be sold. The disappointment of the French is understandable from the fact that *Modeste* was sold, as a prize, for £36,000; based on calculated changes in the consumer price index this would be the equivalent of more than £1,700,000 today.

24 MARTINIQUE 1809, WEST INDIES (NAPOLEONIC WAR)

Commanders: Vice-Adml Sir.Alexander Cochrane & Lt. Genl. Sir George Beckwith v. Adml. Louis Thomas Villaret-Joyeuse.

This was an amphibious operation in which for the third time in less than fifty years this island was taken from the French (see February 12 and March 16). On the two previous occasions, Martinique was restored to France at the subsequent peace treaty, and this time it happened again at the Congress of Vienna 1815 (see 9 June); it seems to have been ordained that Martinique should be French. A pity because if it had remained British, Martinique might have made a distinguished contribution to West Indian cricket.

25 FISHGUARD 1797, WALES (FRENCH REVOLUTIONARY WARS)
Commanders: Col. Lord Cawdor v. Genl. William Tate.
Forces: British: the local Yeomanry, Militia and Volunteers and a large number of the local population carrying pikes, pitchforks and scythes; French 1,400.

This is probably the most bizarre encounter in the whole history of British–French conflict. From the initial planning to the surrender, the French performance was poor; it was based on the hope, without convincing evidence, that revolutionary ideals would inspire popular rebellion. The commander was an Irish-American adventurer from South Carolina nearly 70 years of age, and the troops were little better than riff-raff from prisons and press gangs. After abandoning the original plan of sacking Bristol, the four French ships providing the transport sailed westwards harrying some small merchant ships along the way and raising the alarm as they did so. Reaching Carregwastad Point, near Fishguard, the troops were put ashore at a most unsuitable place for a landing, and the ships then sailed away on other business which for two of them was cut short about two weeks later (see 8 March H.M.S. San Fiorenzo v. Résistance). With no regular British troops in the vicinity, several days were spent in mustering the local militia, and while this was going on some of the local inhabitants, angered by the looting of the poorly-disciplined invaders, attacked pockets of them. The most famous of the locals was Jemima Nicholas, a cobbler nearly 50 years old, who sallied out armed with a pitchfork and single-handedly rounded up twelve of the invaders, then went off for more. As the militia were seen marching towards the French, a number of Welsh women wearing their national dress went along too, and the French mistook their red shawls and black hats for redcoats and capitulated. Embellishing the farcical plot, an unexpected outcome was a temporary, financial panic in Britain that led to a run on the banks and persuaded the government to give the Bank of England authority to issue £1 and £2 notes. The paper money was generally accepted and enabled the Bank's gold to be used for the payment of subsidies to Britain's foreign allies, namely, Austria, Russia, Prussia and Sweden. A further, local initiative was to produce a tapestry, modelled on the Bayeux tapestry, to mark this event, and this is now on display in the town.

27 ORTHEZ 1814, FRANCE (PENINSULAR WAR)

Commanders: Wellington v. Marshal Nicolas-Jean de Dieu Soult, Duke of Dalmatia.
Forces: British and Portuguese about 43,000, French 36,000.

At this stage in the war, the French had been driven out of Spain, and Wellington's army had pursued them into south west France. The immediate objective was to take Bayonne, and in order to do so, the French army had to be pushed eastwards. The first step was to occupy Orthez. The town was protected by a river, the Gava de Pau, the crossing of which and the capture of the town were achieved by tactical feints, something of a Wellington hallmark, and the French retreated to Toulouse. Bayonne was now isolated from the French field army, and the way was open for the British under Maj. Genl. Beresford (see 4 March H.M.S. Diadem) to occupy Bordeaux after an absence of nearly four hundred years. French casualties were 4,000 including 1,350 prisoners, and many of the new French recruits deserted; British casualties were little more than half this number.

28 KAVERIPAK 1752, INDIA (CARNATIC WARS)

Commanders: Captain Robert Clive v. Raja Sahib.
Forces: British, 380 Europeans, 1,420 sepoys & 6 guns; French, 400 Europeans, 4,000 sepoys & 9 guns.

Soundly beaten at Arcot and Arni (see 25 November and 3 December), Raja Sahib rallied his shattered forces and, urged on by the French, proceeded to lay waste the country to the west of Madras. Thomas Saunder, the Governor at Madras, despatched Clive to deal with this aggression. Approaching the enemy camp at dusk, Clive's force ran into an ambush and came under heavy fire from French artillery and infantry that was continued by both sides for two or three hours. Seeking a way to break out, Clive sent a company officer to reconnoitre and he reported that it would be possible to take the French in the rear. Immediately, Clive detached a party for this purpose, and it was able to get within 50 yards of the French before opening fire. The surprise was complete; the French took to their heels leaving the guns behind, and Raja Sahib's troops joined in the chaotic withdrawal.

This was a decisive victory with tangible benefits. First, British prestige was greatly enhanced at the expense of the French. Secondly, the army of Raja Sahib and the French Governor-General, the Marquis Dupleix was so devastated that it was disbanded. Thirdly, there were considerable territorial gains – always prized in the eighteenth century.

28 H.M.S. MONMOUTH (64 GUNS) & OTHERS V. FOUDROYANT (80 GUNS) & OTHERS 1758, SPAIN (SEVEN YEARS' WAR)

Commanders: Adml. Henry Osborn v. Rear-Adml. Duquesne de Menneville.

Osborn was cruising with the Mediterranean squadron outside Cartagena where Rear-Adml. de la Clue Sabran had taken refuge with his six ships bound for the West Indies from Toulon, when he found his way barred by the enemy. *Foudroyant* and two other ships were reinforcements from Toulon which were intercepted by the British squadron before they were able to make port. Outnumbered, the French ships scattered at the British approach, but *Orphée* (64 guns) was soon taken and another smaller French ship of the line was driven aground. Duquesne's flagship, *Foudroyant,* sailed off into the night hotly pursued by *Monmouth.* A better idea of the difference in fire-power of the antagonists can be obtained from a comparison of their respective broadsides – *Foudroyant* at 1,944lbs. (almost a ton) against *Monmouth's* 1,164 lbs. Notwithstanding this difference, *Foudroyant* struck her colours at 1.00 a.m. with 134 killed compared with 30 dead in *Monmouth. Monmouth's* captain, Arthur Gardiner, was killed in action whereupon the first lieutenant, Robert Carkett, took over until the end, and he was given command of the prize. Duquesne was taken prisoner to England, and the British caught up with de la Clue Sabran the following year in Lagos Bay, where he died of his wounds (see 17 August).

Duquesne came from a family of sailors and was at sea as a midshipman in his early teens, he was of Huguenot stock, and it was not until he received his certificate of (Roman) Catholicity that his career could advance. Meritorious service against the British, and African pirates brought him to favourable notice and appointment in 1752 as Governor-General of New France (Canada). In Canada, he quickly took firm action to improve the efficiency and discipline of the militia and the general administration. These efforts were not well received by the settlers, but were necessary in order to carry out the king's orders which were to secure the Ohio valley against the New England colonials. Duquesne's first expedition was a partial failure, and it prompted more local criticism. Undeterred, Duquesne organized another the next year in the course of which several victories were won against the New Englanders, and forts were built including Fort Duquesne which is now Pittsburgh (see 24 November, Fort Duquesne). Duquesne's aggressive policy when Britain and France were still at peace was a factor in Britain's decision to enter the Seven Years War against France in 1756 (but France was not alone in provocative activities – see 10 June, Newfoundland). On his return to France, Duquesne was able to convince the king that the criticisms levelled against him were not justified, and he resumed his naval career. Now it was brought to an end, but the king, who seems to have liked him well, granted him a generous pension, and Duquesne died a rich man with a house in Paris and another in Antony.

Captain Arthur Gardiner's death restored his honour. He had been Byng's flag captain when the French captured Minorca (see 25 March H.M.S. Sheerness et al.; & 17 August, Lagos Bay), a defeat that caused Byng to be shot, and one in which other senior officers, to their dishonour, were generally thought to have had responsibility. Gardiner's death was taken to have removed any stain on his character.

28 THREE FRIGATES V. THREE FRENCH FRIGATES 1760, ISLE OF MAN (SEVEN YEARS' WAR)

This was an unusual action in that the French ships were privateers from Dunkirk which had sailed as a squadron commanded by a notable privateer, François Thurot. The expedition was financed as a joint stock company, and it was originally intended to coincide with the French invasion of Ireland. However, the devastating defeat at Quiberon Bay (see 20-22 November) had made such an invasion impossible, and for the remainder of the war, French naval activities were limited to privateering. Initially, Thurot cruised in Norwegian waters, but then appeared off the Irish coast and occupied Carrickfergus at the mouth of Belfast Lough. Further action was precluded because Thurot and the senior officer of the troops on board were no longer on speaking terms. After a few days in port, the ships were at sea again and were intercepted by three Britsh frigates, in the fighting that ensued Thurot was killed and his ships were captured.

28 H.M.S. SYBILLE (44 GUNS) V. LA FORTE (50 GUNS) 1799, BANGLADESH (FRENCH REVOLUTIONARY WARS)

Commanders: Captain E. Cooke v. ?

In less than two hours, *Sybille* totally dismasted *La Forte* and took her as a prize, but Cooke died of his wounds. *Sybille* herself had been taken as a prize (see 17 June H.M.S. Romney v. Sybille) five years previously, and this was one of the actions in which she was engaged in the East Indies.

MARCH

4 H.M.S. DIADEM (64 GUNS) V. LA VOLONTAIRE (48 GUNS) 1806, SOUTH AFRICA (NAPOLEONIC WAR)

Commanders: Cdre. Sir Home Popham v. ?

Popham had escorted the invading force to Cape Town (see 8 January Blueberg), and his ships were at anchor in Table Bay when a French warship, *La Volontaire*, approached from the south with two others. *Diadem* was under Dutch colours, but once the French were within hailing distance the British colours were run up and Popham called on *La Volontaire* to surrender. The order was promptly obeyed without a shot being fired. *Volontaire* had on board 271 prisoners, mostly from the Queen's and 54th. (West Norfolk) Regiments, who had been taken in the Bay of Biscay. Between 4 October 1805 and 30 March 1806, Popham's squadron captured, retook or destroyed 11 enemy ships.

Popham has been described as energetic, ambitious, lacking in judgment but with a talent for amphibious operations, and he now proceeded to demonstrate the validity of this opinion. Without any orders or authority to do so, he persuaded the commander of the army he had escorted to the Cape, Major- General Baird, to join him in an attack on the Spanish colonies in South America (Spain was an ally of France at this point in the war). The expedition set off in April arriving in the River Plate in June, and the troops were landed. Surprise, not to say astonishment and some luck, enabled the British to take the capital, Buenos Aires, on 28 June. The territory of which Buenos Aires was the capital encompassed the whole of modern Argentina, Uruguay, Paraguay and Bolivia, and the army of barely 1,000 men was totally inadequate to consolidate the initial success. The colonists re-captured the city, the relief force failed, and Popham was court martialled and severely censured for leaving his station in South Africa. On the other hand, the City of London, wishing to reward a senior officer who was conscious of the importance of seizing trade from an enemy, presented Popham with a sword of honour. Baird's second-in-command, Brigadier General Beresford, commanded the South American troops and a few years later, he and Popham both served with considerable credit in the Peninsular War.

5 (EST.) FRESNAY-LE-VICOMTE 1420, FRANCE (HUNDRED YEARS' WAR)

Commanders: Earl of Huntingdon v. Marshal of France Rieux.

The Earl of Salisbury, Henry V's lieutenant in Lower Normandy, was conducting a successful campaign in Maine in the course of which, after capturing Ballon, Beaumont-le-Vicomte, and Montfort-le-Retrou, he was besieging Fresnay when he was told that a French army was marching to relieve the town. Salisbury's confidence in the capability of his troops convinced him that he could continue the siege without that part of his army which he detached to meet the French in open battle. The Earl of Huntingdon was placed in command of the detachment that confronted the enemy a few miles south of Fresnay. The French army included a number of mercenaries, a large proportion of whom were Scots, and the Scots were so confident that they had with them their treasury containing the money for the payment of the troops for the campaign; the result showed this confidence to be seriously misplaced. Details of the battle are lacking, but it is reasonably clear that the English were heavily outnumbered and that they obtained an overwhelming victory. There is information about the French casualties – 3,000 were killed, and the prisoners included Rieux, 6 Scottish knights, 500 men-at-arms, the standard of Sir William Douglas, the Scottish commander, the Scots' treasury and all of the baggage. After this battle, Fresnay quickly surrendered and Salisbury continued his advance.

5 BAROSSA 1811, SPAIN (PENINSULAR WAR)

Commanders: Lt. Genl. Graham v. Marshal Claude Victor.
Forces: British 5,200; French 7,000.

The French had occupied a large part of southern Spain and were now besieging Cadiz, an important port for supplies. Early in January, part of the besieging force was sent off to Badajoz that was still held by the Spanish and Portuguese, and their departure was seen as an opportunity to raid and destroy the French siege works. The overall command was given to the supine and incompetent General La Peňa with Graham commanding the British contingent, including some Portuguese, and Barossa was fought exclusively by these troops. In order to attack the French position from the rear, troops were landed a few miles south of Cadiz, but the line of march ordered by La Peňa left the flank exposed, and this brought about the battle of Barossa. The French, moving against La Peňa's army, occupied Barossa Hill on the flank, and Graham was obliged to turn his force to drive them off it. The British regiments attacked up the hill, and in the process they beat off two French, downhill, counter attacks; finally, the French were driven off the ridge at the cost of heavy casualties. Although the British were out-numbered three to two, the French were beaten again when they made a flank attack by four columns that were decimated by the British infantry firing at fifty yards from two lines. The action was finished by a charge of the King's German Legion. British casualties were 1,238; French 2,062, including 2 generals, 400 prisoners and 6 guns.

At Barossa, Sergeant Patrick Masterson of the 87th.Regiment captured from Sous-Lieutenant Edmé Gillemin of the 8th.. of the Line the first French eagle to be taken in battle, an achievement that brought him a commission and kindled great popular enthusiasm in Britain; later, another French regiment at Barossa, the 45th. of the Line, suffered a similar humiliation, it lost its eagle to the Royal Scots Greys at Waterloo. The 87th. Regiment was known in the Peninsular War for its battle cry 'Faugh-a-Ballagh' (Gaelic: "Clear the Way"), now the motto of the Royal Irish Fusiliers, who still celebrate the anniversary of this victory at which the principal toast is 'Barossa'.

After the battle, the Spanish Cortes (Parliament) wished to award Lt.Genl. Graham the rank of Grandee of the First Class, but he was so incensed by the performance of La Peňa and the failure of the Spanish to provide any support that he declined the honour. For more on this unusual character - see 18 June, Osma.

6 ST. JAMES-DE-BEUVRON 1426, (A.K.A. ROUT OF ST. JAMES), FRANCE (HUNDRED YEARS' WAR)

Commanders: Sir Thomas Rempston v. Arthur de Richemont, Constable of France.

Forces: English 600 : French 16,000.

This is one of the more extraordinary engagements in this war, and it should be noted that the numbers engaged, and the description of the battle are all taken from French chronicles. The regent of France, the Duke of Bedford, was still in England (see 10 August, Le Mans), and relatively minor operations were being conducted in Brittany. In an age when alliances were ephemeral, to say the least, the Duke of Brittany, Jean V, stands out as a turncoat. Until a few months before, he had been an ally of England, favouring as he did the Burgundian faction in the French disputes, but now on the persuasion of his brother, Arthur de Richemont, he abruptly changed sides. Rempston had established his base in St. James-de-Beuvron; Arthur, recently appointed as Constable of France, no doubt as a reward for signing on with the Dauphin, mustered a considerable force and marched on Brittany to support his brother against the aggrieved English. He decided to lay siege to St. James and began with a bombardment from the artillery with which he was well supplied. Two breaches were made in the walls, and a vigorous assault was made that lasted all day. The defenders then took a very bold and courageous step. Leaving a small number to hold the breaches, the remainder went through a sally port and made their way unseen to the rear of the French. Once in position, they let out their battle cry "Salisbury! St. George!" and threw themselves on the enemy. At the same time, those who had been left to hold the breaches advanced from the other side. Notwithstanding their huge superiority in numbers, the French disintegrated – many were chased into a nearby lake and drowned, the others fled back to their camp where, in panic during the night, they burned their tents, abandoned their artillery and stores and made their way back as best they could from whence they came. One account puts the English booty at 14 'great guns', 300 pipes of wine, 200 pipes of biscuit and flour, 200 frailes (rush baskets) of figs and raisins, and 500 barrels of herrings (truly a Godsend at the beginning of Lent for these religious men). The Rout of St. James makes one French commentator's opinion that: "two hundred Englishmen would put to flight eight hundred or a thousand Frenchmen" a serious understatement.

Richemont's career is interesting in that it illustrates how close the leaders of England and France sometimes were at this period. He was a younger son of John IV, Duke of Brittany, whose widow, Joan of Navarre, had married Henry IV after the death of his wife, and thus he was a step-brother of Henry V, the Duke of Clarence, the Duke of Bedford, and the Duke of Gloucester all of whom were very active in the Hundred Years' War. Richemont's elder brother, John V, Duke of Brittany, conferred on him the title of Earl of Richmond that became Comte de Richemont in French. In the French dynastic struggle between the Orleanists, a.k.a. Armagnacs, and the Burgundians, Richemont at first sided with the former and fought against the English at Agincourt (see 25 October). He was wounded in that battle and was lucky to escape with his life, but he was captured and spent the next five years as a prisoner in England. When he was released on parole, his half-brother Henry V was in the ascendant in France, and Richemont not only changed sides, he persuaded his brother the Duke of Brittany to do the same, for which service Henry granted Richemont the county of Ivry. In 1423, Richemont married the widowed sister of the Duke of Burgundy and now, at the age of thirty, was the brother-in-law of the Duke of Burgundy as well as the brother-in-law and step-brother of the Duke of Bedford, the regent of France after the death of Henry. His prospects were dazzling, but then, apparently because of some quarrel with Bedford, he changed sides again and joined the French claimant, Charles VII, who appointed him Constable of France. As noted above, he persuaded his brother to follow him in changing sides again and went on to become something of a French hero in the final stages of the war.

8 H.M.S SAN FIORENZO (36 GUNS) V. RÉSISTANCE (40 GUNS) 1797, FRANCE (FRENCH REVOLUTIONARY WARS).

Commanders: Captain Sir Harry Neale v. Captain J-B Laroque.

Fought off Brest, *San Fiorenzo* was in company with another frigate, *Nymphe* (36 guns) and *Résistance* was with a corvette, *Constance* (22 guns). *Résistance* was a new frigate which had been one of the small squadron taking troops to Fishguard (see 25 February), and *Constance* had also been in company, now they were in sight of home.The British attack first concentrated on the *Résistance* which was soon taken as a prize and later re-commisssioned in the Royal Navy with the appropriate name of *Fisgard*; *Constance* capitulated shortly afterwards. The British suffered neither damage nor casualties.

8 ABUKIR 1801, EGYPT (FRENCH REVOLUTIONARY WARS)

Commanders: Maj.Genl. Sir Ralph Abercromby v. Genl. Friant.

Following Nelson's victory at the Nile (see 1 August), and the failure at Acre (see see 18 May), Napoleon had returned to France leaving behind a stranded army. The decision was made in London to make an alliance with Turkey and to clear the French out of Egypt. The Turks provided little or no support, and the forthright Abercromby decided to proceed independently. His troops landed in Abukir Bay, the scene of Nelson's triumph, and although the landing was hotly contested, the French were forced to fall back on Alexandria. The British commander had a long military career particularly distinguished for improving conditions of service, discipline and training of officers and men. This action was a brilliant example of the value of his training exercises; 14,000 infantry, 1,000 cavalry and 600 artillery were landed in a single day a feat unparallelled at that time, and which might well have depressed the enemy. Abercromby's career began during the Seven Years' War; to the detriment of his career he was an outspoken critic of the War of American Independence, but excellent service in the French Revolutionary Wars, in the West Indies and in Flanders embellished his reputation, particularly in the eyes of the public. He is commemorated by a monument in St. Paul's Cathedral. For the conclusion of this campaign, see 13 March, Mandora and 21 March, Alexandria .

10 MARBELLA 1705, SPAIN (WAR OF THE SPANISH SUCCESSION).

Commanders: Adml.Sir John Leake v. Adml. de Pointis.

In the War of the Spanish Succession, the outstanding successes of the Duke of Marlborough overshadow the naval operations. In the Atlantic, the principal purpose was to seize the Spanish convoys from South America that were escorted by the French, and in the Mediterranean the priority was to establish a base which could service a fleet in those waters. Gibraltar had been captured from the Spanish in July 1704, but as yet it had no operational value, the anchorage was unprotected, there was little trade, and no harbour works except for a small mole (defensive breakwater). The British occupation was precarious, but Gibraltar was seen to have great strategic potential and the garrison was being reinforced by supplies convoyed from Lisbon. In the course of escorting a large convoy to Gibraltar, Leake's squadron encountered five French ships of the line blockading it, and in the action that followed all of the French ships were destroyed or captured, but for the French, the loss of all the crews was more serious than the loss of the ships. Gibraltar was now secure and its development as a major naval base began.

Sir John Leake had an unusual and distinguished career. He was the son of a non-commissioned gunner who had successfully assumed command of his ship when all of the officers had been killed in action. Following in his father's footsteps, Leake went to sea as a boy and served in the merchant marine as well as in the navy. In an early demonstration of his fighting spirit, in 1689, he sailed his ship of only medium size at and through the boom at Londonderry during the siege (see 1 August) and cleared the way for two victualling ships to relieve the besieged. This action was an important contribution to the victory at the Boyne (see 1 July) in the following year. First rate performances at Barfleur & La Hougue (see 19 May), in the capture of Gibraltar, 1704, as well as at Marbella recommended his appointment in 1708 as commander-in-chief in the Mediterranean. Shortly afterwards, he was victorious at Sardinia and Port Mahon (see 19 September), and finally he went ashore and became one of the naval lords of the Admiralty.

11 VALMONT 1416, FRANCE (HUNDRED YEARS' WAR)

Commanders: Earl of Dorset v. Bernard, Comte d'Armagnac, Constable of France.

Forces: English 1,000 v. French 4,000.

The English garrison at Harfleur had been carrying out a series of raids into the surrounding countryside, and in returning from one of them, Dorset was surprised near Valmont by a much larger French contingent. The first attack by cavalry succeeded in breaking through the English line which, on account of sparse numbers, was stretched across too wide a front. Having broken through, the French rode on to loot the baggage in the rear instead of rolling up the line, and this mistake gave Dorset, in spite of his serious wounds, the chance to rally his men and re-group them in a strong defensive position behind a tall hedge and ditch. The French commander decided to resume the battle the next day and led his men to settle down for the night in Valmont. During the night, the English stole away and marched on towards Harfleur, at dawn they took cover in a wood and there remained undiscovered for the whole of the day; early the next morning they resumed their march this time along the beach. They had not gone far when a strong French force was seen on the top of the cliffs in a perfect position to attack their flank. Impetuously, the French dismounted and charged down the rough tracks in front of them. Naturally, they reached the bottom not as a group but in handfuls, and thereby lost all the advantage of their superiority in numbers. The English had formed a line, and wielding their axes mercilessly, they routed their opponents. The victors do not seem to have been aware that they had not been opposed by the whole of the French army but only by part of it sent out to find out where they had gone, and they were engaged in what was presumably the profitable business of stripping the corpses and throwing the bodies into the sea when the remainder of the French were seen at the top of the cliff. The final phase of the action is astonishing. Losing no time after sighting the French, the English seized their arms, charged up the cliff and routed the troops at the top. Those running away made for Rouen but unfortunately this road passed in view of Harfleur from the towers of which the fighting had been watched by the remainder of the garrison. Immediately, they took to horse and went in pursuit of the demoralized fugitives. Many prisoners were taken, and there was then the very unusual spectacle of two victorious groups entering the town at the same time loaded with loot and prisoners.

13 GENOA 1795, ITALY (FRENCH REVOLUTIONARY WARS).
Commanders: Vice-Adml. William Hotham v. Adml. Pierre Martin.
Forces: British 13 ships-of-the-line and 6 frigates; French 15 ships-of–the-line and 6 frigates.

Fought off Genoa. The French fleet had sailed from Toulon escorting troops for the invasion of Corsica and was sighted on 13 March. Hotham gave the order for a 'general chase' meaning that each ship should advance on the enemy under press of sail and engage the first ship encountered as opposed to forming a line of battle and engaging the opposite number in the enemy's line. The French turned about to return to Toulon. Nelson, captain of *Agamemnon* a small ship of the line with 64 guns, made for *Ça Ira* (92 guns) that had collided with the ship ahead and damaged its rigging. Nelson succeeded in bringing *Agamemnon* under the stern of *Ça Ira* and raking her, that is loosing broadsides through the stern windows, for two hours during which time *Ça Ira* was not able to bring a single gun to bear against her opponent. The French ship was now a wreck and *Sans Culotte*, a huge ship with 120 guns, together with another ship of the line, *Censeur*, came up to take *Ça Ira* in tow. Hotham, whose ships were under-manned, feared that some of the ships in the van might be cut off and signalled Nelson to disengage which he did. The next morning *Ça Ira* was sighted in tow by *Censeur*, and was cut off from the main fleet; a fierce fight ensued in which both French ships were dismasted and taken as prizes. The carnage aboard the French ships was appalling, about 400 of *Ça Ira's* crew were killed or wounded out of a complement of 1,300, and about 350 in *Censeur*. In addition to the ships and prisoners, the British were able to replenish ammunition and powder from the magazines of the captured ships.The invasion of Corsica, taken by the British the year previously (see 1 August, Calvi), was abandoned.

13 H.M.S. LIVELY (32 GUNS) V. TOURTERELLE 1795, FRANCE (FRENCH REVOLUTIONARY WARS).

Commanders: Lt. G. Burlton v. Captain G. Montalan.

Fought off Cape Ushant, *Lively*, a frigate, engaged *Tourterelle* ('Turtle-dove') and two other ships. After a spirited action in which *Tourterelle* was badly damaged and dismasted, she was taken as a prize together with the other two French ships, but in spite of her defeat, *Tourterelle* belied her name and damaged *Lively* quite severely with red-hot shot. Lt. Burlton must have been delighted with his victory as he was standing in for the regular commander of *Lively,* Captain Lord Garlies, who was ill on shore, and the prize money was the larger because of that.

13 MANDORA 1801, EGYPT (FRENCH REVOLUTIONARY WARS)

Commanders: Maj. Genl. Sir Ralph Abercromby v. ?

This battle was the second act after Abukir on March 8. The British expeditionary force on its march on Alexandria was confronted by the larger French army. The initial French attack was driven back, they were then routed, and the British continued their advance. For the final thrilling instalment of this campaign, see March 21, Alexandria.

13 H.M.S. LONDON (98 GUNS) & H.M.S. AMAZON (38 GUNS) V. MARENGO (80 GUNS) & LA BELLE POULE (40 GUNS) 1806, CANARY ISLANDS (NAPOLEONIC WAR)

Commanders: Captain Sir Harry Neale v. Rear Adml. Charles Alexandre Durand, Comte de Linois.

The two British ships were part of the Channel Fleet under the command of Vice-Adml. Sir John Borlase Warren and were standing to windward of the main force when they sighted the French ships which were returning from three years in the East Indies. A running fight took place, and after several hours, with the British fleet approaching, the two French ships surrendered having sustained in total 65 killed and 80 wounded, including Linois whose wounds were serious. Following strict protocol, Adml. Linois' sword was surrendered to Vice-Adml. Warren in *Foudroyant* and not to the captain of *London*. British casualties were much smaller – 13 killed and 25 wounded. In recognition, the first lieutenant of *London* was promoted to commander, but the crews had to wait until medals were issued in 1849. The first lieutenant of *Amazon* was killed in the action, and his successor, the next in seniority, was given command of the prize and ordered to take her to port. Ordinarily, this would have been followed by promotion to commander, but this did not occur because Captain Parker of *Amazon*, nephew of Lord St. Vincent, lost his influence when his uncle left command of the Channel Fleet. The promotion was stymied for six years and shows that merit was not always sufficient to secure promotion in the navy.

Rear Adml. Linois had a long and creditable career even though he was mostly on the losing side. He entered the navy at 15, and from the start he showed the courage and determination that brought him rapid promotion. He lost his left eye at Ile de Groix (see 23 June) and was taken prisoner for a second time but secured early release. He was a senior officer at the Nile (see 1 August), and then came to notice in command (unsuccessfully) at Algeciras Bay (see 13 July). In the short, uneasy peace following the Treaty of Amiens, Linois was sent to the East Indies as commander of a small squadron. The presence of a larger British squadron prevented him from taking Pondicherry, but he withdrew to the Ile de France (Mauritius) from which he conducted a successful campaign against British merchant shipping as far afield as the China Sea. There followed an egregious error – he mistook a convoy of 20 East India merchant men for a fleet of warships and allowed the convoy to escape. Accusing Linois of making the French flag the laughing stock of Europe, Napoleon, who ruthlessly castigated mistakes of his commanders, caused the scathing dispatches of his minister of marine to be published in the *Moniteur*. He then showed his displeasure in a more practical way by ignoring opportunities to release Linois through prisoner exchanges. Linois was left a prisoner in England until the restoration of Louis XVIII eight years later (curiously, in 1810, while in captivity, he was created a count of the Empire). The king appointed him governor of Guadeloupe in April 1815, but he supported Napoleon during the return of the Hundred Days, and in August he was obliged to surrender the island in the face of a British assault. Linois was then tried by a military court and acquitted. At this point, he retired to Versailles where he lived until his death at 95 with the rank of honorary vice admiral conferred in 1825.

13 CONDEIXA 1811, PORTUGAL (PENINSULAR WAR)

Commanders: Wellington v. Marshal Michel Ney.

Wellington was now on the offensive, intent on pushing the French out of Portugal, and this action was one of a series between the vanguard of Wellington's army and the rearguard of the French. Wellington displayed skilful, tactical manœuvring and was able to dictate the line of withdrawal, and although Ney's reputation was built on offense, 'the bravest of the brave', he was also capable in managing a retreat. The French were left with no alternative but to retreat to the frontier.

13 H.M.S. AMPHION (32 GUNS) & OTHERS V. LA FAVORITE (44 GUNS) & OTHERS 1811, LISSA (NOW VIS) CROATIA (NAPOLEONIC WAR).

Commanders: Captain William Hoste v. Rear Adml.Edouard Dubourdieu

Forces: British 4 frigates (152 guns and 880 men); French 6 frigates and 4 smaller vessels (200 guns and 2,500 men).

The Adriatic was the scene of considerable naval activity during the Napoleonic War, partly in support of military operations in Italy and the Balkans, and partly because of efforts made by both sides to defeat the blockade system. Napoleon's Continental System was intended to cripple Britain's trade, thereby reducing its financial resources, by prohibiting neutrals and French allies from trading with Britain; Britain imposed a counter-blockade. Considerable hardship was inflicted on both sides, but Britain's naval supremacy gave it much greater success with counter-vailing measures, notably supervised smuggling. For this purpose, commercial depots were established at Gibraltar, Heligoland, Malta, Lissa and elsewhere at which clandestine trade flourished. The French squadron with Venetian support had been ordered by Napoleon himself to capture the British base at Lissa and to hold it. To this end, 500 troops had been embarked and 6 heavy guns. Their marked superiority in numbers made them confident of success leading the Rear Admiral to tell his officers as they approached the British ships: "this is the happiest day of our lives". Dubourdieu decided to copy Nelson's tactics at Trafalgar by attacking in two divisions, and then overwhelming the enemy with boarding parties. Hoste proved to be a much better tactician.

He was Nelson's favourite protégé, and he began with a signal to his ships that echoed Nelson's at Trafalgar, "Remember Nelson" is all it said, and it evoked a strong, inspirational response. Going into battle, the British ships were so closed up in line ahead that there was no room through which the two French divisions could sail. Hoste also changed the usual British tactic of firing into the hull of the target to aiming instead at the masts and rigging. Finding his ship difficult to manœuvre, Dubourdieu now decided he would lead a boarding party himself onto Hoste's ship, and with sword in hand, he stood at the head of his men on the fo'c's'le. Hoste, however, had another surprise in the form of a howitzer loaded with hundreds of musket balls, and as the flag ship, *La Favorite*, drew near the howitzer fired and annihilated the boarding party including Dubourdieu; the ship drifted out of control onto the rocks of Lissa and was set on fire by the crew eventually exploding. The two other frigates in *La Favorite's* division were soon so severely damaged by double-shotted broadsides that they surrendered. The final count was 1 French frigate destroyed, 2 captured and 3 escaped. Morale in the British ships was so boosted that in celebration several ballads were composed by crew members. Literary shortcomings are compensated by authentic experience – the authors were actually present, here are some excerpts:

"Then now, my boys, brave Hoste did say,
We conquer, or, like Nelson die!"
Remember Nelson was the word…
At that we mann'd the rigging and gave three hearty cheers,
"To sink or die!" was each man's cry, or bang the proud Monseers…
"in Spain let Mars decide the day,
Hoste and his squadron shall rule the sea!"

Although never in overall command, Hoste had a distinguished career in the Adriatic; he was created a baronet in 1814, and he married Lady Harriet Walpole with whom he had three sons and a daughter. He conducted sea trials with steam ships and later commanded the royal yacht, but his health was always poor after his strenuous service in the Adriatic, and he died from tuberculosis at the age of 48. An extraordinary legacy of the British occupation of Lissa is that the local population of Vis, having learned about Hoste and his men playing cricket there while it was a British base, formed the William Hoste Cricket Club in

2003. This came to the notice of Saumur (France) Cricket Club and they arranged to visit Vis and play a match against W.H.C.C. The contest aroused great interest and featured on the national TV as the lead story in the evening news programme. The British Embassy in Zagreb helped in various ways including the donation, courtesy (unwitting) of the British taxpayer, of a box of cricket balls. Thus, the spectacle of a French team playing the quintessential English game against a local team named after the principal opponent of the French in the Adriatic nearly two hundred years later and at the British base of operations.

With six defeats on this day, March 13 is clearly a date that constitutes a French 'ides of March' in their battles with the British; it would have been better had they stayed in bed.

14 CASAL NOVO 1811, PORTUGAL (PENINSULAR WAR).

Commanders: Wellington v. Marshal Michel Ney.

This engagement bears a close resemblance to Condeixa March 13. Once again, the vanguard of Wellington's advancing army met the rearguard of the French commanded by Marshal Ney, and success came to Wellington more through tactical manœuvre than by heavy fighting. Generally, casualties were light except for the Light Division which on this occasion was under the temporary command of Sir William Erskine who was unnecessarily reckless in his orders. This was particularly deplorable because the Light Division could fairly be regarded as the crack corps in Wellington's army having been brought to this standard of efficiency by Sir John Moore (the hero of Corunna, see 16 January) and Robert Craufurd (see 19 January, Ciudad Rodrigo). Under the command of Craufurd, the Light Division had made a devastating counter-attack against Ney's troops at Bussaco (27 September) in which their casualties were 177 against 1,200 French. Ney might have thought that on this day the balance was to some degree restored.

15 FOZ DO AROUCE 1811, PORTUGAL (PENINSULAR WAR)

Commanders: Wellington v. Marshal Michel Ney.

This battle followed Casal Novo on March 14 as the French continued their retreat towards Spain. Ney is often referred to as "the bravest of the brave" and was an impulsive, but brilliant, commander in the field who often led his troops in action notably at Waterloo where he had five horses killed under him. As is often the case with men of his temperament, Ney sometimes committed serious errors of judgment, and this battle is an example. In fighting a rearguard action, Ney was apparently disobeying the orders of his superior, Marshal Massena, and he took up a position in which his troops' line of withdrawal across the river behind them was by a single, damaged bridge. The rifle companies of the Light Division were able to get behind the French in the vicinity of this bridge, and this led to panic in one of the French infantry regiments. The French colonel in command was captured and also the regimental eagle, but Ney was able to restore a semblance of order by leading a charge in person. The French withdrew, but Wellington did not continue his close pursuit because he had out-run his supply train.

16 MARTINIQUE 1794, WEST INDIES (FRENCH REVOLUTIONARY WARS)

Commanders: Vice Adml. Sir John Jervis & Lt. Genl. Sir Charles Grey v. ?

A combined operation in which the army was assisted by a naval contingent that made a significant contribution by hauling their cannon overland. The landings began on February 5, and virtually the whole island was occupied by March 16. A French frigate was also captured and commissioned in the Royal Navy. British casualties were small, but the French sustained heavy losses. Jervis and Grey were excellent choices for command. They were friends, familiar with the West Indies, and with amphibious operations. They acted with energy and success (see 4 April, St. Lucia), but they also had a serious weakeness. Their looting and extortions gravely alienated a population royalist in sympathy who might otherwise have been disposed to support the British against the French revolutionaries, and this proved to be a major strategic error. By contrast, Wellington, when he advanced into France, was at pains to suppress looting in order to discourage guerrilla warfare (see 10 November Nivelle), and in his later campaigns Henry V showed similar strategic sense as did Marlborough (see 23 May Ramillies). The island was returned to the French at the Treaty of Amiens 1802.

17 H.M.S. DIAMOND (38 GUNS) V. COASTAL CONVOY OF 10 SHIPS 1796, N.W. FRANCE (FRENCH REVOLUTIONARY WARS)

Commanders: Captain Sir Sidney Smith v. ?

This engagement is typical of many along the Channel coastline in the Anglo-French wars. Under attack from some armed vessels of the Prince of Bouillon (in command at Jersey), the convoy of ten ships had taken refuge in Erquy, and Sir Sidney decided to attack them. A large gun at the harbour entrance was quickly silenced, but a battery of three 24-pounders continued to fire, and it was decided to attack the battery with a detachment of marines and seamen. These men were put ashore, and when they saw that their way was blocked by troops, they proceeded to climb a precipice and take the guns. In spite of heavy small arms fire from the shore, all the ships of the convoy were burned by boat parties. For more about Sir Sidney see 18 May Cape Carmel.

Erquy's biggest excitement today is the Annual Scallop Festival, the town has proclaimed itself the capital of the scallop – Coquille Saint Jacques.

18 H.M.S. TELEGRAPH (16 GUNS) V. L'HIRONDELLE (16 GUNS) 1799, FRANCE (FRENCH REVOLUTIONARY WARS).

Commanders: Lt. J.A.Worth v. ?

Fought off the Ile-de-Bas, although this can only rank as a lightweight encounter, it is an interesting example of rather makeshift practices in the conduct of war at this time. *Telegraph* was a brig that had been hired by the Admiralty for naval service; *L'Hirondelle* (Swallow) was also a brig, but she was a privateer that is to say a privately owned vessel commissioned by the French government to fight the British. The owner received no payment for his ship and his services but was entitled to keep whatever he could capture, and the crew joined in the proceeds. The French commissioned thousands of privateers during the Revolutionary and Napoleonic Wars. In this instance, the action lasted three and a half-hours during which time both sides made unsuccessful attempts to board the adversary. Finally, badly damaged, *L'Hirondelle* surrendered. As a privateer the owner could expect no compensation, whereas the British owner as a lessor could presumably expect his ship to be returned at the end of the lease with any damage made good.

Incidentally, those famous British sea captains Sir John Hawkins and Sir Francis Drake operated mainly as privateers.

21 EAST SCOTLAND 1708, (WAR OF THE SPANISH SUCCESSION)

Commanders: Adml. Sir George Byng v. Rear Adml. Claude, Comte de Forbin-Gordanne

Forces: British 18 warships v. French 5 warships & 15 transports (6,000 troops) & 15 privateers.

Disillusion in Scotland with the recently enacted Act of Union suggested to the French that a descent on Scotland would relieve Marlborough's pressure in Flanders. An invading force was assembled in Dunkirk under the command of the Comte de Gacé (soon to be created Marshal Matignon), and de Forbin commanded the ships. Lengthy delays in the departure were caused by the weather and the misfortune of the 20-year old Chevalier de St. George, son of the deposed James II, in contracting measles; the Chevalier, the 'Old Pretender', was to provide the necessary rallying point for the dissidents. Eventually, the expedition departed on 17 March, but a gale caused it to shelter in Nieuport, and it did not arrive in the Firth of Forth until 21 March with Byng's squadron close behind. Contacts on the shore were discouraging, and de Forbin chose not to attempt a landing, instead he sailed north towards Inverness, but seeing scant chance of success he returned to France. The French ships were encrusted with fewer barnacles than the British and were able to sail faster, but in the chase one of the French ships, the *Salisbury* that had been captured from the British was taken as a prize by a ship of the same name that had been built to replace her. De Forbin has been much criticized for his decisions because when the British became aware of the plan, they recalled ten regiments of experienced infantry from Marlborough's army, and this was the French purpose. An unexpected benefit to the French was the shock to public confidence in Britain leading to a run on the bank that caused Godolphin to transfer all of the bullion to the Tower and to suspend payments; however, this near-hysteria soon subsided. This is not the only time that fear of a French invasion led to a run on the bank (see 25 February Fishguard). Having spent a month at sea, the Britsh regiments returned to Flanders.

This action was small stuff in the respective careers of the two commanders. Byng began his naval service under Charles II and James II, but then in 1688 William of Orange made him his agent in trying to persuade naval captains to support his claim to the throne against James II. After William's enthronement, Byng's promotion was rapid suggesting that his agency had met with royal approval. But Byng was no mere courtier, in 1704 he was prominent in the British fleet that captured Gibraltar from Spain, and in the subsequent battle against the relieving fleet (see 13 August, Velez Malaga). He thwarted the Jacobites again in 1715 by intercepting French supplies to the Old Pretender who for five months controlled a large part of Scotland. A great victory over the Spanish in 1718 raised him to the peerage, and in the final six years of his life he served as First Lord of the Admiralty. De Forbin had an unusually colourful career which began when he ran away to sea and joined the navy. Conspicuous bravery brought rapid promotion, and at 30 years of age, he was a member of a French embassy to Siam. He remained in Siam after the embassy returned home having been appointed a grand admiral of the fleet, general of the armies and governor of Bangkok. These distinguished appointments did not content him for long, and after two years he returned to France where he became a privateer with Jean Bart, a great French naval hero. Captured by the British, he was briefly a prisoner at Plymouth but escaped and saw further service against Spain. However, this unsuccessful sortie to Scotland ended his active career at 42, and he retired to the country to write his memoirs.

21 H.M.S. PETERELL (16 GUNS) V. LA LIGURIENNE(16 GUNS), CERF (14 GUNS), JOLLIET (6GUNS) 1800, FRANCE (FRENCH REVOLUTIONARY WARS)

Commanders: Captain F.W. Austen v. Lt. F-A.Pelabend.

A coastal action fought off Cape Couronne between Sète and Marseille. The French ships were escorting a convoy along the coast to Marseille when *Peterell* attacked, and hard fighting was often carried on within 200 yards of the shore. *Cerf* and *Jolliet* were soon driven ashore, and after a running fight *Ligurienne* was taken within point blank range of two shore batteries. With the escorts out of the way, *Peterell* captured two merchant ships both loaded with wheat. *Ligurienne* was only two years old, and a curious feature of her construction was the fastening of planks by screw bolts so that she could be taken apart and re-assembled.

Notwithstanding this sterling performance, Austen is better known today as one of Jane Austen's two brothers who served in the Royal Navy. He advanced through the service, and twelve years later he was in the Baltic as Flag Captain of Rear-Admiral Sir Thomas Williams (see 7 January H.M.S. Doris et al., and 8 June H.M.S. Santa Margarita et al.), with his wife and children on board, a scene of domestic togetherness in an improbable setting that his sister might have embellished for our pleasure.

21 ALEXANDRIA 1801, EGYPT (FRENCH REVOLUTIONARY WARS) 'BACK BADGE DAY.'

Commanders: Maj.Genl. Sir Ralph Abercromby v. Genl. Baron de Menou

Forces: British 14,000, French 10,000.

The French were trying to turn back the British invasion of Egypt that had begun on March 8 at Abukir, and there had been another battle at Mandora on the 13th; this was the decisive meeting. The Gloucestershire Regiment – then the 28th. Foot – fought with particular distinction on the right of the line. The French attacked at dawn and the 28th.became isolated. When the French cavalry were observed preparing to attack in the rear, the order was immediately given "Rear rank 28th., Right about face.", and showing exemplary discipline, they waited until the French were almost on them before delivering one devastating volley which caused such heavy casualties that their opponents were obliged to withdraw. For gallantry in fighting back-to-back, the regiment was given the honour of wearing the cap badge on the back as well as the front of the cap, and the regiment continues to celebrate 'Back Badge Day' on 21 March. In total, the French suffered 3,000 casualties, including three dead generals, against British losses of 1,464 but these included Abercromby (See 8 March Abukir) who was mortally wounded while exposed to danger in front of his troops. He was buried at Malta.

Following this defeat, Cairo and Alexandria were surrendered to the British who returned Egypt to Turkish rule. The French troops were returned to France. While in Egypt, the French commander, de Menou, converted to Islam; it is difficult to imagine that happening today when western forces are fighting in Moslem countries.

A surprising result of this victory was the acquisition of the 'Rosetta Stone' which now adorns the Egyptian collection of the British Museum. When Napoleon invaded Egypt in 1798, his entourage included a commission of scholars and scientists who were to report on the past and present condition of the country in preparation for its regeneration and the restoration of its former prosperity as a French colony (such were the romantic policies of revolutionary France). Nelson's annihilation of the French fleet at the Nile (see 1 August) had left the French army stranded, but at first they carried on with their plans and in the reconstruction of Fort Julien at Rosetta (Rashid) the Stone was unearthed. Captain François Bouchard recognized its significance and sent it to the Institut de l'Egypte that had been established by some of Napoleon's savants. The Stone is inscribed in three languages – hieroglyphic, demotic, and Greek – and this enabled hieroglyphic to be translated for the first time through the Greek. The Treaty of Alexandria 1801 set the terms of the French surrender and included the transfer of the Stone to Britain; the inscriptions in the British Museum read: "Captured in Egypt by the British Army in 1801" and "Presented by George III". Egyptian authorities are now demanding the return of the Stone.

24 MARGATE 1387, ENGLAND (HUNDRED YEARS' WAR)

Commanders: Earls of Arundel and Nottingham v. ?

Fought off Margate, the French were attempting an invasion of Britain in alliance with Castile, but the allied fleet was routed with 110 ships either captured or sunk. Not surprisingly, this victory put an end to the possibility of an invasion.

25 H.M.S. SHEERNESS V. PRINCE OF WALES 1746, SCOTLAND (WAR OF THE AUSTRIAN SUCCESSION)

Commanders: Rear Admiral John Byng v. ?

This single ship action had larger consequences. The Jacobite rebellion began in 1745 when Prince Charles Stuart (Bonnie Prince Charlie) landed in the west Highlands and raised a small army which was able to advance as far as Derby. At first, the Jacobites acted independently, but their initial success revived French interest in an invasion of England, and money and supplies were promised. In the event, the French commitment to the enterprise was too small and the planning abysmal. The invasion force was to have sailed from Boulogne for Dungeness, but at the last moment the commander, the duc de Richelieu, discovered that not all of the ships could leave the anchorage on one tide, and it was possible that when the ships arrived at Dungeness, it might be low water. By the time the French were ready, the Jacobites were in retreat and already back in Scotland. Attempts were made to land money and supplies, and Lord John Drummond succeeded in landing at Montrose in December with 1,200 men of the Royal Écossais Regiment (there were about 200 French at Culloden), but after this, Admiral Byng's ships prevented most of the supplies, on which the Jacobites depended, from getting through. When *Sheerness* drove *Prince of Wales* ashore on the Sutherland coast this was the last straw. The loss aggravated the disadvantage of the Pretender at the battle of Culloden three weeks later, and the insurrection was over. Admiral Byng went on to an even more unfortunate end than Charles Stuart, he was convicted of 'failing to do his utmost to take or destroy the enemy's ships' in the loss of Minorca and was shot on his own quarterdeck (see 17 August, Lagos Bay).

25 CHANDERNAGORE 1757, W. BENGAL, INDIA (SEVEN YEARS' WAR)

Commanders: Col. Robert Clive & Rear Admiral Sir Charles Watson v. Governor M.Renault

Forces: British 700 + 1600 Indian troops; French 457 + 2,337 Indian troops.

Chandernagore (now called Chandarnager) was a fortified settlement on the Hooghly River about 20 miles up-stream from Calcutta. It was occupied by the French in collaboration with the Nawab of Bengal, and the outbreak of the war in Europe justified the plan to capture the fort. Following the initial attack on the town, the French retreated into the fort, and the Nawab's troops deserted. At this juncture, a Britsh naval squadron under the command of Rear Adml. Sir Charles Watson arrived and bombarded the fort. After a vigorous action, the French surrendered, and most of the British casualties were sailors. Although Britain and France were officially at war, in effect, this was a private one - Clive and his troops were employed by the East India Company, and their opponents were part of the French East India Company

(*Compagnie des Indes*). The loss of Chandernagore meant the end of French influence in Bengal, and in Clive's words: "an unexpressable blow to the French Company".

The timely arrival of the warships was made possible by a previous hydrographic survey and drafting of charts which enabled the ships to navigate the shoals. Such operational chart-making was one of the keys to British success in amphibious operations world-wide (see 27 July, Louisbourg).

30 H.M.S.LION (64 GUNS), FOUDROYANT (80 GUNS), PENELOPE (36 GUNS) V. LE GUILLAUME TELL (84 GUNS) 1800, MALTA (FRENCH REVOLUTIONARY WARS)

Commanders: Captain M. Dixon, Captain Sir Edward Berry, Captain H. Blackwood v. Rear Adml. D.Decrès & Captain Saulnier.

Le Guillaume Tell was one of the two French ships of the line to escape after the Battle of the Nile (see 1 August), and she took refuge in Malta. *Le Guillaume Tell*, taking advantage of a favourable wind, left Valetta at night, and after the moon had set, she was first sighted by *Penelope* who fought her much more powerful enemy throughout the night inflicting considerable damage. The under-manned *Lion* then came up and continued the action until she was unable to stay in touch with the enemy. *Foudroyant* laid her opponent alongside, and although nearly unrigged by a broadside, she was able to reply with a triple-shotted broadside that crashed through the hull of the French ship. *Le Guillaume Tell* refused to surrender until reduced to a floating hulk and was towed off as a prize to Syracuse, Sicily; she was later commissioned in the Royal Navy as, appropriately, H.M.S. Malta. This engagement has been described as "perhaps the hottest action that any enemy vessel ever brought to bear against ships of His Majesty". French casualties were more than 450; British total, 18 killed and 109 wounded. An idea of the ferocity of sea battles in this period can be obtained from the ammunition expended by *Foudroyant* – 161 barrels of gunpowder, 1,200 32-pounder round shot, 1,240 20-pounder round shot, 100 18-pounder round shot and 200 12-pounder round shot; the total is 30 tons of round shot fired into a wooden ship at very close quarters.

An interesting feature of this engagement is the use of rockets for signalling purposes. As soon as the departure of *Guilleaume Tell* from

Valetta was observed, the British batteries sent up rockets to alert the British squadron, and later *Lion* used rockets to guide the pursuit of the rest of the squadron.

The principal credit for the victory goes to Captain Blackwood and *Penelope*. On the French side, Rear Adml. Decrès played a hero's part; he was personally involved in the fighting being at one stage on board *Penelope*, finally, severely wounded, he was taken prisoner. Decrès had already earned a reputation for personal bravery and initiative in battle, and in March 1801, Napoleon himself presented him with a 'sword of honour' for his part in this action; six months later he became Napoleon's Naval Minister, a post he held until Napoleon's first abdication in 1814.

APRIL

2 SERINGHAM 1753, INDIA (CARNATIC WARS)

Commanders: Major Stringer Lawrence v. M. Astruc.

Seringham was an outpost that was successfully attacked by the French, but Major Lawrence arrived with about 1,000 British troops and drove them out. Three months later, Lawrence and Astruc confronted each other again on a much larger stage, and Lawrence showed decisively that Astruc was not a match for him (see 7 July Trichinopoly). Even small scale victories in the ongoing conflict between Britain and France in India were important because of the influence they exerted on the attitudes of the indigenous rulers, whose support was essential to European plans for lucrative, trade organizations.

3 NÁJERA (A.K.A. NAVARETTE) 1367, SPAIN (HUNDRED YEARS' WAR)

Commanders: Edward, the Black Prince v. Henry of Trastamara & Bertrand du Guesclin

Forces: English 24,000 including 5,000 archers; French-Spanish 29,400.

Edward who, in addition to being Prince of Wales, was also Prince of Aquitaine led his army from Aquitaine across the Pyrenees into Navarre in support of Pedro, the King of Castile, whose half-brother, Henry of Trastamara sought to usurp him. The Prince's army included a number of able field commanders with long experience in France, such as the Earl of Pembroke, John of Gaunt (Duke of Lancaster), and Sir John Chandos. Clever tactics trapped the enemy in a place still known as the 'the Ravine of the English', and the archers devastated the enemy cavalry. The Spanish were driven off, many drowning as they tried to cross a small river, and the French surrendered. English casualties were 100, the Spanish had 7,000 killed, and the French at least 500; the French commander, du Guesclin, was taken prisoner, and this time his ransom was set at 100,000 gold doubles (see 30 September, Auray).

As a measure of his appreciation, Pedro presented Edward with a magnificent red spinel gem, later known as the Black Prince's Ruby. Henry V wore this jewel at Agincourt (October 25) where it narrowly escaped destruction, but now, set in a Maltese cross, it is in the centre of the English imperial crown. The victory at Nájera brought only a temporary benefit to Pedro; two years later Henry of Trastamara fought him again and killed him in personal combat. The campaign ruined the health of the Black Prince, his finances, and any prospect of sound rule in Aquitaine.

Some five hundred years later, this battle provided Conan Doyle with the background for his favourite historical novel, 'The White Company', which he considered more serious work than his series about Sherlock Holmes.

3 SABUGAL 1811, PORTUGAL (PENINSULAR WAR)

Commanders: Wellington v. General Jean Reynier
Forces: British 30,000; French 10,000.

This was another rearguard action by the French who were retreating from Portugal (see 13 March Condeixa). Their force was an army corps covering the withdrawal of the main body. When the British attack was about to begin, fog descended and the assault troops, except for the Light Division, halted waiting for further orders. Unfortunately, under the temporary command of the inept Maj.-Genl. Sir William Erskine (see 14 March,Casal Novo), the Light Division continued to advance and was confronted by a superior French force that counter-attacked. This was beaten off at unnecessary cost, and the Light Division went forward again. The main attack began after the fog lifted, and the French were forced to withdraw; they were then were left with only one position in Portugal, namely, Almeida. British casualties were 200, the French 1,500.

4 ILE DE RHÉ 1758, FRANCE (SEVEN YEARS' WAR)

Commanders: Adml. Sir Edward Hawke v.?

Forces: British 7 ships of the line with 3 frigates; French 5 ships of the line, 6 frigates and a convoy of 40 ships.

The French had sailed from Rochefort bound for Louisbourg, Nova Scotia, when they were intercepted by the British, and all of the French ships were driven ashore on the Ile de Rhé. The French were unlucky in that Admiral Hawke, who had earned a reputation for courage and daring, was in command, for few would have dared to pursue so close inshore. Some four months later, the British captured Louisbourg (see 27 July), then the strongest fortress in North America, but if the convoy destroyed by Hawke had got through the outcome might well have been different. For more information about Hawke see 14 October Cape Finisterre II and 20-22 November Quiberon Bay.

4 ST. LUCIA 1794, WEST INDIES (FRENCH REVOLUTIONARY WARS).

Commanders: Adml.Sir John Jervis & Lt. Gen. Sir Charles Grey v. ?

This amphibious operation was a continuation of a campaign that began at Martinique (see 16 March), and the island was captured after brief resistance.

5 KARIKAL 1760, INDIA (SEVEN YEARS' WAR)

Commanders: Rear-Adml. Samuel Cornish & the Hon. Major George Monson v. Governor M. Renault.

Forces: British 300 Marines, 100 Europeans and 300 Indian sepoys; French 200 Europeans and 200 sepoys.

Karikal was a port in the delta of the Cauvery River, about 80 miles south of Pondicherry, that served as a gateway to the trading centres of Tanjore and Trichinopoly. Governor Pigot of the East India Company and Admiral Cornish determined to seize Karikal by means of an amphibious operation. Lt Col. Eyre Coote put Monson, formerly of H.M. Footguards but now of the 84th Regiment, in command of the land forces, including 300 marines, and they were put ashore about 4 miles from the port. The garrison surrendered after less than stubborn resistance.

The 84th. Regiment, later the York and Lancaster, was raised in January 1759 as a result of urgent requests from the East India Company for additional military assistance, and it was sent to India immediately. The first colonel was Eyre Coote who was later c-in-c India (see 15 January Pondicherry and 22 January Wandiwash). The regiment was disbanded at the end of the war in 1763 when many of the officers and other ranks enlisted in the service of the Company.

Rear-Admiral Cornish was something of a rarity having begun his naval career as a common seaman, and it continued steadily but unremarkably until his moment of true glory in 1762. He was joint commander at the capture of Manila from Spain, an operation that has been described as one that for luck and daring has seldom been matched. Incidentally, the support of the East India Company for the attack on Manila was unenthusiastic because local officials stood to lose some very lucrative private trade. Such conflicts of interest were a feature of both British and French operations in India in the eighteenth century.

M. Renault had no success in the war. He had been the Governor of Chandernagore until Clive drove him from it (see 25 March), and he seems to have contributed to the weakening of the French position in India.

5 GINGEE FORTS 1761, INDIA (SEVEN YEARS' WAR)

Commanders: Col. Eyre Coote v. ???

Each of the three forts at Gingee, about 20 miles from Pondicherry, was built on a steep hill, and they were connected by a curtain wall nearly two miles long. Built at a height of 800 feet, they were protected by a moat 80 feet wide and the main walls were over 60 feet thick. Although considered to be impregnable, the forts had previously been captured by treachery and by determined night attack, and, already demoralised by the defeat at Pondicherry (see 15 January), the French surrendered to Coote without a prolonged struggle.

6 H.M.S. AMETHYST (42 GUNS) V. NIEMEN (44 GUNS) 1809, FRANCE (NAPOLEONIC WAR)

Commanders: Captain Michael Seymour v. Captain Dupotet.

Fought in the Bay of Biscay, Captain Seymour first sighted the enemy on the previous day and gave chase. Contact was lost during the night but was re-established and shots were exchanged, then, when *Amethyst* was able to get to close quarters, the fighting became more severe. A succession of broadsides from *Amethyst* brought down *Niemen's* main and mizzen masts, and with her hammock netting on fire, she ceased firing and surrendered. Towards the end of the battle *Amethyst* had also lost her main and mizzen masts, her casualties were 8 killed and 37 wounded; French casualties were 47 killed and 73 wounded. *Amethyst's* achievement is endorsed by the fact that she was hindered by having two officers and thirty-seven men away aboard prizes and was holding sixty-nine prisoners on board. *Niemen* was only three months old and was bound for Mauritius with naval stores; she was towed to England and taken into the Royal Navy, appropriately under the command of Captain Seymour (see 10 November, H.M.S. Amethyst) who was created a baronet in honour of his performance.

7 BADAJOZ 1812, SPAIN (PENINSULA WAR)

Commanders: Wellington v. Genl. Armand Phillipon.

Badajoz was a strong fortress that stood in the way of Wellington's advance into Spain, and the siege began on March 16. The attacks were strongly resisted, and Wellington's troops suffered heavy casualties. Finally, the fortress and town were taken, and there followed three days and nights of such unprecedented acts of pillage and rape in celebration of the victory as would arouse the admiration and envy of the most violent soccer hooligan (but see 8 September, San Sebastian for another view). As Wellington once expressed it: "there is no crime recorded in the Newgate calendar that is not committed by these soldiers, who quit their ranks in search of plunder". Nevertheless, in the round, Wellington admired the Peninsular Army, and when he saw the casualty returns of Badajoz, Wellington, not normally so affected, wept.

8 TAILLEBOURG (A.K.A. THE SAINTES) 1351, FRANCE (HUNDRED YEARS' WAR)

Commanders: Sir John Beauchamp v. Marshal of France Guy de Nesle the Sire d'Offremont & Marshal of France Arnaud d'Endreghem.

King John II had just succeeded his father to the French throne and set out to make his mark by retaking the province of Poitou. Edward III became aware of his intentions and sent Sir John Beauchamp, brother of the Earl of Warwick and Governor of Calais, to Bordeaux with orders to repel the invasion. He was fortunate in that the French preparations took so long that Beauchamp had time to bring in reinforcements and to organize his army. The French were besieging the town of Saintes, and when the English relieving force arrived, the two armies met near Taillebourg. An interesting tactical feature of the battle was the French decision to copy the English practice of dismounting most of the men-at-arms to fight on foot. Unfortunately, this change did not make any difference, the French were decisively beaten – 600 were killed or taken prisoner, and the two marshals were among the prisoners. King John paid a large ransom for the release of Guy de Nesle, and he was soon back in action against the English (see 14 August Mauron)

8 MASULIPATAM 1759, INDIA (SEVEN YEARS' WAR)

Commanders: Lt. Col. Francis Forde v. Le Comte de Conflans

Forces: British 346 + 2,400 Indian troops; French 600 + 2,000 Indian troops.

This was a siege of the most important French fortress in this part of India, and the British were able to invest it because of their victories at Condore (see 7 December) and Rajahmundry (see 9 December). After a heavy bombardment with guns landed from the naval squadron, the fort was taken by storm and virtually the whole French force surrendered. The immediate result was to substitute British influence for French at the court of Hyderabad. The Seven Years' War was proving to be an excellent opportunity for the East India Company to drive from India its commercial rival, the French East India Company (*Compagnie des Indes*).

De Conflans was a Vice Admiral with over 50 years' naval service, but it was the French practice for senior naval officers also to hold military rank and this accounts for his presence in India. Unhappy though his confrontations with the British in India were, much worse was to follow when he returned to France with a sea going command (see 20-22 November, Quiberon Bay).

10 H.M.S. ASTRAEA (32 GUNS) V. GLOIRE (36 GUNS) 1795, FRANCE (FRENCH REVOLUTIONARY WARS)

Commanders: Capt. Lord Henry Paulet v. ?

Three French frigates, sighted by a British squadron patrolling off NW France, scattered. *Astraea*, sailing faster than the other two ships in consort, overtook *Gloire*, and after an engagement that lasted five-and-a half hours, the last hour of which was at close quarters, *Gloire* surrendered. The masts and rigging of both ships were badly damaged, but the French casualties of 40 killed and wounded were five times the British number. Lt. Talbot of *Astraea* was promoted to commander for his part, and eventually, in 1847, Navy General Service Medals were awarded to the survivors.

10 TOULOUSE 1814, FRANCE (PENINSULA WAR)

Commanders: Wellington v. Marshal Nicolas-Jean de Dieu Soult, Duke of Dalmatia.

Forces: British with Portuguese and Spanish 46,573; French 42,000.

This was the final battle of the Peninsular War. Wellington with his Portuguese and Spanish allies had chased the French, commanded by Marshal Soult, out of Spain, and they were now campaigning in what had been the province of Aquitaine (an English possession for three centuries from 1152). Soult had been given a bloody nose in two or three earlier encounters (see 10 December Nive and 13 December St. Pierre) and had retreated into the fortified city of Toulouse. After severe fighting, the French continued their retreat, and the civic authorities invited Wellington into the city. Wellington was there when Colonel Ponsonby arrived to inform him officially that Napoleon had abdicated, and that the war was over.

Wellington's conduct of the Peninsular War was an important factor in the defeat of Napoleon – 'the Spanish ulcer' Napoleon described it. Soult had not been able to stop Wellington's advance, but he had a distinguished military career beginning as a private in the pre-revolutionary infantry and rising to the rank of marshal in 1804. Soult was Napoleon's chief of staff at Waterloo, an appointment that some have regarded as a factor in Napoleon's defeat. Subsequently, by skilfully switching sides, Soult had a prominent government career under several regimes usually serving as minister of war and president of the council; he was largely responsible for the French conquest of Algeria in the 1840s.

11 TREATY OF UTRECHT 1713, THE NETHERLANDS (WAR OF THE SPANISH SUCCESSION)

A series of treaties were signed between the European powers that had been engaged in the war during the previous eleven years, and this one was between Britain and France. The territorial gains of Britain laid the foundations of the British Empire – France ceded: Newfoundland, Nova Scotia, the Hudson's Bay Territory, and the island of St. Kitts and agreed to demolish the fortifications of Dunkirk. France also acknowledged the legality of the Hanoverian succession and undertook not to support the claims of the exiled Stuarts, in spite of which on 24 October 1745 Louis XV, in the Treaty of Fontainbleau, entered into a military alliance with Charles Edward Stuart.As is so often the case with treaties, this was of little consequence, three years later the promise to recognize the Hanoverian succession was renewed (see 18 October, Treaty of Aix-la-Chapelle).

During the war the British, Dutch and Austrian armies commanded by Marlborough and Prince Eugene had gained a series of major victories over the French which aroused some criticism in Britain of the terms of the peace. John Wilkes, for example, described the Treaty as being like the "Peace of God, for it passeth all understanding', but the attributes to Wilkes for his *bon mot* seldom, if ever, acknowledge that James I used the same words to criticize the poetry of John Donne.

The Protocol described Ann as Queen of Great Britain, Ireland and France notwithstanding that Lewis (sic) XIV was also referred to as King of France. In a separate Treaty with Spain, Britain also secured Gibraltar and Minorca. The terms of this Treaty have given rise to a modern dispute. Spain contends that the wording of the Utrecht document precludes any right of the citizens of the Rock to self-determination, but the citizens do not accept this interpretation, and the dispute continues.

11 THE BASQUE ROADS 1809, FRANCE (NAPOLEONIC WAR)

Commanders: Captain Lord Thomas Cochrane v. ?

A French squadron of eight ships had succeeded in slipping out of Brest and anchored in the Basque Roads in preparation for sailing to the West Indies. Cochrane was in command of a group of fireships assembled to attack the anchored ships which were protected by a boom. Attacking at night, the first fire ship broke through the boom, whereupon the French ships cut their cables and all but two ran ashore. The next day the main British fleet, commanded by Adml. Lord Gambier, sailed into the Roads to complete the destruction, but the attack was weak and only three ships were taken and burned, while a merchant ship was recaptured by the French.

This action had political repercussions. Up to this point, Gambier had had a successful naval career and was in command of the Channel Fleet, but his orders of withdrawal to Cochrane and the latter's subsequent criticisms led to his court martial. Thanks to Gambier's political connections, the court had a sufficient number of his friends to ensure his acquittal, but Cochrane, who was also a radical member of Parliament, strongly opposed a Parliamentary vote of thanks to Gambier, and this ruined his naval career notwithstanding that he had been awarded the Order of the Bath for his performance in the Basque Roads. A remarkable character, in 1814 Cochrane was implicated in a stock exchange fraud involving the spreading of false rumours of Napoleon's abdication for which he was imprisoned, expelled from Parliament, and deprived of his Order of the Bath. From these misfortunes he emerged in 1817 in command of the Chilean navy in its war against Spain, and his success in this role led Brazil to enlist his services in its war of independence against Portugal. Returning to Europe, he was employed by Greece in its war of independence but finally resigned because of their lack of support for his novel plans to use steamships in naval warfare. Succeeding his father as Earl of Dundonald in 1831, he worked strenuously and successfully to reinstate his naval career culminating in his command of the American and West Indies Station. He died in 1860, and, perhaps most astonishingly of all, he was buried in Westminster Abbey. Just before he died Lord Cochrane completed his memoirs which are as fascinating as any of the naval novels of this period.

Lord Gambier seems to have led a prosaic life. He is now remembered, if at all, because the Gambier Islands in the South Pacific are named after him; the islands were sighted from a missionary ship in 1797, and the captain gave them the name Gambier. Gambier's entire naval career was spent in fighting the French, and ironically the Gambier Islands were annexed by the French in 1881. Perhaps in recompense, in 1889, Captain Plumper R.N. named an island in Howe Sound, close by Vancouver, Gambier.

11 VILLAGARCIA 1812, SPAIN (PENINSULAR WAR)

Commanders: Lt. Gen. Stapleton-Cotton v. Brig. Gen. Charles Lallemand.
Forces: British 4,000 (1 light & 2 heavy cavalry brigades); French 3,480 (2 cavalry brigades).

This was a cavalry battle, the nineteenth century equivalent of a tank battle. The French were the rearguard of the retreating Army of the South and were confronted by the vanguard of the advancing British force. The French were outflanked by the Dragoon Guards and forced to withdraw, in some disorder, to the main body of their army, 136 were taken prisoner.

Lallemand's career was about to take a dramatic turn. Always a firm supporter of the Revolutionary ideals, he had joined the cavalry at eighteen years of age, and after service in France, Egypt and San Domingo, he had risen to the rank of brigadier-general, baron of the empire and commandant of the Legion of Honour. Commendable progress, but not outstanding under an emperor committed to a policy of *'la carrière ouverte aux talents'*. Napoleon's first abdication in 1814 gave Lallemand his opportunity. Supported by his younger brother, he fomented a rebellion against the newly-crowned Louis XVIII and was saved from the penalties of its failure by Napoleon's return to Paris following his escape from Elba. Immediately, he was promoted to general of division and given the prestigious command of the light cavalry of the Imperial Guard at Waterloo (see 18 June). Showing steadfast loyalty to Napoleon, Lallemand asked to accompany him in exile to St. Helena but was forbidden to do so, although he was allowed to escape to the United States. Once there, he soon came to symbolize the remains of imperial (Napoleonic) glory against the Bourbon and Allied Powers and was exempted from the general French amnesties for his ilk on the ground of incorrigibility. Naploeon died and left Lallemand 100,000 francs in his will, most of which went to pay off his debts that had been largely incurred in trying to establish a military colony with fellow believers in the imperial cause on the Trinity River, Texas, which was then part of Mexico. This venture was the last filibuster incursion from the United States into Spanish Texas, and it, too, failed (although one feels that Davy Crockett and James Bowie would have approved and, perhaps, admired). But fortune favours the brave, and in 1830 a peaceful revolution in Paris enthroned Louis Philippe, and Lallemand was free to return to France. Given his unswerving devotion to the Napoleonic cause, it was singularly appropriate that from 1837-38, he was the Governor of Corsica, the birthplace of his idol. He died in Paris a year later.

12 THE SAINTES (A.K.A. DOMINICA) 1782, WEST INDIES (WAR OF AMERICAN INDEPENDENCE)

Commanders: Adml. Sir George Rodney v. Adml. Comte François de Grasse.

Forces: British 36 ships of the line; French 33 ships of the line.

Fought off the islands called The Saintes near Dominica, this battle was fought when the American Revolution was nearly over, and the French navy, in a rare period of ascendancy over the British, had made a contribution to the American success. Following a somewhat inconclusive victory in Chesapeake Bay that contributed to their final triumph, de Grasse had become a popular hero to the Americans, and now, invigorated by the victory, the objective was to drive the British from the Caribbean. So it was that de Grasse sailed from his base in Martinique with his entire fleet and 15,000 troops to make rendezvous with 12 Spanish ships of the line, and then proceed to capture Jamaica. During the French preparations, Sir George Rodney had arrived to resume command in the Caribbean, and, well-informed of the enemy's intentions, as soon as the French sailed he put to sea in pursuit. Initially, light winds reduced activities to four days of manœuvring in which the poor seamanship of the French redounded to the advantage of the British. There was a number of collisions in the French fleet that cost time and ships, for example, after three collisions in three days, *Zélé*, commanded by Captain Gras-Préville, was dismasted, and this captain had the unusual distinction of fourteen collisions in just over a year.

Action was finally joined at close quarters with the fleets in parallel but opposite courses. In light winds de Grasse ordered his ships to go about and sail in the same direction as their opponents but a number did not do so, and a sudden shift in the wind created further confusion. At this point, by accident or design (the argument continues), Rodney demonstrated an entirely new tactic; he turned his ships and attacked at right angles to the French line. The British ships went through the line in three places and as they did so they were able to rake the ships on each side with devastating results. Six heavily damaged French ships struck their colours, and at the end de Grasse was forced to surrender his 130 gun flagship, *Ville de Paris*, and his sword; in this ship over 400 had been killed and more than 700 wounded. The remaining French ships, many of them damaged, scattered and found shelter in Haiti except for two that Rodney's second–in-command, Samuel Hood, captured later. The invasion of Jamaica was abandoned. Concerning Rodney's tactic of 'crossing the T', although not renowned for innovation, the British Admiralty added it to the 'Fighting Instructions', and a notable application at a later date was at Trafalgar (see 21 October). The Saintes was commemorated in World War II by naming a Battle Class destroyer *H.M.S.Saintes*, and the ship's crest incorporated a purple eagle from Rodney's family crest.

Rodney has a place among the great British naval commanders attested by the fact that a battleship, still in the fleet during World War II, was named in his honour. He entered the Royal Navy aged 13 and influential connections ensured rapid promotion, but his performance soon justified his advancement. He commanded a ship of the line in Hawkes' great victory at Cape Finisterre (see 14 October), and followed this with nearly four years as Governor of Newfoundland. He also had success in the Seven Years' War (see 12 February, Martinique), but his career was impaired through extravagance and avarice that led him to flagrant misappropriation of public funds and abuse of his power of patronage to such a degree that he was obliged to live in France between 1775 and 1779 in order to escape from his many creditors. He was able to return to England in unusual circumstances. Although Britain and France were again at war, the French Marshal Biron, noted for his extravagance, lent Rodney sufficient money to enable him to return to London where the misfortunes of war had made his services urgently needed. Success brought him appointment as a knight of the Bath, and later he was awarded a barony. The colonists in Jamaica were delighted when Rodney brought his prizes into port, and in due course erected a marble statue in his honour that stands in Kingston's Spanish Town Square. Biron did not fare as well. He was an aristocrat with republican sympathies and military ambitions. He steered his way through the political changes in the early days of the revolutionary government, but his generosity was of no account, and his dismal performance in the field led Robespierre to send him to the guillotine in 1793.

The Saintes effectively ended de Grasse's career. After his return to France, courts martial convicted many of his officers for disobeying orders, and although de Grasse was not charged, many held him responsible for the defeat, and he became a public scapegoat.

13 H.M.S. RÉVOLUTIONNAIRE (38 GUNS) V. UNITÉ (36 GUNS) 1796, FRANCE (FRENCH REVOLUTIONARY WARS).

Commanders: Capt. Francis Cole v. Capt. C-A. Durand.

Fought off Ushant, but really not much more than a skirmish, *Révolutionnaire* (captured from the French off Brest two years previously) was detached from a patrolling flotilla of frigates to chase *Unité. Unité* refused to surrender when first challenged but did so after the second broadside. An idea of the action can be obtained from the fact that the French casualties were 9 killed 11 wounded, whereas the British had none.

13 CASTALLA 1813, SPAIN (PENINSULA WAR)

Commanders: Lt. Gen. Sir John Murray v. Marshal Louis-Gabriel Suchet, Duc d'Albufera.
Forces: British 14,800; French 13,500.

Even by the practice of the time, it is a misnomer to describe Murray's force as 'British'; there was the usual assortment of Portuguese and Spanish allies, but in addition there were Sicilian, Anglo-Italian and Calabrese troops. The battle was primarily tactical. The British intention was to prevent Suchet from obstructing Wellington's planned spring offensive. Murray occupied a strong position in and around Castalla, but he was ineffectual in command, and it has been said that his troops gained a convincing victory in spite of him.

15 TOBAGO 1793, WEST INDIES (FRENCH REVOLUTIONARY WARS).

Commanders: Vice-Adml. Sir John Laforey & Maj. Genl. C.Cuyler v. Lt.Genl. Monteil.

This was an amphibious operation in which the island was captured by an attack on the principal fort, mainly by means of a bayonet charge at night. The forces engaged were small, but the actions heroic. Unfortunately, the island was returned to the French at the Treaty of Amiens 1802, after which it was recaptured (see July 1), and finally, joined with Trinidad, it became part of the British Empire at the Treaty of Paris 1814 (see 30 May).

16 PORTO PRAYA BAY 1781, WEST INDIES (WAR OF AMERICAN INDEPENDENCE).

Commanders: Commodore George Johnstone v. Rear Admiral Pierre André Suffren, Bailli de St. Tropez.

Fought off Cape Verde Islands between 10 British ships and 11 French. The French attacked the British ships in the roadstead of Porto Praya but were repulsed and obliged to withdraw. This is one of a series of conflicts that occurred as a result of France supporting the American revolutionary forces.

Suffren was one of the most brilliant and aggressive of all French admirals. He joined the navy when he was 14 and although taken prisoner by Hawke at Cape Finisterre II (see 14 October) and again by Boscawen at Lagos (see 17 August), he was able to continue his career and rose to be appointed to command the Brest fleet. Before he assumed this command, he fought a duel with the Prince de Mirepoix, who had taken offence because Suffren refused to reinstate two of the Prince's relations dimissed from the navy for misconduct, and Suffren probably died as a result of a wound, but officially he died from apoplexy.

19 H.M.S. FOUDROYANT (86 GUNS) V. PÉGASE (74 GUNS) 1782, FRANCE (AMERICAN WAR OF INDEPENDENCE)

Commanders: Captain John Jervis v. ?

A stellar victory for Jervis over a newly-built French ship-of-the-line. The French suffered heavy casualties, and the badly damaged ship was taken as a prize; there were no British casualties except for Jervis himself who was hit by a flying splinter of wood that gave him two black eyes. Relish was given to this victory by the fact that *Foudroyant* had been captured from the French and fitted out for service in the Royal Navy (see 28 February H.M.S. Monmouth et al.). Jervis had already seen considerable service, but his promotions had been steady rather than spectacular; this success changed everything. In recognition of his victory he was knighted and the Order of the Bath conferred on him. Jervis went on to become an admiral of the fleet, and as Nelson's commanding officer in the Mediterranean earned his sincere affection and respect – by no means an easy thing to do.

Another well-known contemporary commander against the French with whom Jervis was associated was General Wolfe, the victor at the Plains of Abraham (see 13 September). Wolfe and Jervis had been at school together, but more to the point Jervis commanded a ship that took Wolfe's troops up the St Lawrence River and landed them in position to climb the cliff to the Plains of Abraham. Jervis' greatest victory was in 1797 over the Spanish fleet that was attempting to join the French fleet for the invasion of Britain, and for which he was created Earl St. Vincent.

20 H.M.S. INDEFATIGABLE (40 GUNS) V. VIRGINIE (44 GUNS) 1796, CHANNEL (FRENCH REVOLUTIONARY WARS)

Commanders: Captain Sir Edward Pellew v. Captain J. Bergeret.

At this time, Captain Pellew commanded a flotilla of frigates patrolling in the western approaches of the Channel (*Révolutionnaire* was one of this flotilla – see April 13), and when *Virginie* was sighted, they gave chase. After a pursuit of fifteen hours, *Indefatigable* caught up with *Virginie* and brought her into action. Considerable damage was sustained by each ship, and *Virginie* surrendered when the other British ships came up.

Captain Pellew had a most distinguished career chiefly, but not exclusively, in fighting the French, first in command of frigates, and later as an admiral. He was made a baronet earlier in 1796 for exceptional bravery and resource in saving all aboard *Dutton,* a troop transport that had gone aground and was breaking up in Plymouth Sound. He served as member of Parliament for Barnstaple in 1802-4 and was created Viscount

Exmouth for his services as commander-in-chief Mediterranean. His Mediterranean command extended into peace-time after hostilities against the French had ceased, and in August 1816 he led a fleet in the bombardment of Algiers in order to persuade the Bey to cease holding Christians in slavery; the guns accomplished what diplomacy had failed to do. A policy that President Bush might well approve (for another example of a pre-emptive strike see 17 August, Lagos Bay).

21 H.M.S MARS (74 GUNS) V.HERCULE (74 GUNS) 1798, FRANCE (FRENCH REVOLUTIONARY WARS)

Commanders: Captain Alexander Hood v. Captain L'Heritier.

Fought off Brest, both were ships-of-the line, i.e., battleships, *Mars* was part of the British squadron patrolling off Brest under the command of Viscount Bridport, Hood's cousin. *Hercule* was sighted and damaged by *H.M.S. Ramillies*; *Mars* took up the chase and found *Hercule* at anchor in the Passage du Raz. For about an hour the ships exchanged broadsides, and then *Hercule* struck her colours. *Mars* had 71 killed or wounded, *Hercule* 315 and 390 taken prisoner. Hood and L'Heritier were both mortally wounded.

Hood was a member of a most distinguished naval family. Another cousin, Viscount Hood, was the brother of Viscount Bridport, Viscount Hood was second–in-command at the Saintes (see April 12), and Alexander Hood's brother, Samuel, fought the French in various places from 1782 until his death on active service in the East Indies in 1814 by which time he had reached the rank of vice-admiral.

26 BEAUMONT-EN-CAMBRESIS, 1794 FRANCE (FRENCH REVOLUTIONARY WARS)

Commanders: Duke of York & Maj. Genl. Otto v. Genl. Renée-Bernard Chapuy.

Forces: British 12 cavalry squadrons, Austrians 6 cavalry squadrons; French 20,000 infantry.

The French sent a strong force to relieve the siege of Landrecies, and while forming up along a ridge under cover of a fog, the fog lifted enabling the Duke of York to mount an attack under the immediate command of Maj.Genl.Otto. A vigorous cavalry charge was directed against the French left which caught the French facing the wrong way, and they fled along the way they had come in great disorder. Their casualties were about 7,000 of whom 3,200 were sabred; at least 350 were taken prisoner including Genl. Chapuy and 41guns. British and Austrian casualties were about 400. Put this down as a brilliant performance by the cavalry. The Duke of York was the second son of George III who has been pilloried, probably unjustly, in the nursery rhyme:

Oh, the brave old Duke of York,
He had ten thousand men;
He marched them up to the top of the hill,
And he marched them down again.

A much earlier version names 'the King of France' in place of the 'Duke of York'.

29 CUDDALORE 1758, INDIA (SEVEN YEARS' WAR)

Commanders: Rear-Adml. Sir George Pocock v. Rear-Adml. Comte Ann Antoine d'Aché de Serquigny.

Fought off Cuddalore between 7 British ships of the line and 9 French ships as each country sought to establish supremacy in trade with India. The British and French factories, i.e., trading settlements, were in a line running down the Coromandel Coast which had no harbour and was only safe for shipping during the south-west monsoon season from April to September; command of the sea was essential to trade and military operations at this time of the year. The French base was in Mauritius and the British at Bombay. In a vigorous action the French lost one ship and had 600 casualties against 100 British and were forced to withdraw, but the rigging of the British ships was too damaged to permit pursuit. Pocock considered that the three ships at the rear of his line of battle were too slow in getting into action, and their captains were court-martialled; two were dismissed their ships and the other acquitted. In August, Pocock and d'Aché fought again a little further south, off Negapatam (see 3 August), and the outcome was similar. The French broke off the engagement, but the British ships were not able to pursue. The following season d'Aché reinforced by three ships of the line was delayed because his base at Mauritius could not victual the additional crews, and a detour had to be made to Madagascar for supplies. His squadron arrived on the Coromandel Coast in September to engage in a fierce but indecisive action with Pocock (see 10 September Pondicherry), before both fleets withdrew to their winter bases. In the 1760 season, d'Aché did not put in an appearance at all, he was ordered to remain in Mauritius against the possibility of a British attack, and then his ships were seriously damaged by a typhoon. The end came for the French in India in the following year (see 15 January Pondicherry).

MAY

1 GUADELOUPE 1759, WEST INDIES (SEVEN YEARS' WAR)
Commanders: Cdre. John Moore & Brig. John Barrington v. ?

Moore was in command in the Leeward Islands (part of the Lesser Antilles), and with 10 ships of the line and 6,000 troops, he was ordered to take Martinique and Guadeloupe. Martinique was too strong for his force, and after three days he moved on to Guadeloupe. A third of the troops were soon afflicted with fever, but, in the manner of the times, vigorous devastation of crops and plantations compelled the islanders to surrender one day before a relief force arrived from Martinique. The surrender proved to be a blessing because the sugar-planters gained access to a lucrative market (with bitter complaints from British planters) and British consumers were well-content. As so often is the case, the halcyon days were short, and when the war ended Martinique and Guadeloupe were returned to France (see 10 February, Treaty of Paris), although this provision was strongly criticised on the ground that the fur trade of Canada was a poor bargain compared with the sugar trade of Martinique and Guadeloupe. On the other hand, the disgruntled British sugar planters were presumably restored to good humour; impossible to please everyone.

2 MEAUX 1422, FRANCE (HUNDRED YEARS' WAR)
Commanders: Henry V v. Bastard of Vaurus.

On the march from Dreux (see 20 July), Henry's army, still suffering from disease, took Vendome and Beaugency, paused briefly outside Orleans, and then turned north towards the rivers Yonne and Marne where their ally the Duke of Burgundy had extensive territory. On the way to Meaux, the towns of Villeneuve-le-Roy and Rougemont were taken, and at the latter Henry found it necessary to hang the garrison and destroy buildings. One reason for this extended march lasting into the winter months was to entice the Dauphin into a set battle, but this was refused, and it is a minor mystery of the history of this phase of the war that there is no record of the whereabouts of the Dauphin's army. Arriving at Meaux, Henry prepared for the siege with his usual care and attention to detail, and it was expected to be lengthy because the fortifications were strong, and the population included a motley collection of English deserters, Scots, Irish, and French ruffians who were outlaws organized under the banner of the Bastard of Vaurus; these men would have to fight, literally, for their lives. As the siege went on sickness began to take its toll, and in December the river Marne, which formed part of the defences of Meaux, flooded; it swept away the bridge of boats that had been constructed to connect the besieging forces across the river and flooded the front trenches. Not the least of Henry's strengths was unusual determination in the face of adversity and setbacks, he persevered when others were weakening and was rewarded for his tenacity when the defenders started to falter. This deterioration began when the defenders sought to bring surreptitiously into the town as a new commander, the famous Guy de Nesle (not to be confused with a predecessor see 8 April Taillebourg & 14 August Mauron), and the attempt failed in comical circumstances. Guy and 40 followers succeeded in creeping through the English lines at night, but when Guy was crossing the moat on a plank, it broke and he fell into the water. Scarcely able to move in his armour, efforts to pull him out failed, and he and his group were taken prisoner. The day after this debacle the garrison rushed out of the town and into the market, which was protected by a wall and a canal, so that their defence could continue. The English army closed in and attacked the market successively and implacably from the north, west, east and south, hammering the enemy into submission. Appeals for a relieving force went unheeded, and the capitulation was signed.

To general satisfaction, the Bastard of Vaurus was hanged from the tree that he used to hang those of his captives unable to pay the ransom. Others less notorious met the same fate because this siege was the longest ever undertaken by Henry and by the time it was over tempers were short. The fall of Meux was also a psychological victory in that all of the other Dauphinist fortresses in Northern France, except for St. Valery, Guise, and Le Crotoy, quickly surrendered after only nominal resistance. The siege of Meaux has been described as "perhaps Henry's masterpiece", and it became an epic, as such it was a fitting finish to Henry's brilliant career, for less than four months later, at the age of 35, he died at Bois de Vincennes. Henry was one of those who contracted a disease, probably dysentery, at the siege of Dreux (see 20 July) and it became worse at Meux. After dealing with post-victory business at Meux, Henry joined Queen Catherine in Paris where he attended to more civil business pertaining to his position as Regent of France, but this was cut short by an appeal from his ally, the young Duke of Burgundy, for help in relieving the siege of Cosne. En route for Cosne with the army, Henry became so ill that he could no longer ride and had to be carried in a horse litter, when this, too, was beyond his endurance he took to his bed at Bois de Vincennes and died there. He is buried in Westminster Abbey.

Unquestionably, Henry stands in the first rank of British military commanders, principally because of organizational and tactical skills, great personal courage, the training and discipline of his army, and, perhaps above all, the ability to raise the morale of the troops he commanded to unprecedented heights, as well as inspiring the general population. Less well known is the grasp he showed of the importance to England of sea power, and his appreciation of how necessary this was to success in France is well beyond that of other mediæval commanders. Before he died, he had created a royal fleet of 6 great ships, 8 barges, and 10 balingers (small vessels capable of transporting about 40 soldiers) that must be regarded as the foundation of the royal navy. Moreover, Henry's ordinances for fleets and armies are grounds for putting his name forward as the founder of English international and maritime law. The various alliances that Henry made also showed him to be an adroit diplomat. All in all, he is a serious candidate for the accolade of the most capable English monarch.

Meaux next has a place in French history as the town in which, in 1546, the first Huguenot (Protestant) community was established.

3 LOCH NAN UAMH 1746, SCOTLAND (WAR OF THE AUSTRIAN SUCCESSION)

Following his defeat at Culloden, barely two weeks before, Bonnie Prince Charlie was a fugitive with a substantial price on his head, 'hiding in the heather' and inspiring many romantic myths the while. His immediate objective was to escape to France, and it was not the French navy that offered him assistance, but French privateers financed by Antoine Walsh, a ship owner of Nantes of Irish descent who had made a fortune in the slave-trade. Walsh had provided the ships that carried the Jacobites to Scotland the previous July, and now, with impressive speed, had sent two ships to bring his hero back. Unfortunately, the two ships ran foul of three British cruisers in Loch nan Uamh, about 22 miles west of Fort William, and it was not until September that Charles Stuart was taken back to France. In characteristic Stuart fashion, the rest of his life was an anti-climax of failed relationships and alcoholism.

3 CAPE FINISTERRE I 1747, SPAIN (WAR OF THE AUSTRIAN SUCCESSION)

Commanders: Adml. Lord George Anson v. Cmdre. Marquis de la Jonquière.

Fought off NW Spain between a British squadron comprising 14 ships of the line, and a French squadron of 9 ships of the line and 26 armed transports carrying troops. The French intention was to land a substantial body of troops in Canada, capable of recapturing Louisbourg and taking British settlements in Nova Scotia and Newfoundland. The battle turned into a running engagement when the French ships sought to escape westwards, and Anson ordered a general chase (see March 13, Genoa). After three hours, all of the French warships had been captured and 6 of the armed transports, 3,000 prisoners were taken. This was a crushing victory, but spare a thought for the French colonists in Canada most of whose supplies and reinforcements did not arrive, and it reduced their ambitious offensive plans to mere raids and skirmishes.

Anson was raised to the peerage after this action. He is in the first rank of naval commanders, and his four-year voyage round the world is one of the great tales of naval heroism. He also proved to be an excellent administrator being First Lord of the Admiralty in two governments.

H.M.S. Anson, one of the most modern battleships in the Royal Navy in World War II, was named after him.

De la Jonquière fought well but is not as distinguished. In the previous year, he had been obliged to bring back to France the bits and pieces of a major expedition (see June 16 Louisbourg I). He was taken prisoner at Finisterre, and after his release two years later, he was appointed Governor of Canada where he died, just in time to avoid having to answer charges at the court of Versailles of illegal pelt trading. A settlement was named after him, now the City of Jonquière, that has recently achieved a modicum of fame as the place in which is located the first Wal-Mart store in the world to be unionized, this was followed by the immediate announcement that the store would be closed – at the time of writing the incident continues.

5 FUENTES DE ONERO 1811, SPAIN (PENINSULA WAR)

Commanders: Wellington v. Marshal André Massena.
Forces: British & Portuguese 37,000; French 47,500.

The French were attempting to relieve the siege of Almeida, and Wellington fought a defensive battle to prevent them. Two particular performances in the heavy fighting spread over three days were: the brilliance of Major General Craufurd (see 19 January Ciudad Rodrigo) and the Light Division in covering the withdrawal of badly battered battalions by means of infantry formed in squares against repeated attacks by French Dragoons; and the bayonet charge of the Connaught Rangers ('The Devil's Own') that finally cleared the village of Fuentes and ended the battle. The result was a narrow victory for Wellington, and the French were forced to withdraw; the siege of Almeida continued and succeeded. Allied casualties were 1,800 and the French 3,300. Wellington described this battle as "the most difficult I was ever concerned in … … and if Boney had been there, we should have been beaten." Notwithstanding casualties nearly twice as many as those of his enemy, and the failure to raise the siege of Almeida, Massena claimed Fuentes as a victory. Napoleon, however, took a different view: "His Majesty is distressed, as we all are, to see his army retire before a British force so inferior in numbers." Massena was replaced by Marshal Marmont.

8 TREATY OF BRETIGNY 1360, FRANCE (HUNDRED YEARS' WAR)

This treaty resulted from the decisive English victory at Poitiers (see 19 September) where the French king, John II, was captured and imprisoned in England. A few months after the battle a truce had been agreed, and two treaties, known as the Treaties of London, were negotiated both of which were aborted. The first failed because the English Parliament objected to it, as well as King Charles of Navarre who alternated between alliance with England (see 3 April Nájera) and with France. Further efforts were made, and another draft was prepared that was more favourable to the English than the generous terms in the first one; not surprisingly the second draft was rejected in France.

Edward III was now out of patience and decided to invade France again; he was an experienced and masterful commander strongly supported by the nobility and population at large, and his preparations were far more thorough than was usual in that period. He landed at Calais on 28 October, 1359 with probably the largest English army to invade France to that date and with his best generals in the van. Divided into three divisions respectively under the command of the king himself, Henry, Duke of Lancaster (a.k.a. Earl of Derby), and the Prince of Wales (the Black Prince), they marched south. The immediate objective was Reims, traditionally the place for the coronation of French kings after anointment with the sacred oil of St. Rémi, and where Edward intended to be crowned king of France in order to endorse his claim to the throne. The French offered no opposition to this march mainly because the country was in a state bordering on chaos. As the king was a captive, there was a regent who was handicapped by a revolt of some of the nobles, a serious peasant uprising, and gangs of disbanded soldiers known as Free Companies who roamed at will pillaging the countryside.

Edward and his men spent Christmas besieging Reims and sending out reconnaissance and foraging parties. In one of these raids, Geoffrey Chaucer, the poet, was taken prisoner. He was with the army as part of the household of Lionel, the Duke of Clarence, one of Edward's younger sons, and he was sufficiently well-regarded for Edward to contribute to the ransom for his release – and subsequent adornment of English literature. For reasons not clearly established, Edward broke off the siege in January, ignored Paris and marched on Burgundian territories. On the way, various towns were taken, including Tonnerre where a large amount of Burgundy wine was seized and taken into custody. With all northern Burgundy now in disarray and helpless, the Duke was obliged to ask for terms. On 10 March 1360, a three year truce between England and Burgundy was agreed, and the Duke undertook to remain neutral in any Anglo-French war. Burgundy was also to pay a large indemnity. With flank and rear now secured, Edward marched towards Paris, and on arrival he paraded the army before the walls inviting a pitched battle. The invitation was refused, and they marched away. An extraordinary thing now happened. The regent sent emissaries after Edward seeking peace, and they caught up with him at Chartres. Bretigny, a small village close by, was chosen as the place for the terms to be negotiated between Henry, Duke of Lancaster, the principal English delegate, and the Bishop of Beauvais on the French side (protocol precluded Edward from negotiating in person because the French monarch was not present). The principal English gains were, in general, sovereignty over an enlarged Aquitaine in south west France (roughly equal to one third of France) without the necessity of feudal homage to the French king, as well as Calais. In return, Edward gave up any claim to the French throne as well as surrendering the duchies of Normandy and Tourraine in addition to Anjou, Maine, Brittany and Flanders. King John II's ransom was fixed at 3 million gold crowns with release on parole when 1 million had been paid. This ransom led to the introduction into the coinage of the franc. As surety for the payment, John gave as hostages two of his sons, several princes and nobles, four citizens of Paris and two each from nineteen principal towns of France. The terms of the Treaty were ratified and sworn at the Peace of Calais five months later by Edward and John and their eldest sons. Two years later, one of John's sons, the Duke d'Anjou, escaped from England, and John, who was in France trying to raise the ransom money, felt honour bound to return to England where he died in 1364. The Treaty of Bretigny brought to an end this phase of the Hundred Years' War in which the English were victorious, and coincidentally or otherwise, Edward replaced French with English as the national language for the first time since 1066.

10 ST. KITTS 1667 , WEST INDIES (ANGLO-DUTCH WAR)

Commanders: Cdre. John Berry v. Antoine Lefebvre de la Barre & Abraham Crijnssen.

Forces: British 12 frigates; Franco-Dutch 22 ships.

In this Anglo-Dutch war, the French came in on the side of the Dutch. Having taken New Amsterdam (renamed New York in honour of the Duke), the English directed much of their effort against Dutch colonies in the West Indies, and against French possessions in the same place. In spite of the inferiority in numbers, Berry attacked with such vigour that five enemy ships were burned, and several others were sunk; the remainder sought refuge in the harbour of St. Kitts, but Berry took his ships in after them and completed the destruction. Another British squadron arrived six weeks later to continue the good work (see 25 June, Fort St. Pierre).

10 WILLEMS 1794, BELGIUM (FRENCH REVOLUTIONARY WARS)

Commanders: Duke of York v. Genl. Jacques Philippe Bonnaud.

The French attacked the British but got much more than they bargained for. The British heavy cavalry charged, and the French cavalry fled, the British then charged again and routed the French infantry. The French lost 14 guns and 450 prisoners, the British about one-quarter of that number. Here was a member of the Royal family earning his keep and keeping alive old traditions.

11 H.M.S. PHOEBE (36 GUNS) V. LE GRAND FERRAILLEUR (16 GUNS) 1800, WESTERN APPROACHES (FRENCH REVOLUTIONARY WARS)

Commanders: Captain R.Barlow v. ?

Ferrailleur (Fencer) was a privateer out of Bordeaux, but in 16 days had not made any captures. Now she was taken into custody by the indefatigable *Phoebe.*

Captain Barlow in *Phoebe* exemplifies the contribution of the British frigates, their commanders and crews in the long wars against the French (see 10 January, 19 February, 21 February, and 20 December).

12 OPORTO (DOURO RIVER) 1809, PORTUGAL (PENINSULA WAR)

Commanders: Wellington v. Marshal Nicolas-Jean de Dieu Soult, Duc de Dalmatie.
Forces: British & Portuguese 29,000; French 20,000.

This battle was fought shortly after Wellington arrived in Portugal and marks the beginning of the campaign to drive the French out of Portugal and Spain which was accomplished five years later. The French had captured Oporto from the Portuguese about two months earlier, but after getting some of his troops across the river, Wellington was able to take the town without too much difficulty, and the French retreated northwards to Spain. French casualties 300 killed and wounded, Allies about 125.

14 ST. PIERRE & MIQUELON 1793, CANADA (FRENCH REVOLUTIONARY WARS)

This was an amphibious operation against these two islands off the coast of Newfoundland. Then, as now, the islands were important because of their valuable fishing rights. A small force was sent from Halifax and quickly conquered the islands. Under the Treaty of Paris 1814 (see 30 May) the islands were restored to France and now represent all that is left of the considerable French empire in North America. If it had not been for the Treaty, these islands would have passed to Canada and would have made the management and conservation of the Grand Banks fishery easier and more efficient.

15 BONN 1703, GERMANY (WAR OF THE SPANISH SUCCESSION)

Commanders: Marlborough v. M. d'Alègre.
Forces: Britsh & Allies 40,000; French 3,600.

At the start of the campaigning season of 1703, the strategic situation faced by the British and the Dutch had become much more difficult because the Elector of Bavaria had entered into an alliance with the French, a decision that next year Marlborough would give him cause for bitter regret (see 13 August Blenheim). In the meantime, Marlborough had a deep personal sorrow, his beloved eldest son, Jack, had died of smallpox, and he was severely grief-stricken. The Dutch had shown a clear preference for sieges rather than set battles, and it was decided to open communications through the upper Rhine to the allies of Baden and the Habsburg Empire by capturing Bonn. After Bonn had been taken, the offensive in the Spanish Netherlands would be resumed. All went smoothly, after only 18 days Bonn capitulated, and the garrison was allowed to go to Luxembourg. The attackers' casualties were about 600 and the French 860, an unusual ratio for a siege.

16 QUEBEC (ST. FOY) 1760, CANADA (SEVEN YEARS' WAR)
Commanders: Genl. James Murray v. Genl. Duc de Levis.

This battle followed on from the French defeat at Quebec (see September 13, Plains of Abraham). The French had retreated up the St Lawrence River to Montreal, and in the spring of 1760 an army of 8,500 French and Indians commanded by the Duc de Levis marched on Quebec. At St. Foy, just outside the city, they were confronted by a British force of about half their number which they forced to withdraw into Quebec. The French besieged the city but were kept at bay by superior artillery fire until a British naval squadron arrived which destroyed the French supply ships. The French then abandoned the siege and made their way back to Montreal leaving behind the sick and wounded as well as 40 siege guns. Four months later, the French capitulated at Montreal (see September 8).

James Murray made his military career in Canada. He arrived as a Lt. Colonel in 1757 and commanded a brigade at the capture of Louisbourg (see July 27). He continued as one of three brigadiers under Wolfe at the Plains of Abraham (see September 13). Murray and his troops were at the capitulation of Montreal, and Murray became the military governor of the Quebec district until 1763 when New France was ceded to Britain at the Treaty of Paris (see 10 February). He was then appointed as the first civil governor of Quebec. In 1782 he was in command at Minorca and was court martialled for surrendering it to the French and Spanish; however, he was acquitted and promoted to general. This outcome is in marked contrast to the fate of Admiral Byng who in 1757 was shot for failing to raise the French siege at Minorca (see 15 January, Pondicherry & 17 August, Lagos Bay).

16 ALBUHERA 1811, SPAIN (PENINSULAR WAR) "THE DIEHARDS' DAY"

Commanders: Marshal Sir William Beresford v. Marshal Nicolas-Jean de Dieu Soult, Duc de Dalmatie.
Forces: British, Spanish & Portuguese 35,000; French 24,200.

Beresford had been ordered to reform and re-organize the Portuguese army. He did so vigorously and successfully and was given the Portuguese rank of Marshal. Beresford had been sent by Wellington to mount a counter–offensive on the border of Spain and Portugal in the course of which he was besieging Badajoz, and Soult was marching to raise the siege. Beresford, on the advice of Wellington, chose to stand at Albuhera. It was one of the bloodiest battles of the Peninsula War, characterized by what has been described as 'the incompetence and worse' of Beresford's subordinates, but it is also known for conspicuous courage and tenacity on the part of the 57th. Regiment, later known as the Duke of Cambridge's Own Middlesex Regiment. Outnumbered, these troops, together with the Fusiliers, succeeded at the expense of heavy casualties in driving off the French. At the end of the action, the casualties of the 57th. were 420 rankers out of 570 and 20 out of 30 officers. The commanding officer, Colonel Inglis, while severely wounded, continually rallied his men with the cry of "Die hard, my men, die hard", and since this battle the nickname of the Regiment has been 'The Diehards'; it is the only regiment in the world whose nickname has entered the language. Albuhera is one of the Honours inscribed on the Regiment's Colours, and any toast drunk at the celebration of this battle ought to be coupled with 'The Diehards'.Finally, the French retreated, and the siege of Badajoz was resumed.

The French defeat has been attributed to errors by Soult, but he said afterwards that "The Day was mine, but they would not run away."

17 H.M.S. THETIS (36 GUNS) & H.M.S. HUSSAR (28 GUNS) V. NORMAN & 4 OTHER SHIPS 1795, U.S.A. (FRENCH REVOLUTIONARY WARS)

Commanders: Captain A. Cochrane & Capt. J. Beresford v. ?

The British ships were looking for French supply ships, and at dawn they sighted five large French ships at the mouth of Chesapeake Bay.

They attacked immediately and soon took all five. British casualties were only 8 killed and 12 wounded. Both Cochrane and Beresford went on to become admirals.

Thetis, a sea goddess and mother of Achilles in Greek mythology, was a popular name for ships in the British, French and Spanish navies, but it has proved to be ill-omened in the British service. This particular *Thetis* was sold in 1814, when it seemed that with Napoleon incarcerated on Elba the war with France was over, and another larger frigate of the same name was launched in 1817. This vessel left Rio de Janeiro in light winds and fog in December 1830 carrying a substantial amount of bullion, and in the evening of the following day, she crashed into a rocky headland and foundered. Nearly all the bullion was recovered later by ingenious not to say dramatic methods; and the captain, who had only taken over command the day the ship sailed, suffered only the loss of one year's seniority. The next calamity to befall a British *Thetis* was to a new submarine of this name in 1939. She sank, in Liverpool Bay, on her first dive, while still under trial, with the loss of 99 people including a number of civilians. The disaster seems to have been due to composite errors, but in the fashion of the times, it is now the subject of conspiracy theories..

A Spanish frigate, *Thetis,* met with a more conventional misfortune while Spain was in alliance with France. She was taken off Finisterre in October 1799 by *H.M.S. Ethalion,* and what a prize! She was carrying specie valued at 1,411,256 dollars and a cargo of cocoa, but it is not known if 'Pusser's kye' was then a naval staple second only to rum. The French frigate, *Thetis,* was captured in 1808 (see 10 November, H.M.S. Amethyst).

18 CAPE CARMEL (A.K.A. ACRE III) 1799, ISRAEL (FRENCH REVOLUTIONARY WARS)

Commanders: Captain Sir Sidney Smith v. Rear –Adml. Perrée & Napoleon

Napoleon had gone to Egypt with the intention of conquering the Ottoman Empire thus opening the way to India, but the British naval victory at Abukir Bay (see 1 August) had cut him off from France. Consequently, he decided to march his army back to Europe and was supported by a French flotilla of eight ships with a battering train of siege artillery and equipment. En route to Acre, the French had taken Jaffa (now Tel Aviv) by storm, and now, sixty miles further on, exhilarated by this success, Napoleon attempted to repeat the feat of Richard the Lionheart in 1191 and drive the Turks from Acre. The defence of the city was reinforced by Sir Sidney Smith's small British flotilla the guns of which protected most of the city, and its first contribution was a brilliant operation that captured or destroyed the French flotilla transporting the siege train. The arcs of fire of the British ships compelled the French to confine their assaults to the north-eastern sector of the city, but all of their assaults were repulsed largely by guns brought up by Smith to cover breaches made in the walls and by flank fire from the ships. In fierce fighting during the last days of the siege, Djezza Pasha, seated in view of the French, was to be seen paying 50 piastres for every French head, while the French made sixteen unsuccessful night attacks. The number of casualties, including eight generals, widespread disease, and the arrival of Turkish reinforcements sent the French into full retreat to Cairo pausing only to massacre the prisoners and poison their own wounded (arguably a humanitarian act). The would-be conqueror of Egypt and the East left the army behind (see 8 March Abukir) and managed to slip back to France in a corvette, where within a few months he climbed out of the political disorder to become the First Consul and soon Emperor. Later, he said of Sir Sidney Smith: "That man caused me to miss my destiny"; perhaps he had contemplated emulating Alexander the Great's conquest of India.

Sir Sidney's outstanding performance at Acre was recognized by a vote of thanks in both the Lords and the Commons, and the award of a pension of £1,000 p.a. Napoleon's chagrin would have been greater if he had realized that only a year before this battle Smith had been a French prisoner-of-war but managed to escape and make his way back to Britain where he rejoined the Navy. Smith had a colourful career. Entering the Navy at 13, he quickly distinguished himself in early battles against the French and was a post-captain five years later. Between 1789 and 1791, he was advising the King of Sweden in the maritime war against Russia, for which services he was awarded a Swedish knighthood subsequently confirmed by George III. Strongly invidualistic, Smith found it difficult to co-operate and was unkindly referred to by his contemporaries as the 'Swedish knight'. However, his abilities were such that he continued to be promoted and became a rear admiral in 1805. Two years later, he succeeded in taking the Portuguese royal family from Lisbon to safety in Brazil from under the nose of an invading French army. Having made a successful career in fighting the French, after Smith retired, he went to live in France where he felt his personality was better appreciated than in Britain; but by this time Napoleon was confined to St. Helena. (see also 3 January H.M.S. Diamond and 19 December Toulon).

19 BARFLEUR & LA HOUGUE, FRANCE 1692 (WAR OF THE LEAGUE OF AUGSBURG)

Commanders: Adml. Edward Russell et al. v. Adml. Comte de Tourville.

Fought off the Cherbourg peninsula and the Channel Islands, this was the beginning of a major fleet action (96 allied ships v. 111 ships) that went on for five days. An Anglo-Dutch fleet engaged a French fleet in light winds, and the action was interrupted by a thick fog; after a partial resumption both sides anchored for the night. In this phase, the French flag ship was badly damaged. Action the following day was limited by light winds and an unfavourable tide but resumed in earnest the next day when the French ships were forced to shelter in several bays with the allied ships anchoring outside. Serious damage was sustained by the French on May 22 when three large ships-of-the-line were burned in Cherbourg Bay by the English Red Squadron under the command of Sir Ralph Delavall. During the next two days, the action was completed in the Bay of la Hougue, principally by the English Blue Squadron commanded by Vice-Admiral George Rooke, where all of the French ships that had retreated there were burned. In addition to the naval ships, the French transports and store ships were also destroyed. The French were attempting to land an army in England in support of the exiled James II (which explains why the English and Dutch were allies, William of Orange having taken James'place) but this battle put an end to the plan. With this commanding victory, the English sailors established a decided superiority over the French marine and ended Colbert's dream of French supremacy at sea; except for a few brief intervals, this mastery continued throughout the eighteenth century until Trafalgar (see 21 October) was, to say the least, 'game, set and match'.

The commanders on both sides were prominent officers. Tourville was a marshal of France, as well as an admiral, with extensive naval experience. In the Third Dutch War (1672-74) he had commanded a French ship which fought with the English against the Dutch at the battles of Solebay and Texel, but his actions against the English fleet were not particularly successful because of excessively cautious tactics. A year after Barfleur, Tourville again confronted Delavall who was in command of a large convoy of some 400 ships. Although the convoy was at his mercy, the larger part of it was able to escape for which Tourville is generally blamed, although Louis XIV took no action against him. Delavall was not so fortunate; he was found to be mainly to blame for the loss of a hundred ships and relieved of his command of the Channel fleet. William III came to his rescue because Delavall had brought to him the loyalty of the Navy on his accession in place of James II for which service Delavall was knighted, and now he was appointed one of the Lords Commissioners of the Admiralty. A good example of the truth of the old saying that three things are required for a successful career – luck, influence and merit, but any two will do.

19 ALMAREZ 1812, SPAIN (PENINSULA WAR)

Commanders: Lt. Genl. Sir Rowland Hill v. ?
Forces: 4,500 British + 2,500 Portuguese; French 1,000.

The French occupied 3 forts guarding the key bridge over the river Tagus. In the face of heavy fire, Fort Napoleon was captured, and a substantial part of the garrison hastily retreated towards the bridge of Almaraz. The pursuing British captured the bridgehead, and the garrison of Fort Ragusa fled in a panic. The bridge was destroyed, and the forts demolished. The key link between two French armies was now broken. For more on Hill's achievements and career, see 28 October, Arroyo dos Molinos; 20 February, Bejar; 30 October, Puente Larga; and 13 December, St. Pierre.

19 H.M.S. NORTHUMBERLAND (74 GUNS) & H.M.S. GROWLER (12 GUNS) V. ARIANNE (44 GUNS), ANDROMAQUE (44 GUNS) & MAMELUKE(18 GUNS) 1812, FRANCE (NAPOLEONIC WAR)

Commanders: Captain H. Hotham & Lt.H.Anderson v. ?

As the French ships were leaving L'Orient, Hotham brought his ships inshore to engage, and by skilful manœuvring he caused his opponents to run aground close to Ile de Groix. *Northumberland* now set up a steady bombardment that forced the French crews to seek safety ashore, and this was continued by *Growler* when *Northumberland* stood off to repair her rigging. All of the French ships were destroyed by fire and explosions. British casualties were small – 4 killed and 23 wounded.

Fifteen years previously, the impending appointment of Hotham to command a frigate had given rise to a mutiny (see 4 January H.M.S. Blanche), but he was obviously a capable commander and had been able to rise to command a ship of the line.

An incident aboard *Northumberland* the year previously gives a glimpse of another side of daily life aboard. The captain's clerk and his assistant were found guilty by court martial of forging certificates of leave and absence for which they charged between one and seven pounds (roughly three to twenty-one weeks' wages for an able bodied seaman). Although each man was able to produce an excellent certificate of good conduct, the captain's clerk was sentenced to 500 lashes around the fleet and his assistant to 50 lashes.

20 LINCOLN 1217, ENGLAND (ANGLO-FRENCH WARS) "THE FAIR OF LINCOLN"

Commanders: William Marshal, Earl of Pembroke v. Comte de la Perche.

This battle was part of a civil war in which the royalists supporting the child king, Henry III, son of John, fought the forces of the Dauphin of France, Louis, who was backed by some of the barons as a rival candidate for the throne. The insurgents were besieging Lincoln castle when they were attacked by a relief force. There was fierce fighting in the streets, and the French commander was killed, nevertheless, as about half of the knights surrendered, the battle came to be looked on as something of a farce and was dubbed the Fair of Lincoln (for the final instalment, see 24 August, Sandwich).

The Earl of Pembroke had risen from being a younger son of a minor noble to regent of England at the time of this battle; his advancement was due to the patronage of Henry II in return for services rendered to him and his sons and also to marriage to an heiress; an example of social mobility in feudal times. In the next century, Pembroke's descendants were prominent in the Hundred Years' War (see 26 August, Crécy; 21 October, Auberoche; 2 December, Aiguillon; 3 April, Nájera).

Incidentally, it was during an earlier siege of Lincoln castle that King Stephen was captured and imprisoned (see 28 September, Tinchebrai).

20 BASTIA 1794, CORSICA (FRENCH REVOLUTIONARY WARS)
Commanders: Captain Horatio Nelson & Lt. Col. W.Villettes v.
Lacombe St. Michel.

The British fleet in the Mediterrnean was commanded by Adml. Viscount Samuel Hood who wished to find a base. He sent Nelson, in command of *H.M.S. Agamemnon*, to report on the suitability of Bastia, and Nelson made an optimistic assessment that, with the support of naval guns, 500 men would be sufficient. Hood decided to proceed, but the army commander, Lord Dundas, refused to take part without at least 2,000 troops. An angry correspondence failed to effect an agreement, and Hood decided that the navy would act without the army. A force of 1,200 marines and 250 seamen was landed with Nelson and Villettes in command, artillery support was provided by guns landed from the ships and put in place with great difficulty. The town was strongly fortified, and operations were directed against the forts. In the bombardment and counter-bombardment, the defenders of Bastia suffered far more than the attackers, and after about six weeks the French surrendered, some 4,500 troops being taken prisoner. Nelson was lyrical: "At daylight this morning, the most glorious sight which an Englishman, and I believe none but an Englishman, could experience was to be seen: 4,500 men laying down their arms to less than 1,000 English soldiers." During the siege flying fragments hit Nelson in the back, but the wound was not serious, and generally British casualties were only about one-tenth of the French. Throughout the siege, the British were assisted by the local population who had risen against the French, and in a formal expression of support, the Parliament of Corsica passed a motion declaring that all Corsicans were Englishmen and King George III was King of Corsica; Sir Gilbert Elliot was appointed Viceroy. The man who became Corsica's most famous son, Napoleon Buonaparte, had recently begun to fight against Britain and was to continue to do so for twenty years; think what might have happened to the history of the world if this action of his countrymen had persuaded him to join with Britain in fighting the French!

21 TREATY OF TROYES 1420, FRANCE (HUNDRED YEARS'WAR)

A few months after the capture of Rouen (see 20 January), Henry V had a great piece of luck. The two rival parties in France, the Armagnacs and Burgundians, met to arrange to join together against the English invaders. As a preliminary, the Armagnacs acted as if they thought the alliance would proceed more smoothly if the Duke of Burgundy were out of the way and murdered him. The result was that the Burgundians and Queen Isabella (her husband Charles VI was incapacitated by insanity) appealed to the English for assistance against the Armagnacs, and Henry was quick to take advantage of his opportunity. On 21 May 1420 the Treaty was signed and sealed in the Cathedral, and it declared that after the death of Charles VI, Henry and his successors would succeed to the French throne, and in the meantime he would be the Regent of France. The Dauphin was disinherited, and as an additional bar to his succession the Queen, his mother, declared the King was not his father and that he was the illegitimate by-blow of an extra-marital affair. However, the Dauphin did not accept the Treaty thereby ensuring that the war would continue. Later in the day, and also in the Cathedral, the official betrothal of Henry and the king's youngest daughter, Catherine of Valois, was witnessed. The marriage took place on 2 June, and there is reason to believe that it was a love-match as well as a dynastic union, certainly Shakespeare treated it as such in his play 'Henry V' in which for better dramatic effect he puts Henry's wooing into prose instead of blank verse. News of the Treaty generated great enthusiasm and excitement in England, and a solemn procession was made to St. Paul's Cathedral to give thanks for it.

These plans that appeared to promise so much came to an end two years later with the premature death of Henry (see 2 May Meaux). Catherine had borne Henry a son who became Henry VI and was crowned Henri II of France in 1431, but his incompetence was compounded by bouts of insanity, seemingly inherited from his maternal grandfather, and he lost both thrones; he was murdered on the instructions of Edward IV (see 29 August Treaty of Picquigny). However, Catherine achieved some posthumous, dynastic success to compensate for Henry VI. As a widow, she married a Welsh squire, Owen Tudor, and was the grandmother of Henry VII.

21 PORT ROYAL (ANNAPOLIS ROYAL) 1690, CANADA (WAR OF THE LEAGUE OF AUGSBURG)

Commanders: Sir William Phips v.Louis-Alexandre Des Friches de Meneval.

Acadia, on the frontier of New France, was the scene of early conflicts between the French and the colonists of New England. On the French side, hostilities took the form of raids on settlements, often accompanied by Indian allies, and privateering from the Bay of Fundy directed against fishing vessels and the mercantile trade of Boston, Salem, and other ports along the coast; in response, English retaliations steadily increased. These activities were not limited to times when the parent countries were at war, but when that was the case, the level of the North American conflict was raised, particularly with the participation of European troops. The deposition of James II by William III and Mary in 1689 led directly to a serious war with France, and an opportunity for the colonists with a leader who had been able to secure the attention of influential people in London. The appointment of Phips as Provost Marshal of the new Dominion of New England did not survive the fall of James II, but it did not matter because almost at once he was sworn in as major-general to command an expedition against Port Royal, the capital of Acadia, organized by the government of Massachusetts. The expense was defrayed significantly by a subscription raised among the merchants of Boston and Salem – a form of support quite beyond the French settlers. Phips sailed with seven ships armed with 78 cannon, transports, and about 750 troops, more than half of whom were a militia regiment. Having dealt with Castine, Le Havre, and Chedabucto (Halifax) along the way, this force anchored off Port Royal. The defences were in disarray – the fort was incomplete, the guns had not been mounted, there were only about 70 soldiers, and for several years internal quarrels had sapped communal strength. It was painfully obvious that resistance was hopeless, and Meneval surrendered. It is arguable that the initial, oral terms of surrender were abrogated on both sides, but the victors pillaged the settlement severely, a practice general on both sides and worse when Indians ran loose. The soldiers were imprisoned in the church; the governor, Meneval, was confined to his house under guard; the Massachusetts' militia ransacked houses and gardens, seized the wheat and the clothes of the settlers, killed those cattle which were not taken away, and burned the stockade. Phips provided some detail: "We cut down the cross, rifled the Church, pulled down the High-Altar, breaking their images." (for another example of the militant, religious fervour of New England, similar to European practice, at this time see 16 June, Louisbourg I). Before sailing back to Boston in triumph, Phips forced the settlers to take an oath of allegiance to William III and Mary and appointed an administrative council pending a Massachusett's administration.

Phips was an extraordinary character. He was born in modest circumstances in what is now Maine, and learned the trade of ship's carpenter, but then married a wealthy widow. He is next recorded as hunting sunken Spanish treasure, and he succeeded in raising funds in London to finance an exploration in the Bahamas, this had little success, but the second Duke of Albemarle organized a joint-stock company to fund a second expedition which made everyone rich including Phips. Outstanding performance with a joint-stock company brought Phips a knighthood (a practice that continues) as well as the appointment of Provost Marshal of New England. In spite of a failure to capture Quebec later in the year, Phips was appointed by the crown to be the first royal governor of Massachusetts. Except for one important decision, he was not a success in this role; although ample courage and energy enabled him to mount an effective defence of the frontier against the French and Indians, he has been described as "ignorant, brutal, covetous, and violent". At the beginning of his term, the witchcraft mania was at its height, and Phips' crowning achievement was to put an end to the executions and to reprieve all of those who had been condemned. The criticisms made against him were sufficiently strong to have him recalled to England to answer charges, including his assault on and persecution of Captain Richard Short, R.N., but he died of a fever before the investigation had been completed. He was buried in the church of St. Mary Woolnoth in Lombard Street, London, since rebuilt.

Meneval had been appointed governor of Acadia two years before the capture of Port Royal. Although he was honest and anxious to serve well, he was not suited for his position. Querulous and captious, his decisions were often arbitrary and immoderate, more immediately, in spite of being a soldier he failed to build adequate fortifications and to develop a defensive plan. After several months of imprisonment in Boston, during which time he claimed that Phips had robbed him of most of his clothes and money, Meneval returned to France. The lawyer in Boston who held his power of attorney to pursue his claim against Phips had been put in prison, and with Phips as governor, the claim went into abeyance; after Phips' death, he tried, unsuccessfully, through diplomatic channels to obtain reimbursement from Phips' widow and heirs.

22 TOURNAI 1794, BELGIUM (FRENCH REVOLUTIONARY WARS)

Commanders: Maj. Genl. Henry Edward Fox v. Genl. Jean-Charles Pichegru.

At the end of a day of heavy fighting the French occupied the village of Pont à Chin, then, at 9 p.m., the British brigade attacked with colours flying and their bands playing. The French scrambled away as best they could, and an hour later it was all over. Pichegru and his senior officers were dining nearby when the cry "Les Anglais, les habits rouges!" caused a panic, and the French commander-in-chief and his officers were left climbing out of windows to escape. Films have been made of less dramatic stuff.

The French lost 7 guns and at least 6,000 men of whom 280 were beheaded by an Austrian battery which caught them wedged in an orchard. The British and Allied casualties were about 4,000.

23 RAMILLIES 1706, BELGIUM (WAR OF THE SPANISH SUCCESSION)

Commanders: Marlborough v. Marshal, le Duc de Villeroi & the Elector of Bavaria

Forces: British & Dutch: 62,000; French, with Spanish & Bavarians 60,000.

Each side was intent on battle, and when the morning fog lifted both were surprised to find the other side much closer than had been expected. Deployments for battle had to be decided coolly and quickly, and in doing so Marlborough gained an advantage that he did not lose throughout the day. The fact that it was Whitsunday did not inhibit either side, and after the guns had opened up at about 1.00 p.m., Marlborough began with attacks on the flanks. The success of these thrusts led Villeroi into tactical errors, the effect of which was magnified by Marlborough's demonstration of his gift for sizing up a position, and skill at controlling the form and detail of a major conflict. Deciding to make his main assault through the centre, a large scale cavalry action took place in which at a critical point Marlborough himself led two charges sword in hand; in one he was thrown from his horse and was ridden over but was finally rescued and provided with a fresh horse. Five hours after the start, the final Anglo-Dutch attack went in and reduced the French to chaos when the reserves that were rushed to strengthen resistance became entangled with the tents and baggage wagons that had been parked too close to the battlefield. A retreat began which soon developed into headlong flight in which one participant reported that after retreating less than 40 yards the cry of 'sauve qui peut' became general. The French forfeited their entire camp and most of their guns as well as 80 standards and colours; killed, wounded and captured amounted to at least 13,000 against 1,066 killed and 2,560 wounded. Pursuit of the vanquished was ruthless and continued into the small hours of the following day. The victory had strategic consequences. As described by a major biographer of Marlborough: "this victory decided the destiny of the Low countries … after the battle a general revolution followed … and the allies were blessed with a continued chain of conquests". With the French in disarray, forts were surrendered offering no resistance, the principal ones were Louvain (see 25 May), Vilvorde (see 26 May), and Brussels (see 28 May). Showing a grasp of strategy, also adopted by Wellington (see 10 November, Nivelle), Marlborough issued strict orders against marauding and looting in order that the inhabitants might better regard the allies as liberators rather than conquerors. Finally, Ghent, Bruges and Damme were abandoned, and Villeroi was left to plan the defence of the French frontier.

Villeroi was seriously outclassed here; he was a marshal of France but owed more of the rank to the favour of Louis XIV than to merit. His father had been the governor of Louis XIV during the latter's minority, and in time had been made Duc de Villeroi and appointed a marshal. Only six years younger than Louis, an accomplished courtier and a glass of fashion, Villeroi grew up in Louis' company and was a favourite until his death. Promoted rapidly in the army, Villeroi's limitations were soon recognized by his comrades if not by the king. He was taken prisoner at Cremona by Prinz Eugen, although the town was held, and this experience inspired a wicked lampoon:

Par la faveur de Bellone (Bellona)
Et un bonheur sans égal
Nous avons conservé Cremone
- et perdu notre général.

Perhaps no one was bold enough to recite it to the king. Although Villeroi was soon replaced after Ramillies, he did not lose favour, and Louis consoled him with the comment: "At our age, one is no longer lucky." Meanwhile, Marlborough, six years younger, continued to make his own luck.

The catastrophic defeat at Ramilles coupled with losses in Italy decided Louis XIV to seek peace terms, and the allies had a great opportunity to secure a substantial part of their objectives. The opportunity was lost through a combination of self-centred political intrigues in Britain, and serious arguments about strategy between Britain, Holland and Austria in the course of which the Austrian emperor offered Marlborough the governor-generalship of the Spanish Netherlands (Marlborough diplomatically and generously refused). The war continued, and France was able to make good some of its losses and obtain better terms than those it was willing to concede in 1706 (see 11 April Treaty of Utrecht).

Ramillies has achieved such prominence in British military history that four ships of the Royal Navy have been named *Ramillies,* the last being a battleship commissioned in the First World War and taking part in the hunting of the Bismarck in the next one; the ship was the principal of the attack force at Madagascar (see 5 November) where it was damaged by the Japanese but not by the French.

23 FAMARS 1793, FRANCE (FRENCH REVOLUTIONARY WARS)
Commanders: Prince of Saxe-Coburg and the Duke of York v. Genl. Adam Custine.

The French were protecting the road to Valenciennes which was the Allies main objective, but withdrew when attacked, offering only slight resistance. The French commander was guillotined for this defeat and for lack of fighting spirit. This sentence is thought to have been a factor in the subsequent improvement in French performance during these wars.

23 H.M.S. AMAZON (38 GUNS) V. CUPIDON (14 GUNS) 1811, FRANCE (NAPOLEONIC WAR)

Commanders: Captain William Parker v. ?

Cupidon was a privateer brig two days out of Bayonne when taken as a prize. *Cupidon* had a crew of 82 among whom were 4 Englishmen posing as Americans; they were arrested and sent for trial at the Old Bailey charged with bearing arms with the King's enemies. In defence, they pleaded that they were pretending to be Americans while waiting for an opportunity to seize *Cupidon* and sail her to an English port. There was some corroboration for this plea, but two of the accused were proved to have served in another French privateer and were hanged.

25 LOUVAIN 1706, BELGIUM (WAR OF THE SPANISH SUCCESSION)

Commanders: Marlborough v. ?

This fort was about 18 miles from Ramillies, and it fell without offering any resistance two days after that battle (see 23 May).

26 VILVORDE 1706, BELGIUM (WAR OF THE SPANISH SUCCESSION)

Commanders: Marlborough v. ?

In the line of pursuit from Ramillies (see 23 May), Vilvorde, just a few miles north of Brussels, capitulated without waiting for a blast from Marlborough's trumpets.

27 YOUGHIOGHENNY 1754, PENNSYLVANIA,U.S.A. (FRENCH & INDIAN WAR)

Commanders: Lt. Col.George Washington v. Capt. Coleton de Jumouville.

Robert Dinwiddie, the Lieutenant-Governor of Virginia, wanted to establish the claims of the Ohio Company in the Ohio Valley where the Company had been awarded a massive land grant, and pressing these claims met with French resistance centred on Fort Duquesne (now Pittsburgh). Dinwiddie was a member of the Ohio Company, as was George Washington and his brother Lawrence. Dinwiddie mustered a force of the Virginia militia and placed the 22 years old George, then serving as a surveyor, in command. The Virginians marched west and were met by a combined force of French and Indians not far from Fort Duquesne. The French and Indians sustained heavy casualties and a number were taken prisoner. As soon as victory had been secured, the Virginians began constructing a fort that was named Necessity. This action was one of several on either side that served to provoke the Seven Years' War (a.k.a. French and Indian War in North America where the duration was nine years rather than seven), but for other provocations see 28 February *H.M.S. Monmouth* & 10 June Newfoundland.

Dinwiddie was an experienced colonial administrator some of whose taxation policies were controversial, but he also took every opportunity to press the cause of the New England colonists, in particular by promoting inter-colonial co-operation against the French. Until his return to England in 1758, Dinwiddie was very active in raising ranger companies (see 29 November Detroit) and a regiment under the command of George Washington.

28 BRUSSELS 1706, BELGIUM (WAR OF THE SPANISH SUCCESSION)

Commanders: Marlborough v. Marshal, le Duc de Villeroi.

As the capital of the Spanish Netherlands, the political importance of Brussels was probably greater than its military one, but into the bag it went along with the others (see 23 May Ramillies).

29 VOLCONDA 1752, INDIA (CARNATIC WAR)

Commanders: Captain Robert Clive v. M. d'Auteuil.

Volconda lies between Pondicherry and Trichinopoly. A French convoy was proceeding to relieve the forces on Sriringham Island, near Trichinopoly, when it was trapped by Clive, and d'Auteuil was forced to surrender.

29 H.M.S. CARYSFORT (28 GUNS) V. CASTOR (32 GUNS) 1794, FRANCE (FRENCH REVOLUTIONARY WARS)

Commanders: Captain F.Laforey v. Captain L'Huillier.

A dramatic action fought in the Bay of Biscay that could serve as a forerunner of the daring rescue of captured British seamen in Jossing Fjord, Norway, in World War II by *H.M.S. Cossack*. *Castor* was a British frigate that had been captured three weeks before this encounter; she was recaptured and 20 British seamen were released.

The commander of *Castor* when she was captured was Captain Troubridge who later was one of Nelson's 'band of brothers', but notwithstanding distinguished service against the French, he seems to have been unlucky. After his release from captivity, he commanded *Culloden* at the Battle of the Nile (see 1 August), but in his anxiety to get into action he put her aground and was not able to take part. Later, he was appointed to command the eastern half of the East India Station, but on his arrival the command was changed to that of the Cape station, and on his way there his ship was lost with all hands in a cyclone. Napoleon is said to have placed great store on his generals being lucky, and it does not seem that Troubridge would have met this test.

30 DAMME 1213, BELGIUM (ANGLO-FRENCH WARS)
Commanders: Earl of Salisbury v. ?

An Engish fleet of 500 ships attacked a French fleet supporting the invasion of Flanders by Philippe Augustus, and 300 French ships were captured and 100 burned. At this period, naval engagements were mainly static, and the ships, small in size, were largely manned by soldiers. Damme was the port of the city of Bruges, one of the most important cities in northern Europe during the Middle Ages, but owing to the silting of the river Zwijn, Damme is now a small land-locked agricultural community. The English commander, William Longsword, was an illegitimate son of Henry II who obtained his title through a marriage arranged by his half-brother, Richard I. Until the 18th.Century, military men sometimes fought on land and sometimes on the sea, and Longsword is an example. In 1214 he was in command of the right wing of the English-Flemish-German army at the battle of Bouvines where he was taken prisoner and later exchanged. When not engaged in fighting, Longsword was a benefactor of Salisbury cathedral where he is buried, and his splendid effigy can still be seen.

30 PORT-AU-PRINCE 1794, HAITI (FRENCH REVOLUTIONARY WARS)

Commanders: Cdre. J. Ford & Brig. Genl. Whyte v. ?

This action was a continuation of the occupation of Santo Domingo (see 22 September). Cdre. Ford's squadron landed the troops that stormed and took Fort Brizotten after which the French retreated and abandoned the town. The booty included 13,870 tons of shipping and an immense quantity of sugar, coffee, cotton, and indigo.

30 TREATY OF PARIS 1814, FRANCE (NAPOLEONIC WAR)

This treaty was meant to bring to an end the long war against France. The signatories were France and the members of the Sixth Coalition – Great Britain, Austria, Prussia, Russia, Sweden, Spain and Portugal. The terms were surprisingly lenient to the French, but the victors were concerned to assist the newly restored Bourbon monarchy, in the person of Louis XVIII, to establish its position. In Europe, the French frontiers were reduced to those of 1792; and Britain was able to secure a number of islands important to a country with world-wide trading interests – these were Malta, Tobago, St. Lucia and Mauritius. France also promised Britain to end the slave trade, although the trade was not abolished by Britain and its colonies until 1833. An interesting feature of the Treaty with contemporary relevance is that France was permitted to keep the works of art plundered by the French armies. The Treaty also confirmed the abdication of Napoleon on April 11, 1814 and his title of 'Emperor of Elba' with an annual payment from France of two million francs. In the event, the Treaty did not end the war. Barely ten months after it was signed, the Emperor of Elba landed in France and was met with considerable popular support; he seized power, recruited a new army, and marched into Belgium where, literally, he met his Waterloo (see 18 June).

31 ESLA SPAIN 1813, (PENINSULA WAR)

Commanders: Lt. Genl. Sir Thomas Graham v. ?

This engagement was an important prelude to the expulsion of the French from Spain.The left wing of the British army had to advance from Portugal and to swing round the northern wing of the French army.

The first major obstacle was the river Esla, and although it was lightly defended, the river had to be forded in several different places. The cavalry led the way, and many riders had an infantry man hanging on to a stirrup. A number of horses and men were drowned, but a pontoon bridge was built when a sufficient number had crossed. The French were swept aside, and their position was turned. Wellington's march to Vitoria continued (see 21 June) with the hero of Barossa helping to clear the way (see 5 March).

JUNE

I ALCANTARA 1706, SPAIN (WAR OF SPANISH SUCCESSION)
Commanders: Lord Galway v. Marshal the Duke of Berwick.

The British attacked the town of Alcantara, and the garrison, comprising ten French battalions, surrendered with the loss of 60 guns. The French commander was the illegitimate son of James, Duke of York (later James II) and Arabella Churchill, the sister of the Duke of Marlborough who became the scourge of the French in this war. Berwick was born and educated in France, and when his father was deposed in 1688, he went to France and was given various commands in the French Army. Much of his career was spent fighting the British, but never in command against his illustrious- and invincible- uncle. Berwick met a soldier's death being cut in two by a cannonball at Phillipsburg when fighting the Austrians.

I PLACENTIA 1713, CANADA (WAR OF THE SPANISH SUCCESSION)
Commanders: Captain John Moody v. Philippe de Costebelle.

The French Governor, Philippe de Costebelle, surrendered Placentia to the British force and moved to Ile Royale (Cape Breton). This victory marked the end of French efforts to take control of Newfoundland. Placentia (Plaisance to the French) had been maintained as a fort from which to harass British settlements along the coast. Later, the Royal Navy established a base at Placentia, and its crowning glory came in August 1941 when Franklin D. Roosevelt and Winston Churchill met in the Bay and signed the Atlantic Charter. The United States had not yet entered the War, and the Charter was a propaganda manifesto of lofty and unexceptionable aims one of which was to disarm 'potential aggressors' (amongst other things, this might seem to cover the invasion of Iraq by the U.S.A., Britain , and Australia).

1 USHANT (THE GLORIOUS FIRST OF JUNE) 1794, FRANCE (FRENCH REVOLUTIONARY WARS)

Commanders: Adml. Earl Richard Howe v.Adml. Louis Thomas Villaret-Joyeuse.

Fought off Cape Ushant, the most westerly point of France dividing the Channel and the Bay of Biscay, this was a major battle in which both fleets were commanded by senior flag officers. The sides were evenly matched, but Howe's ships sank six of the French and captured a seventh ship-of-the-line without loss; 3,000 French died.

Howe, who was 68 at the time of this battle, had a glittering career largely at the expense of the French. Not only did he find favour with George III, but also with all ranks in the Navy. Nelson referred to him as "our great master in naval tactics and bravery"; and when the Channel Fleet mutinied three years after this battle it was Howe who was able to mediate a settlement on honourable terms with no subsequent victimization of the mutineers.

Villaret-Joyeuse was successful, but not to the same degree as Howe. He was promoted for gallantry at the siege of Pondicherry [see October 16] but was captured by the British three years' later after losing a single-ship action. He was also beaten by Cornwallis in operations in the Atlantic (see June 16). Difficulties developed for him with the new revolutionary government because of his royalist sympathies. He was able to resume his career after Napoleon assumed control, but he was usually on the losing side being forced to surrender Martinique, of which he was the captain-general, in 1809 (see 24 February). Not unnaturally, Napoleon was not best pleased, and it was not until two years later that Joyeuse was given another appointment, this time as a lieutenant-general and Governor of Venice.

A very unusual domestic foot-note is that during the battle a Mrs. McKenzie, on board *Tremendous*, a 74 gun ship-of-the-line, gave birth to a son who was christened Daniel Tremendous McKenzie. Fifty-four years later, Daniel received the Naval General Service Medal with clasp

'1st. June 1794'. Over the centuries, hundreds of thousands of Britons have died fighting the French, but, strange to say, Daniel is not the only one to have been born fighting them, a baby was born in *Goliath*, the first ship in action at the battle of the Nile (see 1 August). It was quite common, though unofficial, for at least a few women to be aboard most ships; they were usually the wives of warrant officers and ratings and might be found doing washing and acting as 'dressers' (nurses) when the ship was in action. One child, born off Leghorn in *Minotaur*, was fortunate in having the great Nelson to stand as godfather; but another had the misfortune to be made an orphan when only three weeks old because both parents, a seaman, Phelan, and his wife, were killed in action between *Swallow*, an 18-gun brig-sloop, and two more heavily armed French escort ships. This hotly-fought engagement took place near Toulon in 1812, close in-shore at 50 yards range, and after *Swallow* had rejoined the squadron, the crew, showing the resource for which sailors are renowned, arranged for the child, Tommy, to be suckled by the wardroom goat – and he thrived on this unusual diet and treatment.

2 MORALES 1813, SPAIN (PENINSULA WAR)

Commanders: Col. Colquhoun Grant v. Genl. Alexandre Digeon
Forces: 1,000 British cavalry; 900 French cavalry.

A relatively minor engagement during Wellington's advance through Spain towards France between a British reconnaissance in force and French cavalry in the rearguard of the retreating Army of the South. The 10th.Hussars, supported by the 18th, made a spirited charge that broke their opponents. This was an excellent start for the 10th. Hussars who had only just arrived from England. British casualties were 10, French 200.

6 ANTWERP 1706, BELGIUM. (WAR OF THE SPANISH SUCCESSION)

Commanders: Marlborough v. Marquis of Terracena.

Following the devastating victory at Ramillies (see 23 May), the French were in disarray as they tried to make plans for the defence of *la patrie*. There were opportunities for Marlborough to occupy a number of strategic locations, and one of them was the great port of Antwerp at the mouth of the Scheldt River. The Spanish Governor had no difficulty in persuading his French garrison to join him in surrender without even a token resistance; to the contrary, the victor was entertained to a feast in the bishop's palace. Antwerp had surrendered only once before in its history, and then after a siege of over a hundred days.

7 BELLE ISLE 1761, FRANCE (SEVEN YEARS'WAR)

Commanders: Cdre A.Keppel & Genl. Hodgson v. Genl. St. Croix.
Forces: British 8,000 + fleet convoy; French 3,000

Belle Isle is at the edge of Quiberon Bay, near the mouth of the Loire, where a number of major naval battles have taken place. At this date, the French Atlantic and Mediterranean fleets had suffered heavy damage (see August 17 Lagos Bay & November 20-22 Quiberon Bay), and Quiberon Bay had become almost an anchorage for the blockading British fleet. There was a French garrison on Belle Isle the destruction of which was the object of this amphibious operation. At first, the attack was hampered by foul weather, but then the British over-ran the entrenchments at Palais, and a 40 days' siege ended with the surrender of the Citadel.

The psychological effect of the victory in Britain and in France was greater than the scale of the operation might suggest. In Britain, the siege caught popular imagination and songs were written about it. In France, the occupation of part of metropolitan France was a humiliation for Louis XV; it was no consolation that the French were granted the honours of war and were permitted to march out of the Citadel in full dress uniform for repatriation to France. Such were the courtesies then, and for a later example, this time in reverse order, see January 16 Corunna.

7 FORT BALAGUER 1813 , SPAIN (PENINSULA WAR)

Commanders: Lt. Col. W. Prevost & Rear Adml. Sir Benjamin Hallowell v. ?
Forces: British 1,000 with 3 guns and support from *H.M.S. Invincible*, four other ships and eight gunboats; French 150 with17 guns and mortars.

This was an amphibious operation in which the navy played the major part. The British were besieging Tarragona, and Fort Balaguer blocked the only road open to a French relieving force, therefore it was necessary to take it. The troops were embarked and landed on 3 June with 2 field guns; a howitzer, two 12- pounders, six 24-pounders and two 8 inch mortars were supplied from the ships. All of this armament and all of the ammunition had to be manhandled by seamen and marines up a steep, rocky hill together with sand bags filled on the beach for the purpose of constructing batteries. When the work had nearly been completed, torrential rain brought it to a standstill, ruined much of it, and destroyed the ammunition. Undeterred, the damage was made good and completed under heavy fire from the defenders. Lt. James of the Royal Marine Artllery then directed the fire of the mortars with such precision that a magazine in the Fort was hit, and the explosion wreaked such devastation that the garrison surrendered before the breaching battery had opened fire. The French lost all of their guns, a large quantity of gunpowder and 110 muskets. The prisoners, including 16 Italian artillerymen, were embarked in the ships for transport to prison camp. With Fort Belaguer in British hands, French relief was not able to reach Tarragona, but unfortunately the cowardice of the commander, Lt. Genl. Murray, led the siege to be abandoned. This must have been very frustrating and disappointing for the inhabitants because when the city had been captured by the French two years before, there followed dreadful reprisals on the civilians in the form of the rape of women and children, wholesale slaughter and the burning of the city. None of this prevented the French commander, Suchet, from being promoted to Marshal for his victory.

Rear Admiral Hallowell was almost at the end of his distinguished service. He had served with Nelson in Corsica (see 20 May, Bastia & 1 August, Calvi), prominently at the Nile (see 1 August) where he made Nelson the eccentric present of a coffin made from a mast of the French flagship and was one of Nelson's 'band of brothers'. He is on record as saying that he had only been at home for 10 months in the 18 years he had been a captain, and this was not an unusual experience; Collingwood, for example, died on active service in 1810 complaining that he had not seen his wife and daughters in the seven years following the outbreak of the Napoleonic War. Hallowell died in his bed as Sir Benjamin Hallowell-Carew having changed his name to benefit under the terms of a will.

8 H.M.S SANTA MARGARITA (36 GUNS) & H.M.S. UNICORN (32) V. TAMISE (42) & TRIBUNE (48) 1796, CHANNEL (FRENCH REVOLUTIONARY WARS)

Commanders: CaptainThomas Byam Martin & Captain Thomas Williams v. Captain J.-B.-A.Fradin & Cdre. Moulson.

Fought westwards of the Scillies, when the two British frigates fell in with two larger French ships of the same class, and a corvette. After a running fight, Martin outmanœuvred *Tamise* and engaged at close quarters, less than twenty minutes later *Tamise* struck her colours. This was tit-for-tat because *Tamise* was originally the British frigate, *Thames,* that had been captured in 1793 and was now restored to its rightful owners; on the other hand, *Santa Margarita* had been taken from the Spanish when they had imprudently joined the French during the War of American Independence, and it remained in the Royal Navy until it was sold in 1836. *Santa Margarita's* senior lieutenant, George Harrison, was promoted to commander for his sterling performance, and those who were still living in 1849 were awarded medals. George was not among the survivors, but his promotion was much better value than a medal 53 years after the event.

Meanwhile, *Tribune* tried to escape with *Unicorn* in pursuit, and the running fight lasted for ten hours with the French displaying greater sailing skill than usual. Finally, *Tribune* had only the mizzen mast left standing, and *Unicorn* was able to engage more closely taking ten minutes longer than *Santa Margarita* to bring *Tribune* to book. *Unicorn* had no casualties, but the French had 37 killed and 15 wounded, including Cdre. Moulson. Thomas Williams was knighted, and by 1812 he had achieved promotion to rear admiral (see 7 January H.M.S. Unicorn & 21 March H.M.S. Peterell).

9 ST. POL DE LÉON 1346, FRANCE (HUNDRED YEARS' WAR)

Commanders: Sir Thomas Dagworth v. Charles de Blois.

The English had conducted a winter campaign which was now continued in the northern part of Brittany. Dagworth had been sent out with a flying column by the English commander, the Earl of Northampton, and several towns were taken. Charles de Blois, in pursuit, finally caught up with the English force on the coast with an army considerably greater in size. The first French attack was beaten back, but the second wave was able to overlap the English line on both flanks and to attack simultaneously from three sides. At this point, the English archers, standing their ground, delivered so many volleys of arrows that "a veritable massacre ensued" and the French were routed.

Dagworth established a considerable reputation for his victories in France, and a French historian has described him as: "The English Achilles who covered himself with glory in resisting with a handful of men the whole army of Charles de Blois". However, Dagworth was only one of a number of English commanders at this period who operated at the same level of excellence.

9 CONGRESS OF VIENNA 1815, AUSTRIA (NAPOLEONIC WAR)

The Treaty of Paris, 1814 (see 30 May) contained the principal terms of surrender for France after Napoleon's first abdication, and it provided for a Congress to be convened for the purpose of re-drawing national boundaries in Europe, the better to preserve peace, and generally to undo everything that Napoleon had done. The Congress began in October, 1814 and its Final Act was signed on 9 June, 1815, barely a week before Waterloo (see 18 June). The principal participants were Russia, Prussia, Austria and Britain, and France joined later. Some monarchs attended in person, but not at the meetings where the negotiations and bargaining were done; Prince von Metternich, the Austrian Chancellor, orchestrated the proceedings in the Viennese style, and many were the balls, banquets and other royal and aristocratic amusements which Talleyrand (of France) encapsulated in "*Le Congrès ne marche pas, mais il danse*". Britain was able to add Cape Colony, Seychelles, Ceylon, Trinidad and smaller colonies to its empire, and to establish itself as the predominant European colonial power. Crumbs that fell from the table for France included Martinique, Guadeloupe and Isle de Bourbon (Réunion). After Waterloo, these provisions were made less favourable to France by another Treaty of Paris (see 20 November).

10 NEWFOUNDLAND 1755 (FRENCH AND INDIAN WAR)

Vice-Adml. the Hon. E. Boscawen had been sent to North America in command of a squadron and with orders to intercept a large French reinforcement for Canada, which, considering that Britain and France were then at peace, was a most unusual instruction. Due to fogs off Newfoundland, Boscawen did not find the main French force, but he sighted three and captured *Alcide* and *Lys*; the other escaped to tell the tale. This event was a factor in the outbreak of war between Britain and France in 1756 (the Seven Years' War), as the Lord Chancellor, Hardwicke, put it Boscawen's limited success was at once "too little and too much"; too little to cause any real military damage to the French, and too much to be explained away as an aggression not precipitating war (but the British were not alone in provocative acts - see 28 February H.M.S. Monmouth et al.).

The French reinforcements had very limited effect. In 1758, the strongly fortified port of Louisbourg fell to an amphibious operation in which Boscawen commanded the fleet (see 27 July), and a year after that Quebec City was taken by Wolfe (see 13 September, Plains of Abraham). When hostilities were concluded by the Treaty of Paris 1763, all of the French possessions in Canada were ceded to Britain.

Boscawen made another important contribution to the British success by crippling French naval power in a spectacular fleet action in Lagos Bay (see 17 August). In addition to outstanding performances at sea, Boscawen had a domestic situation that many might have envied – he had married Fanny Glanville, a notable 'blue stocking', whose conversation, Dr. Johnson said, 'was the best of any woman whom he had met'.

10 HMS SOUTHAMPTON (32 GUNS) V. L'UTILE (24 GUNS) 1796, FRANCE (FRENCH REVOLUTIONARY WARS)

Commanders: Captain James Macnamara v. Lt. François Vega.

Although this action, fought off the island of Porquerolles, southern France, was on a small scale, it was a spectacular performance by *Southampton*. *L'Utile* was lying under the shore batteries on the island, and Macnamara was able to bring his ship within close range before being detected. After three broadsides, Lt. Charles Lydiard led a boarding party, and once their commander had been killed, the French surrendered. *L'Utile* was secured and towed away by Macnamara; she was only slightly damaged and was commissioned as a British sloop most appropriately under the command of Lt. Lydiard.

10 ST. CROIX 1800, FRANCE (FRENCH REVOLUTIONARY WARS)

This was a naval action, typical of many in this period, in which considerable bravery and skill were required. A squadron of the Channel fleet was patrolling Brest when a convoy of coastal ships was sighted at St. Croix in the shelter of a fort. Eight boats were launched from the ships and went inshore under heavy fire from the fort. Three armed vessels and eight merchant ships loaded with supplies for Brest were seized, and 20 others were run on to the rocks. The prizes were sent to Plymouth. Notwithstanding the great risks involved, operations of this kind were never short of volunteers. Lieutenants were put in command and welcomed the opportunity not only for substantial profit from prize money, but also for the chance to demonstrate their competence and performance under fire thereby enhancing their promotion prospects.

13 SENS 1420, FRANCE (HUNDRED YEARS' WAR)

Commanders: Henry V v. ?

The siege of Sens marked a new phase in the Hundred Years' War. As a result of the Treaty of Troyes (see 21 May) Henry was now the Regent of France, heir of the king, Charles VI, and he had married the king's daughter, Catherine of Valois, on June 2. These provisions disinherited the king's son, the Dauphin, who refused to accept the Treaty and began his rebellion. Nominally, the armies of France and England were now joined under Henry's command against the army of the Dauphin in which there were those from the parts of France that took his side as well as a number of mercenaries. From the French point of view, there was a civil war between the Burgundians and Armagnacs (Dauphinists), but Henry, who believed in the legitimacy of his claim to his French possessions to the point of fanaticism, saw the conflict as one in which a large number of French supported him against treasonous insurgents. Henry had marched at the head of his new army, after a honeymoon of only one day, against Sens, about 40 miles from Troyes. Charles VI, as well as the Duke of Burgundy, and both courts went with him. Only feeble resistance was offered by the garrison, and it surrendered after 6 days.

It so happens that it was the Archbishop of Sens, Henri de Savoisey, who had married Henry and Catherine, so he cannot have been on the side of the Dauphin; perhaps the capture of Sens enabled him to reside again in his see. The architect of Sens cathedral, William of Sens, also made an important contribution to the church in England. After a fire destroyed the choir of Canterbury Cathedral in 1174, William was responsible for the reconstruction of it and the eastern part of the building. This commission may have owed something to the murder of Thomas Becket in the cathedral four years before, and the subsequent efforts of Henry II to atone for it, but in any case, Thomas probably knew William because he lived in a monastery at Sens during his exile from England, 1166-70.

13 TRICHINOPOLY I 1752, INDIA (CARNATIC WARS)

Commanders: Major Stringer Lawrence v. Jacques Law & Chanda Sahib.

Forces: British 400 +1,100 sepoys and 100,000 Indian allies; French 900 + 2,000 sepoys and 30,000 Indian allies.

The French were besieging Trichinopoly and were handicapped by the incompetence of Law. Lawrence with Clive second-in-command was in command of the force sent to raise the siege, and these two soon demonstrated a mastery over Law. In the first attack, the British force advanced under heavy fire and then dominated in an artillery duel, so that the British marched unapposed into the town of Trichinopoly. A French night attack was beaten back, and they withdrew across the Coleroon River to the island of Sriringham (a.k.a. Srirangam). At this point, Clive proposed that the British army should be divided with one part sent a few miles north to Samiaveram in order to block the road from the main French base at Pondicherry, and the remainder be kept back to attack Sriringham. Clive commanded the northern contingent and duly repulsed a French relief effort. Lawrence then deployed his troops against Chanda Sahib's camp, and a heavy bombardment created such havoc that a large number of the Indian troops deserted. Three weeks later, without any realistic hope of being relieved, Law surrendered. 800 French were taken prisoner together with 2,000 sepoys, and 41 guns were captured.

The French defeat had wider, unfortunate consequences; it marked the beginning of the end of French ambitions for an empire in India. Two years later, the leader of the French in India, the Marquis Joseph-

Francois Dupleix was recalled to France where he sued the French East India Company (*Compagnie des Indes*) for money he claimed he had spent on its account. The law suit was unsuccessful, and Dupleix died in 1763 discredited and in poverty. He possessed great talents as an organizer and diplomat and at one point was on the verge of establishing a French empire in India, but lack of military acumen and inability to work with others brought failure.

Chanda Sahib's end was abrupt. He had been relying on the French to secure his succession to the nawabship of the Carnatic, but shortly after his capture at Trichinopoly, he was beheaded by one of the Indian allies of the British, and his head was sent to Mohammed Ali, the rival claimant, who was supported by the British in order to secure their "protectorate" in that part of India.

13 CUDDALORE 1783, INDIA (AMERICAN WAR OF INDEPENDENCE)

Commanders: Genl. Sir James Stuart v. Genl. The Marquis de Bussy-Castelnau with Tipu,Sultan of Mysore.

Forces: British 1,660 Europeans; 9,340 Indian troops. French: 3,000 Europeans; 8,000 Indian troops.

Strictly speaking, this was a battle between the English East India Company and its French counterpart (*Compagnie des Indes*). It took the form of an attack on the fort at Cuddalore which guarded the port used by the French for supplies and reinforcements. There was heavy fighting in which British casualties exceeded the French, but the latter were driven from their trenches and obliged to retreat into the fort. Simultaneously, there was a naval action off Cuddalore that was inconclusive. A peace treaty between Britain and France signed on June 28 led to the withdrawal of the French troops and ships.

An unusual feature of this engagement is that one of the French prisoners was a Sergeant Bernadotte, then 21 years old. Bernadotte supported the French Revolution and ten years after Cuddalore he was a brigadier-general; in ten more years he was a marshal of France. At Wagram, where Napoleon defeated the Austrians in 1810, Bernadotte suffered a serious setback to his French career. After the battle, he issued a general order claiming that his troops had a large part in the victory, but so incensed was Napoleon by this extravagant exaggeration that he stripped Bernadotte of his title and ridiculed him in front of senior officers. Four months later, in an astonishing change of fortune, Bernadotte was elected Crown Prince of Sweden, wrested Norway from Denmark in 1814, and became king of Sweden and Norway in 1818; his heirs continue to reign. Notwithstanding his advancement under Napoleon, in 1812 he joined the coalition against Bonaparte and continued in it until the final victory at Waterloo. At the time of Napoleon's first abdication in 1814, Lord Castlereagh, the British foreign secretary, and Metternich, the Austrian chancellor, seriously considered making Bernadotte King of France instead of Louis XVIII, but, perhaps in consolation, he was able to negotiate a subsidy from Britain to assist him in taking Norway from Denmark. In a remarkable career in which loyalty to the flag appears to have played no part, Bernadotte went from a private soldier in the Bourbon army to general in the Republican army to marshal of France, short-listed for the French monarchy, and finally king of Sweden and Norway. Napoleon's policy of careers open to talent could not have a better exemplar.

13 HMS DRYAD (44 GUNS) V. PROSERPINE (42 GUNS), IRELAND 1796 (FRENCH REVOLUTIONARY WARS)

Commanders: Captain Lord Amelius Beauclerk v. Captain E. Pevrieux.

This engagement was connected with those on June 8 (H.M.S. Santa Margarita &c.), *Proserpine* had lost contact with the other French ships in a fog, when she was sighted and chased by *Dryad*. Although having a much larger crew, *Proserpine* tried unsuccessfully to avoid action and was obliged to surrender. *Proserpine* began a new career in the British navy as *H.M.S. Amelia*, and Edward Durnford King, senior lieutenant in *Dryad*, was promoted to commander for his part in the victory. British casualties were 2 killed and 7 wounded compared with 30 French dead and 45 wounded.

15 KAISERSWERTH 1702, GERMANY (WAR OF THE SPANISH SUCCESSION)

Commanders: Prince Nassau-Saarbrücken v. Genl.Jules-Armand,
Marquis de Blainville

Forces: British & Allies 22,000; French 5,000.

William III died in March 1702 and was succeeded by his sister-in-law, Anne. In spite of personal feelings, before his death William had chosen Marlborough to assume command of the British army, and to command the Anglo-Dutch army in the alliance against Louis XIV in the War of the Spanish Succession. In England, compliance with his wishes was relatively easy because John Churchill and his wife Sarah were great favourites of Anne, but in the Netherlands overall command by him was politically unacceptable, and the compromise was a military handicap.

Kaiserswerth was an important fortress on the Rhine that was occupied by the French, and the siege of it three months after William's death was Marlborough's first action in command. The garrison put up a stout resistance, but a relief force arrived after it had been obliged to surrender with the full honours of war. British casualties were 2,900 and French 1,000.

By a tactical manœuvre for which he was to become renowned – even by the French (see 13 September, Bouchain) – Marlborough then put his army in a position to make a flank attack on the French army marching across his front that would certainly have resulted in a victory. The Dutch generals would not agree to an open battle, but when Marlborough insisted that they join him in watching the French march by, they had the grace to admit that they "had lost a fair opportunity of giving the enemy a fatal blow".

De Blainville is not prominent in military history, but his descendants feature in the eighteenth century history of North America. Pierre-Joseph Céloron de Blainville was active in enlarging the settlement of New France (Quebec) and became a prominent fur trader. In 1749, he commanded a French-Canadian army of regulars, militia, and Indians that marched through the valley of the Ohio and its tributaries with the intention of asserting the sovereignty of the King of France and rather quaintly planted lead plates recording the claim as he went along. This effort succeeded for several years in keeping the New England colonists east of the Alleghenies – an early attempt by the Virginians led by the young George Washington to persuade the French to withdraw failed – but all was lost in 1763 when France was obliged to surrender all of its North American territories by the Treaty of Utrecht (see 11 April). Nevertheless, the Blainville name lingers on in Quebec; the city of Sainte Thérèse is named after Céloron's daughter.

16 LOUISBOURG I 1745, CANADA (WAR OF THE AUSTRIAN SUCCESSION)

Commanders: Col. W. Pepperell & Cdre.Peter Warren v. Louis du Pont Duchambon, Acting Governor of the Fort.

Louisbourg on the north-east coast of what is now Nova Scotia was strongly fortified and strategically important in commanding the entrance to the St. Lawrence River as well as serving as a port of call for French ships returning to France from the East Indies and the Pacific. The operation owed much to William Shirley, the Governor of Massachusetts, who was impressed by the reports of two returned prisoners of war (one of whom was John Bradstreet - see 27 August) that the defences were weaker than was supposed, and the morale of the garrison was low. Shirley was vigorous in organizing the expedition including the transport of troops from Boston. An additional inspiration to the New England force was religious fervour; the Methodist preacher, George Whitefield, supplied a motto *'Nil Desperandum Christo Duce'* (No need to despair with Christ as your leader) – adapted from Horace, and the senior chaplain, Parson Moody, carried an axe with which 'to hew down the altars of Antichrist at Louisbourg'. The besieging troops were the Maine Militia supported by the British Navy. During the close blockade of the harbour, a French ship of the line, *Vigilant*, tried to land ammunition and other supplies, but the British ships took the ship as a prize, and then forced their way into the harbour under the guns of the fort. The garrison, demoralized by the loss of supplies, was in a state of mutiny and the Governor surrendered.

The fall of Louisbourg was something of a sensation. Built at enormous expense, it was the largest French fortress in Canada, and now it had been taken by part-time soldiers; conversely there was great celebration throughout New England. Valuable prizes of merchant shipping and their cargo were taken, Pepperell was awarded a baronetcy and Warren was promoted to Rear-Admiral.

The following year the French planned to recapture Louisbourg, take Annapolis Royal, destroy Boston and harry the whole New England coast; it was much the largest effort France had ever made to secure its North American colonies. A fleet of 54 ships left La Rochelle intending to link with troops from Quebec, but it encountered violent storms in the Atlantic and was forced to take shelter in Halifax harbour. The commander in chief, the Duc d'Enville, was one of three thousand sailors and soldiers who died of a plague; the second in command attempted suicide; and the third in command, de la Jonquière, led the remnants of the expedition back to France without having fired a shot (see 3 May Cape Finisterre I); such was the disorder that one of the ships was reduced to cannibalism. However, all was not lost, in 1748 to the great chagrin of the men from Maine, Louisbourg was returned to France by the Treaty of Aix-la-Chapelle in exchange for Madras (See 18 October). Ten years later, it was re-captured by the British in order to clear the way for the attack on Quebec (see July 26, Louisbourg II and September 13, Plains of Abraham).

Louisbourg is now a National Park incorporating an impressive reconstruction of the fort and settlement. The official Parks Canada website includes a number of pictures of it.

16 BAY OF FUNDY EXPEDITION 1755, CANADA (FRENCH AND INDIAN WAR)

Commanders: Colonels Robert Monckton & John Winslow v. Captain Duchambon de Vergor & Abbé Le Loutre.

Forces: British and Colonial 2,270; French 475 supported by a band of Micmac Indians converted to Christianity by Le Loutre.

This was a series of small engagements in the Chignecto Isthmus, connecting New Brunswick and Nova Scotia, that had much larger consequences, and it also illustrates the involvement of the New England colonists in hostilities against the French in North America. The principal objective was to enhance the British settlement of Nova Scotia by destroying the French forts that stood on the *de facto* boundary between it and Acadia. Monckton was in command strongly supported by the Governor of Massachusetts, William Shirley (see 16 June Louisbourg I), and the expedition was organized and assembled in Boston. Thirty-one vessels sailed from Boston for the Bay of Fundy where they disembarked near Fort Beauséjour. The opposition was feeble; Vergor was an unpleasant, debauched character, and his troops mainly occupied themselves with heavy drinking and looting their own garrisons. The Fort was surrendered without serious resistance, and Winslow led his colonial troops north to Fort Gaspereau which surrendered immediately on 17 June; on the same day the French abandoned Fort Jemsag (St.

John), their last remaining fort in Acadia. These actions were the first definite steps in the conquest of Canada and in the defeat of the French in most of their colonies around the world.

Monckton enlarged Beauséjour and renamed it Fort Cumberland in honour of the commander-in-chief of the British army; then, at the order of the Governor of Nova Scotia, Charles Lawrence, he burned a number of Acadian villages and deported about a thousand of the inhabitants. He became colonel–commandant of the Royal American Regiment, and at the Plains of Abraham (see 13 September) he stood as Wolfe's senior brigadier general. Abbé Le Loutre who seems to have carried militant Christianity to extremes in inciting his Micmac converts to attack British settlements with savagery, escaped to Quebec and took passage to France, but his ship was captured by the British and he was held prisoner for eight years. Vergor's father, as the acting governor in command, had surrendered Louisbourg in 1745 (see 16 June) and to complete the family's dismal military performance against the British, Vergor was at the Plains of Abraham (see 13 September).

16 OPERATIONS IN THE ATLANTIC 1795 (FRENCH REVOLUTIONARY WARS)

Commanders: Vice-Adml. Sir William Cornwallis v. Vice-Adml. Louis Thomas Villaret-Joyeuse.

The antagonists met off the north-west coast of France, and the French had the weight of numbers on their side (30 ships to 8), but the British, who were escorting a fleet of troop transports, fought with such determination that the French withdrew. The victory has been ascribed to excellent discipline; faultless behaviour; and bold but sound tactics. Vice-Adml. Cornwallis was the brother of Genl. Cornwallis, and although he is not as notable in British military history - no great battle is associated with his name – the resolution he showed in the rigorous blockade of Brest in the early years of the long war with France deserves the highest commendation. For the less successful career of Villaret, see June 1 Ushant.

16 QUATRE BRAS 1815, BELGIUM (NAPOLEONIC WAR)

Commanders: Wellington et al. v. Marshal Michel Ney, Duc d'Elchingen & Prince de la Moskova.

This battle was a prelude to Waterloo in which Napoleon tried to drive a wedge between the British, their allies, and the Prussians. At first, the allied force was out numbered, but later British reinforcements reversed the balance. For most of the day the French held the advantage, but in the evening a successful counter-attack launched by Wellington decided the issue. According to plan, the British withdrew to a position barring the way to Brussels ready for Waterloo.

Simultaneously with Quatre Bras, Napoleon was giving the Prussians what Wellington described as 'a damnable mauling', and forced them to retire towards Wavre from which they were able to march to Waterloo and arrive at the crucial moment.

17 H.M.S. ROMNEY (50 GUNS) V. SYBILLE (44 GUNS) 1794, GREECE (FRENCH REVOLUTIONARY WARS)

Commanders: Captain the Hon. William Paget v. Cdre. Jacques-Mélanie Rondeau.

An unusual engagement fought in the Aegean Sea with both ships at anchor. Paget was escorting a small convoy of merchant ships when he saw *Sybille* lying at anchor with three merchant ships. He anchored his own ship within range and called on the French to surrender, this was refused, and after about seventy-five minutes of firing the French capitulated together with the merchant ships. Paget's ship was greatly under-manned with 266 to 380 in *Sybille*, but the French casualties were much greater than the British. *Sybille* was taken into the Navy with the same name and saw extensive service throughout the Revolutionary Wars and the Napoleonic War, capturing at least seven ships and destroying over twenty.

Paget had considerable success in taking prizes; by 1805, on return from sea, he estimated conservatively that his prize money amounted to £50,000 or about £2.37 million in today's currency. Exhilarated at the thought, he hastened from Portsmouth up to London to speak to his sweetheart, but two weeks later, as sailors are prone to do, he was regretting his haste.

18 H.M.S. NYMPHE (36 GUNS) V. CLEOPATRE (40 GUNS) 1793, CHANNEL (FRENCH REVOLUTIONARY WARS)

Commanders: Captain Edward Pellew v. Captain Jean Mellon.

Fought off Start Point, Devon, and the first successful single-ship action of the war. The action began with elaborate ceremony. As soon as the ships were within hailing distance, Pellew called his crew from quarters to man the shrouds from which they shouted "Long live King George III"; and as the French king had been guillotined only six months earlier, the French replied with "*Vive la Nation*", Pellew then put on his hat as the signal to commence hostilities. From the start, the rigging of the two ships was intertwined, and an early shot from *Nymphe* carried away the wheel of her opponent rendering the ship unmanageable. A boarding party from *Nymphe* brought an end to the proceedings. The French captain was mortally wounded, and as he lay dying he tried to eat the French signal code but ate his commission by mistake! In the final scene of this rather theatrical affair, Pellew called out that he would give ten guineas to anyone who would cut the rigging holding the ships together, and two seamen promptly climbed the shrouds and did so. French casualties were about 60 killed and 150 prisoners were taken; British had 23 killed and 27 wounded. The prize was taken into Portsmouth and commissioned into service in the British Navy as *L'Oiseau*. Captain Mellon was buried in Portsmouth churchyard.

Captain Pellew's distinguished career has been described in respect of another of his victories (see April 20, H.M.S. Indefatigable), and as a reward for this victory he was knighted. On this occasion, his brother, Israel, who also had an impressive record of service at sea (at Trafalgar the French flagship surrendered to him), was with him in *Nymphe*.

18 OSMA 1813 SPAIN (PENINSULA WAR)

Commanders: Lt. Genl. Sir Thomas Graham v. Genl. Honoré Reille.
Forces: British and allies 20,000; French 10,000.

This was not much more than a heavy skirmish. The French, marching to a new position, were surprised by the British on their way to the important battle of Vitoria three days later. After a brief stand, the French retreated having sustained 120 casualties against 60 British. The British commander is more interesting. A Scottish country gentleman, he had no thought of an army career until his wife (a great beauty and the subject of a famous Gainsborough portrait) died in France in 1792, and her coffin was desecrated by a French rabble. This wanton and pointless act so incensed Graham that he determined to fight the French wherever he could, and as this event occurred at the beginning of a war with France that was more or less continuous for twenty-three years he had plenty of opportunities.

He began by raising his own regiment, the 90th., that became known as the 'Perthshire Grey Breeks' from the colour of their trews. There was nothing amateurish about Graham's military capabilities, and it was Sir John Moore's dying wish (see January 16, Corunna) that Graham be promoted to Major General. Graham was prominent at Barossa (5 March), Corunna (16 January), Ciudad Rodrigo (19 January), Esla (May 31), Salamanca Forts (27 June), Tolosa (27 June), Vitoria (21 June) and San Sebastian (8 September). He was the son of the Laird of Balgowan, and at the end of his active service he was raised to the peerage with the title of Baron Lynedoch of Balgowan and offered a pension of £2,000 p.a. that he declined. He was promoted to general in 1821, and died at the age of 95. It is not known if he considered that his thirst for vengeance had been slaked, but he did something for the convenience of army officers in need of a drink in comfort and privacy – he founded the United Services Club in Pall Mall.

18 SAN MILLAN DE LA COGOLLA 1813, SPAIN (PENINSULA WAR)

Commanders: Major Genl. John Vandeleur & Major Genl. James Kempt
v. Genl. Antoine- Louis Maucune.
Forces: British and Allies 6,500; French 5,000.

The French were marching to join General Reille (see 18 June Osma) when they were surprised by the 52nd. Light Division which made a spirited charge that led the French to flee in disorder losing all of their baggage. The surviving French troops were so badly shaken by this experience that they were unfit to take part in the battle of Vitoria 3 days later (q.v.) and had to be sent off as Convoy Guard. British casualties were 110; French 300.

18 WATERLOO 1815, BELGIUM (NAPOLEONIC WAR)

Commanders: Wellington & Field Marshal Gebhard, Prinz von Blücher v. Napoleon.

This battle is one of the critical battles in world history, hundreds of books have been written about it, and there have been countless analyses of the tactics and performance of the commanders. Wellington commanded an allied force of British, German (the British king was also King of Hanover), Dutch and Belgians, and in addition there was a Prussian army that played a decisive role in the later stages of the battle. When the battle began Wellington had 67,660 troops of whom about 35% were British, and Napoleon commanded 71,947, but he had a significant advantage in artillery – 246 guns against 156. Generally, the French army is considered to have been superior in terms of quality, experience, homogeneity (five languages were spoken in Wellington's army) and even motivation (some of Wellington's troops had been fighting with the French as recently as 1813). Wellington's pithy description of his command was:"the worst equipped army with the worst staff ever brought together".

After a night of heavy rain, the French attacked at 11.30 a.m., and the fighting was hot throughout the day, Wellington described it as "a battle of giants", and it was at Waterloo that the 1st Regiment of Foot Guards acquired their title of Grenadiers for their contribution in the defeat of the Grenadiers of the French Old Guard. Towards the end of the afternoon, the Prussian army began to arrive from Wavre which led to more and more French troops being switched from the main front to resist their attack on the right flank. Napoleon made his final thrust with the Old Guard at 7.00 p.m. It was repelled, and Wellington counter-attacked. Except for some elements of the Old Guard, French discipline collapsed, and by 8.00 p.m. the rout had begun.

Until the fashion changed, it was considered vulgar to use certain words in polite conversation and euphemisms were used instead. In French, the euphemism for '*merde* (shit)' is '*le mot de Cambronne*' the origin of which is an incident at Waterloo. At the end of the battle, when French resistance had collapsed, and the Guard was called on to surrender, their commanding general, Pierre Cambronne, is alleged to have replied "*Merde*" and the "*mot de Cambronne*" was embedded in the language. Incidentally, an earlier, analogous example in German is

'Götz-Zitat' referring to a line in Goethe's play *'Götz von Berlichingen'* containing the phrase *'leck mich am Arsche'* (kiss my arse). Compared to these, "Not Pygmalion likely" (Shaw's *Pygmalion*) for "Not bloody likely" seems pallid.

Tactical mistakes were made on both sides, and Napoleon himself later observed that the greatest general was the one who made the least number of mistakes. By this standard, Wellington was superior on the day, but in the years following the battle Napoleon frequently disparaged Wellington and blamed his defeat on the incompetence of his marshals, the weather, and even the faulty tactics of Wellington. Victor Hugo, whose admiration of Napoleon amounted to idolatory, went further, he said that the victory at Waterloo represented "the absolute triumph of mediocrity over genius". But like any contest, it was only the final result that counted, not the method.

The defeat at Waterloo brought an end to the French Empire in Europe, and an end to more than twenty years of war against the French.

During the war, popular hostility towards Napoleon in Britain was sufficiently strong to put him in a particularly gruesome nursery rhyme in which baby is warned that if "Bonaparte hears you… … Limb from limb at once he'll tear you, Just as pussy tears a mouse", and in the last verse after beating baby to a pap "he'll eat you, snap, snap, snap." Although there was better cause, Hitler did not achieve infamy of this kind. More politely and elegantly, Byron criticizes Napoleon in his poem 'Childe Harold', and conversely Wellington is extolled in Tennyson's 'Ode on the Death of Wellington'. And Waterloo appears in Thackeray's 'Vanity Fair' to provide a vehicle for the disposal of one of the characters necessary to the evolution of the plot.

20 ROCHE-DERRIEN 1347, FRANCE (HUNDRED YEARS' WAR)

Commanders: Sir Thomas Dagworth v. Charles de Blois.
Forces: English less than 1,000 v. French upwards of 4,000.

It is a serious understatement to describe this victory merely as audacious. Roche-Derrien was being besieged by Charles' army and Dagworth was leading a column to its relief. By means of a cross country march at the dead of night through wooded country and without maps, he brought his troops to the edge of the besiegers' camp a little before dawn; surprise was complete and no sentries had been posted.

Initial success in the mêlée was followed by several French counter-attacks, and the capture of the wounded Dagworth, but victory was secured when at daylight the commander of the besieged town, Richard Totesham, was able to organize a sortie and take the French in the rear, releasing Dagworth in the process. The French were put to flight, and as many as half the army were killed or captured including Charles de Blois, who was badly wounded, his two sons, and most of the senior nobles and gentry. Charles slowly recovered while a captive in Brittany and was then taken to England serenaded by eight guitarists en route. Imprisoned in the Tower, he found himself in the company of David II of Scotland who had been taken prisoner at the battle of Neville's Cross in which Scotland, fighting in support of its French ally, sustained heavy losses. Charles paid his ransom and was released only to be finished off by the English at the battle of Auray (see 30 September). This victory on the offensive and without the use of archers was unusual for the English in this war.

Through his mother, Dagworth was partly a Plantagenet and thus related to Edward III; for those interested in genealogy, he is also 19 times great grandfather of Charles, Prince of Wales and 17 times great grandfather of Winston Churchill, and neither has any reason to be embarrassed by this ancestor (see 9 June St.Pol de Léon).

20 CHIGNECTO BAY 1704, CANADA (WAR OF THE SPANISH SUCCESSION)

This is an early example of a European war giving the colonists in New England a legitimate reason to fight the French in North America, although neither side was scrupulous in observing the legalities (see 16 June Louisbourg I & Bay of Fundy Expedition; and 29 November, Detroit). Benjamin Church led an attack from New England on several Acadian settlements around Chignecto Bay and Minas Basin at the northern end of the Bay of Fundy in retaliation for a French raid on Maine earlier in the year. Les Mines (Grand Pré), Pipigiguit, Cobequid (Truro), and Beaubassin were all captured.

20 PORT-LA-JOYE (CHARLOTTETOWN) 1745, CANADA (WAR OF THE AUSTRIAN SUCCESSION)

Flushed with their success at Louisbourg (see 16 June) and disappointed with orders against plundering, the troops from New England went the short distance to Ile Saint Jean (Prince Edward Island) and raided and destroyed the French settlement of Port-La-Joye.

21 ST. LUCIA 1803, WEST INDIES (NAPOLEONIC WAR)

Commanders: Cdre. Samuel Hood & Lt. Genl. William Grinfield v. ?

This amphibious action is decidedly dèja vu. St Lucia had been captured from the French in 1794 (see April 4) but had been evacuated a year later. On this occasion, the main fortress on the island was stormed, and the French capitulated leaving it in British hands until its independence as a member of the Commonwealth in 1979. Following up on this conquest, the two commanders went on to take Tobago (see 1 July). Cdre.Hood had a distinguished career in which he was made a baronet and rose to be a Vice-Admiral but is probably second to the famous Admiral Viscount Samuel Hood who was his cousin (see 12 April The Saintes).

21 VITORIA 1813, SPAIN (PENINSULA WAR)

Commanders: Wellington v. King Joseph Bonaparte & Marshal Jean-Baptiste Jourdan.

Forces: British, Portuguese & Spanish about 79,000; French about 68,000 but with nearly twice the number of guns.

Wellington's offensive had forced King Joseph, Napoleon's eldest surviving brother, to abandon Madrid, and he was retreating northwards covered by the French army under Jourdan. In the opening stages of the battle, fighting was heavy, and when French resistance finally collapsed in the face of Wellington's main attack the retreat became a rout in which the French lost all of their guns. This victory was not only a strategic triumph, it was also a logistical achievement of the first order-en route to the battle Wellington had marched his army 400 miles in 40 days, and this gave rise to the quip that 'Wellington's supplies were always hunting for his army; Joseph's army was always hunting for its supplies.' A memorable coincidence was that the success repeated the performance of the Black Prince at or near here some 450 years previously (see 3 April Nájera).

An outbreak of looting meant that the French were not seriously pursued, and nearly all of their army's supply of cash, estimated to be about S$2 million, was stolen (Wellington banned all promotion in the 18th. Hussars because of their looting).

This battle effectively ended the French occupation and control of Spain, but it had wider repercussions. In Germany, where three weeks earlier an armistice had been agreed, the Allied powers were encouraged by the victory at Vitoria to resume hostilities, and three months later Napoleon was decisively defeated at Leipzig.

The Russians were so enraptured by the news of Wellington's victory that they celebrated with an official Te Deum – the first ever for a foreigner's victory. In London, the Prince Regent, always dazzled by military performance, ordered the most 'splendid and magnificent fête' ever held in England, and it was attended by 8,500 people, 1,200 of whom sat down to dinner. In Vienna, Beethoven, who also seems to have been impressed by martial performance, composed 'Wellington's Victory' in honour of Vitoria; earlier he had dedicated his 3rd. Symphony to Napoleon but cancelled the dedication when Napoleon made himself emperor, and the Symphony became Eroica. On the other hand, Napoleon was so enraged by the result that he cancelled a present he had intended for his brother Joseph. The present was an expensive watch ordered from Breguet in Paris with an enamelled map of Spain on the case, and it passed into the possession of Wellington who certainly had better reason to keep Spain in memory.

King Joseph's coach was one of the more attractive items looted. Among the treasures it contained was the silver *pot de chambre* of the King; this was taken into custody by the 14th. Light Dragoons (now the 14th. Hussars) and, christened 'The Emperor', it was used at mess functions for drinking toasts of champagne, after which the pot was placed ceremoniously on the drinker's head. Of much greater value, in the coach there were some priceless pictures belonging to King Ferdinand VII who had been deposed by Joseph, and these passed into Wellington's hands.Wellington acquired another memento of Vitoria. Amongst the booty was Jourdan's baton of a marshal which Wellington sent to the Prince Regent; the Prince was so delighted that in return he ordered a British field marshal's baton be sent to Wellington. Unfortunately, such a baton did not exist, and one had to be quickly designed and made in order to comply with the royal command. Jourdan suffered larger disappointments than the loss of personal belongings. For his defeat at Vitoria, he was dismissed from his command but did not have to wait long for revenge. In 1814, he was in favour of Napoleon's abdication and switched his loyalty to the new king, Louis XVIII. After Napoleon's ignominious exile to St. Helena, Jourdan prospered, he was made a count in 1816 and a peer of France in 1819; he nimbly changed sides again in the revolution of 1830 and served briefly as the foreign minister, finally becoming governor of *Les Invalides*, the famous military hospital. Napoleon's corpse was brought from St. Helena in 1840 and interred in *Les Invalides*, but Jourdan did not live to be in charge of it.

21 SYRIA 1941 (WORLD WAR II)

Commanders: Genl. Henry M. Wilson v. Genl.Henri Dentz, High
Commr. of Syria & Lebanon.

In 1941, when Britain and the Commonwealth were alone in fighting Germany and Italy, the Vichy French who governed in part of France after the surrender were supported by most of their colonies and mandates including Syria and Lebanon. The most active theatre on land was North Africa, and Operation Exporter, the invasion of these two countries from Palestine, was to prevent the Axis from using them as a springboard from which to launch operations against Egypt, and also to provide a base for supporting anti-British factions in Iraq thus endangering oil supplies and communications. Dentz had already permitted Luftwaffe planes to refuel on their way to Iraq, and the invasion by Australian, Indian, British, two Free French brigades and an Israeli Palmach brigade began. The Vichy *Armée du Levant*, including a Foreign Legion regiment, resisted strongly, but the invaders, assisted by naval bombardments and attacks from the air, reached their objectives in a few weeks. Hostilities ceased on July 12 when Dentz surrendered at Acre, but French resistance would have been more protracted if Turkey had granted the Vichy request for permission to transport reinforcements through its territory.

Among the Israelis was Moshe Dayan who later became a famous general in the Israeli army; he was acting as an interpreter for the Australians when he lost an eye in action , hence his well-known black eye patch, and he was awarded the Military Cross.

French fighting French in support of the British is faintly reminiscent of the Burgundians standing with Henry V against the king of France in the Hundred Years' War.

22 MAJOR OFFENSIVE SWEEP 1356, FRANCE (HUNDRED YEARS' WAR)

Commanders: Duke of Lancaster v. King John II
Forces: English about 2,500 v. French about 25,000.

A feature of Edward III's campaigns in the Hundred Years' War was the use on occasion of a *Grande Chevauchée* or Major Offensive Sweep. The main objective might be punitive to destroy the enemy's sources of supply, or to intimidate the population who had supported the wrong side, or to draw enemy forces away from some other area; such expeditions also gave the invaders opportunities for loot and the commanders for booty, ransom money, and supplies which would defray the costs of the war. This campaign was in support of the King of Navarre who had a large number of properties in Normandy, and to some degree kinship because the royal house of Navarre was Norman. Loyalty was never a characteristic of mediæval alliances, and that between France and Navarre was no exception. In brief, the Kings of France and of Navarre fell out, the King of Navrre was taken prisoner by the King of France while dining as the guest of honour at a banquet given by the latter's son, and Navarre's younger brother appealed to Edward III for support. The immediate response was Lancaster's Sweep through Normandy.

The French were besieging the three main Navarre towns, namely, Evreux, Pont Audemer, and Breteuil, and it was Lancaster's purpose to raise these sieges and capture what he could. His army landed from Southampton at La Hogue and four days later began their campaign. The French fled before the advance and Pont Audemer offered no resistance. The French fortified town of Conches was taken without difficulty and set on fire. The next day Breteuil, 10 miles from Conches, was taken without opposition, and large quantities of victuals were loaded into it against future sieges. As Evreux had surrendered before the campaign started, the objectives had now been attained, and the raiders started for home. At this stage, the French army finally appeared in overwhelming numbers just after Verneuil, a strongly fortified town and castle, had been taken by assault after two days of fighting. Lancaster did not have sufficient men to engage the large French army, and by skilful tactics he was able to withdraw with his large amount of booty and prisoners for ransom. On the way back to La Hogue, there were two ambushes; in the first 60 men-at-arms lay in wait all of whom were killed by 15 English men-at-arms, in the second, the redoubtable Robert Knollys, who had come from the base camp at Montebourg with seven men-at-arms to meet the victorious heroes, was ambushed by 120 French. It is reported that Robert and his companions slew 117 French and held the other three for ransom.

The expedition was concluded on July 14 – in less than a month 2 fortresses had been captured, 2 sieges raised, 2,000 horses taken, numerous prisoners, and all at the cost of very few casualties. The English having eluded him, John II marched back to resume the siege of Breteuil, but he made little headway against determined resistance, and when he received news of English hostilities in the south he was glad to grant easy terms of surrender to Breteuil and go back to Paris.

Politically, Lancaster's remarkable effort led Philip of Navarre to enter into alliance with England and to do homage to Edward for his Norman properties. For some years, England and the Navarre-Normans fought as allies, and Joan, the daughter of this King of Navarre and the widow of the Duke of Brittany, married Henry IV, also a widower. Although Joan was on good terms with her step-son, Henry V, after he succeeded to the throne, she was accused of trying to kill him by witchcraft and imprisoned without trial for three years from which she was released by Henry's death bed wish.

22 QUIMPER RIVER 1800, FRANCE (FRENCH REVOLUTIONARY WARS)

This was an action similar to that at St. Croix (see 10 June). This time boats were sent off to attack a coastal convoy in the Quimper River. As the boats approached, the convoy took refuge further up stream, whereupon the boats' crews were put ashore to blow up a battery and other coastal works. Like other places in Brittany, Quimper was the scene of some of the earliest Anglo-French contests, especially in the fourteenth century.

22 LEQUEITIO 1812, SPAIN (PENINSULA WAR)
Commanders: Cdre. Sir Home Popham v.Major Gillort.

An amphibious operation in which a small British fleet, comprising 2 ships-of-the-line, 5 frigates, 2 sloops, and several smaller vessels and 1,000 marines, combined with Spanish guerrillas to support Wellington by diverting French troops. This battle was the beginning of this strategy, and it involved the conquest of a fort and a fortified convent. These objectives were gained with the capitulation of the French garrison. Popham then moved further along the coast to occupy Bermeo and Plencia and succeeded in creating further turbulence that affected the plans of the main French force.

Popham was an interesting character not least because he was the twenty-first child of his mother. In the early part of his naval career he seems to have engaged in some kind of personal trading in India and the Far East. This led to a fierce dispute with the East India Company that ended in a court judgment for Popham in the amount of £25,000. He was next arraigned by the First Lord of the Admiralty, Lord St. Vincent, (see 19 April H.M.S. Foudroyant) on suspicion of dishonesty in the repair of his ship in Calcutta, but in a spirited defence, Popham took his case to Parliament where he was not only exonerated but also established maladministration on the part of the Admiralty. Notwithstanding these distractions, Popham made a major contribution to the Navy by inventing a vocabulary code of signalling that greatly extended the range of orders and instructions available for the direction of a fleet. It was his code that enabled Nelson to send his celebrated signal at Trafalgar. In his activities off the coast of north-west Spain, he was still able to exercise paternal care because one of his daughters was on board with him. (See also January 8, Blueberg, March 4, H.M.S. Diadem, & July 6 Castro Urdiales I).

23 PLASSEY 1757, INDIA (CARNATIC WAR)
Commanders: Colonel Robert Clive v. Siraj-ud-Daula
Forces: British 784 + 2,100 Sepoys and 12 guns, mostly field guns; Bengalis 50,000 + 50 French gunners and 53 guns, mostly heavy.

The Bengalis were in alliance with the French in this part of India, and Clive was seeking to replace Siraj-ud-Daula, the Nawab of Bengal, with one of his entourage who was plotting to usurp him. Treachery in the Bengali army and first class leadership gave Clive an overwhelming victory that led Pitt the Elder to describe him as "the heaven-born general", and his elevation to the Irish peerage as Baron Clive of Plassey. Siraj-ud-Daula was caught trying to escape from his capital and stabbed to death on the orders of the victorious usurper, after which his corpse was paraded through the streets on an elephant. Clive's "man" was now installed as Nawab of Bengal, Orissa, and Bihar.

23 ILE-DE-GROIX 1795, FRANCE (FRENCH REVOLUTIONARY WARS)

Commanders: Adml. Sir Alexander Hood v. Vice-Adml. Villaret de Joyeuse.
Forces: British 14 ships-of-the Line ; French 12 ships -of- the line.

Alexander Hood had been raised to the peerage as Viscount Bridport in recognition of his contribution to the victory at the Glorious First of June (see 1 June Ushant) and was now in command of the Channel Fleet. The fleet was at sea to protect an expedition to Quiberon Bay in support of the Royalist insurgents in the Vendée. The French fleet was taken by surprise off the Ile-de-Groix and took avoiding action but were not able to escape. Three French ships were captured and 670 French were killed or wounded; British casualties were 144. The French had been in an unsuccessful action a week previously (see 16 June, Operations in the Atlantic), and the survivors must have been anxious to return to port but not with another hammering on the way. For more on Villaret de Joyeuse, see June 1 Ushant.

24 SLUYS 1340, BELGIUM (HUNDRED YEARS' WAR)

Commanders: Edward III v. Adml. Quiéret
Forces: English approximately 120 - 160 ships; French about 190.

Sluys (L'Écluse) was the sea port of Bruges, at that time, a major European trading centre. The French ships were anchored and lashed together in fours in a defensive formation of three lines unable to manœuvre, and the English fleet was able to get to windward and attack with the sun behind them. First, the archers loosed a storm of arrows, and then the men-at-arms boarded the target ship and fought hand-to-hand with those not disabled by archery. Methodically, most of the French fleet was captured or destroyed. The estimate of the casualties is approximate, but the French probably lost 16 – 18,000 men including Quiéret and another admiral, the English 4,000; Edward III was wounded, but his crushing victory established his reputation and prestige at home and abroad. In France, it resulted in the devastation of the Norman ports and put an end to French hopes of launching an invasion of England. This battle was the first major engagement in the Hundred Years War, and it also gave rise to an early 'anti French joke' albeit French in origin. In the course of the battle, many of the French were forced off the decks of their ships into the sea, and King Philip's clown was heard to ask: "Sire, do you know why the English are cowards? Because, unlike the French, they dare not jump into the sea".

24 WILHELMSTAHL 1762, GERMANY (SEVEN YEARS' WAR)
Commanders: Ferdinand, Duke of Brunswick v. ?

Ferdinand had family connections with Prussia and Britain, and his army comprised Prussian infantry and British cavalry. He was an able commander who secured a tactical advantage that resulted in a rout of the French following a splendid cavalry charge led by the first rate Lt.Genl. the Marquis of Granby; this performance was a vast improvement on that of a previous British cavalry leader under Ferdinand's command. After the battle of Minden (see August 1) Lord George Sackville was cashiered for refusing an order to charge. Ferdinand was so well regarded by the British that he was offered the position of commander-in-chief of the British army in America when the revolution began, but he refused.

24 HMS DIDO (28 GUNS) & H.M.S. LOWESTOFFE (32 GUNS) V. MINERVE (40 GUNS) & ARTÉMISE (36 GUNS) 1795, S.OF FRANCE (FRENCH REVOLUTIONARY WARS)
Commanders: Captain George H. Towry & Captain Robert G. Middleton v. Captain Perrée & Captain Charbonnier.

These frigates had been ordered to reconnoitre the opposing fleet, and they met between Toulon and Minorca. Although *Minerve* was considerably larger and more powerful, *Dido* attacked and fought for nearly four hours including repelling a boarding party. *Lowestoffe* rendered valuable assistance principally by damaging *Minerve's* masts and rigging, and then chasing *Artémise* which had done almost nothing to assist *Minerve*. *Minerve* surrendered when so severely damaged as to be almost unmanageable. *Lowestoffe* was not able to catch *Artémise* before it reached Toulon, and the failure of *Artémise* to support *Minerve* was in unfavourable contrast to the performance of *Lowestoffe*. *Minerve* was taken as a prize and then into service in the Royal Navy as a 38 gun frigate. Towry was put in command as a reward for his spirited conduct in this action, and his first lieutenant was promoted to commander.

Perrée was one of the prisoners and among the wounded; he fought again after his release but died of wounds received in a violent action against no less a person than Rear-Admiral Nelson (see 18 February H.M.S. Foudroyant et al.)

25 FORT ST. PIERRE 1667, WEST INDIES (ANGLO-DUTCH WAR)

Commanders: Rear Adml. Sir John Harman v. Antoine Lefebvre de la Barre.

This can be regarded as the last part of the action begun at St. Kitts (see 10 May). Harman arrived with another squadron and found the French ships at Fort St. Pierre where in a spirited action he destroyed them. Harman then went on to take Cayenne and Surinam from the French, but this had little effect on the war because hostilities ended a month later at the Treaty of Breda. Harman was one of several senior naval officers who began service in the republican, Commonwealth navy of Cromwell and had then smoothly transferred into the navy of that always pragmatic king, Charles II.

26 TOLOSA 1813, SPAIN (PENINSULAR WAR)

Commanders: Lt. Genl. Sir Thomas Graham v. General M. Foy
Forces: British, Portuguese & Spanish 30,000; French 12,000.

Here was Graham pursuing his vendetta against the French (see Osma, 18 June) and succeeding in capturing this fortified town. The French were obliged to retreat into France, where the Peninsular War was ended at Toulouse (see April 10).

General Foy was an interesting character. His exceptional military capability led to his rise through the ranks of Napoleon's army, and this in spite of his political opposition to Napoleon in the post-revolutionary period in which he voted against the Consulate and later the creation of the Empire. At Waterloo, Foy commanded the 9th Division in the fighting around Hougoumont, and afterwards he retired from military life. In 1819, he was elected to the Chamber of Deputies where he showed a flair for oratory, and for the ten years until his death, he was the leader of the liberal opposition. His funeral was marked by a mass demonstration against the Bourbon monarchy in which 100,000 took part – substantially more than were in the French Army at Waterloo, a year later the Bourbon monarchy was superseded.

27 DOUAI 1710, BELGIUM (WAR OF THE SPANISH SUCCESSION)

Commanders: Marlborough v. General Chevalier d'Albergotti.

Forces: British and Allies 60,000 (not all were directly engaged); French 7,500.

This was one of the numerous sieges that were the principal form of military engagement at this period. The Allied armies were continuing to push the French back towards France, and in Flanders there was a number of fortified cities. The fortifications at Douai were strong, but the besieging engineers devised the clever plan of diverting the river Scarpe into the river Sensée thereby largely draining the double ditch surrounding Douai and simultaneously creating a large flooded area south of the city. Taking rather longer than usual, the surrender was made after about two months and the Allied army with its siege train moved on to Béthune (see 29 August). Casualties were Allied army 8,009; French 2,860.

27 DETTINGEN 1743, GERMANY (WAR OF THE AUSTRIAN SUCCESSION)

Commanders: King George II v. Marshal Andrien Maurice, Duc de Noailles & Genl. Louis, Duc de Gramont.

Forces: Anglo-Germans 40,000; French 60,000.

This defeat of the French prompts the thought that two French dukes were not a match for a British king. The battle could make a Hollywood epic. George II was a dominating figure; always at the centre of the action, he personally led his troops in attack with his sword in hand, and when required could be found sighting the guns of the artillery. The French infantry and cavalry were reduced to panic and disorderly flight, many drowning in the River Main while trying to swim across it. This is the last occasion when a British monarch led his troops in person, although the King's second son, the Duke of Cumberland, was also in the field at Dettingen and fought with outstanding bravery, three years later he was in command at Culloden. In a junior role, James Wolfe, destined for distinction at Louisbourg and the Plains of Abraham (see 27 July and 13 September), also played a part. French casualties were 6,000 compared with Anglo-German losses of 2,400.

27 SALAMANCA FORTS, 1812 (PENISULA WAR)

Commanders: Wellington v. Major Duchemin.
Forces: British & Allies 5,600; French 800 + 36guns.

The forts at Salamanca were three convents that the French had fortified, and in order to do so they had demolished most of the old university quarter which leaves one to speculate on the feelings of the inhabitants after the war had moved on. The fighting was desultory, but Wellington had to capture Salamanca in order to be able to continue his offensive. Never at his best in sieges, Wellington's preparations were inadequate, and this prolonged the struggle. The French finally capitulated having suffered 200 casualties and 600 captured; British casualties were 430, and the offensive continued. The next year, the British and their allies put in a much better performance at Salamanca (see 22 July).

28 CUDDALORE 1748, INDIA (WAR OF THE AUSTRIAN SUCCESSION)

Commanders: Major Stringer Lawrence v. Marquis Joseph-Francois Dupleix
Forces: British 600 Europeans & 400 Indian troops; French 800 Europeans & 1,000 Indian troops.

The French had been trying unsuccessfully to capture Fort St. David, the principal base of the East India Company in that part of India and turned their attention to Cuddalore, a fortified outpost about two miles to the south. The French tactic was a surprise night attack, but Lawrence was aware of the plan and set up a decoy with the result that the attack was instantly repulsed with murderous fire. Most of the French fled without firing a shot and retreated to their base at Pondicherry. This engagement cast a long shadow before because it was the first encounter between British and French troops in India, and the epilogue proved to be the same as the prologue.

29 H.M.S. JASON (38 GUNS) & H.M.S. PIQUE (36 GUNS) V. SEINE (46 GUNS) 1798, BAY OF BISCAY (FRENCH REVOLUTIONARY WARS)

Commanders: Captain C. Stirling & Captain D. Milne v. Lt. J-G.Bigot.

After a chase *Pique* was the first to engage *Seine*, and the fight continued for five hours until at midnight *Pique* with main topmast shot away was obliged to break off. *Jason* took over and *Seine* was completely dismasted. All three ships went aground at Pointe de la Tranche, near La Rochelle, but at daylight action was resumed until *Seine* surrendered. *Jason* was hauled off by a third frigate, and *Seine* was refloated, but *Pique* was bilged and had to be destroyed. Milne and his crew took over *Seine,* and he was later given commamd of her (see 20 August H.M.S. Seine). This was the second time that Milne's career advanced on the strength of the capture of ships of the French navy, *Pique* had been captured from the French in the West Indies three years earlier, and Milne had commanded the boarding party being promoted for his performance (see 4 January H.M.S. Blanche). *Seine* was carrying soldiers, and the total complement was 610 of whom nearly half were casualties, 170 killed and about 100 wounded; total British casualties were 8 killed and 18 wounded. Milne advanced to the rank of commodore, and in the latter part of the Napoleonic war, he served off the coast of Spain with Cdre. Sir Home Popham's fleet in which service he enjoyed some of the comfort's of home because his wife, two children and a maid were on board with him (see also 21 March H.M.S. Peterell and 3 July H.M.S. Milford).

JULY

1 MONTEREAU 1420, FRANCE (HUNDRED YEARS' WAR)
Commanders: Henry V v. ?

Following the quick success at Sens (see 13 June), Henry's Anglo-French army moved on towards Paris and invested Montereau. This town was of particular interest to the young Duke of Burgundy because it was on the bridge here, less than a year before, that the Armagnacs slew his father, John the Fearless, at the beginning of a meeting intended to cement a rapprochement between the two houses (see 2 July Pontoise). The fact that the murder of his father was retaliation for the assassination of Louis, Duke of Orleans, the Armagnac leader, by John thirteen years before, and more recently the murder of the Comte d'Armagnac by a Paris mob incited by the Fearless did nothing to assuage the feelings of his son. After the town had surrendered on 23 June and the castle on 1 July, the Duke went to the parish church and ordered his father's coffin to be opened, the remains were placed in a fresh coffin and sent to Dijon for interment in the family vault. Henry was indeed lucky to find France so bitterly divided.

1 BOYNE 1690, IRELAND (WAR OF THE LEAGUE OF AUGSBURG)
Commanders: King William III v. ex- King James II
Forces: English plus Dutch, Danish and French Huguenot 36,000;
Irish18,000 and French 7,000.

This battle has several facets. William had replaced James II as King of England in 1689, the outcome of the 'Glorious Revolution'. He had a claim to the throne in his own right through his mother, the eldest daughter of Charles I, and he was married to Mary, the daughter of James II, thus he was the nephew and son-in-law of his opponent. William ruled jointly with his wife as William and Mary (their monogram can be seen on their splendid addition to Hampton Court Palace), and as the Prince of Orange in Holland he had become the leader of the Protestant countries of Europe against Louis XIV of France. At this period in European history, Roman Catholics and Protestants fought and persecuted each other with all the animosity now shown by Sunni and Shiite Moslems, or by Jews and Arabs. A major cause of James' downfall in England was the alarm aroused by his conversion to Roman Catholicism, and when he was forced to go into exile, he went to France where Louis XIV gave him military support to help him regain his throne, and at the same time attack the principal Protestant leader. The Boyne was partly civil war, and partly Roman Catholics against Protestants personified in this instance by the French and the English. It remains only to add that Louis XIV had so vigorously persecuted his Protestant subjects, known as Huguenots, that at the end of the seventeenth century some 400,000 had gone into exile, and three regiments of them under their own commanders stood "with Billy at the Boyne".

There was hard fighting at the beginning when the Dutch and Huguenot infantry forced the crossing of the River Boyne. Their commanding general, the Count von Schomberg, was killed during this phase; and as a further illustration of the strange mix at this battle, he had been a Marshal of France until obliged to leave that country with the Huguenots. Yet another curious coincidence was the presence of the Duke of Berwick, the illegitimate son of James II and Arabella Churchill whose brother, John, became the Duke of Marlborough. Berwick fought with distinction, but his uncle was not present at the Boyne; later Berwick became a general in the French army and a Marshal of France. James II had had considerable military and naval experience, and a good reputation as a commander, but his tactics at the Boyne have been strongly criticised. The battle was over by mid-afternoon, and William was able to occupy Dublin a few days later, James II having retired to France at the double. It is noticeable that although the combined casualties were in the order of 3,500, the Jacobite French lost only six men.

1 TOBAGO 1803, WEST INDIES (NAPOLEONIC WAR)

Commanders: Cdre. Samuel Hood & Lt. Genl. William Grinfield v. ?

This action in which the French garrison capitulated after limited resistance was really a continuation of the capture of St. Lucia (June 21). After securing that conquest, the two commanders moved on to Tobago and took it into custody. By way of background, the Treaty of Amiens 1802 ended the first phase of the war against France and her allies, and by this treaty the many colonial islands which had been conquered by the British, including St. Lucia and Tobago, were returned to their previous owners. Hostilities resumed in 1803, and in the first flush of enthusiasm St. Lucia and Tobago were re-taken, British ownership being confirmed at the Treaty of Paris in 1814 (see 30 May).

Cdre.Hood had an outstanding naval career in which after early service with his even more distinguished cousin, he sailed with Nelson, and at the Battle of the Nile (August 1) he was one of those who boldly took his ship inshore of the anchored French ships. He was also in action at Copenhagen when the Danes, foolishly allied to the French, lost most of their fleet. So far as the French were concerned, Hood's final action was in the evacuation of the British forces at Corunna (see 16 January); he was commander-in-chief of the East Indies fleet when he died of a fever at Madras.

2 PONTOISE 1419, FRANCE (HUNDRED YEARS' WAR)

Commanders: Earl of Huntingdon & Captal de Buch v. ?

Immediately after the fall of Rouen (see 20 January), Henry V took several diplomatic initiatives in order to consolidate his victories. He made a truce with the Armagnac and Burgundian factions of France and arranged a conference with the Duke of Burgundy and Queen Isabella, who were the effective rulers of France due to the recurring insanity of Charles VI. After a month the conference had not yielded any definite agreements (but it did establish the basis for the Treaty of Troyes – see 21 May,) and it broke up. Henry wasted no time in taking other steps. Suspicious, with good cause, of the behaviour of the Duke of Burgundy he abrogated the truce and ordered a surpise attack on the strongly defended town of Pontoise. The Captal de Buch from Gascony, a steadfast supporter of English campaigns, led a storming party through the night and by means of scaling ladders they got over the walls undetected until they were seen opening one of the gates. Huntingdon's orders were to approach Pontoise from the other side and enter by the gate that their comrades had opened. This bold plan nearly failed when the second column lost its way and was almost too late, but it recovered in time to join in overwhelming the garrison. A huge quantity of military stores was the major part of the booty, and the success alarmed the French to the point of panic. The king was removed to Troyes and two months later the Duke of Clarence was at the gates of Paris. Unfortunately, the consternation at the French court was sufficient to persuade the Armagnacs and the Burgundians to band together against the invader, and if they had organized future resistance on such a platform it would have gone very badly for the English. However, personal feelings took precedence over national interest, and at the beginning of the meeting intended to establish the new alliance, the Armagnacs ambushed the Duke of Burgundy and murdered him (see 1 July Montereau). Unsurprisingly, the new, young Duke and Queen Isabella immediately appealed to Henry for help against the Armagnacs, and the Treaty of Troyes spelled out the price for this assistance. The Treaty was signed with great pomp and ceremony on May 21, 1420, and Henry went to Troyes from Pontoise with the Duke of Burgundy and with a sizeable army at his back. Not only did he seal the treaty, he became betrothed to the king's daughter, Catherine, and married her on June 2. The dynastic plans failed two years later with Henry's early death because his only son, Henry VI, less than a year old when he succeeded, was eventually murdered. Queen Catherine had an unexpected dynastic achievement. In her widowhood, she secretly married a young Welsh squire, Owen Tudor, and one of her grandsons, Henry Tudor, was crowned Henry VII in 1485.

2 DONAUWOERTH (A.K.A.SCHELLENBERG HEIGHTS) 1704, GERMANY (WAR OF THE SPANISH SUCCESSION)

Commanders: Marlborough v. Comte d'Arco
Forces: Allied army 52,000; Franco-Bavarian 14,000.

This battle was a prologue to the main event at Blenheim (see August 13). Marlborough had marched his Anglo-Dutch army south to relieve the French and Bavarian threat to Vienna. This was a remarkable feat in itself because throughout the march the right flank of Marlborough's force was exposed to a French attack from across the Rhine. On the way, to shake up the Elector of Bavaria, he had burned some 300 Bavarian villages. The French and Bavarians were dug in on a large and prominent hill from which by skilful tactics they were driven into the town, and then from it. British infantry led the resolute storming of the Heights of Schellenburg a feature of which was their shouts and yells while charging; for a time at least these yells expressed the determined aggressiveness of the British infantry akin to the more famous 'Rebel Yell' of the Confederates in the American Civil War. French casualties were about 10,000, and the Allies about half that number.

3 FRÉTEVAL 1194, FRANCE (ANGLO-FRENCH WARS)

Commanders: Richard I (the Lion Heart) v. Philip Augustus.

Richard had extensive lands in France that had been inherited from his parents, Henry II and Eleanor of Aquitaine. The King of France, in the manner of feudal organization, wished Richard to do homage to him, and this was a cause of continual disagreement between them. The two had temporarily co-operated in the Third Crusade until Philip, pleading ill health, returned to France, whereupon he immediately sought to take Richard's possessions by force. Richard's pursuit was delayed by his imprisonment by Leopold V of Austria, but once back in France he set about recovering his property. Richard's military capabilities were considerable, and at Fréteval he inflicted the first of several defeats on Philip who lost not only his baggage but also the royal seal.

Fréteval had earlier connections with the English monarchy. It was here in July 1170 that the rapprochement between Henry II and Thomas Becket, Archbishop of Canterbury, took place, but it lacked substance, and on 29 December 1170, Thomas was slain in his cathedral by four of Henry's knights.

3 ACADIA 1654, CANADA (NORTH AMERICAN COLONIAL WARS)

Major Robert Sedgewick, in reprisal for French attacks on British shipping, led a fleet of the new Puritan Commonwealth of New England from Boston that swept aside French power in Acadia, capturing Fort St. Marie, Port Royal, and Fort Penobscot. Cromwell's military forces were as irresistible in the New World as in the Old. However, the conquest was not permanent, by the Treaty of Breda 1667, at which Charles II could be relied on to try to ingratiate himself with the French, Acadia was returned to France. The treaty did not define the boundaries of Acadia thereby ensuring that the dispute over the territory would continue.

3 GUADELOUPE 1794, WEST INDIES (FRENCH REVOLUTIONARY WARS)

Commanders: Vice-Adml.Sir John Jervis & Lt. Genl. Sir Charles Grey v. ?

An amphibious action in which for small losses Jervis captured the island; it was later recaptured by the French, but it was for small gains because the Royal Navy had destroyed most of the French shipping. The crowning moment of Jervis' career came the following year when he had an overwhelming victory over a Spanish fleet off Cape St. Vincent and was raised to the peerage as Earl St. Vincent.

3 H.M.S. MILFORD (74 GUNS) & OTHERS 1813, FIUME (A.K.A. RIJEKA) CROATIA (NAPOLEONIC WAR)

Commanders: Rear-Admiral Sir Thomas Fremantle v. ?

Fremantle's objective was to attack Fiume as a trial run for an attack against a strongly defended port. Fiume had four shore batteries each with 15 heavy guns and a garrison of about 350 French troops. The attack was hampered by an adverse wind and current, but sustained fire from a ship of the line proved too much for the defenders, and the battery was stormed by marines; after possession was taken, the guns were turned around and used to bombard the other batteries in French hands. While this was going on, another party of marines took a battery that had been under fire from the ships, and this cleared the way for a combined charge into the town by seamen and marines. At first, the attackers were under musket fire from the windows of houses and a field gun in the middle of the road, but the defenders were put to flight when the carronades of the ships boats were brought to bear. Remarkably, a dead marine was the only British casualty.

Fremantle had a distinguished naval career in which he served with Nelson in Corsica (see 20 May, Bastia and 1 August, Calvi); in the boat attack on Tenerife where both he and Nelson were badly wounded; and in Nelson's victory over the Danes at Copenhagen. At Trafalgar,

Fremantle was in command of *Neptune* which was the third ship in the line of the Weather Column, only two behind *Victory.* His friendship with Nelson was genuine. There were many in society who were critical of Nelson's relationship with Lady Hamilton and who shunned her company, but Fremantle and his wife maintained close relations with them both. Fremantle's own marriage was unusual. Lord St. Vincent, when he was commander-in-chief in the Mediterranean, had an English refugee family living on board his flagship for over a year, and the family included three teenage daughters. The eldest married Fremantle, then commanding a frigate, and she was permitted to live on board Fremantle's ship (see 29 June H.M.S. Jason).

3 MERS-EL-KEBIR (ORAN) 1940 (WORLD WAR II)

Commanders: Vice-Adml. Sir James Somerville v.Adml. Marcel Gensoul.

This action occurred less than three weeks after the French surrender to the Germans. In the harbour at Mers-el-Kebir was a large part of the French fleet - 2 battleships, 2 battle cruisers, and many smaller warships and supply vessels. The overriding concern of the British Command was to prevent these ships being used by the Germans, particularly in an invasion of Britain. Somerville commanded 17 ships, Force H, including the battleships *Hood* and *Resolution*, and he was ordered to give Gensoul an ultimatum to join the British navy, or to surrender his ships, or to scuttle them, or to sail to Martinique or the U.S.A., and if none of these was acceptable, Somerville was to open fire. The ultimatum was refused, and the British ships opened fire at a range of about 8.5 miles while the French ships were at anchor or had just left their moorings. The flagship, *Dunquerque* was put out of action in four minutes, the battleship *Bretagne* was sunk and another, *Provence,* badly damaged, considerable damage was inflicted on other ships and about 1,250 French crew members were killed. The French heavy cruiser, *Strasbourg*, and several destroyers escaped to Toulon and were scuttled there in November 1942 when the Germans occupied Vichy France. Controversies about the incident and whether it could reasonably have been prevented continue in both Britain and France, but it would seem that whether the British and French were allies or enemies, in the end they were destined to fight.

4 LE QUESNOY 1712, FRANCE (WAR OF THE SPANISH SUCCESSION)

Commanders: Duke of Ormonde & Prince Eugene v Marshal Claude-Hector, Duc de Villars.

As a result of particularly venal, political intrigues, Marlborough had been replaced as Captain-General of the British and Dutch armies in alliance with Austria, and the Duke of Ormonde had been appointed in his place. The siege of Le Quesnoy was a continuation of the subjugation of the line of forts guarding the northern frontier of France in order to clear the way for an offensive into France, but secret negotiations for peace were already in course, and the British participation in the campaign had been put under restraints. The French were similarly averse to open battles of the kind in which Marlborough had always been victorious. The siege began early in June and ended successfully in less than a month, but in different circumstances it might have lasted much longer. Le Quesnoy had been captured by Louis XIV in 1654 and it was the first of the 160 forts to be designed by the famous French military engineer, Sébastian le Prestre de Vauban. By the latter part of the seventeenth century the traditional fortifications of towers linked by curtain walls were useless against the more powerful artillery that had come into use. Vauban's remedy was a star shaped design with straight sided moats with guns mounted on the ramparts behind thick walls and with slits in the walls through which the defenders could rake the moats with hand guns. Two centuries later these fortifications were no longer required, and their demolition made available a wide, concentric swath of vacant land on which many cities constructed attractive boulevards – the Ringstrasse of Vienna is a notable example. The reason that British cities do not have similar ring roads is that urban fortifications of any kind were not required after the fifteenth century. Today, the Vauban fortifications in Le Quesnoy have been carefully preserved and are a principal tourist attraction.

Vauban's career ended in an unusal way. Up to the year before his death he had merited and enjoyed the favour of Louis XIV, and although he was only of the petty nobility he rose to be a Marshal of France. Possessed of extraordinary energy, he was a prolific writer on a wide range of subjects, and his last work, published anonymously, proposed to substitute for practically all existing taxes, a flat tax of 10% on all land

and trade without exemptions; unusually for his time, his concept was supported by a large amount of statistical evidence. Unfortunately, this idea was altogether too radical for Louis XIV and for the aristocracy who were paying little or no tax under the current tax regime, so publication of the book was suppressed. This rebuff came as a huge disappointment to Vauban and clouded the last year of his life. Albeit belatedly, Vauban's idea has found merit with some contemporary tax reformers, and since 1994 it has been implemented by Estonia and seven other countries, including Russia and the Ukraine. Surprising and not the least of his accomplishments, Vauban can be fairly regarded as one of the pioneers of the use of statistics in economics.

4 MAIDA 1806, ITALY (NAPOLEONIC WAR)

Commanders: Maj.Genl. Sir John Stuart v. Genl. Comte Jean Louis Reynier

Forces: British 5,200; French 6,500.

Napoleon had deposed the King of Naples and had his brother Joseph crowned in his place. The British were supporting the deposed king, and Stuart led an expeditionary force to restore the monarchy. Reynier's troops were veterans, but volleys followed by vigorous bayonet charges were more than they could stand, and they were routed with heavy casualties.The British infantry tactics plainly showed that fighting in line was superior to fighting in column. French casualties were upwards of 2,000 including 700 buried where they fell, the British had 55 killed and 282 wounded.

This victory was the first British victory of the Napoleonic War on the Continent, and it gave rise to popular exultation including peals of church bells and panegyrical ballads of which this is an example:

And now! The raptured Muse in martial strains,
Sounds Stuart's triumph on Calabrian plains!
The French appalled! Bold Kempt pursues the blow,
And deals destruction, midst the flying foe;
With horrid crash the clashing muskets meet,
And pierced foes lay prostrate at his feet;
In contest close, the glitt'ring bayonets shine,
Thrust follows thrust and wounds the steel enshrine;

Then countless numbers strew the carnag'd green,
And some by flight escape the blushing plain.

Incidentally, the British efforts on behalf of the deposed king were in vain, but Nelson, who earlier played a major part, took advantage of the opportunity to make advances to Lady Hamilton, the wife of the British ambassador, with notable success.

5 RENNES 1358, FRANCE (HUNDRED YEARS' WAR)

Commanders: Henry, Duke of Lancaster v. Bertrand du Guescalin.

In spite of a two-year truce that came into effect in March 1357, hostilities in Brittany continued, and on the English side Henry, Edward III's right–hand man, commanded. The key to the conquest of Brittany was to capture Rennes, the capital, and the county of Nantes. The French candidate for the Duchy was Charles de Blois who had recently paid most of his ransom and returned to Brittany at Guingamp from captivity in England (see 20 June Roche-Derrien). Henry promptly marched to Guingamp and occupied it, but Charles had already left for Nantes; tarrying only to re-take Roche-Derrien, Henry then proceeded to Rennes for the siege. Without siege engines and with only a small force, Henry was obliged to proceed with a blockade in order to starve the garrison into surrender. Operations had been in course for six months when Henry was informed that a truce had been agreed to which Brittany was a party, but he ignored this and continued the blockade. In June, a third command to abandon the siege was given, but Henry kept this order to himself and offered the garrison terms. A surrender was accepted on the payment of 100,000 crowns, and the truce was acknowledged in Brittany, the more readily following Henry's return to England.

6 TREATY OF EDINBURGH 1560

In the sixteenth century the division of Christendom into Roman Catholics and Protestants introduced a new cause of war in Europe, and in part the Treaty of Edinburgh reflects this change. Mary, Queen of Scots, had succeeded to the throne in 1542 when only 6 days old. Her French mother, Mary of Guise, was principally concerned to maintain Catholicism in Scotland, and her endeavours were firmly supported by the French who saw an opportunity through the marriage of her daughter,

Mary, to the dauphin to unite not just France and Scotland but England and Ireland as well. Mary had been sent to France when she was six years old and pledged to marry the infant dauphin. The French plan unfolded as intended when Mary, aged fifteen, married the dauphin in 1558, the king died next year, and Mary and her husband succeeded to the throne. At this point, as Burns famously observed:

'The best laid schemes o' mice an' men
Gang aft a-gley'

and Francis II, Mary's husband, died. Meanwhile, in Scotland there had been a Protestant uprising that had not been successful, partly because French troops and ships had been sent to quell it. The English could not afford to see the French in command on their northern frontier and sent an army into Scotland. Although the troops were ill-disciplined and the siege of the French in Leith was conducted badly, they were able to prevail because in the course of Sir William Winter's blockade of the Forth six or seven ships under d'Elbœuf were sunk and supplies from France were cut off. The French were obliged to ask for terms, and the Treaty of Edinburgh expressed them; in particular all French forces were compelled to withdraw. Forty three years later, England and Scotland were united when the Protestant James, the son of Mary, Queen of Scots, by a second marriage, peacefully succeeded Elizabeth I as James I of England, and continued as James VI of Scotland.

6 TROUT BROOK 1758, U.S.A. (SEVEN YEARS' WAR)

Commanders: Maj. Genl. J.Abercromby v. Maj. Genl. Louis-Joseph, Marquis de Montcalm.

This encounter was not much more than a skirmish, but some of the leaders are worth a note.

Abercromby often described as 'incredibly inept', or worse, was leading an army, largely comprising colonials with British officers, against the French. Abercromby's second–in-command was Brigadier Lord Howe called 'the best soldier in the British army', and in effective command in this campaign. Howe was an outstanding leader held in the highest regard by his officers and men; he had been appointed colonel of the Royal Americans, an élite colonial regiment, and had carried out an intensive programme of training in fieldcraft and forest fighting. Howe was leading the advance guard in the attack on Fort Carillon (later renamed Ticonderoga) when it met a French scouting party. The French were almost annihilated, but Howe was killed in the first volley. An idea of his reputation is provided by the fact that the colony of Massachusetts Bay paid for a monument to be raised to him in Westminster Abbey. Two of Howe's brothers, William and Richard, had distinguished careers in the army and navy respectively (see June 1 Ushant). Montcalm has a good reputation in French military history and is known for the quality of his leadership. He makes his final appearance on September 13, Plains of Abraham.

6 GRENADA 1779, WEST INDIES (WAR OF AMERICAN INDEPENDENCE)

Commanders: Adml. John Byron v. Adml. Charles Hector, Comte d'Estaing.

The French had opened hostilities against the British in support of the American revolutionaries (10 years later when the French Revolution began, the radical fervour of Louis XVI and his ministers no doubt vanished quicker than the guillotine blade fell, and the thought of this episode in French history is probably an embarrassment to President Chirac). French support was principally naval, and this engagement was a full fleet action in which the British had 24 ships and the French 25 ships of the line plus 10 frigates. Although outnumbered, Byron attacked and inflicted heavy losses – 1,200 killed and 1,500 wounded against 183 killed and 346 wounded. Byron did not, however, succeed in capturing Grenada.

6 CASTRO URDIALES 1812, SPAIN (PENINSULA WAR)

Commanders: Cdre. Sir Home Popham v. ?
Forces: as described for Lequeitio, 22 June.

A continuation of Popham's harrying of the French along the Biscay coast. After repelling a relieving force, the Spanish guerrillas and the sailors and marines effected the surrender of the French Governor together with 150 men and 20 guns. (See 22 June, Lequeitio)

6 2012 OLYMPIC GAMES AWARD 2005, SINGAPORE.

London was awarded the right to host the 2012 Olympic Games after defeating Paris in the fourth and final round of the voting by the members of the International Olympic Committee (IOC). Paris had started odds-on favourites, but careful preparatory work by the London team, and an inspired address by its chairman, Lord Sebastian Coe, twice an Olympic gold medallist, proved to be decisive. The last four rounds of the bidding were:

London	22	27	39	54
Paris	21	25	33	50
Madrid	20	32	31	X
New York	19	16	X	X
Moscow	15	X	X	X

The decision exhilarated a huge crowd that had gathered in Trafalgar Square to hear the result, and some described it as "the greatest victory since Trafalgar" – which seems an injustice to Waterloo. The mood in France was deep despondency not to say despair. It was the third consecutive defeat for Paris in its bid to host the Games, and the public comments were not those of 'good losers'. The Mayor of Paris, Bertrand Delanoe, accused the London committee of cheating; a prominent French basketball player in the U.S.NBA declared the decision proved that the IOC is Anglo-Saxon, and they prefer the English. In the days prior to the vote, President Chirac of France was so forthright in his hostile comments that he might have damaged his own cause. At a meeting in Russia with the German Chancellor and the Russian President, he was heard to say "that the only thing the U.K. has done for European agriculture is mad cow disease". He appeared to be under the impression that cuisine would be an important criterion declaring that "one cannot trust people with such awful cooking. After Finland, it's the country where you eat the worst". Whether the gratuitous insult to Finland had any effect on the vote is not known because the ballots are secret, but Paris lost by four votes and Finland had two delegates. What Chirac chose to ignore is that in 2005 London had more restaurants (11) in the list of the "World's 50 Best Restaurants" than Paris which had only 6, (based on a poll of 600 food critics, chefs and industry experts by the Restaurant magazine) and the World's Best Restaurant was also British. Looking much further back, an English army, sent to south-west France in 1513 in alliance with Ferdinand of Aragon, was quartered in that part of France during the summer, and the food and drink were so disagreeable that 3,000 were afflicted with the flux. The troops mutinied and demanded to be returned home, and a contemporary account refers to the food having too much garlic.

7 TRICHINOPOLY II (A.K.A.GOLDEN ROCK) 1753, INDIA (CARNATIC WAR)

Commanders: Major Stringer Lawrence v. M.Astruc

Forces: British 500 Europeans and 5,000 Indians; French 450 Europeans and 28,500 Indians.

In spite of being heavily out-numbered, skilful tactics and great resolution, including plentiful use of the bayonet, led to the rout of the French and their Indian allies with the loss of their guns. Lawrence had a most distinguished career with the East India Company during which, with the aid of his second–in-command, Robert Clive, he damaged the French forces in India very severely and paved the way for their expulsion. He rose to be commander-in-chief in India with the rank of major-general, but unlike many of those who retired from the Company with a fortune, he fell on hard times and was rescued to some degree through the efforts of Robert Clive who secured a pension of £500 p.a. for him. This was a modest award for a man who is reckoned to be the real founder of the Indian army under British rule (see 2 October Trichinopoly III, and 17 February Madras).

8 RESTIGOUCHE 1760, CANADA (SEVEN YEARS' WAR)

Commanders: Captain John Byron v. Captain François-Gabriel. d'Angeac

Fought between a British squadron and a French squadron in Chaleur Bay in the Gulf of St. Lawrence in the last naval engagement in the North American theatre of the war.

The British continued to assert their ascendancy and defeated the French. Captain Byron, the grandfather of the poet, was beginning his climb towards flag rank. In 1741, while serving as a midshipman in a ship that was part of Anson's squadron sailing round the world, he was ship- wrecked off the coast of Chile, and after a series of terrible hardships he was consigned to a Spanish prison. Six years later, he was able to return home and resume his service. He found the opportunity to write an account of his shipwreck which was of sufficient merit to be used by Byron in his work 'Don Juan'. Known in the navy as 'Foul Weather Jack' because of his unfortunate experiences at sea, Byron's service afloat ended after he was caught in one of the worst Atlantic gales on record. This event also caught the attention of his grandson who, in his 'Epistle to Augusta' (his half-sister) wrote:

"Reversed for him (i.e.Byron himself) our grandsire's fate of yore,
He had no rest at sea, nor I on shore."

D'Angeac was born in New France and made a successful career there. He was the son of a French colonial officer, and he joined the French colonial army at an early age. He fought at Louisbourg in 1745 and 1758 (see 16 June & 27 July) and was wounded in the latter battle. After the futile resistance at Restigouche, d'Angeac led his men into the forest and engaged in guerrilla warfare. After the final surrender (see 8 September Montreal), he went to France. By now, he had earned a reputation for bravery and administrative competence, and he was appointed Governor of the islands of St. Pierre & Michelon, all that were left of the French Empire in North America. In this capacity, he tried to establish friendly relations with the British governor of Newfoundland, but since the advantages were all on the French side, these efforts were unsuccessful. Later, on orders from France, he was compelled to expatriate from his islands approximately 800 Acadians who had settled there following their eviction from Acadia. In Canada today, retrospective complaints of the expulsion of the Acadians by the British seem to have extinguished any recall of d'Angeac's expulsion. Finally, his request for retirement to France was granted with a comfortable pension, but not before he had been able to arrange the appointment of his nephew to succeed him as Governor; an example of nepotism that would seem to justify Napoleon's later insistence on careers open to talent.

8 BOURBON (NOW CALLED RÉUNION) 1810, INDIAN OCEAN (NAPOLEONIC WAR).

Commanders: Cdre. J. Rowley & Col. Keatinge v. ?

Forces: British 5 ships and a small number of troops; French - the garrison.

Bourbon is a small island about 100 miles SW of Mauritius and was a base for French privateers preying on merchant shipping. It was seized in an amphibious operation with the loss of 16 killed and 67 wounded, but all to little purpose as it was returned to France at the Congress of Vienna in 1815 (see 9 June). Bourbon's importance was in keeping the French naval base at Ile de France (Mauritius) supplied with food (see 3 December).

9 OSTEND 1706, BELGIUM (WAR OF THE SPANISH SUCCESSION)

Commanders: Marlborough & Field Marshal Hendrik Overkirk v. Comte de la Motte

Forces: British & Allies 20,000; French 5,000.

Having taken Antwerp, and replete with the feast the defenders of it gave him (see 6 June), Marlborough turned his attention to the neighbouring port of Ostend. The siege began with a naval bombardment that was repeated after completion of the siege works. When the breaching batteries had been mounted in the outer fortifications, de la Motte surrendered. The siege lasted three weeks in contrast to the siege by the Spanish general, Spinoza, one hundred years before which lasted for three years. The besiegers had 1,600 casualties; the defenders 800.

Overkirk was the commander-in-chief of the Dutch army, and he was said to be the only Dutch general in whom Marlborough had confidence; he had accompanied William of Orange to England in 1689 and had become a naturalized Englishman. In spite of Marlborough's good opinion, when Overkirk's death was reported to him at the siege of Lille (see 9 December), his only comment was "Her Majesty will save the pension", such are the effects on personal feelings of protracted fighting.

11 HUY 1705, BELGIUM (WAR OF THE SPANISH SUCCESSION)

Commanders: Field Marshal Hendrik Overkirk v. M. St. Pierre.

Spare a thought for the people who lived in Huy in these years. The town was taken from the French after a siege in 1703 (see 26 August), in June 1705 it was retaken by the French in a surprise attack, and now a month later it was besieged again by Marlborough's troops. The French decided it was not worth the risk of holding it and surrendered after six days. The experience of the civilians in Huy was by no means rare; in the frequent European wars, continental towns and cities changed hands quite often with concomitant depredation of persons and property, in sharp contrast British civilians were spared such experiences.

11 OUDENARDE 1708, BELGIUM (WAR OF THE SPANISH SUCCESSION)

Commanders: Marlborough v. Duke of Burgundy and Duke of Vendôme
Forces: British with Dutch and German allies, 78,000; French 100,000.

Marlborough's second–in-command was his friend Prince Eugene with whom he had developed a strong partnership (see 13 August Blenheim). By contrast, French performance was seriously impaired by antagonism between Burgundy and Vendôme; demonstrating that nepotism is a poor criterion for command, Louis XIV had given joint command to his grandson, the Duke of Burgundy, although Vendôme was far more experienced and had earned respect. Marlborough's tactical skill was outstanding, and its principal feature was a forced march that has been described as the most inspired in history, this march was followed by another – in all 50 miles were covered in 60 hours - and these greatly disconcerted the divided French command resulting in a decisive victory. French casualties were 6,000 killed and wounded and 7,000 prisoners, including 709 officers, compared with 3,000 for the British and their allies. Presaging a larger, active military career, the future George II of Britain, then 24 years old, was actively engaged in the cavalry at Oudenarde (see June 27 Dettingen).

12 AUGHRIM 1691, IRELAND (WAR OF THE LEAGUE OF AUGSBURG)

Commanders: Lieut.-Genl. Godart de Ginkel v. Lieut.-Genl. Marquis de St. Ruth

Forces: British 20,000; French & Irish 20,000.

The Battle of the Boyne (see 1 July) did not end that campaign. It continued into the following year and terminated at Aughrim. The French troops in James II's army at the Boyne had been recalled to France, but the commander and all of the senior officers of James II's army here were French. The British were commanded by one of William III's Dutch generals, and ironically about 11% of his forces were French Huguenots which, under their own field commanders, made an outstanding contribution. The Irish occupied a strong defensive position and resisted so vigorously that towards the end St. Ruth was prompted to proclaim that "the day is ours", but shortly after he was decapitated by a cannon ball and did not live to see that he was mistaken. Tactical errors and a temporary breakdown in command precipitated a sudden and complete rout. The spoils included 11 standards of cavalry and dragoon regiments, the colours of 32 infantry battalions, 9 field guns and all of the baggage; Irish casualties were about 4,000 the British about half that number. In recognition of his performance, de Ginkel was created Earl of Athlone and Baron of Aughrim; the Huguenot cavalry commander, the Marquis de Ruvigny, was created Earl of Galway in the following year. Aughrim was the last major battle fought in Ireland and the most bloody.

13 HYÈRES BAY 1795, FRANCE (FRENCH REVOLUTIONARY WARS)

Commanders: Vice Admiral W. Hotham v. ?

This action took place in sight of Toulon, the main French naval base in the Mediterranean. The French fleet had been at sea when they sighted a small British squadron and gave chase towards Corsica, now a British base (see 20 May, Bastia). The whole British fleet was at anchor there, but adverse winds prevented it from sailing immediately, and when it did so it was the turn of the French to be chased. After five days, the leading British ships, including Nelson's *Agamemnon*, were able to open fire, and soon *Alcide*, the last ship in the French line, was ablaze and surrendered, but before a prize crew could take it over the ship exploded and sank; only 200 of the crew were rescued. Nelson and his colleagues were confident that in spite of the risk of being close to Toulon, a number of other ships were theirs to take or destroy, but their expectations were turned into frustration when Hotham, eight miles astern, signalled the fleet to retire. Hotham was nervous of the proximity to the French coast, but at seventy years of age he had lost the contemporary, aggressive spirit of the navy. Nelson's comment was that: "...Hotham leaves nothing to chance", and he regretted Hood no longer commanded. Sir Gilbert Elliot, now viceroy of Corsica, put it more bluntly: "... [Hotham] is past the time of life for action, his soul has gone down to his belly, and never rises higher now... ...". Hotham's second in command, Vice-Admiral Samuel Goodwin is said to have kicked his hat around the deck in a frenzy of rage when he was called off. The consensus of the critics was that the fruits of victory were large enough to justify the risks involved in their plucking.

13 ALGECIRAS BAY 1801, BAY OF GIBRALTAR (FRENCH REVOLUTIONARY WARS)

Commanders: Rear-Adml. Sir James Saumarez v. Rear-Adml. C. Durand de Linois.

This was the final phase of a fleet action that began when Saumarez attacked the French ships anchored in Algeciras Bay. The French had sailed from Toulon intending to join Spanish ships in Cadiz and transport reinforcements for the French army in Egypt. En route, the French learned that Britsh ships were patrolling outside Cadiz, and Linois anchored in Algeciras Bay, opposite Gibraltar, under shore batteries that were reinforced by Spanish heavy gunboats. Saumarez attacked, but the wind died as the attack began, and the squadron suffered considerable damage with one ship taken as a prize after going aground. Five Spanish ships of the line now sailed from Cadiz to effect a rendez-vous, and the combined force of ten ships of the line set sail for Cadiz. Meanwhile, every effort had been made to repair the British ships, and, leaving one behind, Saumarez now chased the enemy. A night action began in which the Franco-Spanish force numbered nine against five British. In the fighting, one of the largest Spanish ships was set on fire, collided later with another and set it ablaze before exploding. The other ship that had been set on fire also blew up after engaging one of its own ships in the dark and general confusion. A French ship was captured and another narrowly escaped. The immediate result of this outstanding victory against heavy odds was that the reinforcements did not reach Egypt, but there were also strategic benefits. Spanish disgust with the French alliance was confirmed, they insisted on the return of their ships from Brest and relaxed pressure on the Portuguese. Saumarez had a long and distinguished naval career. He held commands at a number of major victories over the French (see April 12 The Saintes; 23 June, Ile-de-Groix; and 1 August, Nile) and was victorious in an exemplary single-ship engagement (see 20 October, H.M.S. Crescent &c.).

13 SENEGAL 1809, WEST AFRICA (NAPOLEONIC WAR)

Commanders: Captain G.H. Columbine v. ?

An amphibious operation carried out by three warships and transports resulting in the surrender of the French garrison. Senegal was returned to France after the Congress of Vienna in 1815 (see 9 June), and it was taken from the Vichy French without opposition in 1942.

15 (EST.) LE CROTOY 1438, FRANCE (HUNDRED YEARS' WAR)

Commanders: John Talbot v. Philip, Duke of Burgundy.
Forces: English 2,500; Burgundians 5,000.

Situated on the north bank of the Somme estuary and the nearest coastal town to Calais, still in English hands, Le Crotoy was of considerable strategic importance; and it was under siege by the Burgundian allies of Charles VII. Talbot, who had enjoyed success during the winter (see 15 January, Ry & 16 February, Pontoise), was ready to relieve the siege and marched from Rouen to St. Valery on the south side of the Somme estuary. Following in the footsteps of Edward III on his march to Crécy, he intended to ford the river at Blanchetaque (see 24 August), and like Edward, he found the enemy in force on the far bank. Talbot immediately waded into the water and led his army across; an excellent performance was completed by scattering the Burgundians with only a few casualties. Talbot wanted to engage the besiegers in open battle, and in an endeavour to force them to do so, he decided to ravage the surrounding country. Looting and burning against little opposition, but without drawing the Burgundians away from Le Crotoy, Talbot re-mustered his troops and marched on the town. At his approach, the besiegers panicked and fled, abandoning their artillery and stores, and were pursued by the garrison of Le Crotoy. Talbot and his men returned to Rouen heavily laden with booty.

15 (EST.) PORT ROYAL (ANNAPOLIS ROYAL) 1613, CANADA (NORTH AMERICAN COLONIAL WARS)

Commanders: Samuel Argall v. René Le Coq de La Saussaye.

Argall was employed by the Virginia Company, and in 1612 he was named Admiral of Virginia and ordered to expel the French from all territory claimed by England. He sailed from England in a ship, *Treasurer*, mounting 14 guns with a crew of 60. The vessel was owned jointly by Argall and Sir Richard Rich, later the Earl of Warwick who subsequently engaged in piracy. After arriving in Virginia, *Treasurer* and a smaller ship were sent to attack French settlements that were being built on territory claimed by the Virginians. In turn, Argall took the settlements of Mount Desert, Saint-Sauveur, Saint Croix, and Port Royal by surprise, butchered some of the livestock, carried the rest off, and burned the buildings and growing crops. On his return to England, there was an enquiry into his attacks on the French, and it was decided that the actions were legal and proper in order to protect the rights granted by the Crown to the Virginia Company. These activities carried on in the name of private corporations with a royal warrant were typical on both French and British sides in the early days of colonization, and not just in North America.

After these exploits, Argall's career progressed. In 1616, he was elected deputy governor of Virginia and ruled the colony in the absence of the governor for three years; his administration was strict, but complaints against it were not sustained. Next, he was the captain of a 24 gun merchant ship in an expedition against Algiers, and on his return he was appointed to the Council of New England thereby confirming his active interest in the colonization of the region. Given the rank of Admiral of New England, he was knighted in 1622, and 1625 found him admiral of a fleet of 28 ships that took many prizes off the coast of France. The most surprising event in his career was the abduction of the North American Indian princess, Pocahontas, in 1613. Argall inveigled her to come aboard his ship in the Potomac River and sailed off with her to Jamestown where she was held as hostage for 8 Englishmen being held prisoner by her father Powhatan, a chieftain of chiefs. Pocahontas was kindly treated in Jamestown and fell in love with and was married to John Rolfe, Treasurer and Recorder of Virginia. In 1616, the Rolfes went to England where Pocahontas became an immediate success in London society – banquets and dances were given in her honour, her portrait was painted by famous artists, and she was received by James I. Early in the voyage back to Virginia, she died of smallpox and was buried at Gravesend. The latter part of the story has suggested the plot for a recent film, 'The New World', by Terrence Mailick which has received complimentary reviews –"… this gifted director's most beautiful film."

15 VELLINGHAUSEN 1761, GERMANY (SEVEN YEARS WAR)

Commanders: Field Marshal Ferdinand, Duke of Brunswick & Lt. Genl. Marquis of Granby v. Marshal, Duc de Broglie & Marshal, Prince de Soubise

Forces: German and British 60,000; French 100,000

A defensive battle in which the allied army was blocking the French advance. Personal feelings impaired co-operation between the French commanders, and this gave the defenders an advantage. The main French attack was made against the British part of the line under the command of Granby, and it was repulsed with considerable losses that caused the French to retreat.

The Marquis of Granby was the heir to the Duke of Rutland and had a brilliant career as a cavalry commander (see 31 July, Warburg and 1 August, Minden), later he became commander-in-chief of the Army, but he is undoubtedly best known because countless pubs were named after him.

De Broglie was a professional soldier with an impressive record, whereas it has been said of de Soubise, a favourite of Louis XV and Mme de Pompadour, that his military career "owed more to his courtiership than to his generalship"; which being the case de Broglie was probably frustrated at Vellinghausen.

17 TOULON 1707, FRANCE (WAR OF THE SPANISH SUCCESSION)
Commanders: Admiral Sir Cloudesley Shovell v. ?

A serious, strategical disadvantage for the British at this date was the lack of a major naval base in the western Mediterranean, and an audacious plan had been developed to remedy the situation. This was no less than the capture of the French naval base at Toulon. Marlborough's principal partner, Prince Eugene, marched an army from Savoy along the coast, assisted by a British fleet, and besieged the city, but as time passed the scale of the enterprise so daunted the commander that the army began to retreat. The navy, however, found a way to strike an offensive blow. Some coastal batteries were destroyed, clearing the way for bomb ketches to get within range of the harbour and lob their missiles into it. After about eighteen hours, two ships of the line had been sunk, and the French became so alarmed that they scuttled their other ships in shallow water intending to raise them later. Eventually, the ships were salvaged, but only a few were fit for further service.

Admiral Shovell came from East Anglia and had a meritorious career in which he held rank in the marine regiment as well as in the navy. He was able to transfer his allegiance smoothly from James to William when the latter took over the monarchy, even commanding the squadron that took William to Ireland to confront James at the Boyne (see 1 July). He took a serious interest in the welfare of his crew to the extent of endorsing the work of the Society for the Promotion of Christian Knowledge. Indirectly, his death led to a very important improvement in the standard of navigation. His squadron was returning to port when it ran on to the outer rocks of the Scilly Islands; three ships of the line were lost with the crews and the admiral. Part of the reason for the disaster was the inaccuracy of the contemporary charts – the Scillies were shown about fifteen miles too far north, but the underlying cause was that there was no reliable method of fixing longitude at sea. Shovell was such a respected and popular officer that the shock of his death led to the Longitude Act in 1714 which offered large prizes for a practicable method of solving the problem (how the solution was found, and who did so is a fascinating story in its own right, see "Longitude" by David Sobel).

Unlike most of the crews, Shovell did not drown. He was washed ashore and was smothered to death by a local woman as he lay semiconscious in the sand; the murder was committed to take a large emerald ring that he was wearing on his finger.

18 ELIXHEM (LINES OF BRABANT) 1705, BELGIUM (WAR OF THE SPANISH SUCCESSION)

Commanders: Marlborough v. Comte de Hornes; Comte d'Alègre; & Comte de Caraman.
Forces: British & Allies 14,000 v. French & Bavarians 15,000.

The Lines of Brabant were a line of forts and fortified positions running for about 70 miles from Namur to Antwerp that made full use of rivers and canals. Marlborough's plan was to force a passage of the Lines as a preliminary to bringing the French to an open battle. The Lines were formidable and to facilitate the attack, Marlborough began with a subtle tactical march at night in order to decoy the main body of the French troops from the target sector. By great effort and perseverance on the part of the common soldiers, in the early morning the allied army started to pass through the Lines at a strong point where the local guards offered little resistance before running away without stopping to give the alarm. When the defenders began to confront their opponents, a pitched battle ensued in which Marlborough himself led a cavalry charge that shattered the first line of the French-Bavarian cavalry and left both d'Alègre and de Hornes wounded. In the charge against the enemy's second line, Marlborough was unhorsed and only rescued by the heroic intervention of his trumpeter. Caraman conducted the retreat of his battalions notably well, but his task was made easier because the pursuit was not pressed as hard as it might have been. The next day, Marlborough attacked the French baggage train and its escort and took another 1,000 prisoners, but the timidity and carping of the Dutch generals meant that another opportunity of striking a really decisive blow was lost. Nevertheless, with 50 miles of the Lines captured and a great deal of *mat*ériel, Elixhem ranks as a major tactical success. French casualties were 3,000 compared to about 100 British.

19 QUEBEC 1629, CANADA (NORTH AMERICAN COLONIAL WARS)

Commanders: David Kirke v. Samuel de Champlain

David Kirke and his brothers were sons of an English merchant trading between London and Dieppe where David was born. The family business led to a good understanding of French commercial activities and ambitions in North America, and to Kirke senior's investment in a company of merchants with intentions of competing with French traders and colonists on the St Lawrence River. The outbreak of war with France prompted Charles I to commission an expedition, financed by the new company, 'to displace the French from Canada'. David and his four brothers sailed for Canada with three ships and made a start that pleased the investors. Proceeding up the St. Lawrence, they took Tadoussac and a supply ship bound for Quebec but decided that Quebec was too well fortified for their force and turned for England. On the way, they met four supply ships sent by Cardinal Richelieu to sustain the settlers of the Company of New France under the command of de Champlain; the little convoy was quickly captured and this made for a triumphant return. Conversely, in Paris, the Kirkes were burned in effigy for treason, it being held that having been born in France, they were French subjects. The net effect was that in 1629 David Kirke was put in command of a larger squadron with which he was able to intercept French supply ships on their way to Quebec. The settlers had already been reduced to starvation, and the latest loss of their supplies compelled de Champlain to surrender.

The Kirkes occupied Quebec until 1632, when by the Treaty of St. Germain-en-Laye, the Canadian territories were returned to France, and de Champlain returned to Quebec. For his sterling work, David was knighted in 1633, and in 1639 was appointed Governor of Newfoundland. Not much is known about his character - to some English writers he is heroic, but their French counterparts have represented him as a pirate. His later career was affected by the civil war – his sympathies were royalist, and consequently he came under investigation by the parliamentarians, but they were not able to find any evidence of malfeasance. In financial difficulties, he died in the 'Clink', i.e., the prison in Clink Street, Southwark in 1654.

20 PONT DE L'ARCHE 1418, FRANCE (HUNDRED YEARS'WAR)

Commanders: Henry V v. Lord Graville.

In order to attack Rouen from the west (see 20 January), it was necessary to cross the Seine, and Henry's plan was to do so at Pont de L'Arche. Here the Seine is broad and deep, but in the river there are several small islands; on the south bank, a walled town defended the bridge, and at the other end stood a square fort. At first, Henry tried to take the town by assault but the attacks were driven back with sufficient force to indicate that something else ought to be tried. A spectacular effort was made about 400 yards downstream from the bridge. The planning and organization of the campaign was much better than the general standard in the Middle Ages (and much later, too), and the equipment included a number of boats and pontoons intended to be used in forcing river crossings, now they were put to use. A pontoon bridge was put across from the south bank to an island and a large number of small boats were carried over it at night. In the early morning Sir John Cornwall led 60 men to the north bank in these boats covered by the fire of the archers on the island. Although there were plenty of defenders on the north bank, they were taken completely by surprise and routed. A bridgehead was established from which the attack on the fort was launched. This attack was reinforced by troops, who had crossed over two other pontoon bridges now in position on either side of the permanent bridge, and the fort fell. With the capture of the fort, the town was cut off, and, possibly over-awed by the audacity of the attackers, it capitulated. The English must have been uplifted by this victory, and the tactics that secured it, but their jubilation was no doubt enhanced by the fact that the Duke of Burgundy, always a very fickle friend, had recently changed sides and most of the defenders on the river bank were his men.

Pont de L'Arche had an earlier, more congenial association with the royal house of England. Following the death of Henry II, who was also Duke of Normandy, at Chinon in July 1189 his son, Richard Cœur de Lion, succeeded him. Richard was acclaimed Duke of Normandy in Rouen cathedral two weeks after his father's death, and there were great festivals and celebrations in honour of the event in the course of which Richard went on a hunt. On the bank of the Seine, his horse stumbled and fell, Richard was in some danger but survived and to celebrate he vowed to found an abbey at the spot. This is the Cistercian abbey of Bonsport.

20 DREUX 1421, FRANCE (HUNDRED YEARS' WAR)

Commanders: Henry V v. ?

After the triumph of the Treaty of Troyes (see 21 May) and victory at Melun (see 18 November), Henry had returned to England for further celebrations including the coronation of his French queen, Catherine, in Westminster Abbey. The Duke of Clarence had been left in charge in France, but this had not been a success. The Duke had been killed in a foolish engagement, and the initiative had passed to the Dauphin, but on Henry's return to France in June, his reputation and achievements were such that the climate of opinion changed immediately. The Dauphin who was besieging Chartres, and all the while boasting of his intention to do battle with Henry if the chance presented itself, now broke off the siege and retreated hastily to the south. Henry conferred in Paris with the Earl of Exeter, who had succeeded Clarence as the king's lieutenant, and the French government, and then proceeded to besiege Dreux the last major stronghold of the Dauphin west of Paris. The town was strongly fortified with a substantial garrison but only a feeble fighting spirit, and they surrendered after little more than token resistance. Uplifted by easy success, Henry and his troops marched on to Chartres, only twenty miles to the south, and were greeted with a joyful welcome from the lately besieged garrison and citizenry alike. Henry's stature in France now befitted that of a king which it was intended he should become on the death of his father-in-law, the infirm Charles VI, and it completely over-shadowed the reputation of the Dauphin, but fate now intervened. Reconnaissance and communications in mediæval armies were always difficult, and the exact whereabouts of the Dauphin's forces was not known so that Henry could only advance in the direction they were thought to have gone when they gave up the siege of Chartres. On the way, the English took the town of Beauregency but not the castle, and while this was invested and a reconnaissance in force had been detached, an epidemic broke out that killed enough besiegers to oblige Henry to lift the siege and move to a healthier location. The reconnaissance had failed to find the enemy, and there is no record of where it went. There were, however, other places holding out for the Dauphin east and south-east of Paris that threatened the communications of the Burgundians (allies of the English) with their territory in Flanders, and it was on these that Henry now marched (see 2 May, Meaux).

20 PONTOISE 1441, FRANCE (HUNDRED YEARS' WAR)
Commanders: Duke of York & John Talbot v.Arthur de Richemont, Constable of France,.
Forces: English 2,500; French 5,000.

After the Duke of Burgundy had broken his alliance with the English (see 15 January, Ry) and joined with Charles VII, the English in France were at a disadvantage for twenty years, but in that time they still had some successes, and Pontoise was one of them. The French were besieging Pontoise when they learned that the Duke of York was approaching with an army for its relief. Boldly forcing a crossing of the river Oise by means of a pontoon bridge made from leather boats brought along in the baggage train for this purpose, the English army began to march towards the French besiegers about fifteen miles away and on reaching them, the timidity of the French enabled supplies for the relief of the garrison to be passed into the town. As the English approached, part of the French army had been sent to reinforce the defences at Paris, and the king retreated from the vicinity of Pontoise, but almost at once he was bundled out of his new headquarters because of a brilliant, tactical, flanking march by a detachment led by Talbot. With a little luck the king would have been captured, as it was he was able to reach St. Denys on the outskirts of Paris. The episode served to diminish further the king's reputation in the eyes of his subjects – a current *mot* in Paris was: "Whenever the French find themselves in a superiority of three to one, they immediately retreat". Unfortunately, lack of supplies, especially food and forage, obliged the English to withdraw to Rouen leaving Pontoise still under siege.

21 ISLE OF WIGHT 1545, ENGLAND (WAR OF THE SPANISH ALLIANCE)
Commanders: Viscount John Lisle, Lord High Admiral v. Admiral of France, Claude d'Annebault

This was only part of an engagement that had begun in June when Francis I of France assembled at the mouth of the Seine a huge invasion fleet (by the standards of that time) of 150 ships and 25 galleys supported by 50,000 men. The king reviewed the fleet as it sailed for the English coast, but the occasion was marred when the flagship, *Philippe*, caught fire, and the substitute, *Grande Maitresse*, went aground. Navigation was never very accurate in the sixteenth century, and so by accident or design landfall was made at the hamlet of Brighton, making the fleet among the first French tourists to visit it. Brighton was irrelevant to the plan of invasion, and so the ships sailed westwards and entered the Solent on 18 July. The English force mustered to prevent the invasion was greatly out-numbered and retired into Portsmouth harbour. The next day with a favourable wind the English put to sea, and an indecisive action followed at the end of which Henry VIII's new, very large ship, *Mary Rose*, demonstrated a lack of sea-worthiness by capsizing and drowning most of the crew; fairly recently, parts of this ship have been raised and are now preserved, at large expense, for public display at Portsmouth. Disease and lack of supplies were now severely affecting the invaders, and in an attempt to bring the English ships out again, the French troops were ordered to invade the Isle of Wight. As soon as they were ashore, they were set upon by the local militia and driven off; an action that might have inspired the Home Guard formed in World War II to repel German invaders, although it seems likely the latter would have been less easily defeated. The following day d'Annebault, frustrated on land and sea, was obliged to return to France, but for the last word see 2 September, Le Tréport.

Viscount Lisle was soon to become Earl of Warwick, then Earl of Northumberland and finally Duke of Northumberland; he played a brief but prominent part in the history of the Tudors. Henry VIII died in 1547 and his only son, Edward VI, was a minor with Northumberland finally becoming Lord Protector. As Edward lay dying in 1553, Northumberland caused him to will the crown to Lady Jane Grey and her male heirs thereby excluding Henry's daughters, Mary and Elizabeth, from succession. An essential part of his plan was the marriage of Lord Guilford, Northumberland's fourth son, to Lady Jane Grey about seven weeks prior to Edward's death. Four days after this death, Northumberland proclaimed Lady Jane queen, but the proclamation was widely rejected, and the strength of popular support given to Mary Tudor was enough to cause Northumberland to surrender to Mary's forces on 20 July 1553. Northumberland and his wife were beheaded for treason on Tower Hill on 12 February 1554. Someone in the crowd (executions were a public spectacle) might have observed 'like father, like son' because Northumberland's father had been executed for treason by Henry VIII shortly after his accession, albeit on trumped up charges. Northumberland's personal motives for the plot are not to be understated, but the broader policy was to secure the Protestant succession, and although it failed on this occasion, it succeeded with the accession of Elizabeth after Mary's death, and with one or two hiccups along the way it has been maintained ever since.

22 H.M.S. BEAULIEU (40 GUNS) & OTHERS V. CHEVRETTE (20 GUNS + 300 MEN) 1801, FRANCE (FRENCH REVOLUTIONARY WARS)

Commanders: Captain Poyntz v., ?

This one is the epitome of derring-do. *Beaulieu* in company with two other frigates, *Doris* and *Urania*, was keeping watch on the combined French and Spanish fleets in Brest when the ships were sighted by *Chevrette,* a French corvette, anchored in Camaret Bay, part of the approaches to Brest. *Chevrette* then moved up the Bay under the shore batteries and brought troops on board; for extra protection a gunboat with two heavy guns was moored at the entrance to the Bay. It had been intended to send a fire ship from *Beaulieu* into Brest but this plan was changed to an audacious attack on *Chevrette.* Lt. Maxwell and six boats manned by 90 volunteers together with 9 boats from the other ships went off at night through the entrance of the Bay towards *Chevrette* six miles away. As they approached *Chevrette*, they came under grape shot and musketry fire, and several were killed or wounded, but they succeeded in boarding, although the firearms were all lost in the process and the attackers were left only with swords and cutlasses. Hard fighting took place in which Lt. Burke of *Doris* dramatically killed the captain of *Chevrette* in single combat, and a lieutenant of marines was killed while defending a wounded midshipman; curiously, many of the wounds of the boarders were made by tomahawks, a weapon perhaps left over from French colonial days in Canada. Cold steel proved to be sufficient to win control of *Chevrette.* She was cut adrift with sails loosened, and as she drifted away the French crew panicked, some leaped overboard and others retreated below and kept up heavy musketry fire on the boarders overhead as well as setting off explosions below the quarterdeck. To clear the upper deck some 20 or 30 French had to be thrown overboard along with the corpses, and the British returned the firing from below using captured weapons. For a long time, *Chevrette* was becalmed under fire from the shore until a light wind took it out of range; it took two hours to subdue the French below decks and in the final tally Britsh casualties were 11 killed and 57 wounded; French were 92 killed, including the captain and 6 officers, and 62 wounded. For his heroic leadership, Lt. Maxwell was promoted to commander.

22 CAPE FINISTERRE III 1805, SPAIN (NAPOLEONIC WAR)

Commanders: Rear Adml. Robert Calder v. Adml. Pierre de Villeneuve
Forces: 15 British ships of the line against 20 French and Spanish ships of the line under French command.

The enemy fleet was returning from the West Indies with Nelson in unsuccessful pursuit, and Calder's force had been detached from the Channel Fleet blockading Brest and Rochefort in order to prevent it from entering the Spanish naval base of Ferrol. The engagement was fought in foggy weather and light winds. Before nightfall, Calder had captured two ships and inflicted damage on the others to the extent that four were obliged to go into dry dock, but because of the weather he did not feel able to continue the action the following day. The French and Spanish casualties were 149 killed, 327 wounded, and 1200 prisoners; British 39 killed and 159 wounded.

Later, in contravention of Napoleon's order to proceed to Brest, Villeneuve took his ships south to Cadiz and then, in October, to his crushing defeat at Trafalgar. Calder thought he had performed well, but his opinion was not shared by his superiors or by his captains, and Nelson's first duty on taking over command of the fleet prior to Trafalgar was to send Calder home to face a court martial. Calder was acquitted of cowardice, but severely reprimanded for not persevering in the action. The verdict brought his active naval career to an end, but in the fashion of the time, it was not an ignominious end because he became an admiral by seniority in 1810 and was knighted in 1815. These subsequent honours may have had something to do with his family connections – his father had served at court – and his wealth. At the age of 17 he was a lieutenant and had taken part in the capture of a Spanish treasure ship for which his share of the prize money was £13,000, a small fortune at that date (for example, for service at sea, a lieutenant's pay was at the rate of £73 a year).

22 SALAMANCA 1812, SPAIN (PENINSULA WAR)
Commanders: Wellington v. Marshal Auguste Marmont, Duc de Raguse.
Forces: British 30,316, Portuguese & Spanish 21,193 with 60 guns; French 49,000 with 78 guns.

After several days of excellent manœuvring for position by both sides, the French were lured into attacking but suffered badly from the British counter-attack led by Wellington's brother-in-law, Maj. Genl. Pakenham and Le Marchant, an outstanding cavalry commander who was killed in the action. Marmont and his deputy were wounded, and the second wave of the British attack routed the French forcing them to retreat throughout the night. British casualties were 3,129, Portuguese 1,627 and Spanish 6; the French had 7,000 killed and the same number taken prisoner, 2 eagles and 20 guns were also captured. This victory considerably weakened the French position in Spain. In recognition of his victory, Wellington was made a Marquess and voted £100,000 but his reaction was prosaic: "What is the use of making me a Marquess?", but the scale of the victory unhinged the mind of the Prince Regent to the extent that in later years he would claim to have charged with the heavy cavalry at Salamanca. Perhaps the greatest compliment on Wellington's performance is that of the French general, Maximilien Foy,whose division covered the retreat: "[Salamanca] classes Wellington nearly on the level of the Duke of Marlborough", another Frenchman is quoted as saying "Wellington beat 40,000 Frenchmen in 40 minutes". An interesting post-script to the battle is that on the site of the position occupied by the French until they were driven off it, there stands a granite obelisk commemorating the French, but nothing marks their conquerors' performance

23 GARCIA HERNANDEZ 1812, SPAIN (PENINSULA WAR)
Commanders: General George Anson & General Bock v. General Maximilien Foy
Forces: British 1,500 cavalry; French 4,000 infantry, 1,000 cavalry.

This action followed immediately after the victory at Salamanca (see 22 July above), and it was fought by the advanced guard of Wellington's army against the rearguard of the French Army of Portugal. Although the numbers engaged were small, it was one of the finest cavalry performances in the Peninsular campaign and brings into notice that for the hundred years preceding Waterloo (1815), the British kings were also Kings of Hanover, and as such German troops were often an integral part of the British forces in the field. On this occasion, there were four cavalry squadrons of the King's German Legion, but the French cavalry, badly battered at Salamanca, did not stand. Charging up hill in pursuit of the cavalry, the Legion were fired on from the flank by three battalions of French infantry formed into a square - the classic formation against cavalry – regardless, the cavalry wheeled and charged at the square with such élan that it broke, and the British cavalry then proceeded to rout the columns into which the remaining French units had been formed. This was one of the very few times that cavalry succeeded in breaking a formed infantry square. Foy's respect for Wellington's capabilities was recorded after Salamanca (see 22 July). British casualties were 150, French 1,400.

25 HARFLEUR 1417, FRANCE (HUNDRED YEARS' WAR)

Commanders: Earl of Huntingdon v. ?

This victory was a repeat of one in the previous year (see 15 August, Seine Mouth). Ships of the Franco-Genoese naval alliance were menacing shipping bound for Harfleur, when they were attacked by an English fleet augmented by prizes taken in the previous success. The English used the same tactics as before, and after three hours the fighting was over. On this occasion, the fruits of victory were greater – four giant carracks seized plus the French admiral, and three months' pay for the French fleet. These two victories seriously damaged French naval power in the Channel, terminated the Genoese alliance and opened the way for the Normandy campaign that was pressed with determination to a successful conclusion.

25 FORT NIAGARA 1759, CANADA (SEVEN YEARS'WAR)

Commanders: Genl. J. Prideaux & Maj..Genl. Sir William.Johnson v.
Captain Pouchot & Colonel Ligneris

Forces: 2,500 British and 900 Iroquois; 600 French and 1,300 French & Indians.

The British were besieging Fort Niagara at the mouth of the Niagara

River, and when Ligneris attempted to relieve the siege he was driven off with heavy losses at La Belle Famille. Pouchot surrendered on 25 July. Prideaux had been killed by the accidental explosion of a shell quite early in the action, and Johnson assumed command.

25 AMANTHEA 1810, ITALY (NAPOLEONIC WARS)

Fought off the coast of Italy to the north of the toe of Italy, this action was typical of many in this theatre of the war. Sea transport was essential to military operations in Italy and the Balkans, and it was incumbent on the navy to cause as much havoc to the supply convoys as possible. Three British ships, namely, a 32 gun frigate, *H.M.S.Thames* (Captain George Waldegrave), and two brigs, *Pilot* and *Weazle*, sighted a convoy of 32 transports protected by 7 gunboats and 5 other armed vessels. They attacked at close quarters and caused the transports to be hauled onto the beach under the town where they were flanked by two batteries. The escorts lined up in front of the transports, but firing from the British ships forced the enemy crews to abandon ship; landing parties then destroyed the batteries, and 28 transports were taken together with 8 of the escorts, while the remainder were destroyed. The convoy had been taking stores and provisions from Naples to Murat's army at Scylla in preparation for the invasion of Sicily, and the loss of the convoy caused the invasion plans to be abandoned.

26 CAEN 1346, FRANCE (HUNDRED YEARS' WAR)

Commanders: Edward III v. Bishop of Bayeux & Comte d'Eu.

Edward had decided on a major campaign against the French and had landed with a large army at St. Vaast on the Cherbourg Peninsula from which he marched eastwards. The most common type of conflict in the Middle Ages was a siege rather than a pitched battle, and Caen is an example. The town, divided by a river, lies outside the walls of a strongly built castle, largely the work of William the Conqueror and Henry I, and before ordering the assault, Edward sent a cleric into the town calling for its surrender with freedom from pillage and slaughter in return. The Bishop of Bayeux scornfully rejected this message and threw the bearer of it into prison. He was not there long; the next day, after some clever tactical marches, Edward launched a vigorous attack. The town was soon taken and as the defenders had no right to quarter after the refusal to surrender, looting was rampant. The castle capitulated and after several days rest the English resumed their march to a very successful conclusion at Crécy (see August 26). An unusual feature of this victory is that the navy had a part in it. After landing the troops, the ships sailed along the coast burning ports as they went, the ships then sailed into the river Orne and reached Caen at about the same time as the army. Thirty French ships were added to the spoils, and there was transport for the prisoners (at least those able to afford a ransom), including the Counts d'Eu and Tancarville, and for the sick and wounded. Incidentally, William the Conqueror and his Queen were buried at Caen, but in the French Revolution William's remains were thrown out in a paroxysm of republican fervour. Another connection with England is, surprisingly, the university. Henry VI did few notable things, but he did found Eton College and King's College, Cambridge, and in his capacity as Henri II of France, he also founded the University of Caen.

26 FORT TICONDEROGA (A.K.A. FORT CARILLON) 1759, U.S.A. (SEVEN YEARS' WAR)

Commanders: General Jeffrey Amherst v. General Bourlamaque
Forces: British 11,000; French 3,500

Almost one year after his brilliant victory at Louisbourg (see27 July), Amherst was continuing his campaign against the French in North America, and he invested Fort Ticonderoga. Since Louisbourg, the French had been unable to receive supplies from France and were obliged to abandon some of their forts, including this one, in order to reinforce the garrison at Quebec (but to no avail, see 13 September, Plains of Abraham). After blowing up the magazine and fighting on the retreat, the French withdrew to the Ile–aux-Noix in Lake Champlain.

27 LOUISBOURG II 1758, CANADA (SEVEN YEARS' WAR)

Commanders: General Jeffrey Amherst & Adml. Edward Boscawen v. Chevalier de Drucour
Forces: British/Colonials 11,600 + 23 ships of the line & 18 frigates; French 4,300 with 234 guns + 5 ships of the line & 7 frigates with 540 guns manned by 3,000.

The strategic importance of Louisbourg to the French is noted in the entry relating to the previous conquest of it (see 16 June). The siege began on 7 June when troops commanded by Brigadier James Wolfe, including a contingent from New England, charged ashore through heavy surf. Fierce fighting followed, and the French sank 6 of their ships to strengthen the defences, the British then destroyed two more and the French surrendered. After the surrender, the remaining French ships were destroyed along with the fortifications. Admiral Boscawen distinguished himself for bravery on a number of occasions particularly in the action at Cape Finisterre (see 3 May and generally, see 17 August, Lagos Bay). Taking advantage of this success, on 8 August Captain Andrew Rollo led troops to Ile St. Jean (Prince Edward Island), overran the settlement of Point-la-Joli (Charlottetown), and built Fort Amherst named in honour of the conqueror of Louisbourg. On the order of Charles Lawrence, Governor of Nova Scotia, Rollo then expelled some 3,500 Acadians, many of whom found their way to Louisiana which was still French territory.

In a similar operation, Wolfe was sent with three battalions to raid and destroy French settlements at the Bay of Gaspé and other places in the Gulf of St. Lawrence – reminiscent of the action taken in the Highlands following the Battle of Culloden in which Wolfe also took part. James Cook, later Captain Cook of international renown, was serving in the naval squadron that escorted Wolfe and his troops, and he took the opportunity to make charts of the Gulf of St. Lawrence which were of great importance in the campaign led by Wolfe against Quebec in the following year (see Plains of Abraham, 13 September).

27 H.M.S. IMMORTALITÉ (42 GUNS) V. L'INVENTION (26 GUNS) 1801, FRANCE (FRENCH REVOLUTIONARYWARS)

Commanders: Captain H. Hotham v. M. Thibaut.

L'Invention was a French privateer sailing out of Bordeaux on her maiden voyage, and when *Immortalité* engaged she had not taken any ships. *L'Invention* was of superior construction and unusual design being 147 feet long and 27 feet in the beam, typically, such a ship would have had three masts but this one had four all of which were rigged in the normal way; the crew numbered 210. According to Captain Hotham, the ship was a good sea boat and handled well, she had been designed by M. Thibaut, and he must have been very disappointed to lose her before he had had time to see how well his brain child performed – *c'est la guerre* seems an inadequate comment.

The previous twelve months were busy ones for *Immortalité*. During that time, she recaptured a merchant ship with its cargo intact, captured two merchant ships, one Swedish, the other Danish, ran ashore and totally wrecked a notorious French privateer as well as capturing a French corvette that had been causing considerable damage to British trade in the Channel. But quite the most intrepid feat was carried out in June while the ship was part of the in-shore squadron watching the port of Brest. The pilot volunteered to go ashore and gather information about the Franco-Spanish fleet in the harbour. He was landed and visited a number of wine shops, drinking with the seamen and troops. He learned that the fleet was to sail on the first easterly wind for Egypt carrying 15,000 troops, reinforcements for the army that had been cut off there after Nelson's annihilation of the French fleet at the Nile, (see 1 August), and that it comprised 20 ships of the line and 2 frigates. The pilot was gone for eight days and was thought to have been captured, but then he returned having forced a fisherman at gun point to take him back to his ship.

Author's Note: An even more dramatic event was planned in World War II. In July 1944 the German army still occupied large parts of Brittany and Normandy including Brest. The 64th. M.T.B. Flotilla (Lt. Cdr. David Wilkie, D.S.C., R.N.R. commanding) was operating in the approaches to Brest (see 3 January, H.M.S. Diamond-*Author's Note*), and in what in retrospect seems a wildly absurd idea, it was decided while the flotilla (8 boats) lay to in the daylight hours off Ushant that if the Road of Brest could not be penetrated that night, then an officer and two ratings would be sent ashore in a dinghy and demand of the first sentry encountered to be taken to the commanding officer. This officer was to be told that an amphibious landing was imminent, and that to avoid unnecessary bloodshed he was to surrender to the 64th. Flotilla with all of his troops. Acceptance of these terms was to be signalled by Aldis lamp to the flotilla lying close inshore. An immediate difficulty was to find an officer able to speak German, but one with a rudimentary grasp of the language was identified, and the scheme was on. That night the Road of Brest proved impassable, and the flotilla moved along the coast until a suitable beach for a landing was found. The next thing was to launch the dinghy, and here the enterprise foundered because the Atlantic swell was too great to permit the dinghy to be launched. A small example of the hare-brained ideas that find a ready acceptance in wartime.

28 TALAVERA DE LA REINA 1809, SPAIN (PENINSULA WAR)

Commanders: Wellington & Captain-Genl. Don Gregorio de La Cuesta
v. Marshals Jean-Baptiste Jourdan and Claude Victor,
with King Joseph Bonaparte in nominal command.

Forces: British 20,000, Spanish 34,000 and 60 guns; French 40,000 and 80 guns.

Through inept leadership and indiscipline the Spanish played little part in this battle.Talavera was Wellington's second action against the French after his return to Portugal in sole command (see May 12, Oporto), and he won a convincing victory. The engagement lasted for two days and a night and was marked by ferocious fighting. Wellington said "never was there such a murderous battle", while for a wider audience Byron declaimed poetically:

"Three hosts combine to offer sacrifice,
To feed the crow on Talavera's plain."

John Croker, a politician, man of letters, and a great friend of Wellington, wrote an epic poem in twenty-one stanzas on this battle in which France is described as "every nation's foe".

Wellington's prowess loses nothing in the telling, and the heavy casualty rate is referred to proportionately but with what seems to be a good deal of poetic licence:

"Ten gallant French the valley strew
For every Briton slain.
On Talavera's plain they lie
No! never to return!"
And
"France,
Leaving to Britain's conquering sons,
Standards rent and ponderous guns,
The trophies of the fray!

The weak, the wounded, and the slain-
The triumph of the battle plain-
The glory of the day!"

The British had 5,363 casualties (more than a quarter of the total force); the French 7,208 and lost 7 guns. Wellington himself was bruised by a spent bullet and all his staff were wounded.

Paradoxically, the French and British troops in the Peninsular War were friendly off the battlefield. At Talavera, there was an unofficial, local truce during which both sides made use of the small stream that divided the armies, and later when the Spanish had failed to evacuate the British wounded, the French even shared their Spanish loot with the British injured (see also 16 January Corunna). Notwithstanding an emphatic victory, lack of adequate supplies and reinforcements obliged Wellington to make a strategic withdrawal to prepare the Lines of Torres Vedras (November 14). Honours and accolades applauded Wellington's success – a peerage as Viscount Wellington and Baron Douro - and the Spanish gave him the rank of Captain-General.

There are two monuments on the site of the battle. The older one is on private property, but the larger, modern one includes a map in the ceramics for which the district is noted and it lists all of the units of the British-Portuguese, French, and Spanish armies that were engaged.

28 SORAUREN 1813, SPAIN (PENINSULA WAR)

Commanders: Wellington v. Marshal Nicolas-Jean de Dieu Soult, Duc de Dalmatie

Forces: British, Portuguese & Spanish 25,000 increasing to 35,000; French 35,000.

Sorauren was the principal battle in a series that took place between July 25 and August 2 collectively known as the Battle of the Pyrenees. Following their decisive defeat at Vitoria (see 21 June), the French were expelled from Spain except for the garrisons at Pamplona and San Sebastian. As soon as he heard the news about Vitoria, Napoleon sent Soult to Spain with orders to replace and, if necessary, to arrest King Joseph, his brother, and to reorganize the army. Soult carried out his orders, and his immediate object was to reinforce San Sebastian and Pamplona. Wellington spread his troops along the line of the frontier and waited for the French attack which was sent in at several mountain passes commencing on 25 July .After these preliminary thrusts, Wellington and Soult confronted each other, and although Wellington's force was outnumbered two to one, Soult's attacks failed completely, and the French were repulsed. Two days later, hostilities were resumed. Soult had decided to withdraw, and although still outnumbered, Wellington launched successful attacks all along the front. At Sorauren, a French division was all but annihilated, and elsewhere transport and baggage were left behind as the French retreated into France. British and Allied casualties were 1,083; French were 4,000.

29 H.M.S. VIPER (12 GUNS) V. CERBERE (7 GUNS) 1800, SENEGAL (FRENCH REVOLUTIONARY WARS)

Commanders: Acting Lieutenant Jeremiah Coghlan v. ?

This was a boat action fought at night off St. Louis in which Coghlan was in command of a cutter manned by 19 volunteers from the squadron and from *Viper* with orders to cut out the brig, *Cerbere*, from under three shore batteries and within a mile of a ship of the line and two frigates. The brig had 87 on board, including 16 soldiers, who were all at quarters, and, at the third attempt, it was towed away under fire from the batteries. British casualties were 1 killed and 8 wounded including Coghlan, who was wounded twice, one being a pike thrust in the leg, and a midshipman who had six wounds; the French had 6 killed and 20 wounded including all of the officers. The best evaluation of the bravery displayed in this relatively small conquest is that the admiral commanding, Lord St. Vincent, presented Coghlan with a sword worth 100 guineas and hoped the Admiralty would grant him promotion, and most tellingly, the officers and crews in the squadron joined with the admiral in giving up their share of the prize money in favour of those who took the active part. Naval medals were awarded for this action, and on return to port Coghlan was commissioned as lieutenant and confirmed in his command. These rewards justified the confidence of the commander of the squadron, Sir Edward Pellew, who several months before this action, had appointed Coghlan to command *Viper* in the rank of acting lieutenant. Pellew himself was well qualified to judge bravery. He was one of the outstanding frigate commanders of his generation (see 13 January, Indefatigable; 20 April, Indefatigable; and

18 June, Nymphe.).

When this event occurred, St. Louis was a place of some importance in the French colonial empire, but in recent years the rise of Dakar has sent it into decline. Even the consolation of dedication as a UNESCO world heritage site is tarnished by the UNESCO site at Gorée Island, 3km. from Dakar, which attracts about three times as many tourists (see 29 December).

31 CRAVANT 1423, FRANCE (HUNDRED YEARS' WAR)

Commanders: Earl of Salisbury v. Sir John Stewart & Count de Vendôme

Forces: English & Burgundians 4,000; French & Scottish 8,000 +.

The Treaty of Troyes 1420 (see 21 May) and the subsequent marriage of Henry V to the daughter of Charles VI had secured the succession of Henry and his heirs to the French throne, and the disinheritance of the Dauphin, later Charles VII, but the plan unravelled with Henry's premature death in 1422 (there is an interesting analogy with a French dynastic scheme involving Mary, Queen of Scots, see 6 July, Treaty of Edinburgh). He was succeeded as king of England by his son, Henry VI, who later was also crowned king of France as Henri II. The Dauphin, however, repudiated the Treaty and war was resumed. Strategically, it was only practicable for England to wage war in France with a continental ally, and at this period it was the Duke of Burgundy. Cravant, in the valley of the river Yonne, was under siege by the Dauphin's army, and the English-Burgundian army under the command of the Earl of Salisbury had marched to its relief. The French and the large Scottish contingent with them blocked the way in a very strong defensive position about four miles from the town, but Salisbury, giving further proof of his military skills, made an outflanking march so that his troops were less than two hundred yards from the walls of the town but with the river in front of them. At this point the river was about 40 yards wide with a bridge and a ford, and the French and Scots were compressed into a strip of land about 150 yards wide; their offensive option was to attack across the river, or defensively to repel English attempts to do so. Notwithstanding their large numerical advantage, the French chose the defensive option. Under a hail of arrows, Salisbury led the left wing through the waist-high river, while the right wing fought with the Scots for the bridge. The fighting was fierce, and eventually, as the French began to give way, there was a sortie from Cravant. Although the garrison there had been weakened by starvation, their appearance at the rear was sufficient to precipitate the flight of the Dauphin's troops. Trapped in a confined space the slaughter began, especially at the bridge where the Scots refused to flee. It has been estimated that 300 – 400 nobles were killed and chief among the 2,000 or so prisoners were the two commanders Sir John Stewart, Constable of Scotland, (who lost an eye), and the Comte de Vendôme. As an indication of the ferocity of the fight for the bridge, many years later when it was being widened numerous skeletons were dredged from the river.

Salisbury started life with a major disadvantage, his father had supported Richard II, who was deposed by Henry IV, the father of Henry V. Salisbury senior was excuted and his estates forfeited, but fortunately, the sins of the father were not visited on the son in their entirety; when he was 21 a part of the estates was restored to him, he was summoned to Parliament, and then embarked on a military career. He was at the naval victory in the Baie de Seine (see 15 August, Seine Mouth) and served throughout Henry V's Normandy campaign. A few months after the Treaty of Troyes, he was rewarded for his services by the restoration of the rest of the family estates, and by his performances he established such a considerable military reputation that after Henry's death in 1422, Salisbury became the principal field commander. His death from a wound early in the siege of Orleans in 1428 was little short of a calamity for the English.

Cravant has been an inauspicious venue in French military history. In 1870, a three day battle in the Franco-Prussian War was fought here in which the French were not able to halt the Prussian advance, although they performed decidedly better than in 1423.

31 FORT ST. FRÉDÉRIC (A.K.A. CROWN POINT) 1759, CANADA (SEVEN YEARS' WAR)

This fort, a little to the north of Fort Ticonderoga, was abandoned as part of the French withdrawal to Quebec (see 26 July).

31 WARBURG 1760, GERMANY (SEVEN YEARS'WAR)

Commanders: Field Marshal Ferdinand, Duke of Brunswick & Lt. Genl. Marquis of Granby v. Chevalier de Muy

Forces: Prussians and British cavalry about 30,000; French about 30,000.

The French were advancing on Hanover (ruled by King George II as Elector) and were confronted by the Prussians and British. The defeat of the French at Warburg was mainly due to the excellent work of the British cavalry commanded by Granby (see 15 July, Vellinghausen) who had succeeded the awful Sackville (see August 1, Minden). Both French flanks were attacked by Granby's cavalry and their casualties amounted to 3,000 including 1,500 prisoners and 10 guns; the French retreated to the Rhine

AUGUST

1 MIREBEAU-EN-POITOU 1202, FRANCE (ANGLO-FRENCH WARS)

Commanders: John, King of England v. Arthur, Duke of Brittany

Internecine conflicts characterize the progeny of Henry II, and here is another example. John succeded his brother, Richard the Lion Heart, as King of England and Duke of Normandy, but Arthur was the posthumous son of Geoffrey, John's elder brother , and he thought he had a better right to the titles. Geoffrey was prominent in every family quarrel and often intrigued with the king of France as a consequence of which Arthur was raised in the French court and was betrothed to the daughter of Philip II. He was now was trying to capture parts of the Angevin empire; his grandmother the Dowager Queen of Henry II and Duchess of Aquitaine before her marriage, was conducting a vigorous defence of her patrimony on behalf of John and had been obliged to withdraw into the castle of Mirebeau to await a relieving force. Arthur was besieging the town and the castle.While the siege was in progress, John led his troops to the rescue of his mother and Arthur was taken prisoner. Arthur's part in the family feuds now comes to an abrupt end; he was taken to Falaise and then to Rouen where he was murdered either by John himself or at his orders. This victory was an isolated event in a string of defeats for John, and he was soon to be driven back to England.

1 LONDONDERRY 1689, IRELAND (WAR OF THE LEAGUE OF AUGSBURG)

Commanders: Major Baker & Colonel J. Michelburne v. Marshal-Genl. C. de Rosen.

The 'Glorious Revolution' of 1688 was bloodless. Exhibiting the stupidity of the later Stuarts, James II, succeeded in uniting most of the country against him, and less than two months after William of Orange had landed with an army half the size of his, James fled to France and the protection of Louis XIV without firing a shot. In mitigation of this dismal performance, it must be noted that a factor was the number of desertions from his army (and navy) to William's cause including John Churchill (later Duke of Marlborough), the second-in-command. In the spring of 1689, James was in Ireland with French reinforcements, de Rosen in command, for the Irish regiments that still supported him, and with the object of invading Britain from there. The dynastic conflict between William, and his wife Mary (elder daughter of James II) on the one hand, and James on the other was subordinate to larger European wars between Protestant and Roman Catholic countries, and initially the latter had more to do with the siege of Londonderry than the former. Only four years before, Louis XIV had revoked the Edict of Nantes and unleashed pitiless persecution of his Protestant subjects; Londonderry was predominantly Protestant, James ardently Roman Catholic, and the inhabitants of the city were terrified that they were to be treated like the French Huguenots. They looked to William and Mary for protection.

In April 1689, James' army was not expecting Londonderry to offer any resistance because the Governor, Colonel Lundy, had declared that it would be futile to try to defend the city. The majority of the population did not agree and determined not to capitulate. Lundy escaped to England where he was imprisoned in the Tower, Baker was elected Governor, and the siege began when thirteen apprentices became famous in history by closing the gates with the army of James only 50 yards away.

It soon became apparent that Londonderry could not be carried by assault and therefore the garrison would have to be starved out by a blockade. A dithering commander kept a relief force in the River Foyle, looking at a boom across the river while the beleagured inhabitants were starving, until two merchant ships carrying food and a naval frigate, *Dartmouth,* commanded by Cdr. J. Leake (see 10 March Marbella and

19 September Port Mahon), broke through the boom. After three days of bombardment without result, James' army marched away to fight another day, although many of them might have wished not to have done so (see 1 July, Boyne).

1 MINDEN 1759, GERMANY (SEVEN YEARS' WAR)
Commanders: Field Marshal, Ferdinand, Duke of Brunswick v. Marquis Louis de Contades
Forces: 54,000 British, Prussian & Hanoverians with 187 guns; French 64,000 with 170 guns.

Thanks to a vigorous attack by the British infantry against the centre of the French line, followed by the repulse of a counter-attack with a bayonet charge, the French centre collapsed. Unfortunately, the commander of the British and Hanoverian cavalry, Lord George Sackville, then disobeyed repeated orders to charge, so that the French were able to retreat to the Rhine in reasonably good order, although their casualties, including prisoners, were 7,086 and 43 guns and 17 standards. The Allied losses were 2,762 and most of them were British. Because of his pusillanimous performance Lord Sackville was court-martialled and cashiered, and by the practice of this period (see January 15, Pondicherry) he could count himself lucky not to have been executed, but he was commonly dubbed 'The Great Incompetent'.

Sackville is, however, an enigmatic character who was perhaps promoted above his level of competence. Early in his army career, while still an infantry officer, at the battle of Fontenoy he led his men so deep into the French lines that he was made a prisoner and his wounds were treated in the tent of Louis XV. Later, he served as a colonel of infantry in Scotland and Ireland. The steady decline in his military performance began with his promotion to major-general and transfer to the cavalry. A badly-managed attack and consequent defeat at St. Malo in 1758 was a precursor of Minden. Following his forced return to civilian life, and presumably as a result of his connections (he was the third son of the Duke of Dorset), in 1775, he returned to the stage as the colonial secretary in the government of Lord North. In this office, he was responsible for the general conduct of the war against the American colonists, and he was largely to blame for the poor co-ordination of the operations from New York and Canada.

Perhaps because he was so far away from the firing line, after Cornwallis had surrendered in 1781, Sackville was the only member of the Cabinet in favour of continuing the war. He left politics when North was dismissed, but in 1782 was created Viscount Sackville and Baron Drayton.

1 CALVI 1794, CORSICA (FRENCH REVOLUTIOARY WARS)

Commanders: Lt.General Charles Stuart &Captain Horatio Nelson v. ?

Unlike the siege of Bastia (see 20 May), which was the prelude to it, at Calvi the army took part in the siege along with marines, seamen, and heavy guns from the ships. The rocky terrain made it extremely difficult to land the guns and put them in place – it took two weeks of very hard manual labour – and this in itself represented an outstanding performance. The bombardment was opened from the Royal Louis battery manned by French artillery men, royalists who had been evacuated from Toulon (see 19 December), it continued through July, and all the while the besiegers were ravaged by malaria, typhoid, heat-exhaustion and dysentery. When it was questionable whether the operation could be continued with the reduced number of healthy men, the garrison of Calvi ran out of ammunition and were forced to fly white flags. It was during this siege that a shell burst sent up a shower of sand and stones that hit Nelson in his right eye, effectively blinding him, but he never wore an eye patch. Nelson, who was never shy in looking for public recognition of his performances, was out of humour at the scant references in the official despatches to his personal contributions to the victories at Bastia and Calvi. In a letter to his wife he summarised what he had accomplished in the campaign: "One hundred and ten days I have been actually engaged, at sea and on shore, against the enemy; three actions against ships, two against Bastia in my ship; four boat actions, and two villages taken and twelve sail of vessels burnt. I do not know of any man who has done more." A busy life indeed, but it has to be remembered that none of these was a single-handed encounter. Sir Gilbert Elliot, newly-appointed Viceroy of Corsica, was a witness of the campaign and made an interesting comparison of the navy and army: "The character of the profession [navy] is infinitely more manly, they are full of life and action, while on shore it is all high lounge and still life." He preferred the navy as a career for his son.

I NILE (A.K.A. ABUKIR BAY) 1798, EGYPT (FRENCH REVOLUTIONARY WARS)

Commanders: Nelson v. Vice-Adml. François Paul de Brueys
Forces: British 14 ships of the line and a small brig (total number of guns 1,026); French 13 ships of the line + 4 frigates and 2 brigs (total number of guns 1,070 plus a shore battery and some gunboats).

There can be no doubt that this victory had a direct effect on the course of history. It thwarted the French drive to conquer India by way of Egypt, and the scale of the triumph demonstrated a marked superiority of the British navy over the French. Napoleon, at this point not yet a Consul, had formulated a strategy to attack British colonial possessions in the East and as a preliminary to attack the Ottoman Empire. He sailed with his army for Egypt, capturing Malta along the way, and fought a successful battle against the Mamelukes in July. The French fleet that had transported him was anchored at the mouth of the Nile in a bay with shoal water behind the ships. Nelson and his squadron had been searching the Mediterranean and finally sighted the French, a few hours before nightfall, anchored in line astern. Nelson immediately gave orders to attack, and the four leading ships, risking grounding on the inshore shoals, sailed round the head of the enemy line so that the French ships were attacked from both sides. Heavy fighting went on throughout the night in the course of which the French flagship, *L'Orient*, a three decker of 120 guns and easily the largest vessel present, was hotly engaged by *H.M.S. Bellerophon*, a two decker of 74 guns. For nearly an hour the *Bellerophon* fought *L'Orient* single-handed, all of her masts were shot away and all of the officers except one were killed or wounded. Finally, when it was seen that *L'Orient* was on fire, *Bellerophon* disengaged and drifted away. The carnage and damage on the French flagship were equally bad.

De Brueys was wounded in the hand and face, then both legs were shot away, but he remained on deck directing operations until he was killed by a cannonball. He believed that: "a French admiral must die on his poop-deck.", and he did. His heroism became a legend in the French navy, and after the battle Napoleon dismissed criticisms of de Brueys' tactics with: "if in this fatal event, Brueys made mistakes, he has atoned for them by his glorious death". Commodore Casabianca, the Flag Captain, was severely wounded early in the fighting, and while he lay on the deck his ten-year old son, on board as a cadet, refused to leave his side, but after the magazine of *L'Orient* exploded they were last seen floating away clinging to a mast. The magazine explosion was massive; an idea of how big can be obtained from the discovery by French archeologists of one of *L'Orient's* cannon, weighing two tons, which had been blown more than 400 yards.

Nelson was among the British wounded concussed by a flying fragment, but the success of his squadron was overwhelming. When dawn broke, it revealed that ten French ships of the line had been taken, one blown up and only two escaped together with two frigates. Those which escaped were under the command of Rear–Admiral Villeneuve who lived to fight, and be taken prisoner, at Trafalgar (see 21 October). British casualties were 288 killed and 677 wounded; the French had 1,700 killed, 1,500 wounded and 3,000 taken prisoner.

Surveying the large amount of wreckage the next day, Nelson said: "Victory is not a name strong enough for such a scene." When Nelson's despatch reached London, there was widespread and prolonged acclamation. Nelson received the freedom of the City of London and several other cities, the King conferred on him the title of 'Baron Nelson of the Nile and Burnham Thorpe' (his birthplace), and astonishingly a fourth verse was written for the national anthem, namely:

"Join we in Great Nelson's name,
First on the rolls of Fame
Him let us sing.
Spread we his fame around,
Honour of British ground,
Who made Nile's shore resound,
God save the King".

Meanwhile, Captain Hallowell of *H.M.S. Swiftsure* devised a most unusual honour. He had a coffin made from a mast of *L'Orient* and presented it to Nelson; it was enclosed in the catafalque in which he was buried in the crypt of St. Paul's Cathedral after the battle of Trafalgar. The Battle of the Nile also inspired a well-known poem, 'Casabianca', by Mrs. Hemans. These verses were a tribute to the son of Commodore Casabianca who refused to leave the side of his wounded father, and it is the first two lines that have passed into the language:

"The boy stood on the burning deck
Whence all but he had fled;"

1 SUMBILLA 1813, SPAIN (PENINSULA WAR)

Commanders: Lt.General Sir Lowry Cole v. General Bertrand Clausel.

A minor engagement that was a post-script to Sorauren (see 28 July). Cole's 4th Division caught up with the retreating French, who did not offer serious resistance and made their escape at the expense of 150 casualties against 48 on the British side.

Clausel served in the Spanish campaign from 1809 but spent much of his time fighting on the retreat (very risky with Clausel in command as he admitted to having had 50 of his troops shot in the process), nevertheless, he earned a good reputation, and when Napoleon returned from exile in Elba for his hundred days, he raised Clausel to the peerage. Napoleon's second abdication cut short Clausel's enjoyment of his new social distinction, and he was forced to flee to the United States to escape prosecution. The general amnesty of 1820 enabled him to return to France where he embarked on a political career which did not preclude him from being promoted to the rank of Marshal in 1831. Demonstrating an adroitness superior to his military performances, he was made Governor of Algeria in 1835, but his aggressive policies and defeat by the Algerian army resulted in his dismissal a year or so later.

The quality of the British commanders in the Peninsula often disappointed Wellington, but Cole was well above the dismal average. As a young man, he had courted Kitty Pakenham, but his proposal was refused, and not long after Kitty married Wellington. Notwithstanding being jilted in favour of Wellington, Cole developed a considerable admiration for Wellington as an army commander and served him with devotion and skill.

2 IVANTELLY (A.K.A. ECHALAR) 1813, SPAIN (PENINSULAR WAR)

Commanders: Wellington v. Marshal Nicolas-Jean de Dieu Soult., Duke of Dalmatia.

Forces: British 12,000; French 25,000.

The French were in the last stages of their retreat after Sorauren (see July 28) and made a stand on a prominent ridge. Wellington's troops were exhausted after a week of heavy fighting and marching, but Wellington, believing that French morale was low after the mauling they had received, decided to attack. His diagnosis proved to be correct, and in spite of being heavily out-numbered, the British smashed the French centre, and the right wing was dispersed; the retreat continued in some disorder into France.

2 H.M.S. BACCHANTE (38 GUNS) & H.M.S. EAGLE (74 GUNS) 1813, ROVINJ, CROATIA (NAPOLEONIC WAR)

Commanders: Captain William Hoste & Captain Rowley v. ?

Twenty-one ships were sighted in the harbour of Rovinj, and the two British ships sailed into it, *Bacchante* leading, and engaged the shore batteries. These were abandoned, whereupon Captain Hoste led the marines ashore and drove the enemy out of the town. The fortifications were destroyed, and although most of the enemy ships had been scuttled, a gunboat and two armed merchant vessels laden with salt were captured.

3 NEGAPATAM 1758 INDIA (SEVEN YEARS' WAR)

Commanders: Rear-Adml. George Pocock v. Rear-Adml. Ann Antoine d'Aché de Serquigny.

This encounter was really the second part of an action three months earlier (see 29 April Cuddalore). The two squadrons were roughly equal and fought hard with the French breaking off first, and the British, with badly damaged rigging, unable to mount an effective pursuit. In August 1762, Pocock had a much more decisive result against the Spanish. He was joint commander in an amphibious operation that took Havana and a large amount of booty.

3 SANTANDER 1812, SPAIN, (PENINSULAR WAR)
Commanders: Cdre.Sir Home Popham v. Genl. Dubreton
Forces: A British amphibious force comprising 2 ships of the line, 4 frigates, 2 sloops and several smaller vessels, and 1,000 marines acting with several guerrilla bands against the French garrison.

This action was a continuation of the successful operation at Lequeitio (see 22 June), the purpose of which was to control the northern coast of Spain and to provide support to the guerrilla forces, thus reducing the strength of the French opposing Wellington's offensive against southern France. After some serious fighting, the castle and town were evacuated by the defenders leaving Popham in possession of the only good harbour between Ferrol and the French frontier.

4 CALAIS 1347, FRANCE (HUNDRED YEARS' WAR)
Commanders: Edward III v. ?

Following his overwhelming victory at Crécy (Cressy) the previous year (see 26 August), Edward III had marched his army north and laid siege to Calais, an important town not only because of its proximity to England, but also for its position in the cross-Channel wool trade. The inhabitants made a stalwart defence and resisted for nearly a year until starvation finally forced them to capitulate. In those days, the usual result when a city or town surrendered after resisting a siege was rapine and pillage, but on this occasion Edward III was persuaded not to follow this practice provided six burghers, ransom for the population, were executed instead. Six agreed to these terms, but they were spared, it is said, on the intercession of Queen Philippa. The Queen's compassionate nature has gone down in history, and a lasting memorial to her is Queen's College, Oxford founded by her chaplain but named for her.

More than 500 years later, the six burghers were immortalized by Auguste Rodin in one of his major works, the statuary "Les Bourgeois de Calais". Although the work was commissioned by the town council of Calais in 1894, when completed, the work so infuriated them that it was not displayed in front of the town hall until 1925 – thereby demonstrating how ill-suited politicians are to pass judgment on works of art. Several replicas of the statue have been made, and there are several in the United States, including one at Stanford University, and a fine bronze replica stands in the Victoria Tower Gardens hard by the Houses of Parliament, somewhat incongruously placed next to a statue of Mrs. Pankhurst, leader of the women's suffrage movement.

Calais remained an English possession for more than 200 years during which time Henry VIII incorporated it in his kingdom and summoned members from Calais to the parliament. Assimilation failed, however, and it was finally re-taken in 1558 during the reign of Henry's daughter, Mary. The district was named *'Pays Reconquis'* (the Reconquered Territory), and Mary is reputed to have said that after her death the word 'Calais' would be found written on her heart.

9 BATAVIA (DJARKATA) 1811, JAVA (NAPOLEONIC WAR)

Commanders: Genl. Sir Samuel Auchmuty v. Genl. Jan Willems Janssens

Forces: British 5,344 Europeans 6,616 Indians; French/Dutch 17,000 including 500 French light infantry.

Napoleon had made his brother, Louis Napoleon, King of the Netherlands, and consequently the Dutch resumed their alliance with France. The British campaign to conquer Java was planned by the Governor General of India, Lord Minto, who sailed with the invading fleet. Batavia, the capital, was taken without resistance, the French/ Dutch army having retreated to a strongly fortified position a few miles away at Cornelis.

Janssens, now the Governor-General of the Dutch East Indies, had unsuccessfully opposed the British at Cape Town five years earlier (see 8 January, Blueberg). Minto, previously the Viceroy of Corsica (see 20 May, Bastia), had also directed the capture of the islands of Bourbon (see 8July) and Mauritius (see 3 December, Ile de France) in 1810; and so he denied Napoleon any benefit from the Dutch East Indian Empire. General Auchmuty was an interesting character. Born in New York City in 1758, the son of a clergyman, he fought as a loyalist during the American Revolution, and after that war he joined the army in England. Successful service in India and Egypt (see 8 March Abukir) earned him popularity and a knighthood; he was commander-in-chief at Madras when the Java expedition set out, and he finished his army career as commander-in-chief in Ireland.

10 LE MANS 1425, FRANCE (HUNDRED YEARS' WAR)
Commanders: Earl of Salisbury v. ?

A marriage had caused the English impetus in France to weaken. One of Henry V's younger brothers, Humphrey, Duke of Gloucester, married Jaqueline, countess of Hainault and Holland in her own right, who had been previously married to the Duke of Brabant and from whom she had obtained a divorce. Her ex-husband assumed control over the territories of Jacqueline, and she was determined to get them back in which endeavour she was strongly supported by her new husband. Humphrey and Jaqueline landed in Flanders at the head of a mercenary army and quickly occupied her patrimony. Humphrey then decided to exploit this success and invade and ravage the Brabant domains which gave rise to a crisis. The Duke of Brabant was one of a junior branch of the house of Burgundy and a cousin of the Duke, the major ally of England in France. The Duke of Burgundy challenged Humphrey to a duel and although the challenge was accepted, the duel did not take place. The Duke of Bedford, now regent of France and demonstrating his diplomatic skills, was able to mollify the Duke of Burgundy sufficiently to keep the alliance intact, and the war continued albeit in a lower key. This was the background to the siege and capture of Le Mans. The Earl of Salisbury landed in France in the summer of 1425 with a batch of new recruits and proceeded to advance westwards from Paris against the towns in possession of the Dauphin. After several conquests along the way, he arrived at Le Mans, the capital of Maine, and this town soon capitulated as did its neighbour, Mayenne. The campaign came to a halt because the Duke of Bedford was obliged to return to England to settle a new dispute in which the rambunctious Duke of Gloucester was now embroiled. Humphrey, the protector of England, was feuding with his uncle, Cardinal Beaufort, who was the Chancellor and head of government. Their dispute was disrupting both the civil and military administration and sapped the national energy, giving some relief to the French.

Five hundred and nineteen years later, almost to the very day, Le Mans was again liberated, this time by the U.S. 5th. Armoured Division as it broke out of the Normandy beachhead.

10 BREST 1512, FRANCE (WAR OF THE HOLY LEAGUE)

Commanders: Lord Howard v.Jean de Thenouenal.

This battle was part of the ill-conceived campaign of Henry VIII (see 25 September Tournai) in which victories yielded few benefits. An English fleet of 45 ships drove a French fleet of 39 ships into Brest or onto the rocky coast with heavy losses. In the action, the English losses were 1,600 men and two ships.

11 ISLAND OF SCHIERMANNIKOOG 1799, FRIESLAND, NETHERLANDS (FRENCH REVOLUTIONARY WARS)

Commanders: Captain F. Southeron v. ?
Forces: British light squadron comprising a frigate, a sloop, a brig and a cutter; French 3 gunboats.

This was a small scale action in which the notable feature was the skilful navigation required in narrow and shallow channels. The French gunboat, *Crash*, was taken as a prize and two days later the gunboat, *Undaunted*, was added to it. A third gunboat, *Vengeance*, was driven ashore and burned. A shore party then either spiked the enemy guns or brought them back on board, and all without any casualties. The result was gratifying because *Crash* had been captured by the French almost exactly a year before. An excellent description of the difficulties of sailing in the inshore waters of this part of Europe is given in Erskine Childers novel 'The Riddle of the Sands'.

13 BLENHEIM (BLINDHEIM) 1704, GERMANY (WAR OF THE SPANISH SUCCESSION)

Commanders: Marlborough & Prince Eugene v. Marshal Camille, Comte de Tallard & Maximilian II, Elector of Bavaria
Forces: British, German & Dutch 52,000 with 66 guns; French & Bavarians 56,000 with 90 guns.

Blenheim is invariably on the short list of decisive battles in world history. For over forty years, French armies had fought across Europe without sustaining a major defeat, but the humiliation at Blenheim destroyed this reputation and further territorial ambitions. France was put on the defensive for the remainder of the reign of Louis XIV, and Marlborough was established among the greatest military commanders of all time.

By a night march that took the French commanders by surprise Marlborough brought his allied army into position on the north side of the Danube. The French made tactical errors that Marlborough was able to exploit, but the fighting was fierce, and in the late afternoon the outcome was still in balance. At this point, Marlborough asked Prince Eugene to send him reinforcements, which he did without hesitation, although his troops were severely pressed as well; all commentators on the battle commend Eugene highly for his response. Marlborough himself took command of the sector in the counter-attack which broke the French resistance, and retreat quickly turned into a rout, except for the émigré Irish regiment, the 'Wild Geese', that fought notably well. 10,000 infantry in Blenheim, encircled by the British, surrendered after their general, in panic, had ridden off straight into the Danube and drowned. Upwards of 3,000 French cavalry were driven to the same fate by their British counterparts. In total, Marlborough's casualties were 6,000 killed and 6,500 wounded, but on the other side the French prisoners alone numbered 13,000, including Marshal de Tallard and 40 generals, and the killed, wounded and missing amounted to 30,000. The French lost 47 guns, 25 standards and more than 40 colours, the army's treasury, cases of silver, more than 3,000 tents, about 100 fat oxen ready skinned – and 34 coaches with French ladies! The intangible losses were significant. Some of France's finest regiments were badly mauled at Blenheim, and the new recruits were not of the same quality. Then there was the wider effect on morale – both of the French and their opponents. Prior to Blenheim, decades of triumph had built up in the French army a sense of invincibility, and conversely, a feeling among their opponents that they were bound to lose (similar, in reverse, to the relationship between the British and French naval personnel prior to Trafalgar – see 21 October). All of this was blown away at Blenheim. As one French general later acknowledged: "[we] had too good an opinion of [our] own ability - and were excessively scornful of [our] adversaries". The cities of Ulm and Ingolstadt soon fell, and the Elector of Bavaria lost all of his territory; in the rest of Europe, a new confidence emerged to confront French ambitions of conquest. English adulation was formally recognized by the gift of the royal manor of Woodstock with 16,000 acres on which to build, also at national expense, a splendid palace in which, by a most appropriate turn of events, Sir Winston Churchill was born one hundred and seventy years after Blenheim.

Marlborough's reputation was largely earned fighting the French, but as a young soldier his early military experience was fighting with the French after Charles II had made an alliance with the French against the Dutch. Throughout his military career Marlborough distinguished himself. He received public recognition and commendation from Louis XIV for bravery at the siege of Maastricht in 1674, and in April of that year Louis appointed him as a colonel in one of his English regiments. Subsequently, he served under the distinguished French Marshal, Turenne, who prophesied distinction for the handsome Englishman. These expectations were amply realized at Blenheim and subsequently, but not at all in the manner that Louis XIV and Turenne would have wished.

Prince Eugene and Marlborough commanded jointly for the first time at Blenheim and began there a warm collaboration resulting in a number of celebrated victories (see 11 July Oudenarde, 11 September Malplaquet).No doubt due to his early service with the French army, Marlborough seems not to have harboured any particular hostility towards the French and treated his distinguished prisoners with courtesy, but in sharp contrast, Prince Eugene nursed a bitter hatred of Louis XIV and the French monarchy. His mother was a niece of Cardinal Mazarin, chief minister of Louis XIII, and Eugene was born in Paris. His father was exiled twice as a result of intrigues at court, and his mother's bitterness at her husband's treatment passed undiluted to her son. A serious error of judgment by Louis XIV then exacerbated this feeling. Because of poor physique as a child, Louis denied Eugene a military career and sought to force him to enter the church. Eugene and his brother left France for Vienna where Eugene enlisted in the Austrian army and swore not to return to France except with his sword in hand. Rapid promotion led to his appointment as a general of cavalry at 26, and he gained a crushing victory over the Turks at Zenta in 1697. Napoleon was to say of him that he was one of only seven great strategists of all time whose campaigns were worth studying by posterity. In Germany, Prince Eugene is known as Prinz Eugen, and a German heavy cruiser in World War II was named in his honour.

Joseph Addison wrote his poem, 'The Campaign', in honour of Blenheim, part of which is:

'Twas then great Marlboro's mighty soul was prov'd … …
In peaceful thought the field of death survey'd,
To fainting squadrons sent the timely aid,
Inspir'd repuls'd Battalions to engage,
And taught the doubtful battle where to rage.

But Robert Southey in his poem, 'The Battle of Blenheim', had a different perspective:

"Great praise the Duke of Marlboro' won,
And our good Prince Eugene. … …
And everybody praised the Duke,
Who this great fight did win
'But what good came of it at last?'
Quoth little Peterkin.
'Why that I cannot tell', said he,
But 'twas a famous victory."

13 VELEZ MALAGA 1704, SPAIN (WAR OF THE SPANISH SUCCESSION)

Commanders: Adml. Sir George Rooke v. Adml.Louis Alexandre de Bourbon, Comte de Toulouse
Forces: Anglo-Dutch 51 ships; Franco- Spanish about the same.

Gibraltar had been captured from the Spanish by Rooke and his fleet on 24 July, 1704, and the French ships had joined their Spanish allies in an attempt to re-take it. The action was hard fought and lasted for more than eight hours at the end of which time both sides set to repairing the considerable damage sustained, but during the night the Franco-Spanish fleet withdrew leaving Rooke with a strategic victory in that he was able to consolidate his occupation of the Rock. The British casualties were 695 killed and 1,663 wounded, the Dutch had 400 casualties; Franco-Spanish casualties were 1,500 killed and more than 3,000 wounded. A French frigate and two Spanish galleys were sunk.

Rooke had a successful career with a notable performance at Barfleur and La Hougue, and at Vigo Bay(see 19 May; and 12 October respectively) and is generally regarded as the greatest seaman of his age of any nationality, but his capture and defence of Gibraltar, important though it has proved to be, ironically lost him his command, and he never went to sea again. Rooke had Tory friends in Parliament who claimed that the capture of Gibraltar was a greater victory than Blenheim (see above), these assertions so infuriated the Whigs, the party of Marlborough, who were in power that Rooke was not employed again. Not the least of Rooke's achievements was that in a period when corruption in high places might be said to have been the norm, he could fairly claim on his deathbed that "I do not leave much, but what I leave was honestly gotten. It never cost a sailor a tear or the nation a farthing".

The Comte de Toulouse was the third illegitimate son of Mme. de Maintenon and Louis XIV but was later legitimized by the King. As a prince of the blood, he was appointed an admiral at the age of 5, and when he was 12 he went with his father to the Netherlands and was wounded at the siege of Naumur. Notwithstanding his premature appointment to flag rank, Toulouse performed creditably in the navy and always demonstrated great courage. He married in middle age and his grandson, Louis-Philippe, was King of France from 1830-1848.

Gibraltar was formally ceded to Britain by the Treaty of Utrecht in 1713 (see 11 April) and is still a British colony to the great dissatisfaction of the Spanish, but it is worth noting that for 751 years it was a Muslim possession, followed by 242 years in Spanish hands, and now 300 years and counting as British.

13 H.M.S. BELLONA (74 GUNS) & H.M.S. BRILLIANT (36 GUNS) V. COURAGEUX (74 GUNS) & 2 FRIGATES (32 GUNS EACH) 1761, SPAIN (SEVEN YEARS' WAR)

Commanders: Captain R. Faulkner & Captain J. Logie v. Dugne de L'Ambert.

Sighting the French ships while patrolling off Vigo, the two British ships chased them all through the night, and the action began at 6.00 a.m. A clever manœuvre by Captain Faulkner confused the French, and *Courageux* struck her colours at 7.09 a.m. *Courageux's* complement was 700, and she suffered 240 killed and 110 wounded; *Bellona* had 6 killed and 28 wounded; and the French captain died of his wounds in Lisbon. *Courageux* had been bound for San Domingo with property worth £320,000 and the ransom money for five prizes. The French frigates escaped.

13 BILBAO 1812, SPAIN (PENINSULA WAR)

Commanders: Cdre. Sir Home Popham & Genl. G. Mendizabal v. Genls.Rouget & Caffarelli
Forces: British 3 ships of the line, 4 frigates, 2 sloops, several smaller vessels and 1,000 marines + 6,000 Spanish; French 7,000.

This action was the climax of Popham's amphibious operations in support of Wellington's advance towards France (see 22 June, Lequeitio & 3 August, Santander). The Spanish attacked Bilbao from the land side, and simultaneously Popham's marines took Portugalete at the mouth of the Bilbao River. This series of actions by Popham were an intelligent use of sea power in a larger campaign and were made possible by the overwhelming superiority established by the Royal Navy at Trafalgar (see 21 October); they are also a convincing rebuttal of Wellington's complaint after San Sebastian (see 8 September).

14 MAURON 1352, FRANCE (HUNDRED YEARS' WAR)

Commanders: Sir Walter Bentley v. Guy de Nesle, Marshal of France.

A major battle in the War in which de Nesle, returned from captivity as a prisoner of war (see 8 April Taillebourg), decided to repeat his unsuccessful tactic at Taillebourg . Before the battle was joined the French were drawn up in full view of the English, the better to demonstrate that they greatly outnumbered their opponents. Then, in the manner of chivalric ritual, de Nesle sent his herald to offer Bentley the chance to march away unmolested provided his force would leave France. These terms were refused, and the battle began. The English were in a position similar to that at Crécy, standing on a hill top protected by a hedge and ditch with the knights dismounted in the centre and archers on each flank. Most of the French cavalry were dismounted and placed in the centre, the remainder were intended to out-flank the archers. On the right of the English line, the French were successful and the archers were dispersed, but the attack on the left failed and when the main attack went in up the steep slope it was repulsed, and the counter-attack was so vigorous that it turned into a rout. Two thousand of the French army were killed, and the casualties included de Nesle together with a large number of knights. Among the fallen knights were 89 of the newly-formed Order of the Star that King John II had established to rival the

Order of the Garter. The defeat spelled the end of his Order.

14 H.M.S. SUCCESS (32 GUNS), GENEREAUX (74 GUNS), NORTHUMBERLAND (74GUNS) V. JUSTICE AND DIANE (42 GUNS), 1800, MALTA (FRENCH REVOLUTIONARY WARS)
Commanders: Captain S. Peard v. ?

The British ships were part of the squadron blockading Malta (see 4 September), and the two French frigates attempted to escape from Valetta during the night. The British ships gave chase, and *Diane*, which was seriously undermanned, having put men ashore to assist the garrison, soon surrendered to *Success*, but *Justice* got away in the darkness. *Success* suffered a setback a few months later. She was captured near Toulon by a squadron that had been able to sail from Brest during a gale and was taken into the French navy. The ignominy was soon over; in less than a year she was recaptured and returned to the fold.

15 SEINE MOUTH 1416, FRANCE (HUNDRED YEARS' WAR)
Commanders: John, Duke of Bedford v. Guilleaume de Montenay
Forces: English 100 ships including 4 carracks v. French 150 ships including 8 carracks.

The English fleet sailed into the Seine estuary in order to raise the French siege of Harfleur which, following its capture the year before (see 22 September), Henry V intended to develop as a military base in France similar to Calais. Recognizing that their own navy was inadequate for the task at hand, the French had made a naval alliance with Genoa, at that time the most formidable navy in Europe with carracks of superior design and performance. A carrack was the battle ship of its day; large and with a high poop and prow on which were placed archers, crossbowmen, and those operating the primitive artillery. The method of combat was similar to that on land, namely, hand to hand fighting with one ship trying to board another. The French ships were anchored close together as they had been at Sluys (see 24 June), the English fleet bore down on its opponents with all sails set, and individual ships then grappled together. Fighting went on for seven hours and ended when four Genoese carracks had been captured and another driven ashore and wrecked; the remainder took refuge in the harbour of Honfleur. The siege of Harfleur was over, and the English fleet entered the town to the cheers of the inhabitants. Some of the ships were sent back to England with prisoners and the wounded, including the Duke of Bedford.

Jubilation in England was no less fervent than at Harfleur, and when the king received the news, he galloped straight to Canterbury from Hythe and ordered a Te Deum to be sung at which he was accompanied by Sigismund, soon to be Emperor (see 25 October, Agincourt). Harfleur was an important link between the English army in France and England, and the victory consolidated the victory at Agincourt (see 25 October). The French persisted in their attempts to isolate Harfleur, and there was a replay of this battle less than a year later (see 25 July, Harfleur). Bedford was the third son of Henry IV and had been given the duchy two years before by his brother, Henry V. Bedford worked closely with his brother and continued his programme after his death in 1422. At first he was successful (see 17 August, Verneuil), and military performance was enhanced diplomatically by his marriage to the sister of the Duke of Burgundy. A notable achievement was the coronation of Henry VI of England as Henri II of France at St. Denys on 16 December 1431, the only English monarch to be so crowned. Regrettably, Henry VI and II proved to be so incompetent that he lost both crowns. Eventually, lack of money to prosecute the war, dissensions in England, but above all the defection of the Duke of Burgundy to the Dauphin reduced the Duke's policies to ruins, and he died at Rouen in 1435 where he was buried in the cathedral.

15 YORK FORT 1696, CANADA (WAR OF THE LEAGUE OF AUGSBURG)

Captain William Allen captured York Fort in Hudson's Bay from the French.

15 Obidos 1808, Portugal (Peninsular War)

Commanders: Maj.-Genl. Sir Brent Spencer v.Genl. Delaborde
Forces: Four companies of British riflemen; French divisional rearguard.

Really no more than a skirmish, but it is included as the first success of the British army in the Peninsular War, and the troops engaged, the 60th. and 95th. Rifles, were in the first phase of a distinguished history. The 60th. had its beginning as the Royal American Regiment fighting the French in Canada, and in the West Indies (see 16 June, Bay of Fundy & 6 July, Trout Brook), and it was brigaded with the 95th. to form a brigade of Riflemen. In course of time, the 60th. became the King's Royal Rifle Corps, now The Royal Green Jackets. The 95th. was formed in 1800 as an 'Experimental Corps of Riflemen' to act as skirmishers and became the Rifle Brigade in 1816. Sir John Moore (see 16 January, Corunna) was largely responsible for the training of these troops in their new tactical role, and Wellington's standing orders laid down that the brigade of Riflemen should always form the vanguard when the army moved. The brigade fought in this formation at Obidos and Roliça (see 17 August), but then a tactical change was made, and the 60th. and 95th. were re-formed as the Light Brigade and ordered to provide a company to cover each of the other brigades in Wellington's force. The rifle companies were the first units in the British army to be armed with a rifle, the 'Baker', in place of the Brown Bess musket; the Baker was accurate up to 300 yards compared to 50 yards for the musket, and this difference was the basis of the new tactics of these units of the infantry, but use of the bayonet remained a constant, and as the Baker was shorter than the musket, the bayonet fitted to it was made longer than the standard issue. The shortcoming of the Baker rifle was the time it took to reload; by comparison the longbow of the Middle Ages had an effective range of 200 yards, and a skilled archer could fire six arrows per minute, but such skill required constant practice, and it had been lost. Interesting to note that the rifle companies' practice of shooting at individuals was, at first, regarded as unethical; the traditional tactic of firing volleys at a mass of the enemy was the honourable method of execution – even though there was no practicable alternative.

The rifle companies all wore green jackets instead of the traditional red, and they became the élite of Wellington's victorious army.

A rifle company in the Peninsular War is the subject of a series of eulogistic novels by Bernard Cornwell in which one Sharpe is the dashing hero, and catching popular interest, these have been made into films and videos; nothing has been lost, and some things have been added, in the telling. Generally thought to be a 'good read'. A prototype Peninsular War novel with a Rifleman in the 95th. Regiment as the hero is 'Death to the French' by C.S. Forester.

16 GUINEGATE (A.K.A. BATTLE OF THE SPURS) 1513, FRANCE (WAR OF THE HOLY LEAGUE)

Commanders: Henry VIII v. ?

The English with German reinforcements (Henry was in alliance with Austria and Spain) were besieging Thérouanne (see 23 August) when a large force of French cavalry moved to attack but were intercepted at Guinegate. The Allied attack was so fierce that the French fled without a fight, and their flight was such a scramble that the action was derisively dubbed the Battle of the Spurs, but this name has also been applied to Courtrai 1302, where a large contingent of French cavalry was spectacularly routed by Flemish infantry. The prisoners taken at Guinegate included the Duc d'Orleans, the Duc de Longueville and the eminent but elderly Bayard – *le Chevalier sans peur et sans reproche*. The ransom money was most useful in defraying the cost of the campaign.

17 VERNEUIL 1424, FRANCE (100 YEARS' WAR)

Commanders: John, Duke of Bedford v. Count d'Aumale, John Earl of Buchan, Constable of France & Archibald, Earl of Douglas.

Forces: English 9,000 including some Burgundians; French 10,000 plus 5,000 Scots.

The French had suffered serious losses and decided on a major offensive. For this purpose, they had renewed their traditional alliance with Scotland – an obvious ploy when fighting the English. The English troops included a large number of archers who stood behind a line of pointed stakes and repelled a series of charges with volleys from their longbows. A French flanking attack failed when the leader, the Duc d'Alencon was captured. After suffering 7,000 casualties including both Buchan and Douglas, the remaining French and Scots scrambled across the Loire; presumably, the Scots had learned the meaning of *'Sauve qui peut'* beforehand, if not they would certainly have picked it up by the end of the day.

Buchan was the son of the Scottish regent and had been appointed Constable of France; Douglas was Buchan's father-in-law and had had a colourful career of more or less continual fighting, mostly against the

English, and once, while a prisoner of the Percys, fighting with them against Henry IV at the Battle of Shrewsbury. He had also been tried with Buchan's father for plotting the death of the Duke of Rothesay, but they were acquitted. Douglas was made lieutenant general of the French army and Duke of Touraine. In retrospect it might well be that he is now better known as a character in Shakespeare's play: 'Henry IV, Part I'. There he is represented as fighting the King in person at Shrewsbury, and being driven off by the Prince of Wales (the future Henry V), and then pardoned by him.

The Scottish alliance with France was not successful. Although there were 6,000 Scots at Verneuil the original contingent was 10,000, and they were a large proportion of the mercenaries on which the French were forced to depend, but in their case their value was increased because they displayed a fanatical hatred for the English. No doubt it was this feeling that led Douglas, prior to the battle, to pronounce that the Scots would neither give quarter nor expect it. The Scots fought bravely, but in the end they died almost to the last man. Buchan, Douglas and his son, and other gentlemen of rank were killed, and for practical purposes their army in France ceased to exist. Verneuil was one of the bloodiest battles of the Hundred Years' War, and a massive victory for the Duke of Bedford (see 15 August Seine Mouth) second only to Agincourt (see 25 October); it confirmed the international reputation of the invincibility of English archers.

17 LAGOS BAY 1759, PORTUGAL (SEVEN YEARS'WAR)

Commanders: Adml.E. Boscawen v. Vice Adml.de la Clue Sabran.

This engagement between a British squadron of 15 ships of the line against a similar number of French ships continued over three days. The French squadron in Toulon were ordered to Brest in order to complete the French fleet intended to take command of the Channel and permit the French invasion of Scotland. The British ships were refitting and revictualling at Gibraltar when the French put to sea, and although the work had not been completed, they immediately gave chase. During the night eight of the French ships took refuge in Cadiz, and the remainder proceeded towards Lagos. The following afternoon, a running fight began in which the first casualty was the French 74 gun ship, *Centaure* that struck her colours after spirited resistance. During this part of the engagement, the rigging of Boscawen's flagship was damaged so that he was obliged to shift his flag to another ship. The boat which was transferring him was hit while doing so, and in order to prevent it from sinking Boscawen stuffed the hole with his wig. Two of the French ships escaped under cover of darkness, but the remaining four were not so fortunate, they sought refuge in Lagos Bay, although Portugal was a neutral country. The next phase of the battle is generally cited as the principal example of the 'hot chase'. A 'hot chase' is a practice in naval warfare, not sanctioned by law, in which a fleeing enemy may be followed into neutral waters and destroyed provided the action began in international waters. Boscawen gave 'hot chase' to the fleeing French and went after them into Lagos Bay. The French flagship, *Ocean*, was so discombobulated that she ran ashore under full sail, all of its masts went by the board, and she was burned by her crew before they scrambled ashore. The *Redoubtable* went the same way. The other two ships, *Téméraire* and *Modeste*, anchored under the Portuguese guns but were taken as prizes and subsequently commissioned in the Royal Navy. The Portuguese authorities accepted the 'hot chase' argument, perhaps acting as 'the oldest ally', but Boscawen was forthright in his report to the Admiralty, he said it was better to destroy the ships first and argue the principle later. This is the basis for the pre-emptive strike, or as the old saw puts it:

> "Thrice armed is he that hath his quarrel just,
> And four times he who gets his fist in fust."

This battle effectively ended the plan to invade Scotland, and as a reward Boscawen received the lucrative post of General of Marines.

In the line of illustrious naval commanders of Britain during the eighteenth century, Boscawen is prominent. On his mother's side he was related to the Duke of Marlborough, and he honoured the relationship. He joined the navy when he was fifteen and was a captain by the time he was twenty-six. His active service was marked by successive acts of bravery, and he commanded the fleet at the capture of Louisbourg (see 27 July). While serving as a lord commissioner of the Admiralty, the case of Admiral Byng came before him which was particularly bad luck for Byng who was being accused of cowardice in the face of the enemy (see 15 January Pondicherry, 19 September Port Mahon, & 25 March

H.M.S. Sheerness). Boscawen remembered that as a lieutenant, Byng had used his father's influence to leave his ship when it was ordered on a dangerous mission, and he signed the order for Byng's court martial; later, as c-in-c at Portsmouth he signed the order for Byng's execution. Boscawen was renowned for his consideration for the men under his command; during the blockade of Quiberon Bay he ordered a small island to be seized at the mouth of the River Vannes and had it cultivated for the provision of fresh vegetables for his fleet. Ironically, he died shortly after from typhoid contracted on this service. Quiberon Bay was not the only place in which the Royal Navy engaged in horticulture in enemy territory during the Napoleonic War. After Sweden had declared war on the side of the French in 1810, ships of the Baltic fleet made vegetable gardens in Vinga Sound.

De la Clue's service record was more modest. He had commanded at the capture of Minorca, where he was opposed by the wretched Byng and died in Lagos of wounds received in this battle.

17 MARABOUT 1801, EGYPT (FRENCH REVOLUTIONARY WARS)

Commanders: Genl. Sir David Baird v. Genl. Baron de Menou.

This was a minor engagement at end of the Egyptian campaign (see 21 March, Alexandria) in which the Dorsetshire Regiment attacked and captured Fort Marabout, the tomb of a Moslem saint. Although General Baron Menou had become a Moslem, 'Abd Allah Jacques Menou', he surrendered with his troops, but by the Treaty of Amiens, 1802, the British returned Egypt to Ottoman rule. The subsequent career of Abd Allah is not known.

17 ROLICA 1808, PORTUGAL (PENINSULA WAR)

Commanders: Wellington v. Genl. Delaborde
Forces: British 13,500 and 1,500 Portuguese; French 5,000.

This action was a continuation of that at Obidos (see 15 August), and it is a battle honour of the 60th. Regiment (now The Royal Green Jackets). Wellington was advancing southwards down the coast to Lisbon, and the French rearguard sought to delay progress while their main force re-grouped. Misunderstandings and mistakes by some of the British commanders led to an early crisis, but Wellington, giving an early example of his capabilities, was able to rectify the situation. The French had 600 casualties, including Delaborde who was wounded, and lost 3 guns, British losses were 474. Wellington's advance continued.

18 LINCELLES 1793, FRANCE (FRENCH REVOLUTIONARY WARS)

Commanders: Maj. Genl. G. Lake v. ?
Forces: British 3 battalions; French 12 battalions.

The British force had been detached from the siege of Dunkirk to assist the Dutch who had been driven from a group of forts. After trying unsuccessfully to rally the Dutch, Lake led his troops in a bayonet charge that drove the French from the forts in disorder, the guardsmen 'cuffing and hustling the French as if they were a London mob'. This was the first occasion on which British troops met the French in the Revolutionary Wars, and their spectacular performance is generally regarded as the most brilliant one of the year. British casualties were less than 200, the French many more, and they lost 18 guns including 6 that had been captured from the Dutch.

Lake had an excellent military career. He joined the army, as an ensign in the Guards, at the age of fourteen, two years later he was on active service in Germany. He distinguished himself at the Battle of Yorktown in the American Revolutionary War by leading a damaging sortie, and later he repelled a French invasion of Ireland (see 8 September, Ballinamuck). He was appointed commander-in-chief in India in 1801, and shortly before he died he was created a viscount. Lake had the reputation of great calm, self-reliance, and energy, and, above all, he was completely fearless in action. A great leader, he was held in trust and affection by the rank and file.

20 BRENNEVILLE (A.K.A. BREMULE) 1119, FRANCE (ANGLO-FRENCH WARS)

Commanders: Henry I v. Louis VI.

Mainly a small scale cavalry battle with an important result. The fighting was light, but so decisively in the English favour that Louis was glad to make peace on Henry's terms which were to acknowledge Henry's claim to the Duchy of Normandy. Henry I's claim to the Duchy arose from his victory over his eldest brother, Robert, and Robert's capture and imprisonment in England for the remainder of his life (see 28 September, Tinchebrai). Henry was the third son of William the Conqueror, and he had succeeded to the English throne on the death of his elder brother, William Rufus, but only by acting swiftly and cleverly was he able to usurp the claim of his eldest brother, Robert. As was usual with the early Norman kings, Henry spent the greater part of his time in northern France involving England in continental politics to a greater extent than national interest and benefit warranted. Nevertheless, Henry was an able ruler, a successful commander, and a good diplomatist.

Louis VI, known as 'the Fat' or 'the Bruiser', spent most of his time in warfare, often against his own barons, he led his troops in person and became a national hero. In a notable dynastic coup, he was able to arrange the marriage of his son, Louis VII, to Eleanor of Aquitaine, but after 15 years, Louis VII had the marriage annulled on the ground of kinship, but more likely because their children were all girls. Eleanor then married the grandson of Henry (Henry II) bringing to the English crown the vast Aquitaine estates in the south of France.

20 AIGUILLON 1346, FRANCE (HUNDRED YEARS' WAR)

Commanders: Lord Stafford v. John, Duke of Normandy

The reaction of the French to the successes of the Earl of Derby in Aquitaine (see 21 October, Auberoche; 2 December, Aiguillon; 4 January, La Réole) was to raise an even larger army and put it under the command of the king's son, the Duke of Normandy, an unusually inept commander. The Duke decided to recapture Aiguillon and was able to divide his army into four groups, so that by rotation he could maintain continuous operations. In anticipation of the siege, Stafford had brought in plenty of stores so that the strength of the garrison would not be weakened by starvation, and this was demonstrated by several sorties in the course of which supplies were captured or destroyed. Further support was given by the Earl of Derby from his base in La Réole (see 4 January) from which he was able to run the blockade into Aiguillon with supplies and troops. The French did not attempt an assault, and suddenly the situation changed dramatically. Back in England, Edward III had been raising an army too, and it sailed for France in July. Landing in Normandy it advanced rapidly (see 26 July Caen), and with their main army far away in the south, there was consternation at the French court.

Orders were given to abandon the siege and march north. The French left in haste abandoning their tents and leaving behind a huge quantity of supplies. As soon as he heard that the siege had been abandoned, the Earl of Derby set out for Aiguillon, but prudently took the opportunity to capture another town, Villereal, along the way. The English successes in Aquitaine were about to be crowned with even greater glory (see 26 August Crécy).

20 H.M.S. SEINE (38 GUNS) V. VENGEANCE (40 GUNS) 1800, WEST INDIES (FRENCH REVOLUTIONARY WARS)

Commanders: Capt. D. Milne v. S.L.M. Pichot

On sighting *Vengeance*, *Seine* gave chase, and a running fight ensued, vigorously waged by both ships. The action continued until the next day when *Vengeance* struck her colours and was taken as a prize. Milne had been prominent in the engagement two years previously when *Seine* was captured from the French in the course of which his ship, *H.M.S.Pique,* became a total loss after running aground (see 29 June, H.M.S. Jason et al.). *Seine* was re-commissioned in the Royal Navy, and interesting to note that she now had 38 guns instead of 46.

21 VIMEIRO 1808, PORTUGAL (PENINSULA WAR)

Commanders: Wellington v. Genl. Androche-Junot

Forces: British 16,322 infantry + 240 cavalry + 226 artillery with 16 guns and 2,000 Portuguese; French 10,405 infantry + 1,951 cavalry + 700 artillery with 23 guns.

This battle brought to a successful conclusion Wellington's advance on Lisbon (see 15 & 17 August, Obidos & Rolica). The French had marched from Lisbon, which Junot had occupied unopposed in 1807, in order to meet the newly-landed British troops. The action took place in and around the village of Vimeiro about 32 miles north-west of the city. The French attacked confidently in their customary formation of columns of infantry, as many as 30 men broad by 42 deep, supported by guns and skirmishers, and were met by two lines of infantry, 'the thin red line', delivering rolling volleys of fire. A British bayonet charge was a feature of several hours of vigorous fighting, and the British tactics, greatly assisted by clever deployment and the devastating effect of the new shrapnel shells, overwhelmed the French. Regrettably, the British cavalry ordered to counter-attack in the closing stages of the battle went out of control and were cut-up by the French cavalry; this was by no means the last time Wellington was to witness his cavalry perform in this manner, and true to form till the end, they did it on a larger scale at Waterloo. In the later stages of the battle, the pusillanimous British commander-in-chief, Sir Hew Dalrymple, appeared and refused to allow the pursuit. French casualties were 1,500 killed and wounded, and 300 prisoners including 3 generals; British casualties were 720.

General Junot had an uneven career. He began in the ranks of the new Revolutionary Army and quickly earned a reputation for bravery. He was a sergeant at the siege of Toulon where he caught Napoleon's eye and rapid promotion followed; he was a general eight years later and never reluctant to take charge, Napoleon also arranged his marriage for him. Subsequently, Junot's progress stalled. In a series of appointments, Junot displayed erratic judgement and administrative incompetence, finally, he was appointed governor of the Ilyrian Provinces (modern day Balkans), became insane and died twenty years after his first meeting with Napoleon. Junot's marriage was also a failure.

In the months following Vimeiro, a number of notable events occurred on both sides. In Britain, the victory at Vimeiro was greeted with jubilation by the general public (the first victory on land for 15 years), but this mood was quickly replaced by outrage when particulars of the armistice, requested by the French after the battle, were made public. The terms were embodied a few days later in the Convention of Cintra by which Junot and his army were to be repatriated to France in British ships with their property, something that particularly incensed the public, and the aggravation was increased when it became known that 'property' included melted down church plate, two carriages belonging to the Duke of Sussex, and linen of the Portuguese royal family cut up to make shirts for a junior French general. Criticism, in which Wordsworth, Byron and Cobbett, were prominent became so widespread, that a military tribunal was appointed by royal warrant to inquire into the armistice and Convention. Wellington, then only Sir Arthur Wellesley and a junior lieutenant general, and his two superior officers were the subject of the inquiry, and were acquitted, although 'not proven' might more accurately reflect the findings. There was a large political element in the whole affair, but it was a strange experience for a man who had just won an impressive victory. Meanwhile, Napoleon had been busy with political machinations of his own.

In May 1808, by duplicity, Napoleon forced the abdication of the Spanish king, Charles IV, and his son, Ferdinand VII; this enabled the Emperor to move his brother from Naples, where by an imperial decree he had been enthroned in 1806, to Spain and by a similar order to become King of Spain. French armies, directed by Napoleon in person, now invaded Spain to install Joseph in Madrid and to occupy parts of northern Spain. The invasion of Portugal was included in the plan, and a small British force standing in the way of this design was obliged to withdraw (see 16 January, Corunna). As an example of how Napoleon manipulated monarchies, Marshal Murat was crowned king of Naples to fill the vacancy left by Joseph's promotion. Satisfied with the way in which his programme had begun, the Emperor turned his attention to other matters in his empire – Wagram and the rout of the Austrians was the triumph of the 1809 campaign. What Napoleon had no means of assessing was the danger to his empire now about develop with the arrival in Portugal of Wellington, the new commander-in-chief, who was replacing his inept predecessors; the Peninsular War was about to begin in earnest.

22 MENIN 1706, BELGIUM (WAR OF THE SPANISH SUCCESSION)

Commanders: Marlborough v. Comte de Caraman
Forces: British & Allies 30,000; French 5,500.

Considered to be a Vauban masterpiece (see 4 July, Le Quesnoy), Menin was one of the best fortified places in Flanders. The garrison had been reinforced, the magazines and storehouses were full, and controlled flooding had strengthened the defences. The bombardment began on 9 August without waiting for the full complement of artillery, but a week later, in an effort to threaten the besiegers, Marshal Vendôme, commander of the French army, sent out strong columns to attack Marlborough's covering troops. Although these thrusts had some initial success, the siege continued remorselessly, and a week later Caraman surrendered. The garrison was permitted to retire to Douai having sustained 1,101 casualties; their opponents incurred 2,620, more than half of them in the storming assault.

23 THÉROUANNE 1513, FRANCE (WAR OF THE HOLY LEAGUE)

Commanders: Henry VIII v. ?

This was the beginning of Henry's campaign, in alliance with Spain and Austria, against the French, and in the manner of sixteenth century warfare, Thérouanne was besieged. The French relieving force had been resoundingly defeated a few days earlier (see 16 August Guinegate), and Thérouanne surrendered without offering determined resistance. It was not much of a conquest, but it appealed to Henry's pride and perception of himself as a warrior, and it opened the way to Tournai, a more important target (see 25 September).

24 SANDWICH (A.K.A. DOVER OR SOUTH FORELAND) 1217, ENGLAND (ANGLO FRANCH WARS)

Commanders: Hubert de Burgh v. Eustace the Monk
Forces: English 40 ships; French 80 ships.

Following the defeat at Lincoln (see May 20), the French fleet was conveying troops and supplies to England in support of the barons engaged in a civil war against the infant Henry III, and it was intercepted by an English fleet off the coast of Kent. The English manœuvred to attack from windward and were further assisted by the straggling formation of the French ships. The French flagship was well astern at the end of the line, and it was the first to be taken; the English were able to work their way up the line and a large number of the French ships were sunk or captured. This battle is remarkable not only because it was fought by ships under way, when most naval actions were between ships at anchor, but more particularly because the tactics of de Burgh were hardly equalled by any English commander for several centuries. Sandwich was the major English naval victory of the Middle Ages, and effectively ended the French plan to conquer England by exploiting the civil war.

De Burgh possessed considerable ability. In the reign of King John, father of Henry III, he was principally responsible for the suppression of a baronial uprising, which he repeated a few years later; these services led to his appointment as head of the government, and he continued in that office after John's death and Henry's succession. Later, as often happened in mediæval courts, through intrigues he fell from favour and was imprisoned for treason. He made a dramatic escape and was allowed to live in retirement.

Eustace the Monk was a much more flamboyant character. The younger son of a noble family in Boulogne, he spent his youth in a monastery, and shortly thereafter he was accused of misappropriating his master's funds. Declared an outlaw for retaliatory attacks on the property of his former employer, Eustace became a mercenary pirate in the English Channel selling the services of his fleet to the highest bidder. From 1202 to 1212 this was usually King John who was engaged, generally unsuccessfully, in a war against Philip II of France. Eustace raided the Normandy coast and was permitted to establish bases in the Channel Islands, but then he overreached himself by raiding English coastal villages, and John outlawed him. Not long afterwards he was pardoned because the need for his services outweighed his offences. In 1212 Eustace again changed sides because English troops had seized his Channel Island bases. Feisty as befitted a mercenary pirate, Eustace and his merry men raided Folkestone, and in 1215 he assisted the rebel barons against John in the civil war which followed the signing of Magna Carta. In the course of this war, the rebels invited the French Dauphin to claim the English crown in place of John's infant son, Henry, and so it was that Eustace was commanding the French fleet. This led to his dramatic death; taken prisoner in de Burgh's first attack, he was instantly beheaded – perhaps a model for the treatment of contemporary terrorists. The Dauphin, later Louis VIII, fared much better. The Treaty of Kingston, 1217, concluded the civil war, and by a secret provision Louis was paid 10,000 marks (see 20 May Lincoln).

24 BLANCHETAQUE 1346, FRANCE (HUNDRED YEARS' WAR)

Commanders: Edward III v Philippe VI.

Following the siege of Caen (see 26 July), Edward marched his army eastwards intending to link up with a Flemish army that was in the field as a result of an alliance formed at the end of June. In order to effect the rendezvous, it was necessary to cross the River Seine and probably the River Somme both of which were major obstacles. The Seine was the first barrier, and the manœuvres of the French army on the far bank forced Edward to march towards Paris looking for a place where the troops and baggage train might cross. In the meantime, a division was sent under the command of the Black Prince to harass the villages on the outskirts of Paris; St. Cloud was one of those burned in full view of Paris while the main French army and Philippe remained in the city to the great chagrin of the inhabitants. A crossing of the Seine was forced across a damaged bridge at Poissy, and Edward marched towards Airaines with several skirmishes along the way. The immediate objective was to cross the Somme which was too deep to ford and the bridges of which were strongly defended. When the situation was beginning to look critical, Edward was able to bribe a prisoner to lead his army to a place in the estuary where at low tide the river could be forded; the name of the traitor was Gobin Agache, and he is still reviled in French history. The passage across the Somme at Blanchetaque was a causeway wide enough for only eleven men abreast and about 2,000 yards in length. At the low point of the tide, it is about knee deep, and on the other side there were about 500 men-at-arms with upwards of 3,000 infantry including Genoese crossbow men. Archers led the advance across the river, and once within range of the crossbows they came under fire; ignoring their casualties, they pressed on until they had the Genoese within range of their own bows, probably about 150 yards, and then a duel developed. The crossbow fire slackened, and the English men-at-arms charged at the bank and were met in the water by their French counterparts. Fighting in the water in a general mêlée as individuals, the English prevailed and pursued the French out of the river, the Genoese mercenaries fled (their commander, Godemar du Fay, was later wrongfully charged with treachery), and the main English army divided into two wings.

One wing went after the French at Abbeville, and the other down the estuary as far as Le Crotoy burning and plundering as they did so, including a large number of ships in the harbour. Given the inferiority in numbers, the distance that had to be traversed through the ebbing tide, and the lack of any cover or surprise, this was an astonishing triumph. By no means was the least of the benefits from it the boost to the morale of the English troops just two days before the main event at Crécy (see 26 August). Blanchetaque figured again in Henry V's march to Agincourt (see 25 October), and for a similar reason, Henry was looking for a place to cross the Somme. He found that the ford was now protected by lines of palisades behind which stood a strong body of defenders; Henry was obliged to look elsewhere, and it seems the French had learned the lesson Edward had taught them. However, the final outcome was the same in each case, and it is interesting to speculate whether Crécy was a more spectacular victory than Agincourt, or vice versa.

24 FORT CORNELIS 1811, JAVA (NAPOLEONIC WAR)

Commanders: Genl. Sir Samuel Auchmuty v. Genl. Jan W. Janssens.

This battle was essentially a continuation of Batavia (see 9 August). The French troops were entrenched in a strongly fortified position in the hills behind Batavia and were superior in numbers. The British soon occupied the outposts and brought up heavy guns from the ships to bombard the main defences. Assisted by information from a Dutch deserter, an assault party was able to attack the defenders with a spirited charge from the flank, and when the main attack followed, the French were routed, 4,000 were killed or wounded and 5,500 were taken prisoner. Genl Janssens and a few hundred men escaped but were obliged to capitulate a few weeks later (see 10 September, Samarang).

25 WALCOURT 1689, BELGIUM (WAR OF THE LEAGUE OF AUGSBURG)

Commanders: Prince George Frederick of Waldeck v. Duke Louis d'Humiéres & Claude de Villars.

Forces: A German-English army of about 35,000 opposed by a larger number of French.

The English contingent was about 8,000 and was commanded by John Churchill, not yet the Duke of Marlborough. The English were used as shock troops, and they broke the French who suffered heavy casualties. De Villars was at the beginning of a successful career in high command (see 11 September Malplaquet), but d'Humiéres was replaced by Marshal de Luxembourg.

25 FORT DE LÉVIS 1760, U.S.A.(SEVEN YEARS' WAR)

Commanders: Genl. Sir Jeffrey Amherst v. Captain Pierre Pouchot.

This fort was situated on the Ile Royale, or Chimney Island, in the St Lawrence River, but just inside what is now the State of New York; it was intended to protect the approach to Montreal and was named after the Duc de Lévis who had succeeded Montcalm as the French commander-in-chief. Amherst was in the final stages of the campaign that began in 1758 with the capture of Louisbourg (see 27 July) and was advancing on Montreal with the major column of a 3-pronged offensive. The fort was under-manned but was supported by two corvettes that had escaped destruction at Fort Frontenac (see 27 August). The British attacked in a number of small boats, and through skilful manœuvring by the commander, Colonel Williamson, one of the corvettes was captured and re-named Williamson, the other was destroyed. The French troops reinforced by the crews of the corvettes put up a spirited defence but were forced to surrender after three days' bombardment. In recognition of their efforts, the garrison was granted the honours of war. In terms of numbers, but not in importance, the scale of engagements in North America was small – on this occasion 375 French were killed or wounded, the British had 26 killed and 47 wounded. Captain Pouchot was among the prisoners for the second time in two years. He had been captured at Fort Niagara (see 25 July) but then released in an exchange of prisoners; later he was returned to France. This was the last stand of the French in Canada, and Fort de Lévis was re-named Fort William Augustus, for the Duke of Cumberland, the younger son of George II. In retrospect, this might unduly flatter the Duke who militarily has been described "as unlucky as he was incompetent and unimaginative", but he did found the Ascot race meeting.

26 BERGERAC 1345, FRANCE (HUNDRED YEARS' WAR)
Commanders: Earl of Derby v. Comte de l'Isle.

Edward III planned a triple offensive against France, and the Earl of Derby, soon to be the Duke of Lancaster, was put in command of the southern army. Derby was establishing his military and civil base at Bordeaux when he learned that the French had decided to make a stand at Bergerac, about 70 miles to the east. Derby immediately set out with his troops in order to attack Bergerac before its defences could be strengthened. On arriving at Bergerac, the first task was to occupy that part of the town outside the perimeter wall, this was quickly accomplished with the rout of the defenders, and the victors were pleased to find sufficient food and wine for a month. The next phase of the attack was unexpectedly easy. The river was crossed in small boats and a breach made in the walls which the English archers prevented the defenders from repairing. De l'Isle seems to have decided that the town could not be defended against assault, but that it was possible to save himself and most of his men-at-arms; in the dead of night, he rode out at the head of his troops from the side of the town not under siege and they rode on for forty miles before stopping. The next morning, the inhabitants of Bergerac, finding themselves swinging in the wind, were quick to enter into negotiations for the surrender of the town. Derby's army had had a useful and encouraging practice for the larger engagement at Auberoche (see 21 October).

26 CRÉCY 1346, FRANCE (HUNDRED YEARS' WAR)

Commanders: Edward III v. Philippe VI

Forces: English 9,000including 6,000 archers; French 30,000 including 10,000 heavy cavalry.

This was the first major battle of the Hundred Years' War. In July, Edward had sailed from Portsmouth and landed near Cherbourg; Caen was quickly captured – and ravaged (see 26 July). From there the army advanced towards Paris, then to the north-east (see 24 August Blanchetaque), and after a series of marches and counter-marches the English took up a strong defensive position between Abbeville and Calais. The French were surprised to find their opponents there ready to fight and impetuously attacked in the late afternoon. In a heavy thunderstorm, the first wave was led by Genoese crossbowmen fighting as mercenaries, and they were cut to ribbons by showers of arrows from the archers armed with the longbow who had been stationed on each flank. The plight of these hapless men was greatly aggravated by the French cavalry who charged the English position through their decimated ranks. This attack was similarly repulsed as were some twelve to fifteen further attacks made in the moonlight over the next four or five hours. At about midnight, the French retreated with casualties exceeding the total number of the English army and amounting to about 12,000 including 1,500 knights and nobles. Among the dead were Charles, the king's brother, the blind King of Bohemia, and the Count of Flanders, but the king himself was more fortunate in that he was only wounded. These heavy losses were increased by pointless chivalric heroism, notably when the blind King of Bohemia was led into the mêlée by his knights who were bound to him by ropes, and unsurprisingly all were killed. The English losses amounted to two knights and 200 killed or wounded. Edward, Prince of Wales, took part and here took the King of Bohemia's ostrich plumes for his crest and the motto "Ich Dien".

Apart from the magnitude of the English victory, Crécy had other notable features. It established the longbow as a deadly infantry weapon, something akin to the machine gun in World War I, and this dominance lasted for about a century. The skill of the English archers also showed that the thousand-year old belief in the universal superiority of heavy cavalry no longer applied when confronted with the firepower of disciplined infantry. Proficiency in archery depended not only on physical strength – a longbow was six feet long and required a force of 100lbs. to draw it – but also continual practice. In 1365 Edward III had the temerity to ban the playing of football in London, ordering archery practice instead, and it is common in English towns that were in existence in the Middle Ages to have a place or street still named 'The Butts'. Crécy commands a place in any list of outstanding English victories over the French, and it had the immediate effect in Europe of raising England to the status of a great military power.

With the French army in no condition to interfere with his progress, Edward led his troops the short distance to Calais and laid siege to it (see 4 August).

Interesting to note the affinity of the English and French nobility at this date, one year after Crécy, the widow of the Earl of Pembroke was given leave by Edward III to found Pembroke College, Cambridge where French students were to receive a preferential claim to appointments. And years later, after Edward III's death, the king of France commanded a solemn service to be held in the Sainte Chapelle to the memory of a great hero who was also his most dangerous and persistent enemy (see also19 September Poitiers).

The French defeat had an unfortunate repercussion in Scotland. Philip VI urged the Scots to invade England in order to relieve the pressure in France. David II crossed the border with a large army and met the English at Neville's Cross, near Durham; they were routed, David was taken prisoner and was not released until eleven years later.

26 HUY 1703, BELGIUM (WAR OF THE SPANISH SUCCESSION)
Commanders: Marlborough v. M. de Millon
Forces: British & Allies 42,000; French 7,500

Following the capture of Bonn (see 15 May), the campaign of the British and Dutch stalled largely because of Dutch vacillation, as Marlborough pointed out to them: "If you have a mind to Antwerp and a speedy end to the war you must venture something for it." But the heavy defeat of a Dutch army at Eckeren had its effect, and a series of tactical marches represented the action until Marlborough marched his troops towards Huy which lies on the Meuse between Liège and Namur. The town was taken after two days, but the citadel held out longer, eventually surrendering after bombardment from 70 cannon and 46 mortars. The Governor, M. de Millon, who we last saw marching off to Antwerp after the siege of Liège (see 29 October), was now taken prisoner together with the survivors.

A strange distraction at this point was Marlborough's solicitation of the Dutch to permit the Duke of Berwick, the illegitimate son of James II and his mistress Arabella Churchill, Marlborough's sister, to buy and export 8 carriage horses from Holland. Berwick was a senior officer in the French army in which he had a distinguished career, and in spite of being an enemy, permission was given for the transaction.

27 FORT FRONTENAC 1758, CANADA (SEVEN YEARS' WAR)
Commanders: Lt. Col. J. Bradstreet v. Commandant de Noyan
Forces: British & Colonial 3,000; French 150.

The British force had been detached from the main body, proceeding against Fort Ticonderoga (see 6 July, Trout Brook), with the object of seizing Fort Frontenac (Kingston) at the junction of the St. Lawrence River and Lake Ontario. Advancing from New England, Bradstreet led his troops through the Mohawk Valley to Oswego where they embarked in a fleet of small boats and landed three days later a few hundred yards from the Fort. Greatly outnumbered and taken completely by surprise, the French offered no resistance and surrendered. This audacious enterprise was fittingly rewarded – the entire French naval force on Lake Ontario, comprising 9 armed vessels, was captured along with a large supply of provisions, stores and ammunition and, except for two, the ships were destroyed. Fort Frontenac had been the supply depot of all the forts of Upper Canada and the Ohio valley, and the loss of it cut the line of communication between the St Lawrence and the Ohio rivers. This victory was also a major factor in the subsequent French evacuation of the Ohio valley.

29 TREATY OF PICQUIGNY 1475, FRANCE (CAMPAIGN OF EDWARD IV).

The Treaty of Picquigny marks a very rare event in the centuries of conflict between England and France, namely, an English victory without any fighting. Edward IV had regained the English throne in 1471 following the defeat of Henry VI and the Lancastrians at the battles of Barnet and Tewkesbury. Edward was a capable military commander with a clear idea of what had to be done, and to make his victories secure he caused Henry VI to be murdered (Henry's son, the Prince of Wales, had been killed at Tewkesbury). In 1474, the French king, Louis XI was confronted with rebellious nobles and princes of the blood, prominent amongst whom was Charles the Bold, Duke of Burgundy. Charles was Edward's brother-in-law and had supported his efforts to regain his throne in 1470, now they entered into an alliance against Louis. Edward re-asserted Edward III's claim to the French throne and prepared an invasion. The preparations were thorough and were not completed until the summer of 1475. On 4 July 1475, Edward landed in France with what was said to be the largest English army to that date, but unfortunately the Burgundians were ill-prepared. There were marches and counter-marches without battle being joined, and although he had a formidable army, Louis offered, not for the first time, to buy Edward off. The offer was accepted and sealed at Picquigny, west of Amiens. Edward agreed to take his army home on payment of 75,000 gold crowns and an annual payment of 50,000 gold crowns. Louis bargained for the return to France of Margaret of Anjou, the widow of Henry VI, who had been imprisoned in the Tower for four years following the battle of Tewkesbury, and also for the betrothal of Edward's daughter, Elizabeth, to the Dauphin. A similar victory was gained by Henry VII (see 3 November Treaty of Étaples).

Edward's troops were not well-pleased by the settlement, they had enlisted mainly because of the possibilities of plenty of loot that were now to be denied, but pragmatism prevailed and many enlisted in the Burgundian army.

Edward was the eldest son of Richard, Duke of York, and was born at Rouen while his father was campaigning (see, for example, 20 July Pontoise). He used a substantial part of the Picquigny payments to carry out an extensive redevelopment of St. George's Chapel, Windsor, a masterpiece of late mediæval architecture. His capacity for monarchy was greater than that of many of his predecessors and successors, but his besetting sins were lechery and dissipation – some have attributed his death at forty two to sexual excesses.

29 BÉTHUNE 1710, FRANCE (WAR OF THE SPANISH SUCCESSION)

Commanders: Generals Fagel & Schulenburg v. Lt. Genl. de Vauban (the younger) & M.de Roth.

Pace the casualties on both sides, this siege was a secondary engagement. Marlborough and his close friend and colleague, Prince Eugene, were constrained by the politics of the alliance under which they served not to engage in a major battle against the French who had been forced back on the defensive; large plans were set aside, and the campaign of 1710 was reduced to a series of sieges designed to improve the prospects in next year's fighting. Following the surrender of Douai (see 27 June), Fagel and Schulenberg were detached from the main force to invest Béthune, and after a stubborn resistance of about six weeks with no prospect of relief, the French capitulated. General Fagel was Dutch and General Schulenburg was Saxon, both were vigorous and successful field commanders in Marlborough's campaigns.

31 FERRYLAND 1694,CANADA (WAR OF THE LEAGUE OF AUGSBURG)

H.M.S. William & *H.M.S. Mary* defeated 7 French ships off the Newfoundland coast.

The colonization of Newfoundland began formally in 1623 with the grant of a charter to Sir George Calvert for a portion of the Avalon Peninsula, and Calvert's first settlement was at Ferryland. At first, the prospects were promising, but after a few years the harsh climate and disease among the inhabitants caused Calvert to petition for a patent to settle what is now Maryland, where Baltimore takes its name from Calvert who was created Baron Baltimore (Ireland) in 1625 for loyalty to the king. The settlement was vacated in 1629, but taken over a few years later by Sir David Kirke, appointed count palatine of Newfoundland in compensation for the lands he had been obliged to return to France in 1632 (see 19 July, Quebec). Control of Newfoundland and the valuable fishery continued to be contested by England and France, and this action was one of many, until the issue was finally settled in favour of Britain at the conclusion of the Seven Years War (see 18 September, St. John's and 8 September, Montreal).

31 H.M.S. BACCHANTE (38 GUNS) V. TISIPHONE & 2 GUNBOATS, ROVINJ 1812, CROATIA (NAPOLEONIC WAR)

Commanders: Captain William Hoste v. ?

This action, typical of many in the Adriatic theatre, was actually fought between the boats of *Bacchante* and the French ships which were superior to them. Hoste had received information that there were several ships near Rovinj that were carrying ship timber to the shipyards at Venice, and he sent his boats under the command of Lieutenant O'Brien to bring them out. Two merchant men were taken at the harbour entrance, and the British boats then pressed on against the escorts larger in size and more heavily armed than the ship's boats. Audacity and courage carried the day, the French escort vessels were taken together with seven other ships of the convoy without loss on the British side. The French escorts, carrying 72 men, had been intended to provide protection for ships trading between Pola and Trieste.

Following his outstanding performance at Lissa (see 13 March, H.M.S. Amphion et al.), Hoste had returned to England on leave. At home, he was mortified to find that his father, to whom he had entrusted the care of his prize money amounting to tens of thousands of pounds and intended to purchase an estate in Norfolk, had spent it in electioneering in the Whig interest, and in the hope of a bishopric, as well as in matching the extravagance of his rich, political friends. Adding to Hoste's chagrin was the failure to be awarded a knighthood, but his consolation was to be given the choice of a newly-built frigate, and he chose *Bacchante*.

31 VERA 1813, SPAIN (PENINSULA WAR)
Commanders: Wellington v. Genl. Bertrand Clausel.
Forces: British 12,000; French 24,000.

The French were attacking with the object of relieving the siege of San Sebastian (see 8 September) and impeding Wellington's advance into France. After failing to break through, Clausel broke off the engagement during which operation a company of the 95th, Rifles (80 men) held the bridge over the Bidassoa River for two hours without support against the retreating French (see 15 August, Obidos). British casualties were 850; French were 1,300. For something about Clausel, see 1 August, Sumbilla.

SEPTEMBER

1 NAMUR I 1695, BELGIUM (WAR OF THE LEAGUE OF AUGSBURG)

Commanders: William III v. Marshal Louis François, Duc de Boufflers.

At this time, wars in Europe were largely wars of attrition dominated by slow, careful sieges. The location of Namur at the junction of the Meuse and Sambre Rivers, about 35 miles south-west of Liège, gave it considerable strategic importance during centuries of European wars, and consequently it was heavily fortified. It had been captured by the French three years earlier under the command of Vauban, the renowned military engineer of Louis XIV, and now William III invested it. Although William had the useful help of van Coehoorn, who had built the fortifications, his success was one of the most costly sieges in history up to that point – 18,000 casualties against French casualties of 9,000 – and it lasted for 55 days compared with Vauban's 36 days and 2,600 casualties. But as a perspective, when the Germans besieged Namur in August 1914 with 100,000 men they battered it into surrender in 5 days using 540 guns, some firing shells weighing up to two tons, at times at the rate of 20 rounds per minute, and sustained 1,000 casualties; the city surrendered with 50,000 prisoners.

As a result of William's fierce campaigning against the French, he was recognized as the soul of European opposition to Louis XIV's aggressions, and of all France's enemies he was the most deadly and persistent (see also 1 July Boyne).

2 LE TRÉPORT 1545, FRANCE (WAR OF THE SPANISH ALLIANCE)

Commanders: Viscount Lisle v. Adml. of France Claude d'Annebault.

This was the last act in a failed attempt at a full-scale invasion of England by Francis I, who had shared the leading role with Henry VIII at the extravaganza of the Field of the Cloth of Gold tweny-five years before (see 21 July, Isle of Wight). Severely affected by disease, the large French fleet had been repulsed and sailed back to France. After collecting reinforcements, the English went in pursuit, and following another inconclusive encounter off Shoreham on 15 August, they pressed on. On 2 September they landed at Le Tréport, a few miles north-east of Dieppe, and burned it, but this was their last card. Like their opponents, they were afflicted by the plague and forced to return home. Two years later both Henry and Francis were dead.

3 TOURNAI 1709, BELGIUM (WAR OF THE SPANISH SUCCESSION)

Commanders: Marlborough v. Marquis de Surville-Hautfois.
Forces: British and Allies 100,000; French 90,000.

Skilful tactical marching by Marlborough and his close friend and colleague, Prince Eugene, had induced the French to withdraw some troops from Tournai before the siege began in order to reinforce another sector. These troops were lucky because the siege proved to be one of the hardest fought and most unpleasant in modern history. The fortifications were of the latest design and among the defenders was the designer himself, M. de Mesrigny, one of Vauban's ablest colleagues, whose speciality was mining. Mining and counter-mining meant that much of the fighting was conducted in underground tunnels. One of the British camp followers was a Mother Ross who was there with her husband and joined him in the subterranean struggle fighting with pick axes and spades which this Amazon considered to be more dangerous than fighting with swords. The trials and tribulations of the combatants were aggravated by disease and plague, but after about two months the attackers were in a position to storm the citadel into which the French had withdrawn. Without hope of relief, de Surville then surrendered. Some 3,600 French were sent to France on parole to await an exchange of prisoners; they left behind about 1,700 dead and 1,500 wounded. Total British and Allied casualties were in the order of 5,340.

This was the second time the British had besieged and occupied Tournai (see 25 September). Tournai's final entry in British military history is when the Guards' Armoured Division liberated it from the Germans exactly 235 years later to the day.

4 LOTTINGHEN 1522, FRANCE (WAR OF THE HOLY LEAGUE)

Commanders: Earl of Surrey v. ?

A feature of Henry VIII's wars was the unscrupulous way in which all of the antagonists unilaterally abrogated their treaty obligations. Only two weeks after the conclusion of the hugely expensive 'Field of the Cloth of Gold' meeting between Henry and Francis I at which mutual expressions of amity and peace were pronounced, Henry met Charles V of Spain, Francis' enemy, and made a treaty agreeing not to enter into any alliance with France for a period of two years. There followed a foray into France, and not only did the cavalry and pikemen promised by Spain not materialize, but Charles made a separate peace with France. Surrey captured Lottinghen, and, after laying waste the surrounding countryside, he invaded Picardy, but hunger and frostbite so demoralised the army that Surrey withdrew to Calais.

Surrey had a long career in which he, too, managed to change allegiance. In the War of the Roses, he was a Yorkist and was captured in the final battle of Bosworth; released four years later, he held important offices under Henry VII. He was in command of the victorious army at Flodden (see 9 September) and was guardian of England during Henry VIII's absence in France in 1520. His grandson, Henry, Earl of Surrey, was a poet with a place in English literature as the principal author of the English form of the sonnet (see 14 September Boulogne).

4 ALIGARH 1803, INDIA (NAPOLEONIC WAR)

Commanders: Genl. G. Lake v. Colonel P.C. Pedron

Forces: British 1,800 European & 12,500 Indian with 65 guns; French officers and 37,500 Mahrattas with 73 guns.

The Mahrattas were in alliance with the French, and Pedron and his officers trained and commanded the Mahratta army. This army was drawn up in front of the fort which was protected by a ditch 100 feet wide with ten feet of water, and the only means of approach was a causeway. The British aim was to capture Delhi, and Aligarh blocked the way. The British, principally a Highland regiment, covered by heavy artillery fire forced their way across the causeway, eventually blew in the main gate, and fought their way through the fort against strong resistance. French casualties were 2,000 many of whom died by the bayonet or by drowning in the ditch while trying to escape; but Colonel Pedron and several other officers surrendered leaving Bourquien in command; barely a week later he, too, was in the bag (see 11 September Delhi). British casualties were 55 killed and 205 wounded, and Lake wasted no time in continuing the march to Delhi.

Aligarh has since found distinction as a centre of higher education, especially Aligarh Muslim University and its affiliated colleges; and a number of Muslim saints are buried there.

5 MALTA 1800 (FRENCH REVOLUTIONARY WARS)

Commanders: Maj. Genl. Pigot & Captain G. Martin v. Genl. Vaubois & Rear Admiral Villeneuve.

Malta had been captured by Napoleon on his way to the Egyptian campaign in 1798, but following the Battle of the Nile (see 1 August) the island was blockaded by a small British squadron commanded by Captain Martin in *H.M.S. Northumberland*, and starvation forced the French to capitulate. There was one ship in the harbour in seaworthy condition, *Athenienne* (64 guns), which was taken as a prize. *Athenienne* was commissioned into the Royal Navy but had a humdrum career brought to an end six years later by shipwreck on the reefs off Sardinia. Rear Admiral Villeneuve, in command of the ships in the rear of the line at the Nile had escaped, and his next major appearance is at Trafalgar (see 21 October). By the Treaty of Amiens, 27 March 1802, Malta was restored to the Knights of Malta who had ruled it since 1530, but by the Treaty of Paris 1814 (see 30 May), concluded after Napoleon's first abdication, Malta came under British sovereignty as a result of strong objections by the Maltese to the rule of the Knights. Militarily, Malta's finest hour was in World War II during which it resisted frequent, very heavy bombing raids by the Axis powers, and in recognition the island was awarded the George Cross. The George Cross is awarded for "acts of the greatest heroism or of most conspicuous courage in circumstances of extreme danger", and it ranks above all British military and civilian decorations except for the Victoria Cross.

6 LÉAU (ZOUTLEEUW) 1705, BELGIUM (WAR OF THE SPANISH SUCCESSION)

Commanders: Genl. Dedem v. M. Dumont.

The Lines of Brabant were a line of forts and fortified positions running for about 70 miles from Namur to Antwerp that made full use of rivers and canals. Marlborough had been thwarted in his plan to attack the French through the Moselle valley to Saarlouis and turned his attention to the Lines of Brabant which were a much more attractive objective to his cautious Dutch allies. A massive breach was made in the Lines (see 18 July Elixhem), and as part of mopping up operations, a contingent was dispatched to take Léau which was accomplished in eight days.

6 BAHUR 1752, INDIA (CARNATICWAR)

Commanders: Major Stringer Lawrence v. M.Kerjean
Forces: British 400 Europeans and 2,100 Indian; French 500 Europeans and 2,000 Indians + 8 guns.

The British force was seeking to relieve the blockade of Fort St. David. Initially, the British attack made no impression against the French infantry holding firm even when bayonets were crossed in hard hand-to-hand fighting. The turning point came when a crack company of British grenadiers broke through the French centre, at this, the French threw down their arms and fled the field. M. Kerjean, the nephew of the French Governor-General, the Marquis Joseph-François Dupleix, was taken prisoner with 115 officers and men; losses in killed and wounded were heavy.

8 CROWN POINT (A.K.A. LAKE GEORGE) 1755, U.S.A. (FRENCH & INDIAN WAR)

Commanders: Maj. Genl. William Johnson v. Baron Ludwig Dieskau
Forces: British-Colonial 3,500 & 300 Indians; French/Canadians/ Indians 2,000.

The French were intending to invade New England, and Johnson had been appointed by George Clinton, the governor of New York, to stop them. They met at Lake George, and the French were defeated. Dieskau was among those taken prisoner, and the survivors retreated to Fort Ticonderoga; meanwhile Johnson began construction of Fort William Henry (probably named for the Duke of Gloucester, the third son of the Prince of Wales and grandson of George II). Johnson was made a baronet in recognition of his achievements, an award that must have been assisted by his thoughtful re-naming of Lac du Saint-Sacrement as Lake George in honour of George II. He had emigrated to New England in his early twenties and quickly became prominent by showing diplomatic skill, particularly with the Mohawk Indians. Immediately prior to the action at Crown Point, he had been appointed as superintendent of the Iroquois Confederacy. Subsequently, he assumed command at the capture of Fort Niagara (see 25 July) and was with Amherst at the fall of Montreal on the fifth anniversary of this victory.

8 MONTREAL 1760, CANADA (SEVEN YEARS' WAR)

Commanders: General Sir Jeffrey Amherst v. Marquis de Vaudreuil-Cavagnal.

The British had an overwhelming superiority in numbers and had made a three prong offensive on Montreal – Amherst with the main body had advanced from Oswego, General Haviland from Crown Point, and General Murray from Quebec. Once Amherst's troops had joined the others, the French Governor-General asked for terms, and one of the conditions of the surrender was that all of the French troops in New France would lay down their arms; accordingly, the remaining outposts soon surrendered. However, it was not until the Treaty of Paris concluded the War in 1763 (see 10 February) that all of the French territory was formally ceded to Britain.

Amherst was a career soldier whose conquest of Canada greatly enhanced his reputation, he went on to become Commander-in-Chief of the British Army, but George III was moved to point out that great though his services were "they would not be lessened if he left the appreciating of them to others". Amherst, Nova Scotia, and Amherst, Massachusetts, are named after him as well as several other towns in the United States. Murray was appointed military governor of Quebec, and after the Treaty of Paris he became the first civil governor of Quebec, but his opposition to repressive measures against the French Canadians led to his recall (possibly because he came from a Roman Catholic family with pronounced Jacobite sympathies; (see 16 May Quebec)). He seems to have been sympathetic to the French because while he was governor of Minorca he surrendered it to the French, for this he was court martialled but acquitted and was later promoted to general.

8 BALLINAMUCK 1798, IRELAND (FRENCH REVOLUTIONARY WARS)

Commanders: Maj. Genl. Gerard Lake v. Genl. Humbert
Forces: British 5,000; French and Irish rebels about 2,000.

This battle was the last in a series of French invasions of the British Isles over centuries of warfare. During the period in which Napoleon was First Consul of the French Republic, Wolfe Tone, the renowned Irish revolutionary leader, persuaded the French to invade Ireland in support of the Irish rebels. Napoleon himself showed little interest in the scheme, and only three ships and about eight thousand troops were committed. In the event, the first ship with the largest contingent, including Wolfe Tone, was destroyed before it could land and Wolfe Tone was taken prisoner; the second force was never organized; but the third with Wolfe Tone's brother, Mathew, succeeded in putting the troops ashore at Killala. The French were joined by Irish rebels that were hastily trained and equipped by the French. Following a rout of British troops at Castlebar, the antagonists met at Ballinamuck where the result was reversed. The battle lasted for only half an hour before Humbert, putting his hat on the point of his sword, signalled surrender. French casualties were 17 and the other 842 were taken prisoner and later exchanged for British prisoners, but the Irish rebels were ruthlessly pursued and cut down, only 80 out of 1,000 were taken prisoner including Mathew Tone who was hanged. For more on Major General Lake, see 18 August Lincelles.

8 SAN SEBASTIAN 1813, SPAIN (PENINSULA WAR)
Commanders: Lt. Genl. Sir Thomas Graham v. Genl. Emmanuel Rey
Forces: An Allied Army comprising principally Spanish, Portuguese, the Anglo-Portuguese Division, and British Engineers and Artillery; French 3,185 following replacements by sea.

At this point in the Peninsula War, Wellington had advanced to the French border, but before the invasion could begin it was necessary to take the fortresses of San Sebastian and Pamplona (see 31 October). San Sebastian is located in an excellent defensive position and was heavily fortified. The siege was interrupted by Marshal Soult's attacks at Sorauren and neighbouring places (see 28 July) but was resumed after these had been repulsed. The French made a determined defence, and the fighting was fierce. Inevitably, casualties among the storming troops were considerable and the loss of many officers has been held to be a factor in the failure to contain the pillage and looting following the capture of the town, a large part of which was burnt down. The rampage was worse than that at Badajoz (see 7 April), hitherto the extreme example, and it has led to the speculation that just before an assault the soldiers totally suppressed human feelings such as pity and terror, and afterwards the survivors burst out in a degrading catharsis of terrorism and drink. Be that as it may, after the battle Wellington was strongly criticised in the Spanish press for the behaviour of the victorious troops at San Sebastian, but time gives a broader perspective, and in 1925 Queen Victoria Eugénie of Spain opened a cemetery in a flower garden in San Sebastian to commemorate the British soldiers who fought for Spain in 1813 as well as the volunteers who fought in the Spanish civil war in the 1830s. The inscription on the memorial stone reads:

> "England has confided to us their honoured remains
> Our gratitude will watch over their eternal repose."

When the fighting had stopped, Wellington complained about the Navy's inefficiency in the blockade and in the supply of the besiegers prompting an acid reply from the First Lord of the Admiralty: "I will take your opinion… as to the most effectual mode of beating a French army, but I have no confidence in your seamanship or nautical skill". On other occasions, Wellington warmly acknowledged the support he had received from the Navy.

9 FLODDEN 1513, ENGLAND (WAR OF THE HOLY LEAGUE)

Commanders: Earl of Surrey v. King James IV
Forces: English 20,000 v. 25,000 Scots + 5,000 French.

Flodden is generally regarded as an Anglo-Scots battle, but by a treaty with France in 1512, the Scots had taken the field as allies of the French in the War of the Holy League in which England had joined Spain, Austria and others (see 25 September, Tournai). Henry was campaigning in northern France, and James IV took the opportunity to invade England with an army that included 5,000 French troops. The battle was a disaster for Scotland – after several hours of fierce fighting the king had been killed together with many of the senior nobility and upwards of 10,000 troops – it is said scarcely any Scottish community was spared; English casualties were about 4,000. One factor contributing to the defeat was the use by the Scots of the long pike recently introduced from France, this was a formidable weapon against cavalry but virtually useless at close quarters; the English were armed with a shorter pike with a bill hook at the end, and this was a much more effective weapon in the fighting that took place. James IV's widow was the elder sister of Henry VIII, and it was her great grandson, James VI of Scotland and James I of England, who succeeded to the English throne in 1603 when the Tudor line became extinct on the death of Elizabeth.

The Earl of Surrey next met the French in the main at Lottinghen (see 4 September).

9 DENDERMONDE 1706, BELGIUM (WAR OF THE SPANISH SUCCESSION)

Commanders: Marlborough v. M. de Vallé
Forces: British & Allies 6,000; French 2,000.

The first attempt to take Dendermonde stalled, partly because the defences had been strengthened by judicious flooding and partly because of more pressing business at Ostend (see 9 July) and at Menin (see 22 August). Although Marlborough was not in very good health at this time, he remained in the field actively conducting operations and demonstrating to those who cared to observe that Marlborough below par was better than any of the alternatives in better form. General

Charles Churchill, Marlborough's brother, was sent to Dendermonde with reinforcements and 60 more guns, and the siege works were re-opened. Five days later, the garrison surrendered and were made prisoner. This victory brought a bonus in that Dendermonde was of considerable commercial importance to England, and this added to the jubilation at home.

10 PONDICHERRY 1759, INDIA (SEVEN YEARS' WAR)

Commanders: Rear Adml. Sir George Pocock v. Rear Adml. Comte d'Aché de Serquigny

Forces: British 10 ships of the line; French 11 ships of the line

The British had the better of a somewhat inconclusive action at the end of which the badly damaged French ships were obliged to withdraw to the roads at Pondicherry. D'Aché was badly wounded and, discouraged by three successive defeats (see 29 April, Cuddalore & 3 August, Negapatam), he sailed his ships back to Mauritius; the end of French hopes in India was in sight. Three days later, the French lost their Canadian territories as well (see 13 September, Plains of Abraham). This must be one of the worst weeks in French military history.

10 H.M.S. VIPER (12 GUNS) V. A CONVOY 1801, BAY OF BISCAY (FRENCH REVOLUTIONARY WARS),

Commander: Lieut. Jeremiah Coghlan v. ?

At this date, in the British navy the number of ships of the line was approximately equal to the number of smaller vessels, but only ships of the line were directly engaged in fleet battles, i.e., in the Line of Battle. *Viper* was a cutter, and this engagement is typical of what the smaller ships and their crews did. The convoy was making a short passage along the Charente coast when it was sighted by Sir Edward Pellew's squadron, and Lt. Coghlan was ordered to intercept. Coghlan excelled at this kind of work (see 29 July H.M.S. Viper), and he cut out a sloop and drove a brig ashore, but when he went to take possession he was attacked by a large gun brig, two schooners and two luggers. In spite of the odds against him, Coghlan turned towards the enemy, drove the gun brig ashore and forced the others back into harbour. *Viper* received some 24-pound shot in her hull and had one man killed and another wounded.

The previous year, *Viper* had recaptured a transport, *Diamond*, that had been transporting the baggage and horses of the Duke of Kent from Halifax, Canada, where he had been general in command of British forces in North America, a posting that led to Prince Edward Island being named after him. The Duke later became the father of Queen Victoria, and he was so pleased to recover his belongings that he declined Lt. Coghlan's offer to forgo salvage; since the Duke was heavily in debt all of his life, this must be seen as a most generous act. Then, in a single month *Viper* took two prizes – one a schooner with a cargo of cocoa and indigo from French Guiana, and the other a brig with a cargo of wine. A few weeks later *Viper* joined in the capture of a French privateer brig from St. Malo, and in July 1801, back off Rochefort with Sir Edward Pellew's squadron, *Viper* forced a 16-gun corvette into port after an exchange of gunfire.

10 SAMARANG 1811, JAVA (NAPOLEONIC WAR)

Commanders: Genl. Sir Samuel Auchmuty v. Genl. Jan Willems Janssens.

Following their crushing defeat at Cornelis (see 24 August), Janssens and about 600 men fled to Samarang. Auchmuty pursued them, and on 10 September occupied Samarang without loss.

11 MALPLAQUET 1709, BELGIUM (WAR OF THE SPANISH SUCCESSION)

Commanders: Marlborough and Prince Eugene v. Marshal Claude-Hector, Duc de Villars and Marshal Louis François, Duc de Boufflers.

Forces: British & Allies 110,000 + 100 guns; French 80,000 + 60 guns.

The Allied superiority in numbers was off-set by the strength of the position selected by Villars for a defensive battle, and its natural advantages had been greatly enhanced by entrenchments and other works. Fighting was exceptionally fierce involving in turn infantry and cavalry charges; the French were able to repel the first attacks inflicting heavy casualties, but the attackers did not waver and continued to press forward. The French were obliged to retreat but did so in good order under the command of Boufflers after Villars had been wounded, and they earned the admiration of Marlborough himself – "The French have defended themselves better in this action than in any battle I have seen".

Marlborough also described the battle as "very bloody on both sides", and Malplaquet has been labelled 'the bloodiest battle of the eighteenth century', Prince Eugene was among the wounded. Allied casualties were about 18,000 and the French about 11,000. An unusual feature of the engagement was that the Royal Regiment of Foot of Ireland was part of the French army, the 'Wild Geese', (fighting for the deposed, Roman Catholic Stuarts) and also of the British army (fighting for the Protestant Stuart Queen) and at one stage they were in direct conflict.

Villars had a long, successful career as a soldier and as a diplomat; he had been made a duke in 1705, and in recognition of his performance at Malplaquet he was named a Peer of France. At the end of his career, he was promoted to the rare rank of Marshal-General. Older than Villars and not so long-lived, Boufflers was also a well-respected general with years of successful service most recently at Lille (see 9 December); in spite of his age and ill-health, he volunteered to serve under Villars in this campaign, and following the battle he was confirmed in command of the army. Such was the relief of Louis XIV that the troops were rewarded by the distribution of half a million livres. Rewards on the Allied side were less conspicuous, perhaps because by now Marlborough and Eugene were expected to win, and the scale of the casualties had come as a severe shock, but in Britain a coin was struck in commemoration of Malplaquet.

11 DELHI 1803, INDIA (NAPOLEONIC WAR)

Commanders: Genl. Gerard Lake v. Genl.Louis Bourquien.
Forces: British 1,000 cavalry + 3,500 infantry; French [Indian troops] 6,000 cavalry + 13,000 infantry.

Lake, the c-in-c India, was intent on capturing Delhi, and the French in command of the Indian troops sought to repel the advance from Aligarh (see 4 September), by standing in a strong defensive position six miles from the city. Action began with heavy artillery fire from the French, but by very skilful tactical manœuvring, Lake decoyed the defenders from their lines. The British advanced, still under heavy fire, but at a range of 100 yards the infantry fired a volley and charged supported by cavalry and the 'galloper guns', the forerunners of the horse artillery. The result was immediate and spectacular. The Indian troops fled pell-mell, many drowning in the river behind their lines; their casualties were about 3,000 and the loss of 68 guns. British casualties were 478 killed, wounded and missing. Three days after the battle Bourquien and four other French officers surrendered. The British occupied Delhi, and now controlled a huge territory in north eastern India. Ten days after the surrender of the French commanders, Lake was welcomed by the elderly Mogul Emperor who, as a historian of the British army expressed it, "had lived to see the occupants of a few small factories become the masters of India". In 1815, Napoleon recognized the same fact, but from a different point of view – "If it had not been for you English, I should have been Emperor of the East. But wherever there is water to float a ship, we are sure to find you in our way".

13 BOUCHAIN 1711, FRANCE (WAR OF THE SPANISH SUCCESSION)

Commanders: Marlborough v. Marquis de Ravigneau
Forces British & Allies 30,000; French 5,000.

This was a major siege as the British and their allies continued their offensive against France itself. Bouchain was a fortress in the eastern sector of the Lines of *Non Plus Ultra* (approximately, 'No further may you go'). The Lines were a fortified chain of entrenchments, bastions and fortresses extending from the Channel coast to Valenciennes – an eighteenth century version of the Maginot Line of World War II, but superior in design in that they were anchored on the Channel whereas the Maginot Line, fatally, was not. Bouchain stands at the confluence of the Scheldt and Sensée Rivers surrounded by marsh lands that greatly improved its defences. Immediately prior to the commencement of the siege, Marlborough manœuvred his army, inferior in numbers to the French, so brilliantly that the French commander-in-chief, the Marquis de Villars, was completely deceived as to his intentions and decoyed into massing his troops in the wrong place. By means of a forced march – 39 miles in 18 hours with infantry riding behind the saddles of cavalry-Marlborough was able to pass through the Lines of *Non Plus Ultra* at Arleux without losing a man and to put his troops in position to besiege Bouchain. The fortress was one of the strongest remaining in French hands, but the siege was conducted so aggressively and skilfully that the garrison surrendered unconditionally after 34 days with the loss of 24 colours, all arms, 3,000 prisoners and about 2,500 casualties; British and allied casualties were about 4,500. For the whole period of the siege, a French army in larger numbers was less than ten miles from Bouchain, and it points to what has been described as Marlborough's "moral ascendancy" over de Villars, at that time France's most able general, that no serious attempt was made to relieve the garrison.

This engagement was Marlborough's last conquest and command. For ten successive campaigns he fought the French, and he never engaged in a battle he did not win or besiege a fortress he did not take. He has been described as one of history's great commanders, and England has never produced a greater soldier. He lost his command not because of any military failure, but because of the machinations of insidious, self-serving politicians.

13 PLAINS OF ABRAHAM 1759, CANADA (SEVEN YEARS' WAR)
Commanders: Major-Genl. James Wolfe & Vice Adml. Sir Charles Saunders v. Major-Genl. Marquis de Montcalm
Forces: British 4,500; French 10,000.

This battle took place just outside the walls of Quebec, and its importance greatly exceeded the numbers involved. The colony of New France depended on troops, settlers, and annual supplies of all kinds from France transported through the great St Lawrence River, the defence of which centred on Louisbourg and Quebec. Louisbourg had been captured by the British the year before, and its massive fortifications demolished (see 27 July), but the attack on Quebec had been postponed because of the approach of winter and the icing of the river. Now, the invading army was launched from Louisbourg with the newly promoted Wolfe in command at the unusually early age of 32. In June, the fleet and the transports entered the river and in a brilliant feat of navigation, the first large ships of war ever to have passed the notorious traverses of the river below Quebec took up station off and above Quebec itself. The navy was now able to support and supply the troops in their assaults, and to deny the French any supplies from up-stream Montreal. Quebec was too heavily fortified to be taken by siege in the time and manpower available. Wolfe himself was suffering from tuberculosis and gravel that reduced his effectiveness so that at the beginning matters did not go well for the attackers. The French, too, had their problems – Montcalm's command was impaired by the Marquis de Vaudreuil, the

Governor-General, who exercised control over the greater part of the military resources of New France. In addition, the French superiority in numbers was diluted by the fact that they had fewer regular troops than their opponents, and although Montcalm was distinguished for bravery and courage, his skills were principally those of a tactician and field commander. The shoals and dangerous currents in the river, and the precipitous cliffs on which Quebec stands combined to make the conquest of it truly formidable. The French had already been confounded by the appearance of the British fleet so far up-stream and were then to be astounded when they found that during one night British troops had scaled the cliffs about one and a half miles up-stream from Quebec, hauling two cannon with them, and were drawn up on level ground known as the Plains of Abraham. Without waiting to assemble all of his troops, Montcalm sallied out of the city to repel the invaders, and the French fired the first volley, but the British infantry stood their ground, waited until the range had closed to about 40 yards and then loosed a single, perfect volley that halted and shattered the French advance. A few more minutes of firing and a bayonet charge, enlivened by Fraser's Highlanders throwing away their empty muskets after the first volley and charging with claymores as at Culloden, caused the French to retreat pell-mell into the city. The action lasted only about ten minutes, but in that time Wolfe was killed on the battlefield, and Montcalm was mortally wounded. Five days later, after heavy bombardment by the navy, Quebec surrendered, and the remainder of the French force, led by Vaudreuil, escaped to Montreal. The army occupied the Upper Town and the navy marched into the Lower; the whole campaign represented a fine example of inter-service co-operation, loyalty, and harmony. A good case can be made for claiming that although Saunders lacked the genius of Wolfe, his performance during the whole operation was the surer of the two.

Wolfe became a posthumous, national hero following this victory. He is buried, and his flag is displayed, in St. Alfege's Church, Greenwich, where he went to school, and there is a statue of him in Greenwich Park the gift of the people of Canada, although his statue in Quebec has been taken down.There is another fine statue in Westerham, Kent, where he was born. He admitted to a mercurial temperament alternating between exhilaration and despondency but was tireless in the performance of his duties and, possessed of great confidence in his own abilities, he was saved from arrogance by warmth, charm and friendliness. When only 16, and newly promoted to lieutenant, he was acting adjutant of his regiment at Dettingen (see 27 June), continuous service led to rapid promotions, and his reputation spread. Inevitably, his successes, coupled with outspoken criticisms of professional incompetence, resulted in enmities, the final word on which was uttered by George III who, on being told of Wolfe's unpredictable behaviour, remarked: "Mad is he? Then I hope he will bite some of my other generals!"

Society in the mid-eighteenth century was on a small scale, and this probably made inter-service co-operation easier. While British troops were going ashore, *H.M.S. Porcupine* took up station in the channel under heavy fire to cover the landing, and *Porcupine* was commanded by John Jervis, who was not only Wolfe's professional collaborator at Quebec but had also been at school with him. The night before the battle Wolfe had given to Jervis his last will, some notebooks, and a miniature of his fiancée, Katherine Lowther, which she had given him and was to be returned to her. Jervis went on to become a national hero in his own right as the commander of the fleet that inflicted a massive defeat on Spain, then in alliance with France, at the battle of Cape St. Vincent.

The principal pilot in the crucial navigation of the St. Lawrence River was James Cook, later Captain Cook, who became the world's leading maritime explorer of his day (See 27 July Louisbourg II).

Although victory at Quebec made the end of New France virtually inevitable, there were still some mopping-up operations in the following year (see 16 May, Quebec; 25 August, Fort de Lévis; 27 August, Fort Frontenac; and 8 September, Montreal), and formal cession of the territories had to wait until the Treaty of Paris 1763 (see 10 February).

14 BOULOGNE 1544, FRANCE (WAR OF THE SPANISH ALLIANCE)

Commanders: Henry VIII v. ?

Henry, now married for the sixth time and grown older than his years, had revived youthful dreams of French conquests, and in 1542 he made an alliance with Spain against France with the immediate purpose of invading France in the following year. The invasion duly took place, and Boulogne was besieged. In spite of spirited French resistance, the city was forced to surrender, and Henry was exhilarated, but the invasion had been planned as part of a concerted action with Spain which did not happen. The same year, his ally, Charles V, made a separate peace at Crépy with the French king, and by breathtaking incompetence Henry found himself isolated in simultaneous conflict on two fronts – France and Scotland. Fortunately for Henry, at Solway Moss, the Scots managed, against all odds, to replicate the disaster of Flodden (see 9 September), and their defeat temporarily relieved the pressure. The cost of the war, however, was beyond Henry's means, and in June 1546 Henry was obliged to make peace with Francis I by which England kept Boulogne for eight years and then was obliged to return it to France with rebuilt fortifications. Thus, what had been gained militarily was lost politically, and on any cost-benefit analysis it would have been better to have left Boulogne alone; no doubt the citizens of Boulogne would have been the first to agree. Seven months later, to the relief of many, especially the Duke of Norfolk (see below), Henry died.

Notable among the French casualties was François, Duke of Lorraine, who was almost fatally wounded and so scarred that 'the scarred' became his byname; he became a French military hero and was also the uncle of Mary, Queen of Scots.

The governor of Boulogne for the first two years was Henry Howard, Earl of Surrey, now best known for his poetry, but in his lifetime he won royal approval for his military performances and jousting. On his return to England from Boulogne, he succumbed to the ambitions of the Howard family and was outwitted by the intrigues of the Seymours in the last year of Henry's reign. At the age of 30, he was convicted of treason, and he died on the block on Tower Hill. His father, the Duke of Norfolk, would have suffered the same fate if Henry had not died before signing the warrant. Incidentally, capable military leaders who were also poets are rare. Richard I, the Lion Heart, is credited with a song 'Ja Nun Hons Pris' written while imprisoned in Austria; and Henry VIII , though scarcely a capable military leader, has at least 35 musical compositions to his name, the best of which is the song 'Pastime with good company' (popular legend has it that 'Greensleeves' was composed by Henry, but this has not been established). Although only a minor commander who died in Arnhem of his wounds (as did many British paratroopers 359 years later), easily the greatest soldier-poet is Sir Philip Sidney, a contemporary of Skakespeare, whose sonnets are ranked only behind those of the master in any catalogue of Tudor poetry. More recently, there is Rear Admiral Richard Kempenfelt (see 14 December, Ushant), and a vicarious example that comes to mind is Field Marshal Wavell of World War II who, in his retirement, edited an anthology of poetry called 'Other Men's Flowers', second-hand copies of which are still to be found.

16 COVELONG 1752, INDIA (CARNATIC WARS)

Commanders: Captain Robert Clive v. ?
Forces: British 200 European recruits + 500 sepoys with 4 siege guns;
French 50 European + 300 sepoys

The French defeat at Trichinopoly (see 13 June) had diminished French influence in this part of India, and the British Governor decided to attack their fortress of Covelong about 30 miles south of Madras; Clive was placed in command of a force of European and sepoy recruits. Demoralised by a steady bombardment, the Garrison Commander surrendered. The victory was completed the next day with the ambush and capture of a French relief force. The impressive feature of this action was the way in which Clive had succeeded in turning his recruits into a disciplined fighting force from a motley crew who, at first, ran away even at the sound of their own fire, and one was actually found hiding at the bottom of a well a day later.

18 ST. JOHN'S 1762, NEWFOUNDLAND (SEVEN YEARS'WAR)

Commanders: General Sir Jeffrey Amherst v. Joseph d'Haussonville

Following the French capitulation at Montreal (see 8 September), Amherst became governor-general of British North America, and he left Louisbourg with 1,500 troops to expel the French from Newfoundland. Isolated, d'Haussonville soon surrendered St. John's and Fort William. This is thought to be the last occasion on which the British and French fought as principals in North America, but, of course, they were to do so again when the French were allies of the insurgents in the American War of Independence.

18 H.M.S BACCHANTE 1812, VASTO, ITALY (NAPOLEONIC WAR)

Commander: Captain William Hoste v. ?

Raiding in the Adriatic (see 2 August, H.M.S. Bacchante; and 31 August, H.M.S. Bacchante), Hoste sighted an enemy convoy of 26 ships sailing towards Vasto. Light winds prevented *Bacchante* closing on the convoy, and so the ship's boats, under the command of Lieutenant O'Brien, were sent away to intercept. As the boats approached, the merchant ships were run ashore by their crews who then hid in a wood, and the 8 escort vessels each armed with a twelve pounder gun lined up along the shore to protect them. All to no avail, the boats came on, through heavy musket and grape shot, until they were within 50 yards when they fired their carronades, known in the Royal Navy as 'smashers', and then boarded to drive the crews overboard. Concurrently, a party of marines landed and cleared the wood of the others. The prizes were carrying cargoes of oil and almonds, but some were lost in a storm before they could reach Lissa.

O'Brien had had an unusual experience. As a midshipman he had served in *Amphion*, in his next posting he had been taken prisoner and recaptured after an escape. His second imprisonment was in the fortress of Bitche, near Strasbourg, he escaped again, and this time he succeeded in evading re-capture. He wandered about the country for many weeks and finally reached Trieste, there he was able to bribe a fisherman to row him out to a British frigate that could be seen on the horizon. Lo, and behold, the frigate turned out to be *Amphion*, his former ship, Hoste welcomed him on board and later made him third lieutenant.

19 POITIERS 1356, FRANCE (HUNDRED YEARS' WAR)

Commanders: Edward, Prince of Wales (The Black Prince) v.
King John II

Forces: British 6,000; French 20,000.

Early in August, Edward marched out of Bordeaux on his second Major Offensive Sweep, termed C*hevauchée* by the Prince, (see 5 October) with similar objectives, namely, to devastate enemy territory thereby demonstrating the impotence of its ruler; to defeat the enemy in the field; and to join forces on the Loire with two other armies of the north. Once in French territory, after passing through Verizon, systematic looting and destruction began, but on a smaller scale than that in Languedoc. The army was frustrated when it reached the Loire because the river was in spate, and the bridges were either damaged or heavily defended so that it could not be crossed, and no contact with the other English armies was made. Now, restricted in movement by the large train of booty, the army turned for its base, but progress was delayed by a series of marches and counter-marches against a very large French army that was in the field. At last, the two armies came face to face near Poitiers. The French army was organized in four divisions, or 'battles'. The mounted vanguard was commanded by two marshals of France – Clermont, and Audrehem. The second battle was commanded by the king's eldest son, the Duke of Normandy, and the third was under the orders of the Duke of Orleans, the king's youngest brother. The king himself was at the head of the fourth battle. With their huge superiority in numbers, the French took the offensive, and attacked in four successive waves. The first was mainly cavalry supported by some 2,000 Genoese crossbowmen. The mounted knights were decimated by the English archers concealed behind hedgerows and scrub, and Marshal Clermont was killed. The second wave, led by the Duke of Normandy, was principally dismounted men-at-arms, and fierce fighting developed at the English line that finally turned in favour of the English when Edward sent in some of his reserves. At this juncture, the French contributed greatly to their own defeat. When the Duke of Orleans saw how badly the first two attacks had fared, he fled with most of his troops. King John was left with a force still considerably larger than the English, and his men were fresh, whereas the English had been fighting hard for hours. In a masterly decision, Edward decided on a mounted attack and having despatched a small body on a flanking movement, he led a charge. Fierce fighting ensued the result of which was in the balance until Edward's flankers attacked the French in the rear. Most of the French ran off, leaving the King with a small bodyguard who fought heroically until obliged to surrender, and the King was among the prisoners, along with many of the French nobility. The list of the principal prisoners deserves to be recorded: King John II, an archbishop, 13 counts, 5 viscounts, 21 barons and bannerets and about 2,000 French knights and men-at-arms; another 2,000 were killed. The day after the battle the English resumed their triumphal march to Bordeaux where most of the prisoners, who had been released on parole, were honour bound to pay their ransom money by Christmas.

The aftermath of this battle illustrates the 'rules of war' in the Middle Ages. Edward arranged an elaborate banquet immediately after the fighting was finished at which King John was the principal guest and on whom Edward waited with ostentatious ceremony. The leaders of the opposing armies had much in common – the display of personal courage and the conventions of chivalry coupled with a common language, the same religious beliefs, and the enjoyment of similar sports as well as obeying the same canons of behaviour. To a limited extent, this commonality mitigated the cruelty and depravity of the conflicts, but it is very easy to romanticize. King John was taken to London in April 1357 with a ransom set at 4,000,000 gold écus (crowns), and most of southwest France was ceded to Edward. Three years later, John was released in order to raise the ransom money, and while he was engaged in this activity one of the hostages for his return, his own son, escaped, whereupon John, unable to raise the ransom, returned to England of his own volition. Known in France as John the Good or John the Beautiful he died in London still in captivity.

Edward had another considerable victory (see 3 April, Nájera), but he outlived his military achievements proving to be an extravagant and poor ruler of Aquitaine which he was obliged to return to his father, Edward III, and return to England. He predeceased his father and is buried in Canterbury Cathedral where his tomb and accoutrements are still to be seen, but his byname 'Black Prince' because of his black armour seems to be a myth. The Prince's only son succeeded to the throne, as Richard II, on the death of Edward III, but his capacity for government was not much better than his father's. Inadequate revenues led to the imposition of poll taxes that were extremely unpopular (Mrs. Thatcher might have been forewarned), and finally he was deposed by Henry Bolingbroke (Henry IV); he died, probably murdered, shortly afterwards.

Although a small city, Poitiers has a place in European military history as the site of another renowned battle. In 732, Charles Martel defeated a large Saracen army here (sometimes referred to as the Battle of Tours), and ended the threat of any major Muslim invasion of France from Spain.

19 LIMOGES 1370, FRANCE (HUNDRED YEARS' WAR)

Commanders: Edward, Prince of Wales (The Black Prince) v. Bishop of Limoges.

This engagement came about almost by chance. A French army, commanded by the Duke of Berry, had been attacking English towns and castles in Gascony, and when it was approaching Limoges the Bishop, who controlled it, threw open the gates and invited it in. Edward had been on friendly terms with the Bishop, who was a godfather of Edward's son, Richard, and when he heard of the Bishop's treasonous act he flew into one of those violent rages for which he was well-known. Edward was in poor health, but his brother, John of Gaunt, had arrived in Bordeaux, and together they set out on a punitive expedition. Edward was too weak to ride, and he had to be carried in a litter. The Duke of Berry kept his army out of the way, and it took the English only six days to storm Limoges and occupy it. As was usual in those days (and much later), when a town was taken after a siege, the defenders were killed and sometimes some of the inhabitants as well. In this instance it has been widely claimed that after the town was taken, it was sacked giving rise to the name of the 'sack of Limoges' with the Black Prince as the chief culprit. There is, however, reason to believe that this version of what took place is an exaggeration. This was the last battle of the Black Prince.

19 PORT MAHÓN 1708, MINORCA (WAR OF THE SPANISH SUCCESSION)

Commanders: Maj. Genl. James Stanhope v. ?

Port Mahón was by far the best harbour in the western Mediterranean, and it was wanted by the British as a base to counter the French naval base at Toulon (Gibraltar had been captured only in 1704 and had not yet been developed). Admiral Sir John Leake fresh from the capture of Sardinia, arrived with his fleet on 25 August and landed the marines, shortly after Maj. Genl. Stanhope brought his troops from Barcelona and besieged St. Philip's, the principal fortress, which capitulated on 19 September. For the next 100 years, Minorca had a chequered existence. After a heroic siege, it was captured by the French in 1756 (and for his performance on this occasion Adml. Sir John Byng was court-martialled and shot on his own quarterdeck (see 15 January, Pondicherry and 17 August, Lagos Bay), but it was returned to Britain at the end of the Seven Years' War. Re-captured by the Franco-Spanish Army in 1782, it was finally returned to Spain by the Treaty of Amiens in 1802.

19 BERGEN-OP-ZOOM 1799, NETHERLANDS (FRENCH REVOLUTIONARY WARS)

Commanders: Frederick Augustus, Duke of York & Lt. Genl. Ivan Ivanovich Hermann v. Genl. Dominique-Joseph-René Vandamme.

Forces: British & Russian 35,000; French 35,000

The Allies were invading The Netherlands, but their co-ordination was poor, and this gave an advantage to the French. The French launched a strong attack against the Russians and so overwhelmed them that most were taken prisoner. On the other hand, the British repelled the French attack and inflicted heavy losses. The immediate result was that the Allies retreated but advanced again two weeks later. French casualties were 3,000 killed and wounded; Russian 3,500 and 26 guns; British 500. Frederick Augustus, Duke of York, was the second son of George III, who had made the army his career and by this time was commander-in-chief. He was not a success in this role, nor had he been as a field commander, and he has been lampooned in the nursery rhyme beginning "O, the brave old Duke of York/ He had ten thousand men… …". This was a parody of a much older one featuring the King of France, and probably does the Duke an injustice in that he painstakingly introduced a number of reforms in the British army that were sorely needed. He was forced to resign in 1809 because his mistress had been found trafficking in appointments, but he was exonerated and reinstated two years later. He is probably flattered by his statue placed on an imposing column in Waterloo Place, London, at the top of the Duke of York's Steps, because most of the cost was covered by stopping one day's pay from every soldier in the army, and wags said the column had to be so high (124 feet) in order to keep the Duke out of the reach of his creditors.

20 CAEN 1417, FRANCE (HUNDRED YEARS'WAR)
Commanders: Henry V v. ?

Building on his astounding success at Agincourt (see 25 October), Henry now opened a campaign for the capture of the Duchy of Normandy that he considered to be his by inheritance. He landed on 1 August after departing from England with great ceremony. Brushing aside an attempt to oppose the landing at what is now Trouville, the first objective was Caen, the capital of Lower Normandy, about 30 miles away. Two smaller castles were taken as the army marched towards Caen, and the siege of a place the French considered to be impregnable then began. Cannons were now available, sometimes more dangerous to those firing them than to the targets, and Henry had brought a siege train with him that was now put carefully in place. His other preparations were equally methodical, and a continuous bombardment commenced until sufficient breaches had been made in the walls. Henry V was devout, and after hearing three masses, he gave the order by trumpet for the general assault. His brother, the Duke of Clarence, commanded an attack on the east side, and after vigorous fighting his troops were able break into the town, meanwhile, the main thrust had not made progress. On either side of the breach in this sector, the defenders poured down from the walls a mediæval mix of crossbow shafts, rocks, darts, boiling water mixed with fat, lime, and incendiary material that was sufficient to halt the first wave. The king himself then reorganized the troops and, with the Duke of Clarence's men attacking the defenders from the rear, the defence collapsed. In a dramatic scene ideal for a movie, the royal brothers met triumphantly face to face inside the walls. Street fighting continued for some time, French casualties were heavy, and inevitably these included civilians; this was the general experience in contested sieges and was a practical inducement to early surrender. Along with looting and pillaging, the killing of civilians has proved impossible to prevent and was still provoking protests four hundred years later from humanitarians with no understanding of the reality that in wars all manner of bad things happen that are inextricably part of the process and beyond control by rules (see 7 April, Badajoz and 8 September, San Sebastian). As Hazlitt has put it: "The excesses committed by the victorious besiegers of a town do not attach to the nation committing them, but to the nature of that sort of warfare, and are common to both sides. They may be struck off the score of national prejudices."

Caen had previously been captured by Edward III at the beginning of the Hundred Years' War (see 26 July), and in July 1944 there was bitter street fighting here between the Germans and the Canadians during which the inhabitants took refuge in the Abbaye aux Hommes, built by William the Conqueror and the headquarters of Henry V during this siege.

21 ST. JEAN D'ANGELYS 1346, FRANCE (HUNDRED YEARS' WAR)

Commanders: Henry, Earl of Derby v. ?

This was an attack on the town of St. Jean d'Angelys brought about by unusual circumstances. Sir Walter Manny had been taken prisoner and then released with his retinue and given a safe conduct across France. At St. Jean d'Angelys, he was taken prisoner in spite of his safe conduct and held in the castle. Henry, newly landed in France to campaign in Poitou, was enraged when he heard what had happened, and with particular cause because Manny had saved his life at Cadsand (see 10 November); here was a chance to do something in return. Henry immediately broke off the siege of Chateauneuf and forced marched his army to St. Jean. As soon as they arrived, they took the town by assault and released the prisoners. Contrary to the usual practice when a town was taken by assault after refusing to surrender, the victors did not sack the town, accepting the plea that the incident was the fault of an individual and not the citizens. The citizens, perhaps in gratitude or perhaps resigned to their fate, took the oath and became English; they also agreed to bear the cost for the remainder of the war of 200 men-at-arms and 600 foot soldiers.

Sir Walter Manny enjoyed a very successful career in the service of Edward III. He was Flemish by birth and came to England as a squire in the entourage of Phillipa, Edward III's queen. He soon found his true métier as a soldier, at first against the Scots and subsequently against the French. He took a very active part in the war from its commencement up to the Treaty of Bretigny (see 8 May) at which he was one of the English delegates. The ransom money he was able to collect as well as rewards from Edward for his performances made Manny a wealthy man. In the name of his wife and himself, Manny hoped to find favour in Heaven by establishing a Carthusian monastery, London Charterhouse, and a useful practical donation was the gift of land near Smithfield in London for a burial ground for those who had died in the Plague. His two illegitimate daughters became nuns, which invites questions about the mores of the higher echelons of society in those days.

22 HARFLEUR 1415, FRANCE (HUNDRED YEARS' WAR)

Commanders: Henry V v. Sire de Gaucourt & Sire d'Estoutville.

Henry opened his campaign against France by sailing from Portsmouth for the Baie de Seine, also the principal route for the invasion of Normandy in 1944, and laid siege to Harfleur. At the beginning he had 10,000 men, but these were quickly reduced, mainly by disease, by almost half. Harfleur was captured in barely a month, and Henry marched north eastwards towards Agincourt (see 25 October). No commander has ever had a better publicist than Shakespeare was for Henry V; in his eponymous play, he has Henry declaim at the assault on Harfleur:

"Once more unto the breach, dear friends, once more
Or close the walls with our English dead … …"

And much more stirring stuff in the same vein (Act III, Scene 1) concluding with:

"Cry Harry, England and St. George!"

22 SANTO DOMINGO 1793, HAITI (FRENCH REVOLUTIONARY WARS)

Commanders: Cdre. J. Ford & Lt. Col.J. Whitelocke v. ?

Acting on a report from an informer that some of the French settlements in Santo Domingo had royalist sympathies, an amphibious expedition was launched from Trinidad and first occupied Jérémie seizing more than 1,900 tons of enemy shipping loaded with colonial produce. Other isolated settlements were taken until the whole of the French part of the island had been captured. The British occupation lasted for five years during which time thousands died from disease. Eventually, the French resumed sovereignty, quickly followed by independence.

25 TOURNAI 1513, BELGIUM (WAR OF THE HOLY LEAGUE)

Commanders: Henry VIII v. ?

Following the successes at Guinegate and Thérouanne (see 16 & 23 August), Henry laid siege to the important city of Tournai, and it surrendered after only three days. At his coronation in April 1509, the Venetian ambassador had described Henry as "magnificent, liberal and a great enemy of the French", but the campaign of 1513 was undertaken as a member of the Holy League ostensibly in support of Pope Julius II against Louis XII of France, the other members of the Alliance were Spain, Venice, the Holy Roman Empire, and Switzerland. After some initial successes, there were disagreements over strategy, and the members made peace separately. Henry did so in 1518 by the Treaty of London by which time Louis XII had been succeeded by Francis I. Exhilarating though the conquests had been, they proved to be a serious expense, and Henry and his chief minister, Cardinal Wolsey, were relieved to sell Tournai to Francis for 600,000 crowns, and an indemnity to Henry of 12,000 crowns as personal compensation. Wolsey's reward was the bishopric of Tournai. Prior to obtaining its independence in 1830, Belgium had been at different times part of Spain, Austria, France and Holland, but Tournai is unique in that it is the only city in Belgium to have been English. During the rebuilding of the fortifications a large tower was constructed and named the Tower of Henry VIII; the Tower still stands and is one of the tourist attractions of the city.

The Treaty of London was meant to inaugurate a rapprochement with France. Mary, Henry's two year old daughter, was pledged to marry the Dauphin, the French agreed not to support the anti-English faction in Scotland, there was to be a crusade against the Turks, and a treaty of universal peace, but none of these things happened. The Field of the Cloth of Gold, held in 1520 near Calais, endorsed the Treaty but to no effect, and this diplomatic extravaganza utterly failed to improve English-French relations (see 4 September Lottinghen).

25 VENLO 1702, THE NETHERLANDS (WAR OF THE SPANISH SUCCESSION)

Commanders: Marlborough & Prince Nassau-Saarbrücken v. Marshal Louis François, Duc de Boufflers & M. de Varo
Forces: British & Allies 30,000; French 1,100.

Following the successful siege of Kaiserswerth (see 15 June), Marlborough was thwarted in his efforts to engage the French army, partly by the extreme caution of his Dutch allies and partly because the French decided to send reinforcements to various garrisons and to avoid a pitched battle. It has even been suggested that de Boufflers had lost his nerve. In these circumstances, Marlborough planned to provide a platform from which to launch an offensive in 1703, to this end a number of fortified towns were to be captured, and Venlo was the next on the list. A French diversionary tactic was poorly conceived and failed, while the town and citadel were subjected to a most vigorous attack. A surprise assault carried the town, with many of the garrison being put to the sword, and after a week of bombardment by cannon and mortars de Varo, the Governor, surrendered and was allowed to march out of the citadel with the survivors. Allied casualties were 1,100 and the French similar – 839. The victors now full of confidence immediately marched on to Stevenswaert (see 2 October).

27 LIMBOURG 1703, BELGIUM (WAR OF THE SPANISH SUCCESSION)

Commanders: Marlborough v. M. de Reignac.
Forces: British & Allies 16,000; French 1,400.

The French had considered Huy to be nearly impregnable, and its fall after only a few days of resistance (see 26 August) caused gloom and despair. Continued dissension in the Allied command meant that the victory was not pressed home, and finally, towards the end of September, Marlborough was able to attack Limbourg. The siege was routine except for two damaging sorties by the garrison, and once the artillery barrage began, the surrender came after less than two days. Casualties were light – Allies 100 and the French 60; the Governor and the garrison became prisoners of war.

Limbourg was the last of Marlborough's engagements of the 1703 season, the results of which were not the equal of the year before, but crowning glory was less than a year away (see 13 August, Blenheim).

27 BUSACO 1810, PORTUGAL (PENINSULA WAR)

Commanders: Wellington v. Marshal André Masséna
Forces: British & Portuguese 61,000; French 61,500.

Wellington was making a strategic withdrawal to winter quarters in Portugal pursued by the French army which had expectations of taking Lisbon and expelling the British from the Peninsula. Busaco was a prime defensive location dominating the road to Lisbon with a ridge 1,000 feet high. The French had proceeded slowly. According to Masséna's report to Napoleon, they were in a village 8 miles from Busaco, waiting for supplies; however, in the opinion of others they were there to rest his mistress; Marshal Ney's report on his hasty reconnaissance of the Allied position had to be shouted through the bedroom door of his commander. Eventually, the troops were in place, and several attacks were made in columns. Fierce fighting occurred when the French reached the summit of the crest, but the attackers were tired after the climb and were forced back down the slope at the point of the bayonet, or by steady volleys from both British and Portuguese infantry. British casualties were 626, Portuguese 612; French 4,487.

This battle is renowned in the history of the Portuguese army. The year before, Major General Beresford had, on the recommendation of Wellington, been appointed to reform the Portuguese army which he did superbly. Speaking fluent Portuguese, he took a root-and-branch approach to all parts of the army and drafted British officers and NCOs into Portuguese units in large numbers; most importantly, he eliminated appointments and promotions by influence and substituted advancement by merit. At Busaco, the first result of his work was displayed to the great surprise and disconcertment of the French. Various memorials have been constructed at the site of the battle by the Portuguese stimulating a legend of Anglo-Portuguese glory. There is the palace built by Ferdinand II, a cousin of Prince Albert, next to the old Convent which was Wellington's command post, with huge representations of battle scenes in blue and green tiles and it is now a hotel; inside the cell of the Convent where Wellington slept for the last time on the night of his victory there is a plaque to "The Glorious General", and in the garden, the olive tree that Wellington himself planted. Close by is the Chapel of Our Lady of Victory, and a museum dedicated to the battle in which the life-size models of Portuguese soldiers have brown eyes, and the British have blue eyes. Assorted plaques are crowned by a tall obelisk.

Masséna was an unusual character in that he had an excellent military reputation combined with what has been described as "an enthusiastic indulgence in both financial greed and lechery" which he pursued his lifetime long; nevertheless Wellington considered him to be the most able of Napoleon's marshals that he had fought. Masséna enlisted as a volunteer in the French army fourteen years prior to the Revolution and rose to the rank of sergeant before his discharge. Re-enlisting in the Revolutionary Army, his performance in a series of battles in Italy justified his rapid promotion, and he was in the first creation of marshals in 1804. He became the Duc de Rivoli in 1808 in recognition of his earlier victory; finally, after outstanding work at the battles of Aspern-Essling and Wagram, Napoleon awarded him the title of Prince d'Essling. These awards were in spite of two earlier, major scandals of plundering, peculation and corruption, and when he was appointed to command the Army of Portugal in 1810 he was at the height of his career – and almost at the end of it. Defeated by Wellington at Busaco, the Lines of Torres Vedras (see 14 November), and Fuentes de Onoro (see 5 May) Masséna was recalled and never held another active command. Curiously, a village and a town in northern New York State were named for him by the first European settler in 1792 at which date he had only reached the rank of lieutenant-colonel.

28 TINCHEBRAI 1106, FRANCE (ANGLO-FRENCH WARS)

Commanders: Henry I v. Robert, Duke of Normandy

Robert was the eldest son of William the Conqueror, and Henry was the Conqueror's third son. At William's death, Robert had succeeded to the Duchy of Normandy and the second son, also William and known as 'Rufus', was crowned King of England. Many of the principal barons in England held estates in Normandy, their homeland, and if England and Normandy were not ruled by the same person an unstable government was inevitable. Thus, the prime policy of any king of England was to ensure that he was simultaneously the Duke of Normandy. William Rufus was adroit, and when Robert decided to enlist in the First Crusade he raised the money to sustain his purpose by mortgaging the Duchy to Rufus for 10,000 marks. From Robert's departure until his own death, William ruled Normandy as well as England, and in the Duchy he did so more ably than Robert. Robert did not arrive back from the Crusade until a few weeks after William's death in a hunting accident, and in this period Henry, acting with speed and determination, had been able to arrange for his own coronation. In 1101, Robert landed at Portsmouth intent on invasion, but the sides were evenly matched, and Henry was able to negotiate a peaceful settlement which included the payment of a pension to Robert of 3,000 marks p.a. Since this treaty left England and Normandy in different hands, political instability continued, and the battle of Tinchebrai was fought to decide the issue. Robert had served with distinction in the Crusade, but on this occasion his army was destroyed and he was imprisoned for the remaining 28 years of his life. He died in Cardiff Castle, and Henry lived for a year longer.

Henry is generally regarded as an outstandingly able and successful king, and the master politician of his age, but he left a succession problem sown with seeds of civil war. Henry's only legitimate son died in a ship wreck fifteen years before him, and although Henry married for a second time immediately after his son's death, no new heir was born. Henry is said to have acknowledged 20 illegitimate children, but his only legitimate heir was a daughter, Matilda, who became the matriarch of the Plantagenet line.

Matilda was first married to Emperor Henry V of Germany, and after his death she married Geoffrey Plantagenet, heir of the Count of Anjou, and in due course their son was crowned Henry II, but in the nineteen years between the death of Henry I and his grandson's accession in 1154, England was in a state of civil war. Henry I had declared his daughter Matilda to be his heir and made his barons swear fealty to her, but when he died his nephew, Stephen, repudiated his oath of fealty to Matilda and seized the crown. Stephen had the support of some of the barons, and Matilda the others, but she also had a strong base in northern France provided by her husband, further enhanced when Geoffrey completed the conquest of the duchy of Normandy in 1145. There was continual fighting during which Stephen was imprisoned for more than a year, and after his release his writ only ran in parts of his realm. He lost the support of the pope, and just before he died he acknowledged Matilda's son as his heir. This was most fortunate for England because Henry II was one of the most successful of England's monarchs, and conversely unfortunate for France because the Plantagenets for nearly 250 years had extensive territories in France which brought them into conflicts with the French monarchy.

28 WYNENDAEL 1708, BELGIUM (WAR OF THE SPANISH SUCCESSION)

Commanders: Maj. Genl. John Webb v. Genl. Louis-Jacques, Comte de Lamotte

Forces: British 6, 000; French 23,000.

This engagement was a by-product of the siege of Lille (see 9 December). On assuming command of the siege, Marlborough was shocked to discover that only four days' supply of ammunition was on hand, and at once he organized a convoy from Ostend. The immediate threat was from the French force at Bruges to the north which was in course of being reinforced for the express purpose of cutting off supplies to the besiegers of Lille. The convoy, comprising 700 wagons with an escort, left Ostend and the next day were sighted by Lamotte in a thickly wooded area about 12 miles south-east of Ostend, but his way was barred by Webb who had drawn up his badly outnumbered troops in the only clearing that offered the opportunity for a successful attack. The action lasted for two hours; the early stages were dominated by volley firing from the British infantry that led the French left wing to collapse and flee to the right which was thrown into disorder. At this point, General Cadogan appeared with some squadrons of cavalry sent by Marlborough to render any assistance that might be required, and without further fighting the French retreated. The convoy arrived safely with its vital cargo. British casualties were 940, French at least 4,000 and possibly 7,000.

The performance of Webb and his soldiers was exemplary, but unfortunately Marlborough's dispatch commended both Webb and Cadogan. Although Webb acquired great honour and reputation for his victory, he never forgave Marlborough for putting Cadogan's name alongside his when Cadogan's troops had not played an active part, and he greatly marred his case by making it the subject of his conversation on all occasions.

30 MORLAIX (A.K.A. LANMEUR) 1342, FRANCE (HUNDRED YEARS' WAR)

Commanders: Earl of Northampton v. Charles de Blois
Forces: English about 3,000; French upwards of 15,000.

The English army was besieging Morlaix, and the French had collected a much greater number to relieve the siege. They were on the march with this objective when the English, learning of their approach, broke off the siege operations and took up a defensive position about four miles to the east. Their defensive works included a concealed trench within bow shot of the English front line which comprised dismounted men-at-arms with archers on each flank. The French formed up in three large columns behind each other. In the first attack, the leading column advanced on foot, and as soon as it was within range it was decimated by a cloud of arrows, and the survivors took flight (this seems remarkably like World War I infantry marching against machine guns). The first column did not get as far as the concealed trench so that the second wave, consisting of cavalry, did not know it was there and charged into it, and flights of arrows added to their confusion; a few staggered out of the trench but were mopped up in the English line, including the commander, Geoffrey de Charni. At this stage, the Engish withdrew into a wood in their rear to await the third column and prepared to do so by making the position capable of defence on all sides in the manner of a modern 'hedgehog'. This novel disposition baffled the attackers who were unable to penetrate the wood and finally retreated. The relief of the siege of Morlaix had failed. Northampton's army was too small to permit a pursuit of the enemy, and so it marched in the opposite direction to resume the siege. This battle, in which the fighting was fierce and the English tactics imaginative, was the first pitched, land battle in the Hundred Years' War. At this early stage, the nominal cause was the support of Edward III for the claim of John de Montfort to the Duchy of Brittany, and the support of Philip VI of France for the counter claim of Charles de Blois.

30 AURAY 1364, (HUNDRED YEARS' WAR)

Commanders: Sir John Chandos v. Charles de Blois & B.du Guesclin.

This battle brought to an end a war within a larger one. The smaller war was the War of the Breton Succession into which the kings of England and France respectively had been drawn on opposite sides, so that their actions in it were not really distinguishable from the major dispute between them. In support of John de Montfort, who was defending his occupation of the duchy of Brittany, the English were besieging Auray when they were surprised by a French army led by du Guesclin. Chandos had placed his troops in a strong defensive position against which the French could make no impression, and an attack on their flank so discombobulated them that they could not stem a rout in which Charles de Blois was killed and du Guescalin captured. The Treaty of Guérande 12 April 1365 formally ended the twenty years' war, and in it Charles V of France acknowledged John as the Duke of Brittany.

Sir John Chandos was descended from a follower of William the Conqueror and was a lifelong follower and supporter of the Black Prince (Prince of Wales, son of Edward III). He was responsible for the military education of the Prince and had the opportunity to mark his progress at Crécy (see 26 August), Poitiers (see.19 September), and Nájera (see 3 April). As a reward for his services, he was given the lands of the Viscount de Saint-Sauveur in Cotentin (where the D-Day landings were made), and as Constable of Aquitaine (1361) and Seneschal of Poitou (1369), the capital of Poitiers, he proved to be as able an administrator as he was a commander in the field. Chandos was one of the original Knights of the Garter, and at the Treaty of Bretigny (see 8 May) he was a principal negotiator and won the esteem of friend and foe alike. He was killed fighting the French and is buried in France.

Du Guesclin is a national hero of France. Outstanding military performance in the early stages of the Hundred Years' War led to his appointment as Constable of France (essentially commander-in-chief) in 1370. Notwithstanding that after Auray his ransom was set at 40,000 gold francs, the newly crowned king, Charles V, so valued his services that he paid this amount eight months later. However, the benefit of the payment was limited because Sir John Chandos took him prisoner again at Nájera less than three years later (see 3 April). Du Guesclin died besieging an enemy fortress.

OCTOBER

1 ATH 1706, BELGIUM (WAR OF THE SPANISH SUCCESSION)
Commanders: Genl. Overkirk v. ???
Forces: British & Allies 20,000 v. French 2,000.

Following the fall of Dendermonde (see 9 September), Marlborough, intent on securing Brussels for the winter, marched the army to Ath situated on the road from Lille to Brussels. Marshal Vendôme made a vain attempt to delay the siege, and in spite of a spirited defence by the garrison, after 15 days they surrendered as prisoners of war. This action concluded the very successful campaign of 1706 (see 23 May Ramillies).

2 STEVENSWAERT 1702, THE NETHERLANDS (WAR OF THE SPANISH SUCCESSION)
Commanders: Marlborough v. M. de Castellas.
Forces: British & Allies 30,000: French 1,500.

Sweeping on from Venlo (see 25 September) with the objective of clearing the line of forts along the Meuse (Maas) river, Stevenswaert was invested the same day that Venlo was taken. The resistance was weak, and after a week the Governor surrendered and was allowed to march off to Namur.

2 ST. VENANT 1710, FRANCE (WAR OF THE SPANISH SUCCESSION)

Commanders: Marlborough & the Prince of Orange v. Marshal Villars & Brig. de Seloe.

Forces: British & Allies 12 battalions + 5 Squadrons; French 7 battalions.

At this stage in the war, the French in the north-east were on the defensive with the main object of preventing the invasion of France. Marlborough was not in robust health, in Britain he had lost political support, and the Dutch alliance was always difficult to manage. These circumstances were not propitious for a grand offensive strategy, and although Marlborough proposed a drive down the Channel coast to Calais, it was finally decided to limit activities to the capture of the fortresses of St. Venant and Aire (see 8 November) which would give uncontested use of the River Lys, and a broader avenue of attack on the last fortress line of France. Marlborough remained in command of the main army covering the siege, and the Prince of Orange was given command of the siege itself. The defence lacked resolution, and in less than a month the garrison surrendered.

This action does not complete St. Venant's military history – it is also the site of a World War I British cemetery to which extensions were made for those killed in the heavy fighting in 1940 to cover the evacuation from Dunkirk, and British troops continued to fight here even after the evacuation had been concluded.

2 TRICHINOPOLY III (A.K.A. SUGAR LOAF ROCK) 1753, (CARNATIC WAR)

Commanders: Major Stringer Lawrence v. M. Astruc

Forces: 600 Europeans + 5,000 sepoys & Indian cavalry; French 600 Europeans + 3,000 sepoys & 30,000 Indian horse and foot.

This battle was a sequel to Trichinopoly II (see 7 July), and it occurred when Lawrence returned to Trichinopoly with a large convoy and found that he had to fight his way back into the town through strong French opposition. Deciding to take the offensive, Lawrence launched a night attack in bright moonlight and routed the French in a pincer movement in which the British grenadiers advanced with a volley followed by a bayonet-charge. French casualties were 100 killed and wounded together with 200 prisoners including M.Astruc and 10 of his officers, 11 guns were captured. The two defeats at Trichinopoly within three months seriously impaired the plans of the French Governor-General, the Marquis Dupleix, and he was recalled the following year. His successor then negotiated a treaty that brought to an end the Second Carnatic War (see also 13 June, Trichinopoly I; 28 June, Cuddalore; & 28 November Trichinopoly IV).

2 EGMONT-OP-ZEE 1799, NETHERLANDS (FRENCH REVOLUTIONARY WARS)

Commanders: Frederick Augustus, Duke of York v. Genl. Guillaume Brune

Forces: British & Russians 35,000; French 35,000.

This was a curious action in which the Russians overcame the French outposts, and the British outflanked the enemy line and attacked the left and centre. This success enabled the allies to occupy the town of Alkmaar in the centre of the French line of defence, but when they had done so, they found themselves besieged. On 17 October, the Duke of York conceded and signed the Treaty or Convention of Alkmaar, and by it he agreed to withdraw his forces from Holland, and to arrange the release of 8,000 French prisoners of war. The Duke was severely criticised for his decisions, and although his critics were motivated in part by domestic politics, he never again commanded in the field.

General Brune had an unusual career. Twenty six years old at the start of the Revolution, he was already preoccupied with literature but became associated with Danton, an early leader of the Revolution, and later Brune served with Barras and Napoleon in the days of the Directory. Brune's campaign against the Russians and British established his military credentials, and further victories in Italy led to his promotion to marshal in 1804. Then he went to Constantinople as ambassador returning to France to command some coastal defences, and he cleared Stralsund of the Swedes. Afterwards, for reasons never revealed, he was never employed again until he served Napoleon once more during The Hundred Days between Napoleon's escape from Elba and Waterloo. Napoleon sent him to defend Provence which was strongly royalist, but after Waterloo Brune was attacked by a royalist mob in Avignon and killed. He was suspected of participating in the gruesome murder of Princesse de Lamballe, a confidante of Queen Marie Antoinette, by a Parisian mob in 1792; the woman was seized and beheaded, her head was then stuck on a pike and paraded in front of the windows of the Queen in the Temple prison.

4 POITIERS 1346, FRANCE (HUNDRED YEARS'WAR)

Commanders: Earl of Derby (a.k.a. Duke of Lancaster) v. ?

This was the final phase of the Gascony campaign to re-possess the territory that had been lost by the English during the reign of Henry II – the Angevin empire. Derby had been in command from the beginning of the year before, and a series of successes (see 26 August, Bergerac; and 21 October, Auberoche) had now brought him and his small army to Poitiers, the capital of Poitou. On the previous day, Lusignan had been taken by assault, and the general exhilaration carried the troops forward to the next objective fifteen miles away. As soon as the troops reached Poitiers the garrison was called on to surrender; they refused, and in spite of the march of 15 miles, an immediate attack was launched which was beaten off. It would have been reasonable to have rested for the remainder of the day, but instead Derby ordered simultaneous attacks at three separate points on the perimeter.These quickly carried, and though the French commanders managed to escape by swimming the river Clan, most of the garrison were taken prisoner. As was customary, when a town had refused to surrender it was pillaged and some were killed, but to describe the victory as 'the sacking of Poitiers' probably exaggerates the case.

The Earl of Derby was a remarkable man, very successful both as a soldier and diplomat. He was probably the most powerful feudal noble in England of his day, and although he was a great-grandson of Henry III, he was always a loyal supporter of Edward III and became his most trusted adviser. In 1349, he was appointed Edward's captain and vice-regent of Gascony and Poitou, and in 1360 as commissioner for France he was largely responsible for negotiating the Treaty of Brétigny (see 8 May) that ended the first phase of the Hundred Years' War. At one time or another, he was sent on embassies to most of the courts in Europe, and strangely, when David II of Scotland was finally released from his imprisonment in the Tower, he gave Derby the rank of Earl of

Moray. Derby was made Duke of Lancaster in 1351 and his grandson became Henry IV. We might well take the opinion of a French historian as being the most objective: "...Derby was at once...an honourable man, a courageous soldier, and a skilful diplomat"; and purely as a soldier: "These campaigns have imprinted upon the memory of Derby an indestructible glory. This illustrious Englishman displayed all the qualities which in their entirety form the appanage of the truly great."

5 MAJOR OFFENSIVE SWEEP 1355, FRANCE (HUNDRED YEARS' WAR)

Commanders: Edward, Prince of Wales (The Black Prince) v. Count Jean d'Armagnac

Forces: English 5,000 v. many more French than 5,000.

For two years, d'Armagnac, the king's lieutenant in Languedoc, had been harassing English territory in Gascony to the west. The Prince's Sweep (a.k.a.*Chevauchée*) was intended to restore English prestige in the eyes of the Gascons; to pay back d'Armagnac for his depredations; and not least to create a diversion that would assist the northern campaign. Full of enthusiasm fed by the prospects of plunder, the army left Bordeaux and marched south-east towards the Mediterranean. Armagnac's army barricaded itself in Toulouse, and little resistance was encountered so that crops and stores not taken as plunder were burned as were buildings except for religious ones. The most notable destruction was at Carcassone where the lower town, outside the walls, was burned after the inhabitants, now refugees in the upper town, had tried to buy off the Prince with a large ransom. The offer was refused with the disdainful reply that Edward III was not seeking gold but justice- of which, his son might have added, a flaming torch was the symbol. The failure of d'Armagnac to attempt any relief so incensed the inhabitants who were suffering deprivation that they threatened to kill him. A few miles beyond Carcassonne, within sight of the Mediterranean and already burdened with plenty of booty and prisoners, the English turned to return to base. D'Armagnac led his troops out of Toulouse, but on two or three occasions when the English offered battle he refused it, and finally the French marched back to Toulouse in company with the reinforcements that had joined them. Less than ten weeks after setting out, the Prince and his army were back in Bordeaux in nice time for

Christmas and with much to celebrate. For the rest of the winter and through the spring, great efforts were made to consolidate the victory and more than 50 towns and castles of the former English territory were recovered. This work set the stage for the next Offensive Sweep later in the year (see 19 September, Poitiers).

6 HARFLEUR 1440, FRANCE (HUNDRED YEARS' WAR)

Commanders: Earl of Somerset & John Talbot v. Artur de Richemont & La Hire.

The French had retaken Harfleur in 1435, and its loss was a constant threat to one of the main English lines of supply through the Baie de Seine. The small English army was energetic in constructing the siege works around Harfleur including fortifications on the seaward side. The besieged garrison appealed to Charles VII for help, and an army considerably larger than the English one had been sent in response. The French tried one assault from the sea, but this failed in front of the defences that had been prepared, and their casualties were heavy in the two major land attacks. English archery was responsible for most of the casualties in the latter case which suggests that the fighting took place at close quarters because by this date plate armour had been so well developed that an arrow could only penetrate it when fired at close range. By October, the French effort was spent, and they marched off towards Paris only to meet with an unexpected rebuff along the way. The Duke of Burgundy, now in alliance with Charles VII, refused to allow the retreating troops to pass through his territories on account of the pillaging in which they had engaged on their march to Harfleur. With such friends, who had need of an enemy?

6 RUREMONDE 1702, THE NETHERLANDS (WAR OF THE SPANISH SUCCESSION)

Commanders: Marlborough v. Comte de Hornes.
Forces: British & Allies 25,000; French 2,400

Cavalry had been sent the day after the fall of Venlo (see 25 September) to begin this siege at the confluence of the Roer and Meuse rivers, and when the main body arrived a heavy bombardment from 60 cannon and 150 mortars began. Capitulation followed and under the terms of it, the garrison was allowed to march away to Louvain. In spite of unfavourable weather, Marlborough's plan to clear the Meuse (Maas) was proceeding smoothly and was to be completed at the end of the month (see 29 October Liége & Fort Chartreuse).

7 BIDASSOA 1813, SPAIN (PENINSULA WAR)

Commanders: Wellington v. Marshal Nicolas-Jean de Dieu Soult, Duke of Dalmatia.

Forces: British 39,000, Portuguese 25,000, Spanish 25,000 v. French 61,000.

In successive campaigns since April 1809, Wellington had forced the French out of Portugal and Spain, and almost back to France. Soult was constructing field fortifications to block further advance, but at Bidassoa, Soult believed that the estuary could not be forded and had not prepared defences on his side of it. Wellington had been advised that at very low tide the estuary was passable, and this was where he directed the main attack. This thrust met with immediate success, and the troops moved to support attacks further down the line. Badly outnumbered, the French retreated, and the following day the whole of the allied army was able to continue its advance.

9 BARCELONA 1705, SPAIN (WAR OF THE SPANISH SUCCESSION)

Commanders: Earl of Peterborough v. Duke of Anjou (Philip V of Spain).

Following an alliance with Portugal, the British were able to carry the war into Spain, and they did so in the north east in the provinces of Catalonia and Valencia in which there was opposition to the accession of Philip V (the grandson of Louis XIV). Fighting for the cause of the Austrian Archduke Charles, the Earl of Peterborough with 4,000 troops made a brilliant, surprise attack on Philip's French-Spanish army that was blockading Barcelona and took the city. The victory complemented the successes of Marlborough in the northern sector of the war, but later, the advantage was lost by the feeble efforts of Archduke Charles.

Peterborough had a long career as a politician and soldier marred by deficiencies of character. His undoubted cleverness was often used dishonestly, so that he was a liability to any ministry. In his early twenties, he took part in naval operations on the Barbary coast and then became interested in politics. He was strongly opposed to James II and was an early supporter of William III which brought him the title of Earl of Monmouth. Later, he became unduly critical of William and his policies, for which he was sent to the Tower of London for three months. William died in 1702, and by 1705 Peterborough had worked his way back into favour sufficiently to secure his military appointment. His victory and entry into Valencia on January 20, 1706 justified the confidence shown in him, but then, true to form, disagreements with his colleagues and outbursts of his violent temper led to his recall to England and cost him any further advancement. However, he remained active and was ambassador to the Duke of Savoy in 1713, and the philosopher George Berkeley, who was his chaplain, described him as "ambassador extraordinary". Peterboro, New Hampshire is named after him.

At the end of the war in 1713, Philip was confirmed as King of Spain, but at the expense of the Spanish Netherlands (Belgium), Gibraltar, Minorca, Naples and Sicily. He proved to be a weak king, and towards the end of his life experienced bouts of madness. Notwithstanding his weaknesses, his descendant, Juan Carlos, is the King of Spain, and the Bourbons of France have, for practical purposes, disappeared from monarchical history.

9 SAVANNAH 1779, U.S.A. (AMERICAN WAR OF INDEPENDENCE)

Commanders: Brig. Genl. A. Prevost v. Adml. Genl. Comte d'Estaing & Maj. Genl. B. Lincoln

Forces: British 3,200; French & American 6,000 + 39 ships.

In a wild mood of jealousy, revenge and enthusiasm, the French monarchy of Louis XVI declared war on Britain in 1778 in support of the American colonists, and d'Estaing commanded a fleet, including troops, to operate with the insurgents. The French troops were landed near Savannah and linked up with American contingents, while the British were receiving reinforcements from other garrisons. D'Estaing felt he was sufficiently strong to call for the British to surrender "to the arms of the King of France"; surrender was refused, and a siege began. Bad weather and the approach of the hurricane season precipitated an assault that was poorly coordinated – the French arrived at their positions late and attacked early- d'Estaing misdirected some of the American troops into a swamp, and throughout the defence was vigorous. Not surprisingly, d'Estaing's performance greatly disappointed the colonists.

The French-American force withdrew after suffering 800 killed or wounded, of whom 650 were French, and 120 prisoners; British losses were 60. D'Estaing was seriously wounded, and an American cavalry commander, Brigadier Pulawski, was mortally wounded.

Generally, Savannah was typical of d'Estaing's military career. His fleet in the Caribbean was larger than the British, but he was half-hearted (see 6 July, Grenada and 29 December, St. Lucia), and he returned to France in 1780. He entered politics and showed sympathy with the principles of the Revolution but failed in this, too. He was commander of the National Guard at Versailles in 1789 when the royal family was removed, but later wrote in support of Marie Antoinette and was sent to the guillotine in the Reign of Terror. Brigadier Kasimierz Pulawski was quite a different character. The son of a Polish nobleman, he took part in an armed rising against Russian domination, and although this was a forlorn struggle that continued for four years, Pulawski distinguished himself in the hostilities. When the revolt ended with the invasion of Poland by Prussian and Austrian armies, Pulawski went into exile. He was able to assist the Turks against the Russians until they came to terms, and he then went to Paris where he was living in poverty until he met Benjamin Franklin, newly arrived as a Commissioner of Congress. Franklin gave him an introduction to Washington, and this led to his appointment by Congress as Chief of Cavalry. He fought heroically in several engagements and was later authorized to raise and command his own corps. His unit became known as Pulawski's Legion, they were badly mauled at Savannah and lost their leader who had fought against his conception of tyranny since his twenty-first birthday. Brigadier Lincoln went on to serve as Secretary for War from 1781-83 and then passes from notice.

12 VIGO BAY 1702, SPAIN (WAR OF THE SPANISH SUCCESSION)

Commanders: Adml. Sir George Rooke v. Vice Adml. Marquis de Chateau-Renault.

After the failure to capture Cadiz, the Anglo-Dutch fleet made what has been described as "a fortuitous descent upon Vigo", the result of which more than made up for any earlier disappointment. A French fleet had escorted the annual convoy of Spanish treasure ships from America and the Indies to Spain, and the ships came into Vigo harbour where they were protected by a boom with shore batteries at each end, and the French warships drawn up behind it. *H.M.S. Torbay*, a British ship of the line, broke through the boom, and the other ships followed. Chateau-Renault fearing that all was lost gave orders for his ships to be burned, but before this could be done the British had taken 10 of them and 11 galleons as prizes, and every other ship in the harbour was destroyed. Even though some of the treasure had been landed, an enormous amount estimated at £1,000,000 was captured.

There is a reference to Rooke's career in the entry for his victory at Velez Malaga (see 13 August). Chateau-Renault served with distinction in the wars of Louis XIV. He began in the army but transferred to the navy three years later, exceptionally rapid promotion followed, and by 1701 he had reached the rank of vice admiral of France. He was under secret orders to bring the convoy into a French port, and his inability to do so might have been due to fact that there were Spanish officers serving in his ships. In any event, he was not blamed for the disaster at Vigo Bay and was made a marshal of France in 1703, but he never commanded at sea again.

12 ATTEMPTED INVASION OF IRELAND 1798, IRELAND (FRENCH REVOLUTIONARY WARS)

Commanders: Cdre. Sir John Borlase Warren v. Cdre. Jean-Baptiste-Francois Bompart.

On 16 September, Bompart sailed from Brest with 10 ships carrying 3,000 troops for the invasion of Ireland, and course was set for Lough Swilly in north west Ireland. The French squadron was sighted by three British frigates that followed it, and after some difficulties caused by bad weather, an intercepting force of 3 ships of the line and 5 frigates brought the enemy to action in Donegal Bay early in the morning of 12 October. The French were outgunned, and by nightfall the flag ship, *Le Hoche*, had been taken as a prize together with three frigates; the other French ships were able to escape under cover of darkness. The defeat of the invasion attempt was completed in the next six days (see October 13, H.M.S. Melampus et al.; October 18, H.M.S. Anson et al.; October 20, H.M.S. Fisgard et al.), and this action illustrates the strategic importance of Britain's naval superiority.

Sir John Warren had a distinguished naval career. Serving in frigates, in 1794 he had captured three out of four marauding French frigates for which effort he was knighted. In the following year he accomplished the astonishing feat of destroying or taking 220 enemy ships – surely a record in frigate warfare (and his prize money might have been as well). For defeating the invasion, he received the thanks of both the British and Irish parliaments and promotion to rear admiral. A vice admiral in 1805, his squadron captured a French ship of the line and a frigate (see 13 March H.M.S.London et al.). He completed his service in 1813 as an admiral and c-in-c of the North American station.

13 PORT ROYAL (A.K.A. ANNAPOLIS ROYAL) 1710, CANADA (WAR OF THE SPANISH SUCCESSION)

Commanders: Colonel Francis Nicholson; Colonel Samuel Vetch & Cdre. George Martin v. Daniel D'Auger de Subercase.

Following the capture of Port Royal in 1690 (see 21 May), the British and the Massachusetts' colonists failed to establish government and control, but the neglect was about to be made good. The year before, Nicholson and Vetch had failed in an ambitious campaign against Quebec, but now received approval from London for a smaller operation against Acadia (Nova Scotia). Nicholson was the c-in-c of an amphibious force comprising marines, a flotilla of frigates, transports, and a bomb ketch under the command of Martin; in Boston, they were joined by Vetch's contingent of colonial troops, and there were the supplies that had been presented to Nicholson for the expedition, namely: 20 pipes of wine (about 2,000 gallons), 20 sheep, 5 pigs, and 100 fowls. The arrival of the enemy in such force had a formidable effect on the defenders of Port Royal – they were outnumbered about 7 to 1, and the troops from France were mostly young, raw recruits with muskets apt to explode in the hand. The war in Europe was putting a huge financial burden on France, and this had a direct effect on supplies to New France; the pay of officers and soldiers was always in arrears, and supplies were inadequate. The governor, Subercase, was obliged to give his sheets and shirts to the sick and to sell his silver table service to pay for repairs to the fort. When he asked for better support from France, the reply was: "The treasury is empty ... and the king will abandon the colony if it continues to be such a burden." Neglect breeds discontent and discord, and morale sinks. As the governor appointed by the king, Subercase was held responsible by the community, and when the siege began, a few days of brisk bombardment induced a large number of desertions and reduced the settlers to a panic to the point of requesting the governor to surrender. The next day, the council of officers supported the request unanimously, and the capitulation was signed. The terms were honourable to the French in that the garrison was permitted to march out of the fort with drums beating and colours flying; and the garrison, the civil officials, and a few families were sent back to France in three French ships. On arrival, Subercase was accused of negligence by some officers, court martialled and acquitted.

Shortly after the victory, the name of Port Royal was changed to Annapolis Royal in honour of Queen Anne and confirmed three years later at the Treaty of Utrecht (see 11 April) by which Nova Scotia was ceded to Britain along with Newfoundland, the Hudson's Bay Territory, and other places.

Francis Nicholson began his career as an officer in the army, but from his early thirties he was in the North American colonies mainly in civilian appointments, although at this period these were never sharply distinguished from military ones. For fifteen years, he was lieutenant governor of Virginia and persistently championed the defence of New York's frontier against French raids from Canada, but then, as was often the case with both British and French colonial administrators, he was recalled to answer many charges of financial maladministration. These he survived, and he appears in 1709 in association with Vetch. He returned to England after the success at Port Royal and was soon ordered back to North America with promotion to lieutenant-general. A year later, he was made governor of Nova Scotia and Placentia, Newfoundland, and also appointed with a royal commission to audit colonial accounts. These responsibilities were too much for even the most capable administrator to handle, and Nicholson quickly proved it. Predictably, the immediate problems arose out of his auditing of the provincial accounts, and he was soon at loggerheads with his former friend and colleague, Samuel Vetch, and two supply agents of the Annapolis garrison. Most of the government of the province was left to his deputy, Thomas Caulfield. Shortly after the accession of George I in 1714, Nicholson returned to England, where the Whigs were now in power. A lengthy investigation of his conduct began in which Nicholson's association with the Tories was an obvious handicap. He was dismissed from his appointments, and Vetch was appointed to succeed him. Resilient, in 1720 Nicholson was made governor of South Carolina. Opinions of such a controversial figure varied widely. His opponents complained of a vehement temper, vindictiveness, and vanity, Vetch said he was an "illiterate madman". On the other hand, he was supported by his field-officers, fellow governors, and most of the Anglican clergy who extolled his generosity, consideration, and bravery.

Samuel Vetch was a more colourful character than Nicholson. Born in Edinburgh, a 'son of the manse', he grew up in Holland to which his family had been forced to flee to escape Charles II's persecution of the Covenanters. They returned to Britain with William of Orange in 1688, and Vetch joined the army rising to the rank of captain. Showing his spirit of adventure, he then joined the Company of Scotland's ill fated attempt to establish a colony at Darien on the Isthmus of Panama. He returned to New York with the survivors in 1699 and quickly established himself through marriage to the daughter of a wealthy and influential Scottish merchant. A year later, he was engaged in profitable, but illegal, trade with the French in Canada, and when he was obliged to move on to Boston in 1705, he found ways to continue his business of trading with the enemy in Acadia (war between Britain and France began in 1702). Vetch then showed talent as a strategic thinker. His concept of the advantages and method of conquering New France were explained in his paper "Canada Survey'd" and submitted to the Queen and her ministers in 1708. The 'Glorious Enterprise' was approved; Samuel was appointed a colonel and promised the post of governor of Canada when it had been taken; but the resources for the venture were all needed for the war in Europe, and the conquest of Acadia was all that could be managed. Vetch went to London in 1714 to answer the charges Nicholson had made against him, and after he had been exonerated and had been appointed governor, he remained there trying to collect the money due to him, making proposals for the development of Nova Scotia, and applying for vacant colonial governorships. His death in the debtor's prison in London should not obscure his vision of crown and colonists working together for mutual benefit, and for the commercial opportunities that Canada could provide for Britain. Fifty years later, there was still a body of opinion that thought the sugar trade of the West Indies would have been a better bargain than Canada (see 10 February, Treaty of Paris), but time has proved Vetch's ideas to be well-founded, and it can be safely asserted that he helped to provide the spark that replaced the French empire in Canada with British dominion. There is a monument to him on the ramparts of the old fort at Annapolis Royal, and handsome portraits of him and of his wife hang in the Museum of the City of New York.

Subercase, like many sons of the minor nobility, embarked on a military career that oscillated with naval service. At twenty six, his career continued in New France. Commendable service led to his appointment as governor of Placentia in 1702, and in this post he showed energy and imagination, starting farming in order to make good the continual deficiency in supplies from Quebec and France, he also repaired the fortifications and carried out raids against the British settlements. His performance gained him the governorship of Acadia, and although he was the last French governor, he was probably the most remarkable. Repatriated after the defeat at Port Royal, he was offered a posting to Quebec to serve under Vaudreuil's orders, but he refused in disgust and retired to his estates. He died in Cannes-Église, and a ledger-stone in the church marks his grave.

13 H.M.S. MELAMPUS (36 GUNS) & H.M.S. MERMAID (32 GUNS) V. LA RÉSOLUE (36 GUNS) & LA LOIRE (46 GUNS) 1798, IRELAND (FRENCH REVOLUTIONARY WARS).

These actions were a continuation of that of 12 October (Attempted Invasion of Ireland). A boarding party from *Melampus* took *La Résolue*, and their task was made easier by the fact that *L'Immortalité* (42 guns), which was in company with *La Résolue*, gave no assistance. Retribution for *L'Immortalité's* pusillanimity came a few days later (see 20 October H.M.S. Fisgard v. L'Immortalité).

Mermaid engaged *La Loire* and, although heavily outgunned, succeeded in crippling her opponent, but in the process was too much damaged to pursue. *La Loire* remained at liberty for only five more days (see 18 October, H.M.S. Anson et al.; & 20 October, H.M.S. Fisgard et al.).

14 CAPE FINISTERRE II 1747, SPAIN (WAR OF THE AUSTRIAN SUCCESSION)

Commanders: Rear Adml. E. Hawke v. Cdre. Marquis de l'Étanduere
Forces: British 14 ships of the line; French 9 ships of the line, some frigates & a convoy of 252 merchant ships.

For some weeks, the French had been assembling a convoy for the West Indies, and Hawke's squadron found them about 200 miles southwest of Ushant. The French squadron formed up against the British ships, while the convoy was ordered to continue under the protection of one of the larger ships of the line. A running fight took place in which the French fought well but were crushed by weight of numbers, and six ships were taken as prizes. No British ships were lost, and although they were too damaged to give chase, Hawke was able to send a message to the Leeward Islands that the convoy was en route which enabled the British ships on that station to capture 38 vessels. This victory and that of Anson at Cape Finisterre (see 3 May) gave a timely boost to morale in Britain, and the Duke of Newcastle, a senior member of the government, was able to write: "we have more French ships in our ports, than remain in the ports of France… …" Indirectly, the victories led to such an improvement in the blockade of French colonies in the West Indies that by the end of the year, they were on the verge of starvation.

Hawke entered the navy at the age of ten, and thanks to influence he advanced rapidly becoming a post-captain at 29. However, he soon demonstrated that he deserved his advancement by merit, earning a reputation for audacity that was controlled and never impetuous; he also developed new battle tactics that came to be generally adopted. His final naval victory was gained not far from Ushant in 1759 (see 20-22 November, Quiberon Bay), and he went ashore in 1762, then served ably as First Lord of the Admiralty. He was made a baron in 1776 after a lifetime of distinguished service.

16 PONDICHERRY 1778, INDIA (WAR OF AMERICAN INDEPENDENCE)

Commanders: Sir Hector Monro & Sir Edward Vernon v. M. Bellecombe.

The Treaty of Paris, February 1763 (see 10 February) concluded the Seven Years' War, and one of its terms provided that France should regain the trading stations ("factories") in India that it had lost in the war, but in return it was obliged to acknowledge and accept the supremacy of the East India Company. Pondicherry was one of the trading stations, and it was besieged by a British force supported by a squadron of five ships. The defence was stout, but after a month's bombardment the defenders capitulated. During the siege, a French squadron of five ships appeared and attacked the British ships but was beaten off and driven back to its anchorage.

18 TREATY OF AIX-LA-CHAPELLE (AACHEN) 1748, GERMANY (WAR OF THE AUSTRIAN SUCCESSION).

This treaty concluded the War of the Austrian Succession during which there had been several changes in alliances, and the only clear outcome was that Prussia under Frederick the Great came to be recognized as a major European country. Although Prussia was not a signatory, it kept Silesia the conquest of which was the *casus belli*. Austria was obliged to recognize the Prussian conquest and also to cede to Spain the Italian duchies of Parma, Piacenza, and Guastalla. For the rest, it was mainly a matter of restoring the status quo by exchanging captured territory; thus Britain returned Louisbourg to France in exchange for Madras. Nothing was resolved in the struggle between France, Britain and Spain for colonial and trading supremacy, but the Seven Years' War, 1756-63, went a long way towards a final settlement (see 10 February, Treaty of Paris and 9 June, Congress of Vienna). For what it was worth, the French confirmed the Hanoverian succession in Britain and Hanover, but they had done so at the Treaty of Utrecht thirty-five years earlier and promptly broke their word.

Ineffectual as ever and less than three years after his humiliating defeat at Culloden, the Young Pretender, Bonnie Prince Charlie, roused himself from his customary stupor to issue a declaration, as 'Prince of Wales and Regent for his father, James III', denouncing the Treaty. However, an enduring benefit from the Treaty was the inspiration for a major musical composition by George Frideric Handel. George II planned a national celebration of the Treaty that included the performance in Green Park of a new composition by Handel for a wind band. The piece is 'Music for the Royal Fireworks', and a score for strings was added later to permit concert performances.

18 H.M.S. ANSON (44 GUNS) & H.M.S. KANGAROO(16 GUNS) V. LA LOIRE(46 GUNS) 1798, IRELAND (FRENCH REVOLUTIONARY WAR)

Commanders: Captain Philip C. Durham & Captain Edward Brace v. ?

This was another action in the attempted invasion of Ireland (see 12 October). Although quite badly damaged, *La Loire*, on her way back to France, had reached Cape Clear, the south eastern point of Ireland, and there *Anson* and *Kangaroo* caught up and engaged. *Anson's* rigging had been damaged in the previous fight, but after about an hour of vigorous fighting *La Loire* was taken. Including troops, *La Loire* was carrying 664 men, and her casualties were 48 killed and 75 wounded, *Anson's* were 2 killed and 14 wounded. Only 3 ships of the original French squadron succeeded in returning to France. Two of the captured French ships were taken into the Royal Navy, and one of them was appropriately renamed *Donegal.*

20 MONS 1709, BELGIUM (WAR OF THE SPANISH SUCCESSION)

Commanders: Marlborough & Prince of Orange v. Marshal Claude-Hector Villars & Marquis de Grimaldi.

The British and Allied army had taken Tournai (see 3 September) and decided to besiege Mons in order to maintain ceaseless pressure on the French. Mons itself was not vital, but it was strategically located, and Louis XIV saw it rather differently, telling Villars "should Mons follow on the fate of Tournai, our case is undone; you are by every means in your power to relieve the garrison; the cost is not to be considered; the fate of France is at stake." Although the investment of Mons began on 6 September siege works were postponed because a battle between the French and the British and Allied army was imminent. Villars was on the defensive but sought to protect Mons by inflicting serious damage on his opponents in a battle (see 11 September Malplaquet); although he did not succeed in this endeavour, the Allies needed a few days to recuperate from a very hot fight, and it was not until 20 September that the siege was resumed. Wet weather hampered the Allies; on the other hand, the garrison was short of supplies from the beginning, and on 20 October, Grimaldi capitulated. The French were granted the honours of war and allowed to evacuate Mons, but were obliged to leave their artillery behind. French casualties were 980, British and Allies over 2,000.

The British army fought again at Mons in August 1914, but on the side of the French against the Germans; after spirited resistance, in which their rifle fire was so rapid the Germans thought it was from massed machine guns, they were forced to retreat.

20 H.M.S. CRESCENT(36 GUNS) V. RÉUNION(36GUNS) 1793, (FRENCH REVOLUTIONARY WARS)

Commanders: Captain J. Saumarez v. Captain F. Dénian.

On the night before this engagement, *Crescent* was cruising off Cape Barfleur, a few miles east of Cherbourg, when contact was made at dawn with *Réunion* returning from a regular nightly patrol along the English coast in search of prizes. *Réunion* was in consort with a large cutter, *Esperance* (14 guns). A hard fought action lasting more than 2 hours ended with *Réunion* striking her colours and being escorted into Portsmouth; *Esperance* succeeded in escaping into Cherbourg. Out of a crew of more than 300, French casualties were at least 33 killed and 48 severely wounded; by contrast, in the British crew of 257 only 1 man was wounded – a seaman whose leg was broken by the recoil of his gun. The disparity in casualties probably reflects the difference in tactics between the French and the British at this period. The French generally aimed their guns higher in order to damage masts and rigging, whereas the British aimed lower at the hull.

Saumarez was knighted for his performance in this battle. He came from a well-known Guernsey family and saw more varied active service in the course of his long life than most of his contemporaries. A commanding officer at Cape St. Vincent, 14 February 1797, and second in command at Nelson's spectacular victory at the Nile (see 1 August), he was in command as a Rear Admiral at Algeciras (see 13 July), and

Nelson made his maiden speech in the House of Lords seconding the motion of thanks for this victory moved by Lord St. Vincent. Later, in Nelson's renowned ship, *Victory*, Saumarez commanded in the Baltic during the final period of the Napoleonic War. He was made a peer in 1831. Eminently brave, a contemporary described him: "as having the boldness of a lion whenever a sense of duty brings it into action."

20 H.M.S. FISGARD (38 GUNS) V. L'IMMORTALITÉ(42 GUNS) 1798, FRANCE (FRENCH REVOLUTIONARY WARS)

Commanders: Captain T.B. Martin v. Captain J-F. Legrand.

Fought off Brest, *L'Immortalité* had almost escaped from the defeat of the attempted invasion of Ireland (see 12 October) when she was intercepted by *Fisgard.* The two ships were evenly matched, but after a long and well fought action, *L'Immortalité* was taken as a prize; Martin's skill and tactics were such that in Britain this was considered to be one of the most brilliant frigate actions of the period. Ironically, and to rub salt in the wound, *Fisgard* was originally a French ship, *Résistance,* that had been captured off Brest only the year before (see 8 March H.M.S. San Fiorenzo) and taken into the Royal Navy.

21 AUBEROCHE 1345, FRANCE (HUNDRED YEARS'WAR)

Commanders: Earl of Derby (Henry, Duke of Lancaster) v. Comte de l'Isle

Forces: English 1,200 v. French 7,000.

The English army landed at Bayonne in June 1345 to come to the assistance of the nobles of Gascony whose feudal loyalties were to the English kings, but who were being harassed by the French, and at the same time to constitute the third part of Edward III's strategic plan for the conquest of France. By the autumn, satisfactory progress had been made through the country to the east of Bordeaux (see 26 August, Bergerac) and Auberoche had been taken. The French army had retreated in order to re-group and re-equip, and their first objective was to recapture Auberoche; the castle with its English garrison was under siege when the news reached Derby. He gathered a small army of about 1,200 and sent for reinforcements. Although the reinforcements had not arrived, the English marched rapidly towards Auberoche and were able to get within two miles of the town without the French knowing they had done so. There they waited, concealed in a wood, in the hope that the reinforcements would arrive but eventually were obliged to attack without them. Derby devised a skilful plan of attack, making full use of the ground, in which the cavalry were directed to the rear of the enemy camp while the archers sent clouds of arrows into the tents. The surprise was complete, and there were heavy French casualties from the beginning; the *coup de grace* was given by the garrison of the castle. Observing how the fight was going, they opened a gate in the walls and made a mounted charge into the rear of the French who were attempting to fight back. This new front precipitated a rout. In addition to those killed and wounded, many prisoners were taken including Comte de l'Isle. The immediate effects were surprising, French sieges of three towns were abandoned, a campaign in preparation was delayed for six months, and communications with forces in the south virtually ceased. The victory against such odds helped to create in the English army a sense of superiority and in their opponents, a feeling of intimidation. In the best traditions of chivalry (still practised in this period), after the fighting had ended, the Earl of Derby entertained to dinner the senior captives. During these festivities, the Earl of Pembroke arrived with the reinforcements that had been so urgently requested.

21 CAPE FRANÇOIS 1759, HAITI (SEVEN YEARS' WAR)

Commanders: Captain M. Suckling v. ?

A British squadron of three ships of the line was confronted by a greatly superior French squadron but was victorious after an action that lasted for more than two hours. The victory was widely acclaimed at home. Captain Suckling was a career officer who had married the niece of the famous Sir Robert Walpole; however, the family connection that has brought him the greatest reflected glory is that his sister was the mother of Nelson. Suckling was a capable officer who held a number of seagoing commands before being appointed Comptroller of the Navy in which position he was able to put his nephew into posts that were favourable to his career and in which he took the maximum advantage. Nelson's father, an Anglican parson with a modest living, wrote to his brother-in-law asking him to take his son to sea and launch him on a naval career to which Suckling replied: "What has poor Horace (*sic*) done, who is so weak, that he above all the rest should be sent to rough it out at sea? But let him come; and the first time we go into action a cannon ball may knock off his head and provide for him at once." And so, at the age of twelve, Nelson joined his uncle's ship as a midshipman.

The date of this victory coincided with that of the annual fair following the harvest at Burnham Thorpe (Nelson's home), as well as being three weeks after Nelson's first birthday, and it became an annual celebration in the Nelson family until superseded by the supreme anniversary of Trafalgar. However, the story of his own victory that Suckling liked to tell was of a pet monkey belonging to one of his officers which escaped when the ship was cleared for action and climbed the mizzen mast where it stayed until the fighting was finished and the smoke had cleared, whereupon it climbed down and rejoined its master.

21 TRAFALGAR 1805, SPAIN (NAPOLEONIC WAR)

Commanders: Vice Admiral Lord Nelson v. Admiral Pierre, Comte de Villeneuve

Forces: British 27 ships of the line; French & Spanish 33 ships of the line (18 French, 15 Spanish).

In the long history of conflict between Britain and France, this is an epic battle. Some contemporary British historians (but not French) have sought to diminish its importance, but these iconoclastic exercises have been convincingly rebutted and are not worth pursuing. The prelude to the battle was Napoleon's plan to invade Britain, an essential part of which was to secure command of the Channel for at least long enough to cover the voyage of the invasion fleet. In the planning and organization of the enterprise, Napoleon was far from his best and displayed a profound ignorance of maritime matters compounded by not being able or willing to delegate responsibility to anyone better qualified to be in charge. Serious preparations for the invasion began about three years before Trafalgar and, especially in the final twelve months, a series of contradictory orders were given to the French fleets at Brest and Toulon; the Spanish at Cadiz were involved because following their defeat on land in 1795, Spain had become effectively a French puppet, and in 1804 entered the war actively on the side of France, but in a subordinate role. The strategic design was that the French and Spanish fleets would evade the British blockades, and by sailing to the West Indies would decoy the British fleet into pursuit, then by returning to Europe, there would be sufficient time to permit the invasion to proceed unopposed. Implementation illustrated the difficulties created by weather and very slow and uncertain means of communication; the Brest fleet was not able to avoid the blockade and never sailed at all; the Toulon fleet succeeded in passing the blockade unseen, but the rendezvous with the Spanish at Cadiz did not take place because the cables of some of the ships were found to be entangled causing a delay of several hours and, except for one ship, the Spanish contingent was ten days late in joining the French at Martinique. Nelson was in command of the blockade at Toulon, and when he learned the French had sailed, he first went east to scout the Mediterranean, on discovering his mistake, he did not wait for further orders but set course for the West Indies and arrived there nineteen days after the French. Villeneuve, in command of the Combined Fleet, heard of Nelson's arrival three days later, and, ignoring Napoleon's latest order to wait for twenty-five more days for the Brest fleet to arrive, he decided to return to Europe. Nelson followed four days later. The Combined Fleet had almost reached the west coast of Spain when they were intercepted by a British squadron commanded by Vice Admiral Sir Richard Calder (see 22 July, Cape Finisterre III).

The blockade of Cadiz was reinforced by the return of Nelson's ships to Gibraltar, and the stage was set. By way of prologue, there was more chaos in the relationship of Villeneuve and Napoleon. On 3 August, the latter arrived in Boulogne the main port from which the invasion was to be launched as soon as Villeneuve appeared, and to which Villeneuve had been ordered to sail. Instead, Villeneuve deliberately ignored this order and followed an earlier one that instructed him to proceed to Cadiz. On August 26, alarmed by the news that Russia and Austria had decided to resume the war against France and disenchanted with his navy, Napoleon gave orders for the army of invasion to break camp and march to Germany to meet different enemies; there, decisive victories were won at Ulm (v. Austrians, 17 October 1805) and Austerlitz (v.Austrians & Russians, 2 December 1805). Incidentally, this sequence of events disproves a common opinion that it was the victory at Trafalgar which rendered the invasion impossible. Before leaving Boulogne, Napoleon in frustrated rage had described Villeneuve as committing treason and "a wretch who must be sent packing in disgrace… [who] would sacrifice everything to save his own skin". It is true that the nearer Villeneuve found himself to the British fleet, the more despondent he became, and this mood reflected the psychological advantage that the British enjoyed before the fighting began. The British had a long string of naval victories in the years immediately preceding Trafalgar, the crews had been at sea continuously, sometimes for years (e.g., in Nelson's final tour of duty in *Victory* he was continuously at sea for 2 years less ten days), were highly trained and could fire at twice the rate of their enemies; above all crews and officers shared confidence, respect, and liking for Nelson. They expected to win. By contrast the French and Spanish had spent most of the previous years in port, were poorly trained, morale was low, and to aggravate matters no love was lost between the French and the Spanish; the French tended to despise the Spanish who in turn distrusted the French. Villeneuve had told the Minister of Marine that: "Our naval tactics are antiquated. We know nothing but how to place ourselves in line and that is just what the enemy wants."

Villeneuve finally led his fleet from Cadiz on 19 October, a departure attributed in part to the arrival in Madrid of the admiral appointed to replace him. Winds were light, and it took two days for the British fleet to intercept. In spite of his inferior numbers, Nelson intended to have what he called a 'pell mell battle', fought at close quarters in order to inflict maximum damage on the French navy. His tactics were unconventional and dangerous but eminently successful. The attack was made in two columns at right angles to the enemy line, 'crossing the T' (see 12 April, The Saintes), and to emphasise his plan, Nelson had told his captains before the battle that "no captain can do very wrong if he places his ship alongside that of an enemy", an instruction in line with an opinion expressed early in his career that "Lay a Frenchman close and you will always beat him.". The first shots were fired at about 12 noon, and violent, bloody fighting ensued until about 5.00p.m.; by that time, 17 ships of the Combined Fleet had surrendered and 1 had exploded, while no British ships had been lost. Although the Combined Fleet was being overwhelmed from the beginning, eight ships forming the van of the line of battle under the command of Rear Adml. Dumanoir acted in a curious way. Dumanoir ignored an order to turn and join in the action, and he continued to sail away from it; it was not until some two hours after fighting began that he gave orders to his squadron to turn and take part. The manœuvre was badly performed, and it took another hour before they were in position to participate. By this time it was too late, the battle was lost. For his performance, Dumanoir was subsequently brought before boards of enquiry, court martialled at his own request and finally acquitted, in the meantime, the British caught up with him (see 4 November, Ferrol).

In terms of sea battles, Trafalgar was a massacre with more men killed or wounded than in any sea battle during the previous 250 years– British killed or wounded were 1,690, French 4,500 killed or wounded, Spanish 2,400 killed or wounded; in addition, prisoners from the Combined Fleet numbered about 7,000 including Villeneuve, and 20 captains or junior admirals. Nelson was by far the most prominent of the British dead, and the Spanish admiral, de Gravina, also died. Villeneuve's flagship, *Bucentaure,* was the first ship to surrender, and Villeneuve became a prisoner of Captain Israel Pellew of *Conqueror.* A surprising prisoner rescued from the sea was a French woman, Jeannette, who had leapt from a burning ship that later exploded. She was naked when hauled on board the rescue boat, but was clothed by the crew who treated her with kindness, and then by happy circumstance, she was reunited with her husband who was among the prisoners. Immediately after the battle, there occurred a violent storm of hurricane strength that lasted for several days and destroyed a number of the surviving and damaged ships, most of the prizes were lost as well as another 14 ships of the Combined Fleet. Due to the severity of the storm, days after the battle, there were many survivors washed ashore at Cadiz where a local doctor introduced an improbable method of reviving those who were still alive – he pumped tobacco smoke into their lungs with bellows to induce vomiting and to cough up sea water!

Trafalgar secured for Britain unchallenged command of the sea, essential for the development and control of a colonial empire, and it has been fairly described as the most decisive marine battle, both strategically and tactically, in history. The consequences of France's naval defeats were succinctly expressed by Napoleon on his way to St. Helena: "If it had not been for you English I should have been Emperor of the East. But wherever there is water to float a ship, we are sure to find you in our way", or as the U.S.Admiral, A.T. Mahan, put it: "Those far distant, storm-beaten ships, upon which the Grand Army never looked, stood between it and the dominion of the world." Trafalgar was disastrous for Spain, the battle sacrificed the fleet which was the principal support of Spain's imperial power and colonies, and the way was made wide open to colonial independence.

Before his death Nelson was a national hero, and after it his memory was idolised as the 'Immortal Memory'; the column in Trafalgar Square, at 184 feet 11inches, must be one of the largest icons ever made. Honours and rewards were showered on his family (but nothing for Lady Hamilton and Nelson's daughter, Horatia). Nelson's elder brother, William, was made an earl with a pension of £5,000 p.a. plus £90,000 with which to buy an estate (Nelson himself had had the lesser rank of viscount); Nelson's sisters received £15,000 each, and his estranged widow a pension of £2,000 p.a. The men who fought at Trafalgar were not as generously treated – a seaman's share of the prize money was £10.13 equal to about six month's pay. Nelson's body was returned to England embalmed in a cask of spirits of wine (it had first been taken to Gibraltar in a cask of brandy) and it was also interred in spirits. After the body had lain in state for three days in the Painted Hall at Greenwich, where it was estimated that 60,000 viewed the coffin, there was a lavish State funeral in St. Paul's Cathedral. Thousands lined the route, and the procession of royalty, nobility, admirals, generals, soldiers and sailors stretched from Whitehall to the Cathedral – over 1.25 miles. The body was put in the coffin presented to Nelson by Captain Hallowell after the Battle of the Nile (see 1 August), and the coffin was placed in a stone sarcophagus that had been made for Cardinal Wolsey.

Villeneuve was born an aristocrat twenty-six years before the outbreak of the French Revolution. He supported the revolution and renounced his aristocratic origins which greatly assisted his naval career, officers in the royalist navy were almost entirely aristocrats, and the revolution brought their careers to an end in one way or another. At the age of thirty-three Villeneuve was a rear admiral, he commanded the rear division at the battle of the Nile (see 1 August) and led the only four ships to escape that annihilation. Promoted later, he was put in command of the Toulon fleet in November 1804, but was not comfortable in this position, and a few months afterwards he submitted his resignation. In spite of deteriorating relations with Napoleon and his Minister of Marine, the resignation was refused. Villeneuve was taken as a prisoner to England and while on parole he attended Nelson's funeral. He was returned to France where he died, soon after arrival, from stabbing in a hotel at Rennes in April 1806. Some have argued that he was assassinated on orders from Napoleon, and others that he committed suicide because he left a farewell letter for his wife, but the weakness of this view is that

Villeneuve had six stab wounds.

22 NIEUWPOORT 1793, BELGIUM (FRENCH REVOLUTIONARY WARS)

Commanders: ? v. General D. Vandamme

Vandamme was the French commander at Dunkirk, and he had advanced and taken Furnes; now he invested Nieuwpoort garrisoned by British infantry, some artillery, and two German companies. The garrison put up a determined resistance behind the floods they had created and the French made a disorderly retreat. British casualties were small - 46 killed or wounded. In recognition of their resolute defence, Nieuwpoort is a Battle Honour of the Shropshire Regiment.

French revolutionary governments were always quick to punish the failure of military commanders, and Vandamme was placed under arrest but was released a few days later. Vandamme joined the army when he was 16 and made it his career. He supported the revolution, and by the time Napoleon came to power he had attained the rank of general of division. Known for his frank, rough manners and a plundering, dissolute lifestyle, he performed very well on the battlefield and was a faithful supporter of Napoleon who made him a count. Vandamme joined Napoleon on his return from Elba and, now a peer of France, he brought his corps back to Paris after Waterloo in good order. At the Restoration he was at first imprisoned and then exiled, but was allowed to return to France in 1820. He retired to his native village not far from Nieuwpoort.

Nieuwpoort has often figured in European wars most notably in World War I when it was the key to the defence of the Ypres salient. On this occasion, too, flooding was a decisive defence. Six sluices were opened flooding the entire area and halting the German advance but also completely destroying the town.

25 AGINCOURT 1415, FRANCE (HUNDRED YEARS' WAR)
Commanders: Henry V v. Charles I d'Albret, Constable of France & Jean II le Meingre Boucicaut, Marshal of France
Forces: British 4,950 archers + 750 knights; French 3,000 cross-bowmen + 22,000 knights.

Although it proved not to have any lasting strategic importance, Agincourt has always been an epic victory in popular memory and inspired some of Shakespeare's most spirited lines. Fought against odds of more than 4 to 1 (Shakespeare puts them at 5 to 1), it was an annihilating victory in which the French casualties and prisoners alone were nearly twice the number of those who faced them at the beginning. The capture of Harfleur (see 22 September) had taken longer than had been expected, with the result that Henry was obliged to curtail his campaign. Casualties and disease had so reduced the size of his army that Henry decided to march to Calais, an English fortress, to spend the winter, and there recoup and refit for the 1416 season. At this period, France was politically weak with a king, Charles VI, subject to bouts of insanity, and two factions, Burgundians and Armagnacs (a.k.a Orléanists), disputing succession. Henry had negotiated the neutrality of the Duke of Burgundy, but the Armagnacs assembled a strong army which they deployed to cut off Henry's line of march to Calais. This deployment compelled Henry's army to make a series of forced marches, and by the time they reached Agincourt, where the French were prepared for battle, they were tired. The battle was fought on St. Crispin's day, and the night before the battle the French spent hours gambling on the number of prisoners they would take and on the division of their spoils, they were recklessly over-confident; Henry had exhorted his troops, and notwithstanding the heavy odds against them, their morale was high.

For practical purposes, the result was decided in the first thirty minutes. The opening French assault was a number of disorganized cavalry attacks that were repulsed by clouds of arrows, and in their retreat the horsemen trampled on the second wave of troops now advancing. Tightly packed in appalling confusion, many of the French were unable to raise an arm to strike a blow, and Henry attacked ruthlessly with his knights. Simultaneously, the archers laid aside their bows and armed with bill hooks, axes, and swords, they fell on the French who were lying in the quagmire of mud unable to get up because of the weight of their armour. At this stage, with a third of the French army not yet committed Ysambart D'Agincourt led a sally from the castle of Agincourt in an attack on the English camp and baggage. Threatened from the front and rear and with a large number of prisoners still mobile in his field, Henry ordered the prisoners to be killed. This was partially carried out, although the order was cancelled when it became clear that the remnants of the French army were in full flight. Henry's tactics and leadership were brilliant, but the incoherent French tactics contributed greatly to their defeat.

Six weeks before the battle, Charles VI had ceremoniously raised the Oriflamme at the abbey church of Saint-Denis. Originally, the Oriflamme was the banner of Saint-Denis, the patron saint of France, and after his death, it became the sacred banner of the kings of France. It was meant to be carried at times of great national danger, and Charles was certainly correct in regarding Henry V as a great national danger, but the Oriflamme did not prove to be of much material assistance at Agincourt.

After his victory at Poitiers, the Black Prince arranged a banquet and ostentatiously waited on his prisoners (see 19 September), but this was not Henry's style, he made his prisoners wait on him and his nobles.

On this day, France lost half of its nobility. The dead included the Constable, 3 dukes, 5 counts, and 90 barons, altogether about 10,000; the English losses were about 400 most notably the Duke of York who either suffocated in his armour while pinned under a pile of bodies or drowned in the mud (shades of the western front in World War I). Prisoners were an important factor in the economics of war in this period because of the ransom to be collected as a condition of their release, Henry certainly calculated on ransom money to finance his campaign, and others hoped for substantial capital in compensation for the risks incurred, conversely, a family could be ruined by raising the money to pay a ransom (see, for example, 19 September, Poitiers). It was, of course, only the wealthy (nobility) who had the means to pay, and for this reason if there was a choice they would be taken prisoner rather than be killed. Jean, Duc de Bourbon, was a most unfortunate prisoner, he was taken to England, and although his ransom was paid he was never released. Charles, Duc d'Orleans and a nephew of Charles VI, fared rather better in that although he remained in England as a prisoner for 25 years, he was finally released and, a widower on his return to

France, he married for a second time. A son, born when Charles was 68 years old, was crowned Louis XII of France and became known as the 'Father of the People'. Another distinguished prisoner, who died in Yorkshire six years after the battle, was the second in command, Jean II le Meingre Boucicaut. Jean had had an excellent military career prior to Agincourt, principally against the Turks including a notable naval victory at Gallipoli, but he had also been taken prisoner by the Turks and ransomed by them (perhaps this left the family with insufficient funds for another ransom). A champion of the ideals of chivalry, Boucicaut founded the *Dame Blanche à l'Écu Vert* ('White Lady of the Green Shield') an order to defend the female relatives of absent knights.

Henry was gifted in a number of ways. He had strategic and diplomatic skills as well as the qualities of a great commander in the field – tactical appreciation and above all the ability to kindle confidence and loyalty in the common soldiers. There is not much poetic licence in Shakespeare's representation of Henry as the ideal monarch – brave, eloquent, honourable, and efficient to the point of ruthlessness when necessary. Henry was also religious, and he dedicated this victory to St. John of Beverley, Bishop of York, because it was the anniversary of the date in 1037 when St. John's remains were translated from Beverley to York. Agincourt brought some immediate benefits. Diplomatically it brought Henry to the front rank in Europe confirmed in 1416 by the visit to England of Sigismund, later the Holy Roman Emperor, and the conclusion of a Treaty of Alliance at Canterbury which amongst other things was to bring to an end the naval alliance between France and Genoa (see 15 August, Seine Mouth). The extent of the victory made possible the conquest of all of Normandy in successive campaigns culminating in the capture of Rouen (see 20 January) and the Treaty of Troyes (see 21 May). The Treaty confirmed Henry's conquests, acknowledged him as heir to the French throne, and in view of the incapacity of Charles VI, Henry was made the Regent of France, then to bring the settlement within the family Charles' youngest daughter, Catherine of Valois, was betrothed to Henry. It does seem to have been a love match, and at the end of his play, Shakespeare, for better dramatic effect, put Henry's wooing in prose rather than blank verse; they were married on June 2, 1420. The Dauphin did not accept the Treaty, and Henry was obliged to continue the war. Two years later he contracted dysentery at the siege of Melun and Meaux (see May 22, Meaux) and died at Bois de

Vincennes before his thirty-fifth birthday. Henry's successor was his infant son, Henry VI, who was crowned King of France (as Henri II) in Paris in 1431, but incompetent and sometimes insane (like his maternal grandfather, Charles VI) he eventually lost both the kingdom of England and of France. However, the lasting benefit from Agincourt was that it engendered in English people of all classes a sense of national pride and national identity.

Charles I d'Albret was a member of a Gascon family celebrated in French history whose father earlier in the Hundred Years' War had fought on the English side. One reason for the undisciplined behaviour of the French at Agincourt was the refusal of a number of the nobles to accept orders from d'Albret because he was a lesser noble, but he died bravely early in the battle. By way of posthumous revenge, 175 years later one of d'Albret's descendants was crowned Henri IV, the first Bourbon king of France.

Shakespeare's treatment of Agincourt (Henry V, Act 4, Sc.3) is well known, but the battle has other marks in the literature of France as well as of England. The Duc d'Orleans was one of the greatest courtly poets of France, and during his long captivity in England he wrote extensively including poems in English. The earliest known poem of Alain Chartier, a distinguished French poet, is *'Livre des Quatre Dames'* a discussion among four ladies who have lost their lovers at Agincourt. In England the Agincourt carol, *'Deo gracias Anglia'*, was written at about this time and is an early example of political verse with a characteristic note of insular patriotism, as such the first verse is worth quoting:

"Owre kynge went forth to Normandy
With grace and myght of chivalry
Ther God for hymn wrought mervelusly
Wherefore all Englonde may calle and cry
Deo gracias"

This song featured in the 1944 film of 'Henry V' as well as the 1989 version.

Later, Michael Drayton, a contemporary of Shakespeare, displayed his gift of pure narrative in 'The Ballad of Agincourt', which begins with the dramatic line: "Fair stands the wind for France".

There are various monuments and memorials of the battle including one on the actual site. One of the more curious is that Agincourt is the name of a district in Toronto. It was originally an Ontario rural community named Agincourt in order to mollify local French Canadians; the reasons for this extraordinary choice are not known, but perhaps it was meant to intimidate, or historical ignorance might have been a factor. Also, there is an Agincourt cocktail, but it is not worthy of its name.

26 TRIER (TRÈVES) 1704, GERMANY (WAR OF THE SPANISH SUCCESSION)

Commanders: Marlborough v. ???

In the exhilaration of the triumph at Blenheim (see 13 August), the campaign season of 1704 was extended. Looking forward to the next season in which France would be very definitely on the defensive, favourable positions on the Upper Rhine and the Moselle were sought. Trier in the Moselle valley became an objective and was taken in a surprise attack. The city was important in Roman times and had become a commercial and cultural centre that blocked the way through the valley.

Trier is notorious for the extent and ferocity of its persecution of witches in the latter half of the sixteenth century, and for some as the birth place of Karl Marx in 1818.

28 ARROYO DOS MOLINOS 1811, SPAIN (PENINSULA WAR)

Commanders: Lt. Genl. Sir Rowland Hill v. Genl. Jean Paul Girard
Forces: British 10,000; French 4,000.

This was a dashing engagement in which a series of secret forced marches through rough terrain brought the British deep into Spain and in front of the enemy in a howling storm just as dawn was breaking. Having blocked the escape routes and repelled several French attempts to break out, Hill led his entire force in a charge that broke French resistance, and in the panic some of the French fled for 22 miles. French casualties were 300 killed and 1,300 prisoners compared with 7 British killed and 658 wounded.

Hill was a career soldier with the reputation of a paragon of virtue. Affectionately known to his troops as 'Daddy' Hill, he reinforced charm with kindness and thoughtfulness as well as acts of generosity and consideration to common soldiers. Although not endowed with the skills required for overall command, in the field he rendered excellent support to his c-in-c, Wellington, who had ample cause to criticise some of the generals assigned to him under the rigid system of seniority, and who found Hill's reliability and competence in carrying out his orders to be invaluable. About six months later, Hill again commanded successfully in an important strategic action (see 19 May, Almaraz); other Peninsular War actions in which Hill distinguished himself were Oporto (see 12 May), Puente Larga (see 30 October) and St. Pierre (see 13 December). As a lieutenant colonel, Hill had fought and been wounded at Alexandria (see 21 March), and the height of his active service was at Waterloo (see 18 June) where Wellington recognized his worth by putting him in command of the 2nd. Corps on the right of the line. In the final phase of the battle, Hill led the counter-attack against the Imperial Guard, his horse was shot from under him and for a while he was lost from sight in the mêlée. After Wellington resigned as Commander-in-Chief of the British Army, Hill succeeded him. This Sir Rowland Hill is not to be confused with his contemporary of identical name who was the inventor of penny postage.

29 LIÈGE & FORT CHARTREUSE 1702, BELGIUM (WAR OF THE SPANISH SUCCESSION)

Commanders: Marlborough v. M. de Violane & M. de Millon.
Forces: British & Allies 25,000; French 7,200.

Marlborough's rapid advance led by cavalry took the French by surprise, and there was barely time for the garrison to close the doors of the citadel before the leading troops were in the city. After two days of bombardment by heavy guns, a sufficient breach had been made in the wall of the citadel to permit a crack force of grenadiers to make the assault. They carried the day, and building on their success, Lord Cutts, an outstanding cavalry commander, led troops on foot through the outer fortifications killing most of those who stood in their way, then, climbing the ramparts under fire, they so terrified the defenders that they laid down their arms in surrender. M. de Violane and 1,700 of the garrison were made prisoner. Marshal Boufflers had set out on a march to relieve Liège, but found himself out-manœuvred by Marlborugh and forced to withdraw. Lord Cutts had fought well at Namur (see 1 September) and went on to be third in command at Blenheim (see August 13), where his cavalry charges made an important contribution to the victory. Liège capitulated on 25 October, and the guns could now be brought to bear on Fort Chartreuse. Two days of violent cannonade were sufficient to force the garrison to ask for terms, and they were allowed to march off to Antwerp. Altogether the siege lasted thirteen days, one day longer than in August 1914 when the German army invaded Belgium.

Marlborough's victory crowned with success the campaign of 1702 and set the stage for the following year, it also gave a great boost to the morale of the civilian population in Britain and in the Netherlands. Queen Anne, expressing the popular mood, made Marlborough a duke, and when he arrived in the Hague on his way home a huge crowd gathered to welcome him and civic celebrations continued throughout the night. On the other side, although intangible, perhaps the most important achievement of the campaign was the moral ascendancy that Marlborough gained over the French commanders and their troops. As Napoleon himself expressed it: "in war moral factors account for three-quarters of the whole, relative material strength accounts for only a quarter".

29 SANTOLIET 1705, BELGIUM (WAR OF THE SPANISH SUCCESSION)

Commanders: Graaf Noyelles v. ???

At the end of the 1705 campaign in which disagreements with the Dutch on both strategy and tactics had impaired results, Marlborough felt it desirable to accede to urgent requests from the States-General in The Hague to capture and destroy the fortress of Santoliet. This was done without any trouble in a matter of six days which probably indicates its degree of importance.

30 PUENTE LARGA 1812, SPAIN (PENINSULAR WAR)

Commanders: Lt. Genl Sir. Rowland Hill v. Marshals Soult & Jourdan & King Joseph Bonaparte

Forces: British & Portuguese 4,000 with 6 guns; French 5,000 with 6 guns.

Following the spectacular victory at Salamanca (see 22 July), Wellington marched his army to make a triumphal entry into Madrid.

King Joseph had retreated to Valencia with a huge cavalcade of two thousand vehicles (this proved to be a labour in vain because he lost all of his baggage less than a year later after the defeat at Vitoria, see 21 June), and the troops were greeted with scenes of adulation and wild excitement. The enthusiasm of the inhabitants could not make up for the deficiencies that Wellington faced; his army was still outnumbered by nearly two to one, and he was short of supplies including ammunition. The principal objective was to drive the French back into France, and so, after finding it impossible to take the key centre of Burgos, the army was withdrawn into Portugal, the better to campaign in 1813.

The action at Puente Larga was fought by the British rearguard against the advance guard of the French. The fighting took place in heavy rain, at first as an artillery duel until the Portuguese gunners ran out of ammunition, then the French made two attacks and were repulsed both times. During the night the British made an orderly withdrawal having accomplished a successful rearguard action. For more information about Hill, see 28 October, Arroyo dos Molinos.

31 PAMPLONA 1813, SPAIN (PENINSULA WAR)

Commanders: Wellington & General Enrique O'Donnell v. General Cassan.

Pamplona and San Sebastian were the last two places in Spain remaining in French hands. Wellington decided to lay siege to San Sebastian (see 8 September), but simply to blockade Pamplona until starvation compelled the garrison to surrender. The troops and commanders mounting the blockade changed several times, but supplies were always short in Pamplona and the plan worked from the beginning. As the condition of the garrison deteriorated, Cassan asked for honourable terms in return for not blowing up the fortifications to which request Wellington ordered a peremptory answer – if the fortifications were demolished, all of the officers and NCOs and ten per cent of the troops would be shot (literally decimated). As the attack was being prepared, Cassan agreed to surrender personally and to be imprisoned in England provided that the rest of his command could march out with the honours of war. These terms were accepted, and the famished garrison emerged like skeletons.

Pamplona had been occupied by the French since February 1808 when Napoleon had sent a large army into Spain on the pretext that they were on the way to reinforce the French occupation of Portugal. Less than three months later, the Spanish king was forced to abdicate, and Napoleon's brother, Joseph, was crowned king, but his ignominious expulsion from Spain had now been completed.

Up to this time, O'Donnell, Count of Abisal, was the most celebrated descendant of the O'Donnell clan who were part of the Irish Jacobite diaspora following the Battle of the Boyne (see 1 July). Pamplona's international recognition has reverted to a more ancient, but still violent, event, namely, the annual running of the bulls through the streets at the Festival of San Fermin, the reputation of which owes much to Hemingway's "The Sun Also Rises".

NOVEMBER

3 TREATY OF ÉTAPLES 1492, FRANCE (WAR OF THE SPANISH ALLIANCE)

Henry VII was not given to extravagance, and since wars were very expensive they were to be avoided, but policy compelled him to mount a modest invasion of France which began with a siege of Boulogne. The *casus belli* was the effort of Charles VIII of France to effect a union of the Duchy of Brittany with France, and Henry's desire for an alliance with Spain. England entered into an alliance with Spain, the Holy Roman Empire, and Burgundy against France; the army, marched out of Calais on 18 October and laid siege to Boulogne. When the Duchess of Brittany married Charles VIII, it became clear that the union could not be prevented, and Henry was pleased to accept the French offer of terms for the cessation of hostilities. Negotiations concluded with the Treaty of Étaples which declared the two kingdoms to be at peace and, routinely, not to support the other's enemies; Charles agreed to pay substantial cash indemnities – reimbursement for Henry's expenses in Brittany, and the arrears of the payment promised at the Treaty of Picquigny (see 29 August) – a total of 745,000 gold crowns payable at an annual rate of 50,000 gold crowns. In return, Henry agreed to disclaim all historic rights to French territory except for Calais. The disclaimer did not, however, preclude Henry's son and every English monarch up to and including George III from being crowned king of France in addition to England, Wales, Scotland, and Ireland. To illustrate further the ephemerality of such professions, the protocol of the Treaty of Paris 1763 (see 10 February) listed George III, inter alia, as King of France and Louis XV the same, but the latter might reasonably have thought that possession was nine-tenths of the law.

4 FERROL 1805, SPAIN (NAPOLEONIC WAR)

Commanders: Cdre. Sir Richard Strachan v. Rear Adml. Dumanoir -le-Pelley.

This action was a post-script to Trafalgar (see 21 October). Dumanoir was in command of the Franco-Spanish van at Trafalgar, but his ships took little part in the fighting and eventually made their escape. Dumanoir has been strongly criticised for his failure to engage the enemy at Trafalgar, and there were several boards of enquiry and a court martial from which he emerged more or less unscathed. On this occasion, he was leading the four ships that escaped from Trafalgar to a French port when he was sighted by a British squadron that was at sea trying to intercept ships from the Rochefort division engaged in raiding British convoys and shipping. The British chased Dumanoir half way across the Bay of Biscay and captured all of them. British casualties were 24 dead and 111 wounded, French casualties were 750 including Dumanoir who was wounded. After Ferrol, the final tally of the losses of the Franco-Spanish fleet at Trafalgar was 23 ships out of a total of 33. The prizes and their crews were taken to England where two of the ships were taken into the Royal Navy. *Formidable* (Dumanoir's flagship at Trafalgar) became *H.M.S.Brave* but was soon found to be unsuitable for service and was used as a prison hulk. *Duguay-Trouin* had a more distinguished career as *H.M.S. Implacable*. She saw active service in the Baltic and in amphibious operations on the coast of Spain; finally, she became a training ship for boys until at last, with her timbers rotted, in 1949 she was sunk in the English Channel. Prior to sinking, *Implacable* was, except for *Victory*, the last wooden ship of the line afloat.

Strachan was on active service for over 30 years; brave and zealous, he inspired the respect of the crews who served with him; they called him "Mad Dick, who when he swore he meant no harm, and when he prayed he meant no good".

4 FASHODA INCIDENT 1898, SUDAN.

In the centuries of British–French conflict, Fashoda is that very rare event - a victory achieved without a shot being fired. The confrontation arose from irreconcilable colonial ambitions – the British wanted to construct a railway from the Cape of Good Hope to Cairo, and the French to extend their dominion from the west coast of Africa eastwards across Central Africa to the Sudan. The British had occupied Egypt since 1882 with the intention of maintaining a government sufficiently friendly to foreign interests to preserve the security of the Suez Canal, and in Egypt life itself depended on the waters of the Nile. British diplomacy had secured the agreement of the German and Italian governments to keep out of the Nile valley, but not that of the French (perhaps they thought that Napoleon's failure (see 8 March Abukir) gave them a prior claim to suzerainty). Having failed to persuade Britain to withdraw from Egypt, the French developed a plan to build a dam on the Upper Nile which it was thought would obstruct the flow of the Nile waters. Eventually, Jean-Baptiste Marchand and 150 men set out from Brazzaville in 1896 to march to Fashoda (Kodok), which they reached in July 1898, and occupied the fort. Meanwhile, the British had decided that the French could not be allowed to proceed with their plan, but in order to stop it the Sudan had to be brought under control. The country was governed by Abd Allah, the successor to the Mahdi whose army had killed General Gordon at Khartoum, and Abd Allah now commanded this army. An Anglo-Egyptian army under the command of General Sir Herbert Kitchener marched to Fashoda up the Nile Valley, and on the way defeated the much larger army of Abd Allah at Omdurman, where Winston Churchill took part in a cavalry charge with the 21st. Lancers. Kitchener arrived at Fashoda about two months after the French, and with neither side willing to yield, the situation was tense. With their resounding defeat in the Franco-Prussian War still fresh in the memory, and neither the army nor the navy in a condition to wage war, the larger French design was to secure an alliance with Britain against Germany, and so, in spite of popular indignation, the foreign minister, Delcassé, gave orders to the French to march away. Marchand became a public hero and was promoted to commander of the Legion of Honour. The British position in Egypt was confirmed, and the resolution of the Fashoda incident cleared the way for the Entente Cordiale in 1904 which, in retrospect, some would argue was a major victory for the French over the British.

5 MADAGASCAR 1942, MADAGASCAR (WORLD WAR II)

Commanders: Rear Adml. E.N. Syfret & Maj. Genl. R.G.Sturges v.
Armand Annet, Governor-General.

After the French surrender in 1940, Madagascar was one of the French colonies that accepted the Vichy government. The British considered the island to be of strategic importance because it commanded the convoy routes through the Martinique Channel to the Middle East and India as well as having a large, natural harbour at Diego Suarez (a.k.a. Antseranana), and Japanese occupation had to be forestalled. 'Operation Ironclad', a combined operation for the capture of Madagascar, was approved in March and barely seven weeks later, in a remarkable demonstration of the flexibility and long reach of sea power over a distance of more than 9,000 miles from London where the plans were made, No. 5 Commando and two infantry brigades began the assault on Diego Suarez. The action included a *coup de main* that might have been scripted in Hollywood when a destroyer, *H.M.S. Anthony*, went at high speed in rough seas through the narrow entrance of the harbour, exchanging salvoes with the shore batteries, on the way to landing marines behind the French positions. Two days later the French surrendered the port but decided to continue to resist rather than to capitulate. Over 900 miles of coastline along the Mozambique Channel remained in French hands, and inevitably, hostilities were resumed. With more troops from East Africa, commanded by Lieutenant-General Sir William Platt, the principal towns were taken, mainly in amphibious operations; the French retreated to the south, and on 5 November the Governor-General surrendered the island. He was sent off to internment in Durban.

Ironically, the major damage to the British forces was inflicted by a Japanese midget submarine that penetrated Diego Suarez harbour three weeks after its capture and sank a tanker as well as causing serious damage to *H.M.S. Ramillies.* A notable performance in the night before the landings was the skill of Captain Oliver, commanding the cruiser *H.M.S Devonshire*, in bringing a convoy of 34 ships, including several large liners, through reefs that the French considered were too difficult to navigate at night (a similar under-estimate of the navigational skills of the British navy was made at the Plains of Abraham – see 13 Septenber).

Overall, Operation Ironclad was an exemplary combined operation underpinned by what Syfret described as 'most cordial' co-operation between the services. Several months later, after the firing had stopped, and the dead had been buried, administration of the island was handed over to the Free French.

8 AIRE 1710, FRANCE (WAR OF THE SPANISH SUCCESSION)

Commanders: Marlborough & Prince Anhalt-Dessau v. M. de Goësbriand.

Forces: British & Allies 28,000; French 7,000.

Marlborough's political position at home was weak, and he had been obliged to eschew any adventurous plans and to be circumspect; thus he sought only to improve his position for the following year. The sieges of St. Venant (see 2 October) and Aire, conducted simultaneously, were undertaken to this end and completed the campaign of 1710. The main army was positioned to provide cover against any French attack, and a detachment under the command of Prince Anhalt-Dessau was dispatched to besiege Aire. French resistance was much more spirited than at St. Venant, and their efforts were assisted by torrential rains creating a sea of mud and shortages of supply to their opponents. Relief of the hunger of the besiegers came from an incredible source. It is well documented that the local mice had laid up hoards of corn in storehouses under the earth which were discovered by the troops and used to sustain them. Although the siege made slow progress, the French made no serious attempt to relieve the garrison, a reflection of the moral ascendancy that Marlborough had won, and the garrison surrendered being allowed to evacuate to St. Omer. Britsh and Allied casualties were heavy – 7,200; French 1,400.

Prince Anhalt-Dessau was a distinguished commander closely associated with Prussia and had an impressive record of fighting the French. For most of the War of the Spanish Succession he commanded the Prussian contingent and was conspicuous at Tournai (see 3 September) and Malplaquet (see 11 September). Blessed with imagination, he invented the iron ramrod and introduced the modern bayonet, but on a larger scale he established the old Prussian military system that was the foundation of Frederick the Great's successes.

10 CADSAND 1337, BELGIUM (HUNDRED YEARS' WAR)

Commanders: Henry Plantagenet, Earl of Derby v. ?
Forces: English 500 men-at-arms & 2,000 archers; French 5,000

This engagement was the gambit in the Hundred Years'War and was intended as a diversionary tactic. It was something of a vicarious victory in that most of the French army were Flemish who had elected to join them, and the survivors must have regretted the decision. At this juncture in the War, the English enjoyed a marked superiority in tactics and weapons (the longbow), and the Earl of Derby was an experienced and successful commander. Befitting his reputation, when hostilities began Derby rushed forward so far ahead of his men that he was knocked down and then rescued from his dangerous predicament by the bravery of his second-in-command, Sir Walter Manny (see 21 September, St. Jean d'Angelys). The French were dispatched without particular difficulty, 3,000 were killed or taken prisoner including the celebrated Guy, illegitimate brother of Louis, Count of Flanders. A year later the Count of Flanders found it expedient to change sides and ally with the English; the magnitude of this defeat might well have encouraged him to do so. Henry, great, great grandson of Louis VIII of France, the cousin of Edward III and grandfather of Henry IV, fought constantly against the French both at sea (see 24 June, Sluys) and on land. In addition to the earldom of Derby, as he grew older he was granted or inherited the titles of earl of Lincoln, of Leicester, of Lancaster, and Duke of Lancaster. Always loyal to the king, he became the most powerful noble in England, and his great wealth was appropriately symbolized by his sumptuous palace of Savoy from which the eponymous hotel derives its name. In addition to his impressive military services, he played a prominent role in diplomacy, and he was, for example, the principal English participant at the Treaty of Brétigny (see 8 May) that followed the victory at Poitiers (see 19 September). He is buried in the Collegiate Church of Newark.

10 H.M.S. AMETHYST (42 GUNS) V. THETIS (44 GUNS) 1808, FRANCE (NAPOLEONIC WAR)

Commanders: Captain Michael Seymour v. Captain Pinsun.

This was a vigorous action fought at close quarters off the north-west coast of France in the vicinity of the Ile de Groix. In the evening, *Amethyst* sighted *Thetis* running before the wind and gave chase; action was joined and continued for nearly two and a half hours. At one point, *Thetis* rammed *Amethyst*, but the ships broke apart; each ship lost its mizzen mast, and *Thetis'* attempt to board *Amethyst* was thwarted by a broadside that cleared her fo'c's'le of men. Several times, *Thetis* was set on fire and was eventually boarded and seized. By this time, damage to the hull had caused *Amethyst* to make two feet of water, and *H.M.S. Shannon* arrived to take the prize in tow. British casualties were 19 killed and 51 wounded; the French complement included 106 soldiers taking passage to Martinique, and in total 135 were killed and 102 wounded including all of the officers except three; Capt. Pinsun did not survive the battle. *Thetis* (see 17 May) was taken into the Royal Navy as *H.M.S. Brune* and was used mainly as a troop ship. Captain Seymour was one of the foremost frigate captains of the period (see 6 April H.M.S. Amethyst). In February 1809, the city of Limerick awarded him the freedom of the city and presented it to him in a heart of oak box ornamented in gold with a suitable address; he was also presented with a gold medal. Much later, in 1849, survivors of the action were each awarded a silver medal for which an apt inscription would have been 'Better late than never'.

In 1949, *H.M.S. Amethyst*, also a frigate, continued to honour the name in an incident in China's Yangtze River (now the Chang Jiang). The ship had been ordered to proceed up river to Nanking to relieve the guard ship and to evacuate British and Commonwealth citizens caught up in the advance of Chinese Communist troops during the civil war. *Amethyst* came under heavy fire from shore batteries and, severely damaged, ran aground. After several unsuccessful attempts to re-float her she was brought off the mud, and then months of negotiations with the Communist authorities failed; finally, under cover of darkness, *Amethyst* slipped her cable and made a 104 –mile dash down stream for open waters. After running the gauntlet of guns on both banks and making black smoke to eclipse the searchlights of the forts at the mouth of the river, she burst at full speed through the boom and sent the signal: "Have rejoined the fleet off Woosung...God save the King."

10 ALBA DE TORMES 1812, SPAIN (PENINSULA WAR)
Commanders: Wellington v. Marshals Nicolas-Jean de Dieu Soult & Jean-Baptiste Jourdan and King Joseph Bonaparte.

This action was similar to that at Puente Larga (see 30 October). Wellington was on his way to winter quarters in Portugal followed by a larger French army. Alba de Tormes was held as a bridgehead across the Tormes River, and the rearguard comprised British and Portuguese units with 12 Portuguese guns. The French attack began with a lengthy bombardment from 18 guns followed by three assaults by light infantry companies, each of which was repulsed. The next day the bombardment began again, but after a few hours, when it was seen to be having no effect, it was discontinued. The rearguard remained in place for a few more days and then withdrew because the French had been able to cross the river further up stream after the water level had fallen.

10 NIVELLE 1813, FRANCE (PENINSULAR WAR)
Commanders: Wellington v. Marshal Nicolas-Jean de Dieu Soult, Duke of Dalmatia
Forces: British and Portuguese & Spanish 80,000; French 60,000.

Having forced his way across the Bidassoa River (see 7 October) and taken Pamplona (see 31 October) Wellington continued his inexorable march into France itself, and his army now stood closer to Paris than any other of the coalition against Napoleon. Soult had constructed a chain of fortified lines, strengthened with redoubts, on which to make a stand and fight a defensive battle. As at Bidassoa, Wellington again deceived Soult in his plan of attack by feinting on the left against the strongest part of the French positions and launching the main thrust in the centre where the principal point of defence was cleverly outflanked. The battle had begun at four in the morning and by noon the Allied army had attained all of its objectives. Soult began to draw his troops back towards Bayonne, and although fighting on the defensive, it was an expensive day, French casualties were 4,300 and 59 guns were lost; the Allied casualties were 2,700. The victory at Nivelle was inevitably overshadowed by Napoleon's resounding defeat at Leipzig a few weeks earlier, nevertheless the Prince Regent declared himself to be "quite worn out with the joy of…this thrice happy day", and he urged his mother, the Queen, to arrange an orchestral concert and for 'good luck's sake to play *Landes Vater'*. The Queen agreed, and though 'almost drunk with joy herself' promised to join in the chorus. It was following Nivelle that Wellington took firm steps to stop looting of the French civilian population, a policy prompted by the aim of discouraging guerrilla warfare, akin to that which arose in Spain against the French, rather than from chivalric motives. Implementation of this policy included returning a large number of Spanish troops to Spain because due to insufficient rations and recent memories of French ravages in Spain, they were notorious for looting. This decision was made in spite of the fact that it made Wellington's army smaller than the French.

12 BOIS-LE-DUC 1794, NETHERLANDS (FRENCH REVOLUTIONARY WARS)

Commanders: Frederick Augustus, Duke of York v. Genl.Jean Moreau.

A relatively small encounter in which the French army tried to invade Holland by crossing the Meuse River at a time when the dykes were not an impediment. The Duke of York, commanding an army largely comprising Dutch and Austrians, fought back so vigorously that the French were obliged to withdraw and abandon their attempt.

In this battle, Moreau was embarking on a remarkable military career that began when he was a student of law at Rennes. In 1788, he led a students' riot in protest against an attempt by the government of Louis XVI to restrict the authority of the high courts of justice, and when the revolution broke out in the following year, Moreau thankfully abandoned the study of law to join the army. In that time of opportunity, he went in 1792 from the National Guard at Rennes to the Army of the North, and by April of 1794 he had risen to be a general of division in which rank he fought at Bois-Le-Duc. The set-back he received here did not interrupt his upward climb. Following spectacular victories over the Austrians, he became heavily outnumbered and obliged to withdraw to France. He won European renown for a brilliant retreat through the Black Forest and across the Rhine when pursued by greatly superior forces. Back in Paris, at a time of considerable political turmoil, the faction led by the Abbé Sieyès, which overthrew the Directory, offered him the dictatorship, but he declined and supported Napoleon's bid for power. At first, the relationship was cordial, it was even mooted that Moreau should marry Napoleon's favourite sister, Pauline, an honour that Moreau refused, but after Moreau's outstanding victory over the Austrian's at Hohenlinden and that of Napoleon at Marengo, mutual envy and jealousy predominated. Moreau became the focus of those parties opposed to Napoleon's ambition to be emperor, and so Napoleon felt compelled to remove his rival. A dubious charge of treason was laid, and a conviction secured in a kangaroo court. Although Moreau's aged father had been executed on the flimsiest grounds by the revolutionary authorities at Brest, Moreau had such strong support in the army that the death sentence was not a practicable option, and two years of exile was imposed. Moreau decided to spend his exile in the United States, and he bought an estate at Morrisville within convenient distance of Philadelphia and New York. During the eight years he remained there, he established a reputation among liberals and the intelligentsia for his opinions and analyses of European policies, but his military reputation in Europe was such that the Czar made determined efforts to recruit him using as an intermediary Bernadotte, a former French marshal (see 13 June Cuddalore), but now Crown Prince of Sweden and a friend of Moreau. Initially, the overtures were rejected, but after Napoleon's invasion of Russia had ended in disastrous defeat, Moreau changed his mind and decided to fight against France. He arrived in the Baltic in July 1813, and planned with Bernadotte the campaign for the Russian and allied army, thus he was at the battle of Dresden in August. During the battle he was struck by a cannon ball and severely wounded in the legs. Carried to the tent of the Czar on the lances of Cossacks he endured the amputation of both of legs with great composure while smoking a cigar throughout the operation. He died a few days later in Bohemia and was buried in the Catholic Church of St. Petersburg. An indication of the great regard in which he was held by Czar Alexander is that the Czar wrote personally to Moreau's widow and presented her with half a million roubles as well as a pension of thirty thousand roubles.

14 LINES OF TORRES VEDRAS 1810, PORTUGAL (PENINSULAR WAR)

Commanders: Wellington v. Marshal André Masséna.

In the early period of his command in the Peninsular War, Wellington recognized that his resources were limited in both quantity and quality, and for this reason he decided that Lisbon must be made impregnable, and, in the last resort, it would have to provide a place from which the British army could be evacuated. In the autumn of 1809, Wellington and the commanding officer of his engineers made a careful study of the country around Lisbon and designed the system of fortifications known as the Lines of Torres Vedras. The 'lines' were not continuous entrenchments, but a total of 152 redoubts arranged in several lines with complementary fields of cross-fire and connected by roads to facilitate rapid deployment of the defenders. The defence was to be mobile not static. The works were completed by the time the 1810 campaign began and were unknown to the French. Following the defensive victory at Busaco (see 27 September), Wellington marched his troops into the lines to wait for the French, and they were ordered to carry out a scorched earth policy as they withdrew. A preliminary skirmish took place on October 14, and an inspection of the Lines persuaded Masséna that he did not have enough troops to mount a successful assault. The scorched earth policy now began to take effect. Faced with starvation in the field, the French abandoned any hope of breaching the Lines and withdrew to winter quarters at Santarem, but there they continued to starve, and in March 1811, the retreat from Portugal began. The Lines of Torres Vedras was the peak of the French attempt to conquer Spain and Portugal, and within three years they were back in France with nothing to show for the substantial economic and military losses they had sustained, succinctly summarised by Napoleon as the 'Spanish ulcer'.

At the site of one of the batteries in the Lines, there is a monumental pillar surmounted by a figure of Hercules inscribed *'Non Ultra'* ('Not Further'). The Lines of Torres Vedras fully justified this inscription in marked contrast to French fortified lines given the name of *'Non Plus Ultra'* which Marlborough took his army through without losing a man (see 13 September, Bouchain).

16 RUGBY FOOTBALL WORLD CUP FINAL 2003, SYDNEY, AUSTRALIA.

Captains: Martin Johnson v. Fabien Galthie.
Result: England 24 points France 7 points.

Some anthropologists have held that sport is a substitute for war, and this is the justification for including this event. The match was played in pouring rain that got heavier as time went on, and England adapted to the conditions much better than their opponents (irresistible to cite the comparison of similar weather at Agincourt and Waterloo) . A particular advantage was the form of the England fly-half and kicker, Wilkinson, who scored all of the English points (5 penalties + 3 drop goals); by contrast the French kicker missed 5 penalties. Consistently outplayed, the two blatant fouls by French players, punished by yellow cards and 10 minute suspensions, were an indication of peevish frustration, and one of the fouls was so flagrant that it might well have justified the culprit being sent-off. A decisive win that sparked a spontaneous, national celebration enjoyed by many who had little idea of the game itself or how it is played.

18 MELUN 1420, FRANCE (HUNDRED YEARS' WAR)

Commanders: Henry V v. Arneud Guilleaume, Sire of Brabant.
Forces: English 20,000; French 700.

The capture of Montereau (see 1 July) cleared the way to Melun, about 30 miles from Paris, and Henry V marched on it with his Anglo-French army. Melun was strongly fortified, and Henry, mindful of his limited number of troops and the difficulty of getting any more, decided his best tactic was to starve the garrison and inhabitants into surrender. By this time, Henry and his compatriots were well practised in siege warfare, and they made their preparations methodically. Considerable tangible and intangible help was afforded by an unsolicted and unexpected gift from the citizens of London; they had ordered, and paid for, a huge cannon and its transport to France. The army christened the gun 'The London', and it is reported to have done considerable damage to the fortifications as well as to the morale of the defenders. The people of London were proving to be generous to 'the boys in France' (see 20 January, Rouen). An unusual feature of this siege was that fighting took place in the tunnels that were constructed in order to make mines (compare 3 September, Tournai), and one report has it that Henry and the Sire fought hand to hand in the tunnels at least once. After holding out for appreciably longer than Sens and Montereau, Melun surrendered.

The Dauphin had been obliged to reinforce his army with mercenaries and alliances – principally Lombards, Castilians and especially Scots. Although the main body of the Scottish troops was not yet in France, there were enough in the garrison of Melun to lead Henry to persuade the Scottish king, James I, to stand in front of the walls and call on the Scots within to join him. This stratagem failed, but later the terms of surrender specifically required the English deserters and the Scots to be handed over to Henry. Showing the ruthless side of his character, Henry hanged 20 Scots out of hand as traitors to King James; the laws of chivalry prevented him from executing the Sire because of their personal combat, and he was obliged to content himself by putting him in an iron cage.

James was with Henry because in 1406 when Scotland was in a state of civil war, his father, Robert III, had sent him to France for his better protection, and while on passage he was captured by the English off Flamborough Head. James was then 12 years old, two weeks later his father died and he was king, but he was kept at the English court for the next eighteen years. During his captivity he came to admire the English system of royal government, and he married the daughter of the Earl of Somerset, a cousin of Henry. James' father-in-law was one of the better English field commanders in France, and James took part in some of the actions in which Scottish troops were on the other side including Dreux (see 20 July) where he took over command during Henry's temporary absence; this probably accounted for his unpopularity when he returned to Scotland in 1424, but in that frugal country, the cost of the ransom of £40,000 might have been a larger factor.

When Melun had been secured, Henry and Charles VI made a state entry into Paris. Henry, in his capacity as Regent and heir of Charles VI, made the Louvre his residence, and there were English garrisons in the Bastille and the Bois de Vincennes. After a month of government work, Henry and his new bride departed for England via Rouen and received a tumultuous welcome; his brother the Duke of Clarence was left in charge in France.

20-22 QUIBERON BAY 1759, FRANCE (SEVEN YEARS WAR)
Commanders: Admiral Sir Edward Hawke v. Admiral le Comte de Conflans
Forces: British 23 ships of the line; French 21 ships of the line & 4 frigates.

A major victory made possible by outstanding seamanship and bravery. In an effort to reduce the pressure exerted by British successes in North America and India, France planned an offensive in the form of an invasion of Scotland or Ireland. The first attempt had been resoundingly defeated by Admiral Boscawen in Lagos Bay (see 17 August), and another was now set in course. The French fleet was blockaded in Brest, but a gale blew Hawke's ships off station and required them to carry out repairs in Torbay. Their absence gave Conflans the opportunity to put to sea in order to link up with the troop transports waiting down the coast at Morbihan, and their departure was reported to Hawke by spies. Repairs were hastily completed, and Hawke under full press of sail went after the French; they were first sighted near Quiberon Bay, about 100 miles south east of Brest, in stormy weather and poor visibility. The Bay is about 5 miles long and 6 miles wide strewn with rocks and shoals with dangerous tidal races, but in spite of these hazards and gale force winds, Hawke signalled his ships to follow him in a general chase (see March 13, Genoa). It is on record that the master of Hawke's ship, *Royal George*, pointed out to the admiral the navigational dangers they were running to which Hawke replied: "You have done your duty in pointing out to me the danger: now lay me alongside the enemy's flagship." The fighting was so close to shore that thousands were able to watch a full scale fleet engagement in appalling weather. Action on the first day continued into the darkness, and during the night *Thésée* was flooded and sank while trying to open her lower deck gun ports, *Superbe* was sunk by two broadsides from Hawke's ship, and by the next day six French ships including the flagship, *Soleil Royal*, were wrecked or sunk; 2 British ships had gone aground on one of the shoals. On the 22nd, the weather had moderated sufficiently for Hawkes to send crews to burn *Soleil Royal* and *Héros* as well as to rescue the crews of the two British ships aground. Eleven French ships fled into the River Vilaine, some with their guns thrown over board, and eight into the River Charente where constant pounding on the shallow river bottom caused most of them to break their backs, the remainder were either sunk, burnt or wrecked. French casualties were 2,000 killed or captured compared with 270 British. First hand accounts of the action from the French side are given in the comments of two survivors: "The battle of the 20th. has annihilated the French navy and finished its plans.", and "…blunders, proofs of ignorance and then folly, plenty of zeal but no ability, plenty of gallantry but no sense, arrogance without prudence. That sums up what has just happened." This victory terminated plans for the invasion of Britain and extinguished whatever hopes remained to the Jacobites after Culloden of regaining the British crown.

In the European wars of the eighteenth century, religion was a prominent element, and the end of a French invasion also meant that the succession of the Hanoverians was secure, and the identification of Britain with Protestant causes; 'No Popery' became a rallying cry for generations.

After its leading part in this spectacular action , it is sad to report that *Royal George* foundered not in action against the enemy, but as the result of culpable carelessness – see 14 December, Ushant.

For biographical information on Hawke, see 14 October, Cape Finisterre II. De Conflans was past his prime in this engagement which was unfortunate because his opponent was on the top of his form. In the previous war, of the Austrian Succession, Conflans had noteworthy successes on the West Indies station and had risen to be a marshal of France, but his star was now waning. Fighting on land in India, (French naval officers typically held military rank simultaneously), he was beaten at Condore (see 7 December), Rajahmundry (see 9 December), and Masulipatam (see 8 April), and at the age of 69 (Hawke was 54) he had been put in command of the force that was to sail round the west coast of Ireland, land in the Clyde estuary, then continue round the north of Scotland and south to Ostend there to embark a second army that was to be landed on the Essex coast. This audacious plan called for the energies of a much younger man, and qualities of leadership which Conflans, always conscious of his aristocratic standing, never possessed. After Quiberon Bay Conflans did not serve at sea again and died in retirement at the age of 87.

20 TREATY OF PARIS 1815, FRANCE (NAPOLEONIC WAR)

At last the war was really over. This treaty confirmed the earlier attempts (see 30 May and 9 June, Congress of Vienna), but in the light of Napoleon's activities after his escape from Elba, ending at Waterloo, the terms France was now obliged to accept were much harsher. Instead of the frontiers of 1792, the new French frontiers were those of 1790. There was also an obligation to pay an indemnity of 700 million francs, as well as to support an army of occupation of 150,000 men for 3 to 5years. Prussia wanted more but had to wait until 1871, when it was able to dictate its own terms to a defeated France without having to conform to the wishes of allies (in passing, the indemnity in 1871 was 5 billion francs). The signatories to this treaty were Britain, Prussia, Russia, and Austria, and, in the colder climate that now prevailed, France was not invited.

23 H.M.S. COURIER (12 GUNS) V. LE GUERRIER (14 GUNS) 1799 (FRENCH REVOLUTIONARY WARS)

Commanders: Lieut. T. Searle v. Felix Lallermand.

Courier was a hired cutter employed in coastal waters and operating from Yarmouth; *Le Guerrier* was a privateer cutter based in Dunkirk. *Courier* sighted the enemy in the afternoon of the previous day and chased her throughout the night. Action was joined in the morning about 30 miles from Lowestoft, and after nearly an hour of brisk fighting the French ship surrendered. *Courier* had one killed and two wounded; *Le Guerrier's* casualties were four killed and six wounded. Searle was promoted to commander as of this date.

A privateer operated under a letter of marque issued by the government licensing the commander of a privately owned vessel to cruise in search of enemy merchant vessels, the object was to capture ships not to sink them. All countries made use of letters of marque to some extent, and the best known English privateer is Sir Francis Drake; French privateers were particularly active in the eighteenth century wars operating principally from Dunkirk and St. Malo. Privateering could be very profitable, and consequently many of the best seamen preferred to man privateers instead of enlisting in regular naval service; for this reason, all navies were highly critical of this form of warfare, and the practice was formally abolished at the Convention of Paris in 1856. As an indication of the aggravation and intimidation of privateering based on Dunkirk, the Treaty of Utrecht, 1713 (see 11 April), expressly compelled the French to raze the fortifications of Dunkirk, but apparently this was not a permanent solution because there was a similar provision in the Treaty of Paris, 1763 (see 10 February).

24 FORT DUQUESNE 1758, U.S.A. (SEVEN YEARS WAR)

Commanders: Brig. Genl. John Forbes v. Capt. Ligneris
Forces: British & Colonials 6,000-7,000; French 600-700.

Fort Duquesne (now Pittsburgh) commanded the Ohio Valley and was an obstacle to settlement from Pennsylvania. Previous attempts to capture it had failed, but now French resistance was weakening as the war continued, and support from France was made increasingly uncertain by the naval blockade. Forbes made careful preparations for the assault, but when all was ready he found that the garrison had left after destroying the fortifications. He built a new fort named Fort Pitt in honour of William Pitt the Elder, effectively the British prime minister, and shortly after the war ended in 1763, the area around the fort was laid out as a settlement (now the Golden Triangle) named Pittsburgh.

25 ARCOT 1751, INDIA (CARNATIC WAR)

Commanders: Captain Robert Clive v. M. de Saussey
Forces: British- 200 Europeans and 300 Sepoys; French – 150 Europeans and 10,000 Indians.

The Carnatic is the coastal strip extending from Nellore (north of Madras/Chennai) southward to the Tamil country, and at this time it was a dependency of Hyderabad within the Mughul Empire. Together with Bengal, the Carnatic was the most profitable part of India for European traders. Chanda Sahib was the French nominee for the Nawabship of the Carnatic region, and his army included an important French contingent in addition to which he received strategic and tactical advice. Chanda Sahib was engaged in besieging Trichinopoly, and in order to relieve the pressure there, Clive boldly seized the fortress of Arcot, Chanda Sahib's capital. As soon as the news reached him, Chanda Sahib sent his son, Raja Sahib, with a strong force to re-take the fortress. The siege went on for fifty days and came to an end when a final assault was firmly repulsed; the besiegers marched away abandoning several guns and large quantities of supplies. A spectacular feature of the final assault was a herd of elephants with iron head plates which were driven forward to batter down the gates, but when they came within musket shot the animals stampeded and trampled down the soldiers urging them on.

Although Britain and France were officially at peace (see 18 October,Treaty of Aix-la-Chapelle), the terms of treaties made in Europe frequently failed to settle issues that were of great importance thousands of miles away, and sporadic fighting continued in India and North America as each country sought to establish control. This engagement was important in re-asserting British prestige and military dominance in India and was the first of a series of victories that ended French ambitions in the sub-continent (see, for example, 2 October, Trichinopoly III; 23 June, Plassey; and 15 January, Pondicherry).

28 TRICHINOPOLY IV 1753, INDIA (CARNATIC WAR)
Commanders: Major Stringer Lawrence v. ?

This was no more than the epilogue to the more important battle at Trichinopoly two months previously (see 2 October), but spectacular in miniature. After the previous action, the French had withdrawn to Sriringham Island in the Cauvery River and decided that a night attack might enable them to capture Trichinopoly. Acting boldly and bravely, they scaled the outer wall, but then found themselves trapped between the outer and inner walls and under fire from the defenders who had anticipated their move. After sustaining heavy casualties, there was no alternative to surrender and 360 did so. Trichinopoly was a happy hunting ground for Lawrence, he had already had two victories here (see 13 June & 2 October).

29 DETROIT 1760, U.S.A. (SEVEN YEARS' WAR)
Commanders: Major Robert Rogers v. ?

One of the terms of surrender at Montreal (see 8 September) was that the entire French army in New France and its dependencies must lay down their arms. The capitulation of Detroit was part of this condition. Fort Detroit was founded in 1701 by Antoine Laumet de la Mothe Cadillac as Fort Pont-Chartrain du Detroit. Intended to be principally a trading post, it was not particularly successful, and its name was abbreviated to

Fort Detroit in 1751. Under British occupation a fort was built in 1778 on a new site and named Fort Lernault after Captain Richard Lernault, the commandant. Detroit remained in British occupation until 1796.

Rogers was an extraordinary man. On the one hand, a swindler, braggart, and drunkard, and on the other, he showed a genius for a certain type of military operation and has claimed a place in military history as one of the fathers of modern commando soldiering. He grew up in New Hampshire, and in the hard school for survival on the frontier, he took to the life of the forest in the course of which he soon demonstrated qualities of leadership. In his early twenties he was a captain with Johnson at the battle of Crown Point (see 8 September) and impressed him by his courageous scouting patrols, capture of prisoners, and skilful collection of intelligence. A few months later, the Governor of Massachusetts, William Shirley, appointed Rogers as captain and commanding officer of an independent company of Rangers. A series of daring exploits deep in enemy territory against the French and their Indian allies made him a popular hero in Britain and in North America. The Rangers' contribution to the British campaign was in surprise attacks on isolated outposts, harassing supply convoys, collecting vital intelligence about enemy troop movements and deployment, disrupting communications, and not least in waging merciless psychological warfare on the Indian allies of France. The Rangers fought ruthlessly, so that Rogers became notorious throughout New France, and a large price was put on his head. He was with Wolfe at Quebec (see 13 September, Plains of Abraham) and in the final campaign against Montreal (see 8 September) after which he was instructed to take possession of the French outposts in the west – including Detroit. Peace brought out his worst characteristics, he was appointed governor of the important Fort Michilimackinac (a post once held by Antoine Cadillac), but his wretched performance led him to be suspected of treason, and he was brought to Montreal in chains to face a court martial at which he was acquitted for lack of evidence. He visited Britain twice and was able to secure a colonecy in the British army, but then, saddled with large debts, he was confined to a debtors' prison. Rescued by his brother, he returned to America where the War of Independence was about to begin. At first, he seems to have flirted with both sides, but Washington did not trust him and had him imprisoned as a loyalist spy. Rogers escaped and was commissioned to raise a loyalist corps, but he was later replaced as commander, and the unit was renamed. Rogers' career was now over, he returned to Britain where he lived on his half pay and died in a cheap lodging house in London at the age of 64.

DECEMBER

2 (EST.) AIGUILLON 1345, FRANCE (HUNDRED YEARS' WAR)
Commanders: Earl of Pembroke & Lord Stafford v. ?

Following the heavy defeat of the French at Auberoche (see 21 October), the Earl of Derby decided that the best strategy was to secure the valley of the Garonne River against an attack on Bordeaux, and Aiguillon was one of two fortified towns that were on this line. The army was divided into two divisions; one, commanded by Pembroke and Stafford, was sent to take Aiguillon, and the objective of the other, commanded by the Earl of Derby, was La Réole (see 4 January). On the march to Aiguillon, Monségur was captured, but little is known about the conduct of the siege itself except that it did not last long. The citizens may have assisted the English, and if they did, it could be argued that this was not treason because at this date Gascony had been under English rule for two hundred years (the dowry of Eleanor of Aquitaine on her marriage to Henry II). While the Earl of Derby was taking towns and castles in Bordeaux there was a much larger French army only a few miles away commanded by the Duke of Normandy, but it kept conspicuously out of the way.

3 ARNI 1751, INDIA (CARNATIC WAR)
Commanders: Captain Robert Clive v. Raja Sahib
Forces: British - 200 Europeans, 700 sepoys & 600 Mahratta cavalry;
French 300 Europeans, 1,500 sepoys & 3,000 native levies.

This action was in direct succession to the victory at Arcot (see 25 November). Clive lost no time in pursuing Raja Sahib's army in their retreat from Arcot. Initially, they had prepared to stand at Vellore about 20 miles away but had left there to meet French reinforcements who were on their way from Pondicherry. When Clive heard of this plan, he ordered a rapid night march in order to block the way to Vellore, and the two armies came face to face on the morning of 3 December. Clive had selected a strong position on rising ground with swampy paddy-fields immediately in front. The nature of the ground meant that the first enemy assault was not supported by artillery, and they were pinned down by enfilading fire. French troops were used in the second wave but were thrown back by a counter-attack, and the retreat began, gathered momentum, and became a rout. Raja Sahib's indigenous troops fled in groups of 20 – 30, and the French did not stop until they were half way back to their base at Pondicherry. The picture was completed when 700 French trained sepoys surrendered and were enrolled in the British forces. French casualties were 200 killed including 50 French; the British losses were limited to 8 sepoys and 50 Mahrattas. This was Clive's first victory in a set battle, and he showed tactical skills in the selection of his position, and in the deployment of his troops and artillery; determination and resolution marked his forced march by night and his pursuit of a beaten enemy.

3 H.M.S. LAPWING (28 GUNS) V. DECIUS (20 GUNS) AND VAILLANTE 1796, WEST INDIES (FRENCH REVOLUTIONARY WARS)

Commanders: Cdr. Robert Barton v. ?

Lapwing was anchored off St. Kitts when information was received that the French intended to invade Anguilla, about 60 miles north-west of St. Kitts, and she sailed immediately to intercept. When *Lapwing* arrived, the French had already landed and burned the town, but on sighting *Lapwing*, the French commander, decided that 'discretion is the better part of valour', and re-embarked the troops. The two French ships set sail hotly pursued by *Lapwing*; the brig, *Vaillante*, made off and *Decius* surrendered, but *Vaillante's* escape was only temporary, she ran aground and was destroyed by gunfire from *Lapwing*. *Lapwing* suffered only 1 man killed and 6 wounded, but the French casualties, including the troops, were heavy.

3 ILE DE FRANCE (MAURITIUS) 1810, INDIAN OCEAN (NAPOLEONIC WAR)

Commanders: Vice Adml. A.Bertie & Maj. Genl. John Abercromby v. Charles Isidore, Comte De Caen
Forces: British 19 ships + 10,000 troops; French 4,000.

This amphibious operation was the completion of a strategic plan that began with the conquest of Bourbon (see 8 July). Ile de France was the principal French naval base in the Indian Ocean, and as the performance of the French navy deteriorated, maritime hostilities came to depend more and more on privateers who sailed from Ile de France against East India Company convoys. A serious limitation of Ile de France was that it was not self-sufficient and had to import substantial amounts of food, chiefly from Bourbon. Now that these supplies had been cut off, it was time to extinguish any further hostile activity in Ile de France. Fighting did not last long, and the island was taken at the cost of 167 killed, wounded and missing; French casualties were higher, and a substantial number of ships were taken, namely, 7 frigates, 10 sloops, 21 merchant ships and 3 British merchant ships recaptured. Recognizing its strategic location, at the Treaty of Paris 1814 (see 30 May), Britain retained possession of Ile de France, and the new colony reverted to the original name of Mauritius.

7 CONDORE 1758, INDIA (SEVEN YEARS' WAR)

Commanders: Lt. Col. Francis Forde v. Le Comte de Conflans.
Forces: British 500 Europeans, 7,600 Indian infantry & cavalry and 18 guns; French 500 Europeans, 6,000 Indian infantry and 36 guns.

Forde had been sent from Calcutta by Clive, now governor of Bengal, to link up with an Indian ruler who had rebelled against the French. The combined force came within sight of the French and prepared for battle on a flat piece of ground in front of the village, where a field of maize enabled Forde to conceal the British infantry. Taking advantage of their superiority in artillery, the French opened with a barrage at a range of about 1,000 yards followed by an attack on a sepoy battalion on one of the flanks, but at just the right moment the British infantry emerged from their cover and so surprised the French attackers that they fled in confusion. The retreat became a rout when those who had rallied under the cover of the guns failed to hold against the full weight of the British force. The French lost 30 guns and all of their baggage, and the next day the British were able to advance 40 miles against the fort at Rajahmundry (see 9 December).

9 LILLE 1708, FRANCE (WAR OF THE SPANISH SUCCESSION)

Commanders: Marlborough v. Marshal Louis François, Duc de Boufflers
Forces: British & Allies 35,000 v. French 16,000

Following the crushing defeat of the French at Oudenarde (see 11 July), Marlborough held the initiative, and on the strength of it he developed a bold plan in the form of an advance along the Channel coast coupled with an amphibious attack on Abbeville on the Normandy coast in order to establish a forward base for operations within France itself. Mastery of the sea ensured that the main line of attack could be supplied from the sea by the Anglo-Dutch fleet, and the offensive would have outflanked the triple line of fortresses defending the north-west frontier. Overall, the plan showed a grasp of the strategic and tactical possibilities of coordinated land and sea operations that was highly unusual in the eighteenth century; indeed, the novelty and unorthodoxy were sufficient to so alarm the Dutch and other allies that it was stillborn. Accepting the limitations often found in alliances (e.g., World War II), Marlborough decided to capture the fortress of Lille for the benefit of next year's campaign.

Lille was not a trivial target. It was regarded as the capital of French Flanders, and the centre of all trade between the Netherlands and France; second only to Paris, its strong fortifications had been designed by Vauban, the brilliant military engineer of Louis XIV, and are now commemorated by a plaque. Further aids to its defences were given by its location amongst unhealthy marshes, the proximity of other French fortresses that could be used as bases for relief forces, and the vulnerability of the allies' long line of communication. On the other hand, the French were demoralised, and Marlborough was regarded as invincible, rather like Rommel in the desert before El Alamein; as one French commentator put it: "[Oudenarde] reduced us, the owners of a far stronger army, to a difficult and timid defensive… … We were effectively under the orders of M.de Marlborough." In the first phase of the siege, the French advanced an army of 110,000 men to about eight miles of Lille where they were confronted by Marlborough's smaller numbers drawn up in a defensive position. There the French stayed for a week without making a serious attempt to break through to Lille, and then withdrew along the way they had come. The next French counter took the form of a blockade along the River Scheldt to cut off land communication with Brussels, to which Marlborough's response was to arrange supplies through Ostend (see 28 September Wynandael). On the same day as Wynandael, an extraordinary effort was made by the French to relieve the shortage of gunpowder in the beleaguered city. The Chevalier de Luxembourg mustered 2,000 cavalry and 150 grenadiers and gave each horseman 50 lbs. of gunpowder to carry. They put Dutch insignia in their hats and bluffed their way through the allied lines at dusk. Their bluff was not discovered until most had passed through, and then all hell broke loose. As those who had passed through galloped towards Lille, they were fired on and some of the powder bags were ignited and exploded, further explosions were set off by sparks from the hooves of the furiously ridden horses. In minutes, the ground was strewn with dead carcasses, horses, and half burned limbs. Those who had not yet passed through the lines fled towards Douai, but about 40,000lbs.of powder were delivered to the garrison. A less tangible but still important benefit was the boost given to the morale of the defenders by this daring action, which became known as *'l'affaire des poudres'*, and shortly afterwards the Chevalier was promoted to lieutenant-general by Louis XIV. The effort did not make any great difference to the outcome of the siege, on 25 October the city was surrendered, and the attack was now concentrated on the citadel itself, but the French were not prepared to yield Lille without an epic struggle. Next to appear on the scene was their ally, the Elector of Bavaria, who had arrived in Mons from the Rhine (he had been ignominiously expelled from Bavaria after the battle of Blenheim (see 13 August)), and it was decided that he should lead an attack on Brussels. Expecting, wrongly as it turned out, support from the local population, the Elector reached his objective on 25 November and began a bombardment on a limited scale. This only went to show that a normal siege would be required. Any possibility of such a move was destroyed the next day, when Marlborough launched a four pronged attack across the River Scheldt and by nightfall had established a bridgehead thirty miles wide, communication between

Lille and Brussels was now restored and the Elector, in great danger of being cut off from Mons, was sent into precipitate retreat leaving behind his guns and 800 wounded. Another ineffectual and half-hearted effort for relief was easily countered by Marlborough, and the French had nothing left; the end of the siege was only a matter of days. The French army was ordered to winter quarters on December 4, and in the evening of December 9 Boufflers capitulated; in acknowledgement of its courageous defence, the garrison was allowed to march out with Boufflers leading.

Over sixty years old at the time of the siege of Lille, Boufflers was nearing the end of his distinguished military career. He conducted a heroic defence of Namur in 1695 when besieged by William III (see 1 September), and his performance at Lille was up to this standard. The year after Lille, he was in the heavy fighting at Malplaquet (see 11 September) where he assumed command after Marshal Villars was wounded, and then conducted a masterly retreat.

This was not the final episode in the military history of Lille. In World War I it was besieged by a German army whose bombardment destroyed 2,200 buildings, and when they discovered that they had been duped by the defenders, they burned down a whole section of the city. The experience in World War II was less drastic, brief resistance to the rapid German advance was offered by a Moroccan infantry division, and Lille was not liberated until four and a half years later.

9 RAJAHMUNDRY 1758, INDIA (SEVEN YEARS' WAR)

Commanders: Lt. Col. F. Forde v. Le Comte de Conflans
Forces: British 2,500 Europeans & 5,000 Indian troops v. French 6,500 European & Indian

The momentum of the victory at Condore (see 7 December) had carried Forde's army to Rajahmundry, where the battle was fought virtually between the European contingents. No doubt badly shaken from events two days previously, the French were routed.

10 NIVE 1813, FRANCE (PENINSULA WAR)

Commanders: Wellington v. Marshal Nicolas-Jean de Dieu Soult, Duc de Dalmatie

Forces: British 36,000 & 27,000 Portuguese and Spanish; French 62,500.

Wellington was pressing forward into France with Bayonne as the immediate objective; Soult was in Bayonne behind strong fortifications and sought to disrupt the advance by a series of attacks. These were in divisional strength but stoutly resisted, and, on balance, Wellington had the better of a day's inconclusive fighting because his advance was resumed a day or two later (see 13 December, St. Pierre); casualties were almost equal – French 2,000, British and allies 1,800.

During the battle, Wellington received an unexpected windfall when three battalions of Napoleon's German Confederates changed sides under orders from home, a prudent move that was prompted by Napoleon's defeat at Leipzig on 19 October. In a similar vein, French peasants showed a preference for profit over patriotism in having no hesitation or scruple in selling their produce to the British rather than to the French commissariat – prices were higher, coercion less, and part of the payment might be made in sugar. Sugar was highly prized because for seven years the British naval blockade had prevented imports of it from the West Indies.

13 ST. PIERRE 1813, FRANCE (PENINSULA WAR)

Commanders: Lt. Genl. Sir Rowland Hill v. Marshal Nicolas-Jean de Dieu Soult, Duc de Dalmatie

Forces: British & Portuguese 14,000; French 40,000.

This was a continuation of the Nive (see 10 December above). Having failed to halt the British advance on Bayonne, Soult tried again. Hill's detachment was isolated from the main body when the River Nive, swollen by heavy rain, swept away all of the bridges except one, and their difficulties were compounded by mistakes and worse by two of the battalion commanders. The whole front was barely a mile in length which in view of their smaller numbers was an advantage to the British. The French attacked the British left with three times the number of troops but without significant result, and their attack in the centre led to heavy fighting for three hours before a fierce counter attack that included all the available reserves sent the French in retreat all along the line. In the early phase, Lt. Col. Bunbury pulled back with unnecessary haste, and Lt. Col. Sir Nathaniel Pococke not only ordered a withdrawal but he himself fled to the rear where Hill found him. Bunbury was allowed to sell out of the army (perhaps he became the prototype of the phantom character in Wilde's play 'The Importance of Being Earnest') , but Pococke was cashiered. French casualties were 3,300; British 1,773, and Soult withdrew into Bayonne. This was a good performance by Wellington's most reliable subordinate (see 28 October, Arroyo dos Melinos). Four months later, the Peninsula War came to an end at Toulouse (see 10 April) as part of the general surrender of Napoleon.

14 USHANT 1781, FRANCE (AMERICAN WAR OF INDEPENDENCE)

Commanders: Rear Adml. R.Kempenfelt v. Adml. Comte de Guichen
Forces: British 11 ships of the line + 6 smaller ones; French 21 ships of the line.

De Guichen's ships were escorting a large convoy to America, when in foggy weather, they were sighted by Kempenfelt about 150 miles west of Ushant. Deciding that his squadron was too greatly outnumbered to offer battle, Kempenfelt took advantage of careless covering on the part of the French to capture 20 of the merchant ships and scatter the rest; the French escorts were dispersed in a gale and returned to base.

Kempenfelt was from a Swedish family, but his father spent most of his life serving in the British military. Although Kempenfelt acquired a wide experience, including staff appointments, his advancement was slow, and he was nearly 60 before he was promoted to flag rank. Most unusually for his time, Kempenfelt was an officer of wide reading and intellectual tastes who was responsible for many important innovations in signalling, strategy, tactical principles, proper use of various types of vessel, health, and internal discipline; in short, he has been described as one of the most prescient officers in the entire history of the Royal Navy. In spite of these many interests, Kempenfelt found time to write poetry and published a volume of it. His death was a tragic accident. In 1782, his ship, *Royal George*, had taken on stores preparatory to joining the operations for the relief of Gibraltar when a small leak was identified, the repair of which required the ship to be heeled onto her side. When this was done the cargo shifted, the sea flooded in through the open gun ports and the ship quickly sank taking Kempenfelt and many of the crew to the bottom. This disaster inspired Cowper to write his poem, 'Loss of the Royal George':

Toll for the brave-
The brave that are no more
All sunk beneath the wave
Fast by their native shore.
… … …
Brave Kempenfelt is gone
His last sea-fight is fought

Perhaps unintentionally, there is a memorial in Trafalgar Square to *Royal George*, Kempenfelt, and his crew. The four bronze, couchant lions at the foot of Nelson's column were cast from guns recovered from the wreck.

De Guichen was less illustrious. Early successes against English privateers were not sustained, and subsequently he was either on the losing side or in a draw.

15 CONJEVERAM 1751, INDIA (CARNATIC WAR)

Commanders: Capt. Robert Clive v. La Volonté
Forces: British 200 Europeans & 1,300 Indian troops; French 300 Europeans & 400 Indian troops.

This battle followed directly from Clive's victories at Arcot and Arni (see 25 November and 3 December). His superior, Thomas Saunders, Governor of Madras, urged him to seize Conjeveram which was being used by the French to interfere with communications between Arcot and Madras; they had also captured a party of English sick and wounded officers and soldiers and reportedly were treating these men very cruelly. The defenders were in the great temple which had inner and outer walls and was well fortified. La Volonté, a Portuguese mercenary, refused to surrender and threatened to hang two of the wounded officers if the British did not withdraw. Clive ignored the threat, and the bombardment began. After two days, one of the captive officers was forced to mount the breach in the walls, but he was saved by the intervention of the

Indian governor who was secretly in league with the British. That night, La Volonté and his party left quietly leaving all the prisoners behind unharmed. Faced with the departure of his Indian cavalry, Clive sent his troops back to Arcot and returned to a hero's welcome in Madras.

19 FORT ST. DAVID 1746, INDIA (WAR OF THE AUSTRIAN SUCCESSION)

Commanders: British Garrison v. Genl. de Bury.
Forces: British 200 Europeans +2,100 Indian troops; French 900 Europeans +700 Indian troops +6 guns & 6 mortars.

Three months earlier the British had been driven from their base at Madras and were now re-grouping at St, David about100 miles south of Madras, and only 12 miles from the major French base at Pondicherry. Fort St. David was the strongest fortification in British hands in India, and it was essential to hold it. The French force took up position near to the fort, and while deciding on how best to proceed, they were surprised and set upon by a detachment of cavalry from the garrison. The infantry ran away in panic, and only firm resistance by the gunners saved the French from annihilation. Once they were able to disengage, the French retreated to quarters near Pondicherry leaving behind 132 killed and wounded.

19 TOULON 1793, FRANCE (FRENCH REVOLUTIONARY WARS)

Commanders: Vice Adml. Viscount Samuel Hood v. Genl. Jacques François Coquille Dugommier
Forces: British 2,000 marines; French 11,500 .

This was a curious action which began when the municipal government in Toulon invited Lord Hood, whose squadron was blockading the naval base of Toulon, to enter the harbour and defend the city against a republican army marching against it. In 1793, there was a royalist insurrection in western France that quickly spread and briefly became a serious civil war known as the War of the Vendée; the rebels suffered heavy defeats and by the end of 1793, Toulon, which had declared royalist sympathies, accommodated some 50,000 refugees. The last resort was the appeal to Hood for help. They could not have chosen a naval commander more likely to respond to such an appeal. Hood was bold and decisive, perhaps precipitate, and, assisted by part of the

Spanish fleet, he took his ships into the harbour thereby impounding the French Mediterranean fleet. Unfortunately, the government in London did not react to the opportunity in time, and the essential reinforcements arrived too late so that Hood was obliged to withdraw. When he sailed away he took with him three French ships of the line under royalist officers, several thousand refugees, and burned nine other ships of the line. More of the French navy would have been destroyed if the Spanish had not been so dilatory and ineffectual, but the damage inflicted had been considerable.

A particularly interesting part of this engagement is the appearance of two subordinate commanders destined for much larger parts and to meet in opposition later. The greater of the two was a French chef de bataillon (major) of artillery named Napoleon Buonaparte who is credited with devising the successful plan of attack that ended the siege. On the British side, there was Captain Sir Sidney Smith in charge of the destruction of French ships prior to the withdrawal, an unconventional officer – intelligent, eccentric, courageous and independent. There is no record that these two confronted each other at Toulon, but they certainly did so, much to Napoleon's disadvantage, five years later (see 18 May, Cape Carmel).

Dugommier is a distinguished figure in French military history. He was born in Guadaloupe, where he had a large estate, and joined the royalist army at an early age. He reached the rank of major before being put on half-pay, and it was not until the revolution that his military career flourished. At first, he returned to France from Guadeloupe as a deputy to the National Convention, but soon applied to re-join the army. Performance in Italy quickly led to promotion to general of division, and it was in this rank that he fought at Toulon with conspicuous ability, courage, and humanity towards the defeated royalists. The following year he was enjoying success against an invading Spanish army until he was killed by a mortar bomb at the battle of Black Mountain, Figueras. Apart fron numerous street names, he is commemorated by a monument on the ramparts of Fort Bellegarde-Roussillon, and by a Paris Metro station on Line 6. He is buried at Perpignan.

20 TRARBACH 1704, GERMANY (WAR OF THE SPANISH SUCCESSION)

Commanders: Prince Frederick of Hesse-Cassel v. ???

With Trier taken (see 26 October), Marlborough pushed his army further down the Moselle valley towards France and laid siege to Trarbach. This was not as easy as Trier, taking nearly seven weeks to subdue, but it was captured in time for Christmas and the 1704 campaign.

20 H.M.S. PHOEBE (36 GUNS) V. NÉRÉIDE (36 GUNS) 1797, IRELAND (FRENCH REVOLUTIONARYWARS)

Commanders: Captain Robert Barlow v. Captain Antoine Canon.

This action was fought in the dark about 60 miles off Cape Clear, south-west Ireland, and at the end of a long chase by the British ship, towards midnight *Néréide* (Sea Nymph) struck her colours having sustained considerable damage and 75 casualties out of a crew of 330; *Phoebe's* casualties were 13 out of a crew of only 261. Taken as a prize, *Néréide* had a colourful career in the Royal Navy including a mutiny and the recapture of an American merchant ship that had been taken by a French privateer.

Captain Barlow in *Phoebe* exemplifies the contribution of the British frigates, their commanders and crews in the long wars against the French (see 10 January, 19 February, 21 February, and 11 May).

21 SAHAGON 1808, SPAIN (PENINSULA WAR)

Commanders: Lt. Genl. Lord Henry Paget v. Genl. Debelle.
Forces: British 1,200 cavalry with 4 guns; French 800 cavalry.

Unusually, this was exclusively a cavalry engagement in which the French were routed with 120 killed and 167 taken prisoner compared with 2 killed and 23 wounded on the British side. Sahagon marked the limit of Moore's ill-fated advance into Spain (see 16 January, Corunna). The British cavalry have a dismal record during the French Revolutionary and Napoleonic Wars – Napoleon's derogatory opinion was that "the [British] cavalry were greatly inferior to the infantry in everything except appearance"- but this was one of their shining moments and owed much to the ability of their commander.

Paget was the eldest son of the wealthy Earl of Uxbridge, and he was the epitome of the popular ideal of an English cavalry officer – tall and handsome, laconic and brave, as well as a great lover of women. He advanced rapidly in rank during his early military service at a time when commissions and promotions could be readily purchased, but in those early days he soon showed that his capabilities justified his rank. At Egmont-Op-Zee (see 2 October), he re-captured some British guns putting the French cavalry to flight in the process, and four days later his troopers took 500 prisoners. Paget commanded the rear-guard in the retreat to Corunna with great skill against much superior forces (see 29 December, Benavente). Paget's next notable performance was in the boudoir rather than the battlefield. His wife, née Lady Caroline Villiers, had borne three sons and five daughters, but then Paget became enamoured of Charlotte Wellesley, the sister-in-law of Wellington, and herself the mother of four small children. The scandal was immense leading to divorces and a duel on Wimbledon Common between Charlotte's brother, Henry Cadogan, and Paget in which the latter, true to his image, refused to fire after his opponent had missed. Paget's chivalry enabled Cadogan to die a hero's death fighting under the command of his sister's brother-in-law at Vitoria (see 21 June). To complete this vignette, Charlotte and Paget were married and had six children. The scandal had some adverse, military consequences. Wellington had a real need for an able cavalry commander in the Peninsular campaign, but Paget's off the field activities were thought to make him unsuitable for an appointment. However, at Waterloo, he was under Wellington's orders as commander of the cavalry. In that capacity he led a large part of the British cavalry against a French infantry attack with such spirit and determination that 3,000 prisoners were taken, 30 guns disabled and two eagles captured. Unfortunately, as he later admitted, he was at fault in leading the charge because he failed to control the heavy cavalry who advanced too far and lost about half their number. Paget (now the Earl of Uxbridge) at Waterloo is remembered far more often for the manner of his wound than for the heroic charge. Towards the end of the battle, Paget was hit in the leg by a shot as he sat on his horse next to Wellington, and so the story, probably apochryphal, goes, Paget said: "By God, sir, I've lost my leg!" to which Wellington replied "By God, sir, so you have." Be that as it may, the leg was amputated, without anaesthetic, in the village of Waterloo, and the operation was endured with characteristic sang-froid (cf. Moreau, Bois-Le-Duc 12 November). Further honours followed including the marquisate of Anglesey and promotion to Field Marshal; this colourful man lived to be 86.

22 BANTRY BAY 1796. IRELAND (FRENCH REVOLUTIONARY WARS)

Commanders: Vice-Adml. Sir John Colpoys v. Vice-Adml. Justin Morard de Galles & Genl. Lazard Hoche

Forces: British 15 ships of the line v. French 17 ships of the line, 13 frigates, and some transports with 16,500 troops.

The French intended a major invasion of Ireland escorted by the Brest fleet. Incompetence and atrocious weather were the principal reasons for a total failure. In the French Revolutionary Wars and the one immediately following, the Napoleonic War, the French navy was, with some justification, poorly regarded especially by senior army officers; here, for example, is Genl. Hoche in overall command of the Bantry Bay invasion: "Our hateful navy cannot and will not do anything…What a bizarre mixture! The commissioned officers chaotic and divided, organized indiscipline in a fighting service... arrogance, ignorance, vanity and folly". The fleet sailed from Brest on December 16, and at the insistence of Hoche, it left by the unfavourable route resulting in the wreck of one ship with heavy loss of life and the scattering of the others in fog and darkness. Hoche and Morard never made contact with the rest of the fleet which arrived in Bantry Bay during a blizzard on December 22. After a week of continuous gales (and presumably a most unhappy Christmas) the fleet returned to Brest, but not all of them succeeded (see 7 January H.M.S. Doris et al. & 13 January, H.M.S. Indefatigable et al.). For the Royal Navy, this was a victory largely obtained through their opponents scoring several own goals.

23 AVRANCHES 1439, FRANCE (HUNDRED YEARS' WAR)

Commanders: John Talbot v. Arthur de Richemont, Constable of France & Duc d' Alençon.

Forces: English 3,000; French 6,000.

The Duke of Brittany was in one of his periodic alliances with the English, and Avranches, on the borders of Brittany, was under siege by the French. Throughout Europe in the Middle Ages, it was quite usual for siblings, parents and combinations of them to be on opposite sides in the frequent wars, and Avranches is an illustration because Richemont was a younger brother of the Duke. (see 6 March St. Jean-de-Beuvron). Talbot had been sent by the Earl of Warwick to relieve the embattled garrison, and on arrival he deployed his army on the north bank of the river Sée. The French were encamped on the other side of the river between it and the town. Talbot decided on a flanking attack at night. His army forded the river up-stream, wheeled to their right and fell on the enemy who appear to have been still asleep. Chaos erupted, and the French fled without stopping until they were about twenty miles away, only a handful with de Richemont offered any resistance. Richemont left his troops and went to Paris to make his complaints to the king about the poor quality of the army and its equipment. For more on John Talbot, see 16 February, Pontoise.

26 H.M.S. VIPER (12 GUNS) V. LE FURET (14 GUNS), ENGLAND 1799 (FRENCH REVOLUTIONARY WARS)

Commanders: Lt. Pengelly v. Citizen Louis Brevet

Throughout the French Revolutionary Wars and the Napoleonic War that followed, the performance of the French privateers was decidedly better than that of the French navy, although on a smaller scale. The practice of privateering, based principally on Dunkirk and St. Malo, was centuries old, but during times of open warfare it often became part of French maritime strategy, and some famous French naval heroes, such as Jean Bart, were more often privateers than enlisted in the regular force. Suppression of, and protection from, privateers was an important part of Britain's naval effort, and this action is typical of it. *Viper* was a cutter, a small vessel designed for auxiliary service with main fleets and for action against privateers and smugglers. She was patrolling about 20 miles south of Dodman Point, off Falmouth, when *Le Furet* ('Ferret'), a privateer on her maiden voyage from St. Malo, was sighted, *Viper* gave chase, and three hours later was able to open fire. A running fight continued for about 90 minutes when *Viper* was able to loose off two broadsides into her opponent causing her to surrender. *Le Furet* had 4 killed and 8 wounded, including the captain; *Viper* had only 1 man wounded. The prize was taken into Falmouth. Pengelly made something of a name for himself while commanding *Viper* (see 5 January).

Those with an interest in comparing the relative efficacy of the private and public sectors of an economy can find useful case study material in privateering, particularly French, during the eighteenth century.

29 GORÉE ISLAND 1758, SENEGAL (SEVEN YEARS' WAR)

Commanders: Cdre. Augustus Keppel v. ?

Gorée is a small island of volcanic rock, considerably less than one square mile in area and about two miles from Dakar. In the eighteenth century, it was an important staging point in the slave trade, and at various times it was in the possession of the European colonizing powers of Portugal, the Netherlands, Britain and France; during the eighteenth century, it was held four times by Britain and five times by France. This action was the second expedition against the island, and it was soon over. Keppel's squadron conducted a fierce bombardment that forced the French garrison to surrender, and the marines went ashore to occupy the island. As often happened, when the peace treaty was signed to end the war, various places were returned to the original owner, and although Britain had much the better balance in these trades at the Treaty of Paris, 1763 (see10 February), Gorée was a French consolation prize. It became French for the last time in 1817.

Keppel was 33 years old when he fought this battle, but he had already made his mark, first as a boy of 15 during Anson's circumnavigation of the world for which service he was promoted to lieutenant; then, at 24, he commanded a small squadron in a successful raid against the piratical Dey of Algiers whose ships had been preying on British merchant-men. In the year following Gorée, Keppel was prominent in Hawke's sensational performance at Quiberon Bay (see 20-22 November) and commanded at BelleIsle (see 7 June). At the outbreak of the War of American Independence, Keppel, like many Whig naval officers, refused to serve at sea on the ground that the war was unjust; but he served again in command of the Channel Fleet when France entered the war. He rose to be First Lord of the Admiralty and was raised to the peerage as a viscount. From about 1750 onwards, the British navy, with plenty of opportunities to practice, developed considerable skill in amphibious operations, and in so doing the relations between all ranks of the navy and the army became notably harmonious and efficient. Keppel became probably the greatest practitioner of this most difficult operation of war.

The extinction of the slave trade led to collapse of Gorée's economy, but in recent years it has revived as an important tourist centre in which a major attraction is a museum about the slave trade. Doubt has been cast on claims that 20 million slaves passed through Gorée, but the figure seems to have become sufficiently established to justify UNESCO putting the island on its World Heritage List in 1978. There has followed a visit by the Pope in 1992 during which he made an apology to Africa, and in July 2003, President George Bush stayed on the island long enough to deliver a brief, if slightly unctuous, eulogy of democracy and freedom coupled with appropriate regrets for his country's involvement with slavery.

29 ST. LUCIA 1778, WEST INDIES (WAR OF AMERICAN INDEPENDENCE)

Commanders: Rear Adml. the Hon. Samuel Barrington & Maj. Genl. James Grant v. Adml. Genl. Comte d'Estaing.
Forces: British 4 ships of the line + 6 smaller ones & 12,000 troops; French 9,000 troops & 13 ships of the line.

St. Lucia is one of the smaller Windward Islands, the possession of which was hotly disputed by the British and French for more than a century during which time it changed hands fourteen times (see 4 April & 21 June St. Lucia). On this occasion, some of the British invaders sailed from New York to Barbados to rendezvous with others stationed in the Leeward Islands; eluding d'Estaing's superior fleet while en route, the combined force set out for St. Lucia without delay, and the troops landed on 13 December immediately taking a number of key positions. The next day the French ships appeared, but, notwithstanding their marked superiority in numbers, they did not immediately attack their opponents who were at anchor in a bay. By the morning of the 15th. Barrington had moored his ships in a close line across the head of the bay, and d'Estaing delivered two attacks both of which were beaten back. D'Estaing then landed his troops, but they were not able to make any headway against the British entrenchments, and after two weeks of ineffectual efforts on sea and land, d'Estaing re-embarked his soldiers and sailed away to Martinique. The governor's position was now hopeless, and he surrendered St. Lucia on 29 December. St. Lucia passed permanently to Britain by the Treaty of Paris, 1814 (see

30 May) following the first abdication of Napoleon and his exile to Elba. D'Estaing was principally a soldier, and his performance at sea illustrates the weakness of the French practice of conferring military and naval ranks to be held concurrently – for more on d'Estaing see 9 October, Savannah.

29 BENAVENTE 1808, SPAIN (PENINSULA WAR)
Commanders: Lt. Genl. Lord Henry Paget v. Genl. Charles Lefèbvre-Desnouettes
Forces: British 1,000 cavalry (10th. Hussars & King's German Legion cavalry); French 600 cavalry (Chasseur of the Imperial Guard).

This engagement was the second round of Sahagon (see 21 December). Paget continued in command of the British rearguard as the army retreated to Corunna (see 16 January), and aimed to give the infantry time to do so in good order. Paget succeeded in ambushing the French, and he led the charge that drove the French back across the River Cea. The French had 50 casualties and 100 were taken prisoner, including their general who had been slightly wounded. This success persuaded Napoleon that he would not be able to prevent Moore from reaching Corunna, and he handed over command to Marshal Soult, Duke of Dalmatia.

30 GHENT 1708, BELGIUM (WAR OF THE SPANISH SUCCESSION)
Commanders: Marlborough v. Genl. Louis-Jacques, Comte de Lamotte.
Forces: British and Allies 40,000; French 15,000.

In the early days of July, 1708, the French had greatly surprised Marlborough by making a bold dash for Ghent and Bruges and, with the aid of local sympathisers, had occupied both places. This feat greatly affected Marlborough's communications and tarnished his reputation; however, the effect was shortlived because his victory at Oudenarde (see 11 July) and subjugation of Lille (see 9 December) quickly restored the status quo. Five days before Lille surrendered a general order had been given for the French troops to go into winter quarters, but Marlborough was not ready to follow their example even though normal practice would have been to do so. He determined to re-take Ghent and invested it just before Christmas. Lamotte had been discredited by his defeat at Wynandael (see 28 September), and the garrison did not resist for long.

They surrendered having sustained 4,000 casualties, against 4,800 on the British side, and were allowed to evacuate to Dunkirk.

31 CALAIS 1349, FRANCE (HUNDRED YEARS WAR)

Commanders: Edward III v. Geoffrey de Chargny.

This is a strange 'cloak and dagger' event that provides a fitting tale with which to end the year. De Chargny was the French governor of St. Omer who devised a plan by which Calais could be retaken. The governor of the English garrison at Calais was an Italian by the name of Amerigo (it is not known how he came to be appointed, although by this date Italian merchants were well established in the trade of Flanders, or why there were no suitable English candidates), and de Chargny offered him a bribe to open the gates of the town. Amerigo accepted, but then went secretly to England and told Edward III about the plot. Edward designed a counter-plot and told Amerigo to return and pretend to continue with de Chargny's scheme. In the meantime, Edward with his son, the Prince of Wales, and Sir Walter Manny crossed to Calais in disguise and made arrangements to deal with the French. On New Year's Eve, the postern gate was opened to admit the French advance party while the remainder waited outside the main gate, and no English guards were in sight. As soon as the French were inside, a false wall in the courtyard that Edward had ordered to be constructed was pushed down and the English charged out to overpower the confused French. There was drama, too, at the main gate. A guard had been posted on a tower overlooking the drawbridge, and as soon as he heard the noise at the postern gate he pushed a huge stone that hurtled down onto the drawbridge, and the bridge, that had been previously weakened, broke. De Chargny and his followers were not able to go to the assistance of the advance guard, and as they were contemplating what might be done, they were taken in the flanks by the English counter-attack. Simultaneously, Edward (choosing to be incognito) had led a party out of the east gate and the Prince of Wales had led another out of the west gate, they converged on the French and routed them. De Chargny was captured together with a famous French knight, Eustace de Ribaumont, who at one point in the fighting crossed swords with Edward. Although outnumbered, the English prevailed, and in the spirit of chivalry, and no doubt in honour of the date, the captive French nobility were entertained to dinner by

Edward and his knights. De Rimbaud was set free and given various presents by Edward; by merit he advanced in the service of the French crown, and at Poitiers he was Marshal of France and the standard bearer, but that day belonged to the Prince of Wales, the Black Prince, (see 19 September) and was not one for the French to remember.

31 BRUGES 1708, BELGIUM (WAR OF THE SPANISH SUCCESSION)

This merely concluded the events of the previous day. Marlborough was intent on recapturing both Ghent (see 30 December) and Bruges. When resistance at Ghent collapsed, the troops in Bruges abandoned the town and marched away.

REFERENCES

This is basically a reference book, and as such much of it has been compiled from other books of this kind.

The following dictionaries of battles have been particularly useful: 'The Dictionary of Battles (1715-1815)' by Brig. Michael Calvert & Brig. Peter Young , pub. Mayflower Books, N.Y. 1979; 'Brassey's Battles' by John Laffin, pub. Brassey's, London & Washington, 1986; 'Dictionary of Wars' by George Bruce, pub. Harper Collins, Glasgow, 1995; 'The Battle Book' by Bryan Perret, pub. Arms & Armour Press, London,1992; 'Irish Battles' by G.A.Hayes-McCoy, pub. Barnes & Noble, N.Y.,1969; and 'Dictionary of Canadian Military History', ed.D.J.Bercuson & J.L.Granatstein, pub. O.U.P., Toronto, 1992.

Of many standard references: 'The Oxford Companion to British History' ed. John Cannon, pub. OUP, Oxford, 2002; 'The Oxford Companion to Ships and the Sea', ed. Peter Kemp, pub. OUP, Oxford, 1990; and 'Dictionary of Military Biography', ed. Martin Windrow & Francis Mason, pub. Wordsworth, Ware, 1997 were consulted most often. 'The Encyclopædia Britannica' 2001 (CD Edition) & 1947, pub. Chicago also provided a wide range of general information.

Historical works include: 'Economic History of Europe' ed. C.M.Cipolla, pub. Collins/Fontana Books, London, 1973; 'Cambridge Economic History of Europe', ed. J.H.Clapham & E. Power, pub. C.U.P. Cambridge, 1942; 'Economic History of Europe' by S.B. Clough & C.W. Cole, pub. Heath & Co., Boston, 1946; 'A History of Europe' by H.A.L. Fisher, pub. Eyre & Spottiswood, London,1938; 'The Crecy War' by A.H. Burne, pub. Greenhill Books, London, 1990; 'The Agincourt War' by A.H. Burne, pub. Wordsworth, Ware, 1999; 'The Hundred Years War' by E. Perroy, pub. Eyre & Spottiswood, London, 1951; '

England under the Tudors' by G.R.Elton, pub. Methuen, London, 1955; 'Henry VIII' by J.J.Scarisbrick, pub. U. of California Press, Berkeley, 1968; 'Elizabeth I' by J.E. Neale, pub. Jonathan Cape, London, 1952; 'Expansion of Elizabethan England' by A.L. Rowse, pub. Macmillan, London, 1955; 'England in the Eighteenth Century' by Roy Porter, pub. Penguin Books, 1990; 'The Safeguard of the Sea' by N.A.M. Rodger, pub. Penguin Books, 2004; 'The Command of the Ocean' by N.A.M. Rodger, pub. Penguin Books, London, 2004; 'Nelson's Navy' by Brian Lavery, pub. Conway Maritime Press, London, 1995; 'The Wooden World' by N.A.M. Rodger, pub. Collins, London, 1996; 'Broadsides' by Nathan Miller, pub. John Wiley, N.Y., 2000; 'Stopping Napoleon' by Tom Pocock, pub. John Murray, London, 2004; 'Nelson's Trafalgar' by Roy Adkins, pub. Viking Penguin, N.Y., 2005; 'The Story of Canada' by Donald Creighton, pub. Macmillan, Toronto, 1959; 'Britons' by Linda Colley, pub.Yale U.P., New Haven,1992; 'Historians I Have Known' by A.L. Rowse, pub. Duckworth, London, 1995; 'Battlefields in Canada' by M.B. Fryer, pub. Dundurn Press, Toronto, 1986.

Principal biographies are: 'Marlborough as Military Commander' by David G. Chandler, pub. Penguin Books, 2000; 'The First Churchill' by Corelli Barnett, pub. G.P. Putnam's Sons, N.Y., 1974; 'The Duke' by Philip Guedalla, pub. Wordsworth, Ware, 1997; 'Wellington: The Years of the Sword' by Elizabeth Longford, pub. Weidenfeld & Nicolson, London, 1972. The Journal of the Nelson Society, December, 2005, contains a Survey of the Literature associated with Nelson and the number of items, stated to be incomplete, is 242. I have five biographies, including Southey's 'Life', which is not listed in the Survey, and two in particular are: 'Nelson' by Ernle Bradford, pub. Granada, St. Albans, 1977; and 'Nelson' by Tom Pocock, pub. Pimlico, London, 1984; and 'Nelson's Dear Lord' by Evelyn Berckman, pub. Macmillan, London, 1962.

There is, of course, a myriad of websites that vary considerably in quality. Those that have been particularly useful include: www.napoleonguide.com; historyhome.co.uk; napoleonic-literature.com; statistics.gov.uk; maisonstclaire.org; historyguide.org; perso.orange.fr.; cronab.demon.co.uk; bruzelius.info; pbenyon.plus.com; nmm.ac.uk; yale.edu-The Yale Avalon Project at Yale Law School; digitallibrary.mcgill.ca; deremilitari.org; livgenmi.com; biographi.ca [Dictionary of Canadian Biography Online].

INDEX

INDEX OF BATTLES & TREATIES

Boulogne	September 14	1544
Bourbon	July 8	1810
Boyne	July 1	1690
Brenneville	August 20	1119
Brest	August 10	1512
Bruges	December 31	1708
Brussels	May 28	1706
Busaco	September 27	1810
Cadsand	November 10	1337
Caen	July 26	1346
Caen	September 20	1417
Calais	August 4	1347
Calais	December 31	1349
Calvi	August 1	1794
Cape Carmel	May 18	1799
Cape Finisterre I	May 3	1747
Cape Finisterre II	October 14	1747
Cape Finisterre III	July 22	1805
Cape Francois	October 21	1759
Casal Novo	March 14	1811
Castalla	April 13	1813
Castro Urdales	July 6	1812
Chandemagore	March 25	1757
Chignecto Bay	June 20	1704
Ciudad Rodrigo	January 19	1812
Condeixa	March 13	1811
Condore	December 7	1758
Congress of Vienna	June 9	1815
Conjeveram	December 15	1751
Corunna	January 16	1809
Covelong	September 16	1752
Cravant	July 31	1423
Crecy	August 26	1346
Crown Point	September 8	1755
Cuddalore	June 28	1748
Cuddalore	April 29	1758
Cuddalore	June 13	1783
Damme	May 30	1213
Delhi	September 11	1803
Dendermonde	September 9	1706
Detroit	November 29	1760
Dettingen	June 27	1743
Donauwoerth	July 2	1704
Douai	June 27	1710
Dreux	July 20	1421
East Scotland	March 21	1708
Egmont-op-Zee	October 2	1799
Elixhem	July 18	1705
Esla	May 31	1813
Falaise	January 2	1418
Famars	May 23	1793
Ferrol	November 4	1805
Ferryland	August 31	1694
Fishguard	February 25	1797
Flodden	September 9	1513
Fort Balaguer	June 7	1813
Fort Cornelis	August 24	1811
Fort de Levis	August 25	1760
Fort Duquesne	November 24	1758
Fort Frontenac	August 27	1758
Fort Niagara	July 25	1759
Fort St David	December 19	1746
Fort St Frederic	July 31	1759
Fort St Pierre	June 25	1667
Fort Ticonderaga	July 26	1759
Foz do Arouce	March 15	1811
Fresnay	March 5	1420
Freteval	July 3	1194
Fuentes de Onero	May 5	1811

Garcia Hernandez	July 23	1812
Genoa	March 13	1795
Ghent	December 30	1708
Gingee Forts	April 5	1761
Goree Island	December 29	1758
Grenada	July 6	1779
Guadeloupe	May 1	1759
Guadeloupe	July 3	1794
Guinegate	August 16	1513
Harfleur	September 22	1415
Harfleur	July 25	1417
Harfleur	October 6	1440
HMS Amazon	May 23	1811
HMS Amethyst	November 10	1808
HMS Amethyst	April 6	1809
HMS Amphion	March 13	1811
HMS Anson	October 18	1798
HMS Astraea	April 10	1795
HMS Bacchante	August 31	1812
HMS Bacchante	September 18	1812
HMS Bacchante	August 2	1813
HMS Beaulieu	July 22	1801
HMS Bellona	August 13	1761
HMS Blanche	January 4	1795
HMS Carysfort	May 29	1794
HMS Courier	November 23	1799
HMS Crescent	October 20	1793
HMS Diadem	March 4	1806
HMS Diamond	January 3	1795
HMS Diamond	March 17	1796
HMS Dido	June 24	1795
HMS Doris	January 7	1797
HMS Dryad	June 13	1796
HMS Fairy	February 5	1800
HMS Fisgard	October 20	1798
HMS Foudroyant	February 18	1800

HMS Foudroyant	April 19	1782
HMS Immortalite	July 27	1801
HMS Indefatigable	April 20	1796
HMS Indefatigable	January 13	1797
HMS Jason	June 29	1798
HMS Lapwing	December 3	1796
HMS Lion	March 30	1800
HMS Lively	March 13	1795
HMS London	March 13	1806
HMS Mars	April 21	1798
HMS Melampus	October 13	1798
HMS Milford	July 3	1813
HMS Monmouth	February 28	1758
HMS Northumberland	May 19	1812
HMS Nymphe	June 18	1793
HMS Nymphe	February 24	1800
HMS Peterell	March 21	1800
HMS Phoebe	December 20	1797
HMS Phoebe	February 21	1801
HMS Phoebe	May 11	1800
HMS Phoebe	February 19	1801
HMS Phoebe	January 10	1797
HMS Revolutionnaire	April 13	1796
HMS Romney	June 17	1794
HMS San Fiorenzo	March 8	1797
HMS Santa Marguerita	June 8	1796
HMS Seine	August 20	1800
HMS Sheerness	March 25	1746
HMS Southampton	June 10	1796
HMS Speedy	February 3	1798
HMS Success	August 14	1800
HMS Sybille	February 28	1799
HMS Telegraph	March 18	1799
HMS Thetis	May 17	1795
HMS Viper	July 29	1800

HMS Viper	September 10	1801
HMS Viper	December 26	1799
HMS Viper	January 5	1800
Huy	July 11	1705
Huy	August 26	1703
Hyeres Bay	July 13	1795
Ile de France	December 3	1810
Ile de Rhe	April 4	1758
Ile-de-Groix	June 23	1795
Island of Schiermannikoog	August 11	1799
Isle of Wight	July 21	1545
Ivantelly	August 2	1813
Jersey	January 6	1781
Kaveripak	February 28	1752
Karikal	April 5	1760
Kaiserswerth	June 15	1702
La Reole	January 4	1346
Lagos Bay	August 17	1759
Le Crotoy	July 15	1438
Le Mans	August 10	1425
Le Quesnay	July 4	1712
Le Treport	September 2	1545
Leau	September 6	1705
Lequeitio	June 22	1812
Liege & Fort Chartreuse	October 29	1702
Lille	December 9	1708
Limbourg	September 27	1703
Limoges	September 19	1370
Lincelles	August 18	1793
Lincoln	May 20	1217
Lines of Torres Vedras	November 14	1810

Loch nam Uamh	May 3	1746
Londonderry	August 1	1689
Lottinghen	September 4	1522
Louisbourg I	June 16	1745
Louisbourg II	July 27	1758
Louvain	May 25	1706
Madagascar	November 5	1942
Madras	February 17	1759
Maida	July 4	1806
Major Offensive Sweep	October 5	1355
Major Offensive Sweep	June 22	1356
Malplaquet	September 11	1709
Malta	September 5	1800
Mandora	March 13	1801
Marabout	August 17	1801
Marbella	March 10	1705
Margate	March 24	1387
Martinique	February 12	1762
Martinique	March 16	1794
Martinique	February 24	1809
Masulipatam	April 8	1759
Mauron	August 14	1352
Meaux	May 2	1422
Melun	November 18	1420
Menin	August 22	1706
Mers-el-Kebir	July 3	1940
Minden	August 1	1759
Mirebeau-en-Poitou	August 1	1202
Mons	October 20	1709
Montereau	July 1	1420
Montreal	September 8	1760
Morales	June 2	1813
Morlaix	September 30	1342

Najera	April 3	1367
Namur I	September 1	1695
Negapatam	August 3	1758
Nieuwport	October 22	1793
Nile	August 1	1798
Newfoundland	June 10	1755
Nivelle	November 10	1813
Nive	December 10	1813
Obidos	August 15	1808
Operations in Atlantic	June 16	1795
Oporto	May 12	1809
Orthez	February 27	1814
Osma	June 18	1813
Ostend	July 9	1706
Oudenarde	July 11	1708
Pamplona	October 31	1813
Placentia	June 1	1713
Plains of Abraham	September 13	1759
Plassey	June 23	1757
Poitiers	October 4	1346
Poitiers	September 19	1356
Pondicherry	September 10	1759
Pondicherry	January 15	1761
Pondicherry	October 16	1778
Pont de l'Arche	July 20	1418
Pontoise	July 2	1419
Pontoise	February 16	1437
Pontoise	July 20	1441
Port Mahon	September 19	1708
Port Royal	July 15	1613
Port Royal	May 21	1690
Port Royal	October 13	1710
Port-au-Prince	May 30	1794
Port-La-Joye	June 20	1745
Porto Praya Bay	April 16	1781
Puente Larga	October 30	1812
Quatre Bras	June 16	1815
Quebec	July 19	1629
Quebec	May 16	1760
Quiberon Bay	November 20	1759
Quimper River	June 22	1800
Rajahmundry	December 9	1758
Ramilles	May 23	1706
Rennes	July 5	1358
Restigouche	July 8	1760
Roche Derrien	June 20	1347
Rolica	August 17	1808
Rouen	January 20	1419
Rouvray	February 12	1429
Ruremonde	October 6	1702
Ry	January 15	1436
Sabugal	April 3	1811
Sahagon	December 21	1808
Salamanca	July 22	1812
Salamanca Forts	June 27	1812
Samarang	September 10	1811
San Domingo	February 6	1806
San Millan de la Cogolla	June 18	1813
San Sebastian	September 8	1813
Sandwich	August 24	1217
Santander	August 3	1812
Santo Domingo	September 22	1793
Santoliet	October 29	1705
Savannah	October 9	1779
Seine Mouth	August 15	1416
Senegal	July 13	1809
Sens	June 13	1420

Seringham	April 2	1753
Sluys	June 24	1340
Sorauren	July 28	1813
St. Croix	June 10	1800
St. James	March 6	1426
St. Jean d'Angelys	September 21	1346
St. John's	September 18	1762
St. Kitts	May 10	1667
St. Lucia	April 4	1794
St. Lucia	December 29	1778
St. Lucia	June 21	1803
St. Pierre	December 13	1813
St. Pierre & Miquelon	May 14	1793
St. Pol	June 9	1346
St. Venant	October 2	1710
Stevenswaert	October 2	1702
Sumbilla	August 1	1813
Syria	June 21	1941
Taillebourg	April 8	1351
Talavera de la Reina	July 28	1809
Tarifa	January 7	1812
The Basque Roads	April 11	1809
The Saintes	April 12	1782
Therouanne	August 23	1513
Three Frigates	February 28	1760
Tinchebrai	September 28	1106
Tobago	July 1	1803
Tobago	April 15	1793
Tolosa	June 26	1813
Toulon	July 17	1707
Toulon	December 19	1793
Toulouse	April 10	1814
Tournai	September 3	1709
Tournai	September 25	1513
Tournai	May 22	1794

Trafalgar	October 21	1805
Trarbach	December 20	1704
Treaty of Aix la Chapelle	October 18	1748
Treaty of Bretigny	May 8	1360
Treaty of Edinburgh	July 6	1560
Treaty of Etaples	November 3	1492
Treaty of Paris	May 30	1814
Treaty of Paris	November 20	1815
Treaty of Paris	February 10	1763
Treaty of Picquigny	August 29	1475
Treaty of Troyes	May 21	1420
Treaty of Utrecht	April 11	1713
Trichinopoly I	June 13	1752
Trichinopoly II	July 7	1753
Trichinopoly III	October 2	1753
Trichinopoly IV	November 28	1753
Trier	October 26	1704
Trout Brook	July 6	1758
Ushant	June 1	1794
Ushant	December 14	1781
Valmont	March 11	1416
Velez Malaga	August 13	1704
Vellinghausen	July 15	1761
Venlo	September 25	1702
Vera	August 31	1813
Verneuil	August 17	1424
Vigo Bay	October 12	1702
Villagarcia	April 11	1812
Vilvorde	May 26	1706
Vimeiro	August 21	1808
Vitoria	June 21	1813
Volconda	May 29	1752
Walcourt	August 25	1689

Wandiwash	January 22	1760
Warburg	July 31	1760
Waterloo	June 18	1815
Wilhelmstahl	June 24	1762
Willems	May 10	1794
Wynandael	September 28	1708
York Fort	August 15	1696
Youghioghenny	May 27	1754

INDEX OF BRITISH & ALLIED COMMANDERS

INDEX OF FRENCH & ALLIED COMMANDERS

ISBN 142510368-5

9 781425 103682